DATE DUE

| Brodart Co. | Cat. # 55 137 001 | Printed in USA |

TIME AND THE SHAPE OF HISTORY

TIME AND THE
SHAPE OF HISTORY

PENELOPE J. CORFIELD

YALE UNIVERSITY PRESS
NEW HAVEN AND LONDON

For information about this and other Yale University Press publications, please contact:

U.S. Office: sales.press@yale.edu   www.yalebooks.com
Europe Office: sales@yaleup.co.uk www.yaleup.co.uk

Set in Minion and Gill Sans Book by J&L Composition, Filey, North Yorkshire
Printed in Great Britain by St Edmundsbury Press Ltd, Bury St Edmunds

Library of Congress Cataloging-in-Publication Data

Corfield, P. J.
   Time and the shape of history/Penelope J. Corfield.
      p. cm.
   Includes bibliographical references and index.
   ISBN 978–0–300–11558–1
1. Time.   2. History—Philosophy.   I. Title.
   BD638.C67 2007
   115—dc22

                                                                                    2006032506

A catalogue record for this book is available from the British Library.

10 9 8 7 6 5 4 3 2 1

Contents

Illustrations

Every effort has been made to establish copyright claims. In the event of any
query, please contact the author.

Preface

This book takes a new look at the shape of history, as viewed in the context of long-term time. As a historian, I found myself over the years growing increasingly dissatisfied with the way that studies of the past are habitually subdivided into many short and often disconnected periods. I wanted to return to the very long term, but in a different way. Not finding any book that answered my questions, I decided to write one myself. It has been an absorbing process that has led me into enjoyable new terrain, far from my research home-base in the study of eighteenth-century Britain. The outcome has turned into a study that is addressed to all who are interested in the past and its intersections with the present, without any limitation of period or place.

Themes of history and time are not, of course, subject to any professional monopoly. They are studied within so many subject-disciplines, from astronomy to zoology, that historians may indeed appear to be crowded out of the field. After all, Stephen Hawking's phenomenal *Brief History of Time* (first published in 1988) is the work of a physicist with a special interest in the origin of the cosmos and how it can be understood. But these great themes are, fortunately, inexhaustible and open to all. There is always more to debate, whether about time or about history or, as in this study, about the shape of history in time.

Two of the twentieth century's outstanding historians helped to trigger my interest in the question of whether and how it is possible to fit the details together to reveal a bigger picture. These seminal figures were E. P. Thompson, an extraordinary polymath of literature, theory, history and the European campaign for nuclear disarmament, and my uncle Christopher Hill, who grounded his faith in human equality upon the seedbeds of historical change. Debating the rights and wrongs of Marxism(s) and post-Marxism(s) with them over many years was an education in itself. Both would no doubt disagree with my arguments in return – but not with my belief in the illuminating power of history. This book is therefore an indirect but appreciative acknowledgement of valued friendships and intellectual stimulus.

Thanks for unflagging support and interest also go most warmly to my immediate family; and to many friends and colleagues for providing advice, criticisms and references. All the many comments that I have received on Time, the universal theme, have been most welcome, including especially significant exchanges with Humayun Ansari, Sarah Ansari, Vera Bacskai, Sam Barnish, Caroline Barron, Michael Bennett, Margaret Bird, Hugo Blake, John Broad, Alison Brown, Arthur Burns, Zbigniew Ciechanowicz, Mary Clayton, David Clemis, Sean Creighton, Martin Daunton, Michael Drolet, Beverley Duguid, Maaria Farooqi, Paolo Ferrari, Helgard Frölich, Andrew Gibson, Suzanne Gossett, Warwick Gould, David R. Green, Edmund Green, Uriel Heyd, Tim Hitchcock, Peregrine Horden, John Hodgkins, Julian Hoppit, Ahuvia Kahane, Sarah Knott, Kazuhiko Kondo, Reinhart Koselleck, Xabier Lamikiz, David Lewis, Takao Matsumura, Chris Mounsey, Rudolf Muhs, Tadashi Nakano, Avner Offer, Caroline Ogilvie, David Ormrod, Christina Potter, Dave Postles, Roland Quinault, Adam Roberts, Raphael Samuel, Daniel Snowman, Dan Stone, Rosalind Thomas, Benjamin Thompson, Tzu-Chen Yang; and a physicist friend who travels incognito.

The participants at numerous research gatherings around the world have given pertinent comments and criticisms. My cordial thanks to all of them and, in particular, to those at the Royal Historical Society/Royal Society Conference on 'Time: History, Science and Commemoration' in Liverpool (September 1999); and at the Millennial Conference on 'Old Histories – New Beginnings' at University College Chichester (February 2000). The continuing programme of London University's (very long) Long Eighteenth-Century Seminar also provides an ideal research workshop for debates, both formal and informal, about the art and craft of being a historian.

Throughout this project, unobtrusive help has been forthcoming from the staffs of many research libraries, including the various London University libraries, Oxford's Bodleian Library, Nuffield College Library, and the curators of the specialist collection of the British Dental Association Library. Above all, the staff teams in the British Library's Rare Books room have patiently supplied mountains of books on an array of subjects, from tantric sex to men on the moon, and have made working in Rare Books a rare pleasure.

Thinking and writing time is greatly treasured by authors. Special thanks go therefore to Nuffield College, Oxford, for the award of a research fellowship in 1999, when this study was largely planned; and to Royal Holloway, University of London, for a timely period of study leave, when much of the writing was done. In addition, I am grateful for the intellectual companionship of my academic colleagues, and for the perpetual stimulus of Royal Holloway's history students. They will recognise some of the themes that follow.

True gratitude goes as well to Robert Baldock of Yale University Press for wise counsel. He has encouraged, doubted and advised upon appropriate changes to the text, in perfect editorial style. And his colleagues at the Press have been superbly professional. Patrick O'Brien, the doyen of world historical studies, has also provided a judicious mixture of support and scepticism. From his expert vantage point, David Lightfoot gave important advice on the history of languages. Richard Fisher and Tony Morris also offered tonic encouragement, as friends within the publishing world who recognise the travails of book-making. And Sunil Chhatralia not only empathised with my theme but kindly produced illustrative materials for this book and for my *Timeframes* website.

Three anonymous readers for Yale University Press produced, at crucial points in the writing process, trenchant critiques of early drafts of an overlong and overexcited text. This behind-the-scenes labour of collegial support should not go without a public expression of gratitude. Their responses, which helped me transform every chapter for the better, confirm the maxim that 'opposition is true friendship'. Hearty appreciation in this regard goes also to Jacqueline Eales and Susan Whyman for their detailed line-by-line critiques, and especially to Amanda Goodrich for invaluable advice not only on the book's contents but also upon its presentation.

There remains only the agreeable task of recording my last and first thanks, and the dedication of this book, to my fellow time traveller – all of which go, incontestably, to Tony Belton.

Penelope J. Corfield
Battersea, London
April 2006

Starting Points

What this book sets out to do

Historians cannot stop the clocks to put time under the microscope, any more than philosophers or physicists can achieve such a feat. This study accordingly does not start by probing one specific moment and then working outwards. Instead, it examines the shape of history (and not just human history) in time, as it has been considered over the long term. The justification for this longitudinal approach is because that is the way temporality operates, 'in the long', just as space coheres laterally, 'in the round' – both space and time being, of course, simultaneously and integrally linked in what physicists know as space-time.

History has been envisaged in many long-term guises. Does it mark a process of deep-rooted continuity? Or, instead, one of gradual progress? Or one of persistent decline? Or, if avoiding the value-laden terms 'progress' and 'decline', does history consist of unending gradual change, neither systematically for better nor perennially for worse? Or, if pure continuity and gradualism seem inadequate for all the eventualities, does history instead unfold via a series of dramatic breaks? Or perhaps in a sequence of graduated stages? Or, alternatively, do events occur disconnectedly, in a miscellany of random fluctuations? The life-as-jumble viewpoint was once defined succinctly as 'one damned thing after another'. But even that verdict, it may be noted, contains a minimalist message of a sort. Or does history display none of those patterns? Or, by contrast, some elements of all, or some, of them?

Help in answering these questions comes not only from assessments of specific case studies but also by drawing upon the immense repertoire of ideas about the shape of history, as viewed in the long term, that have been formulated within history, science, philosophy, world religions, literature and everyday cultural traditions. Some of the examples that are discussed in the chapters that follow are well known, even if others are not. And, no doubt, readers can think of many more. That should be the case, because there is always more history, past and present, to study, as restless time continually creates more – and as new events and/or new evidence encourage new perspectives upon the past. Nonetheless, the diversity is not so great that it is impossible to find any common ground. The different traditions 'speak' to one another. Out of the many different interpretations, a finite number of organising 'shapes' do emerge again and again; and it is these that have become the major themes for analysis in the following chapters.

Here it may be added that the essential focus is upon this-worldly experiences and interpretations. Teachings from the world's great religions provide a particularly rich corpus of ideas about historical trends and meanings; and such views are considered respectfully at relevant points. However, readers will not find it hard to detect that the assumptions in this study are based upon a secular liberalism. The discussion therefore does not seek to debate the theological validity or spiritual value of beliefs in life or lives *beyond* time, but concentrates upon what can be learned about the shape or shapes of history in this world and within daily lived time.

Having noted that, another starting assumption can also be mentioned briefly. The quest to investigate patterns of history past and present is not intended to imply a passive or fatalistic view of the role of individuals (whether acting singly or collectively) within such patternings. People are not just pawns in a greater game over which they have no control. On the contrary. The sum of what happens, in the eras in which humans live, contains the sum of all human actions and inactions, multiplied by the multifarious factors outside and beyond human control. This study is therefore written in the firm conviction that a better understanding of the dimensions of history, past and present, provides a better understanding of the scope for people to live their lives.

Who are 'we'?

Themes relating to time have a potential relevance that is universal. However, there are many meanings that can be attached to the experience of temporality, so that too much human togetherness should not be assumed. Bearing in mind the diversity of individual and cultural responses, this study generally avoids all collective statements, such as 'we think this' or 'we find that'. Invoking collective pronouns in that manner can easily become a covert form of special pleading, encouraging assent by implying that all reasonable men and women will endorse a common viewpoint. That is not always the case; and the arguments in the following chapters do not imply that either.

There are some occasions, however, when it is appropriate in a study with global themes to refer to all people, as one species. In this book, therefore, the personal pronouns, 'we', 'us', 'ours' are used infrequently but, when they are, it is specifically in contexts that are understood to apply generically and non-controversially to all fellow humans. An example is 'we talk', which is a species indicator of *Homo sapiens*, even though not all individuals actually do so.

The resulting discussion is offered as part of a world conversation, to all who are or who seek to be students of history. Examples are cited from specific times and places, but the underlying themes are ones with a general application. We all carry around various assumptions about the past and how it relates to the present. What those are and might be are the subjects of discussion here.

Starting definition of time

Time refers both to long duration and to continuously unfolding change within that duration. The resultant combination is a uniquely dynamic process, which stretches to embrace the immense reaches of the past, the immediate here-and-now of the fleeting present, and the potentially vast expanses of the future. The elasticity of temporality is impressive but it operates nonetheless within a detectable framework. Time can accordingly be measured, whether in terms of specific spans of time (a day, a month, a year, a millennium) or in terms of micro-moments, such as the instant when this sentence began to be written, in the first nanosecond of half an hour past midday on a specific date in May 2005.

Tellingly, too, the term is used with many colloquial variations to invoke a subjective awareness of temporal unfolding, that intersects with human hopes and fears. So it is possible to talk of 'gaining time' or 'making time'. Or 'doing time' or 'wasting time'. Or even, on the part of bored people idling restlessly with nothing to do, 'killing time', although no one so far has managed to strike a fatal blow.

Two effective terms, previously not much used but now coming into wider currency, capture the twin perspectives of the immediate moment and the experience of the long term. The *synchronic* indicates everything that occurs more or less simultaneously at a synchronised moment in time. It stands proxy for any set of contemporary circumstances that all happen together or virtually together. To give a practical example, mechanical engineers in the twentieth century invented synchromesh gearing, to smooth the process of changing gears at speed into a near-immediate friction-free synchronisation. By contrast, the *diachronic*, which literally means during or through-time, refers to any protracted span of time, from years to millennia. This term therefore stands proxy for the long term – and, from a human perspective, refers especially to the great temporal span that stretches far beyond an individual's personal experience.

To historians, it is axiomatic that the synchronic is always in the diachronic – in that every short-term moment contributes to a much longer term. And the converse is also true. The diachronic is always in the synchronic – in that long-term frameworks always inform the passing moment as well. To invent a new word on a par with synchromesh, the seamless linkage of the momentary with long duration could be termed *diachromesh*.

Together, these different diachronic/synchronic perspectives combine to allow a full view of time, not just as it seems at any split second but as it also operates when the split seconds accumulate massively and inexorably to become millennia.

Starting definition of history

Terminology can famously stretch to cover many meanings and the term 'history' has imperceptibly become elasticated. It can refer to the unfolding past generically; and/or to the study of the past as a specific subject of inquiry; and/or, much more loosely, to whatever are taken to be the meanings or 'messages' of the past. There are many possibilities – from history as narrative or story to history as myth, history as morality tale, history as national pride, history as heroic destiny, history as group therapy, history as autobiography, history as applied methodologies, history as record, history as judge, history as avenger, history as betrayer, history as a compound of lies and villainy, or history as mess and muddle.

Those who doubt the value of studying the past often enjoy quoting, above all, the famously snappy verdict associated with Henry Ford, the US impresario of the new mass automobile. 'History is bunk,' he was reported as saying in 1916. Later chided for this remark under cross-examination in the witness box, Ford partially retracted: 'I did not say it was bunk. It was bunk *to me.*' His revised view, however, did not manage to obliterate the terse impact of the original dictum. Indeed, it remains in circulation almost one hundred years after its first avowal, testifying paradoxically to the power of historical memory to retain information through time. Ford's debunking phrase accordingly remains available for repetition by those who want to rubbish elements of the past, or to snub those who study the past, while his wording simultaneously represents a certain type of brisk businessman's no-nonsense anti-traditionalism – which is very much part of history.

Throughout this book, these overlapping usages are disentangled by varying the terminology. When used without any further qualification, the term 'history' is here taken to refer to the entire past or, as dictionaries specify, the 'aggregate of past events in general' (and not just events in the human past). It embraces anything or everything up to and including the immediate micro-moment before 'now', as well as the legacies of earlier times that survive into the present. Such a definition in itself contains multitudes. It is at once 'up close and personal' and far, far distant in time and place. Meanwhile, when the intention is to refer to 'history' in a more specific sense, then amplified phrases are used such as 'the study of history', 'the meanings of history', 'the evidence of history' and so forth. The general point is to differentiate between, on the one hand, the past as *the subject* of retrospective analysis and, on the other hand, *the many and varied interpretations/studies of the past* that are generated by all who look back on things that have 'gone before'.

That said, it should be noted that some sceptical theorists prefer instead to define history simply as 'what historians write'. This was said to me, dismissively, by a colleague in 2001, when I told him of the subject of this book. It is a view-point which assumes that 'the past is dead' and is completely inaccessible to later generations. The sceptics further point out that a silent redrafting occurs, when one era in time is described in the language of another.

Thus, in one way, historians are outwardly flattered as the 'creators' and 'designers' of history. Yet, at a deeper level, they are being debunked, with the implication that they merely invent their 'stories' freely as they write their books. Such an assumption implies that there is no external evidence against which historians check, reference and debate their arguments – and the assumption would further mean that there would be no way of telling whether one study of history is more reliable or plausible than any other. The only criteria for judgement would become aesthetic ones: who tells the better story? And, since readers often disagree, there could be no way of deciding between their differing verdicts. One story would be as potentially good as any another. So – to take an extreme example – it would become hard to find grounds upon which to refute the claims of Holocaust deniers.

Therefore 'history' is not merely created or designed by historians but 'history' as the unfolding past is what historians write *about*. And their own books, once launched into the world, join that vast panorama of things that have happened. Moreover, as already noted in the preface, the historians have no professional monopoly. The past is investigated by physicists – like Stephen Hawking – who debate the origins of the cosmos, as well as by archaeologists, astronomers, botanists, biologists, geologists and geogra-phers, to name just a few. No study begins from a blank mind, outside time, so historians share rather than invent history. Even more importantly, too, ideas about the past, especially the human past, do not emerge just from the world of scholarly research. Collective memories, stretching well beyond each passing generation, circulate attitudes, beliefs and emotions about things that have gone before, generating communal repertoires that are both commem-orated and contested. There is always an interesting interaction (including mutual feedback and, sometimes, opposition) between scholarly assessments and popular attitudes, as seen in the diversity of media representations of history. But here again none has a monopoly in generating or circulating viewpoints about the past.

Thinking beyond the immediate moment, both retrospectively and prospectively, is a human characteristic. It is part of a shared and living process of *diachromesh*. Thus 'history' as the past – including all that has gone before, up until the micro-moment before the present moment, and including the legacies of the past in the present – is something that appertains to all.

A note on calendars

This study adopts a secularised version of the Christian calendar, which currently forms the international standard. It is used in its 'Gregorian' format, as reformed by Pope Gregory XIII in 1582 and as now minutely adjusted by astrophysicists to synchronise measured time with the geophysical time of the universe. Under this system, dates are counted both backwards and forwards from year 1. Hence there is no 'zero' standing outside time. Traditionally, the first year AD (*Anno Domini* or year of the Lord) is taken as marking the first year of Christ's life, while 1 BC was the last year before Christ. In recent years, however, a secularised version of the nomenclature is slowly emerging into use for cross-cultural overview studies. The framework chronology remains unchanged but the period BC is represented as BCE (before the Common Era) and the period AD becomes CE (the Common Era). It is not a terminology that pleases everyone – but its application is intentionally global.

Times past in this study are thus specified, when appropriate, as occurring either before or in the Common Era (BCE/CE). But a special notation is not required in all cases. So dates that appear without further qualification can be taken as referring to the most recent two thousand+ years of history – the Common Era (CE) in which we now live.

Translations from the Christian calendar into other global calendars are also routinely possible, although differing definitions of the year-length mean that calculations are often complex. Taking one date as an exemplar, the first day of January 2000 CE has various alternative designations. In Japan, it marks the ending of the eleventh year of Heisei (the Imperial regnal year). In the zodiac-based system as celebrated in traditional Chinese popular culture, it occurs within the Year of the Hare. In the Muslim world, it falls within the lunar year 1421 of the *Hijra* (Latin *Hegira*) dating from Muhammad's migration to Medina. In the Hindu notation, the year is 1922 of the Saka Era. And, in the Jewish calendar, it is year 5761, as counted from the designated start of the world (*Anno Mundi*). As these examples imply, many people are accustomed to using more than one calendrical system at the same time. The dates in this study, while cited in the international standard, are therefore potentially convertible into all parallel notations.

These popular calendars, it may be noted, all operate with manageable numbers. For their own specialist purposes, the world's astronomers also share a common counting system which focuses upon successive twenty-four-hour spans. Each day-and-night has its own separate notation, with fractions to mark subdivisions. The sequence starts at midday on 1 January 4713 BCE in the classical Roman (Julian) calendar, counting backwards and forwards from then. Midnight GMT on 31 December 1999 CE thus appears as Julian number J 2,451,544·50. Totals such as these, however, remain far too large for easy reference or daily use, other than by specialists.

Theoretically, too, it would be possible to start a year-count from the scientifically calculated origin of the universe some 13 to 15 billion years ago (defining a billion as a thousand million), and then to scroll forwards from that. It would offer a daily reminder of the vast extent of past time. So 2000 CE would equate to Cosmic Year 15,000,002,000 plus or minus an error range of 1–2 billion. Yet such a formulation entirely lacks user-friendliness, so that for daily use it is more convenient to rely upon historically created calendars, as scientifically updated by the global research community, and now adopted within an international framework. The plurality of usages among different communities makes it clear that the details of time measurement are matters of social convention. Nonetheless, the very fact that these differing systems can all be converted from one into another shows that there is also a singular process at work, within which all interpretations of the past are shaped.

How the book is organised

Historical themes interpreted longitudinally form the subject of this study. Such an arrangement means that the book as a whole is not organised primarily by chronology, although some sections are. Instead, each chapter discusses a different aspect of the developing argument so that, taken together, the chapters act as separate spokes in a collectively turning wheel.

Highlighted examples of ways of 'shaping' history are also inserted as short self-contained sections. These case studies, *indicated with a distinctive typeface*, bridge between the chapters, acting as chapterlinks that hold the turning spokes together. Particular themes that are discussed are: time travel; time cycles; time lines (or long-term trends); time ends (apocalypses); time names; time pieces (or time measurement); and human responses to 'time power'. For readers without any background in the formal study of history, these bridging sections or chapterlinks, which are located at the end of each main chapter, offer possible starting points. For all comers, meanwhile, the overall argument runs throughout the book, unfolding in the sequence in which it was written (and rewritten).

How history is located within a temporal framework of cosmic time is the subject of the first chapter. Various debates and definitions are reconsidered. And the assumption that there are no constants within the cosmos – a viewpoint sometimes (wrongly) associated with Einstein and relativity – is rejected. After that, three chapters (2–4) examine three central and inter-locking dimensions of history. These are identified as continuity (persistence; tradition), gradual change (evolution) and all forms of rapid, frictional and discontinuous change (turbulence; upheaval; revolution).

Human interpretations of long-term trackways through time are then analysed in the second half of the book. Chapter 5 looks at 'ages' in history and calls for a rethink about 'modernity', which has become overused, while chapter 6 explores stage theories, which divide historical time into tidy stages as a way of looking back at the past and sometimes forecasting the future as well. Such divisions are suggestive about long-term changes but can lead to crude categories that then become stretched too thin. For example, 'capi-talism' as a stage in world history (like its pairing with 'modernity') is thus revealed as overdue for a critical reconsideration. Chapter 7 returns to reassess the longitudinal 'shapes' of history, arguing for a threefold approach. And the final chapter 8 considers how the intertwined components of continuity and different forms of change apply to human experiences, of the past, present, and anticipated futures.

Halting the journey at the very end is a brief coda. It revisits the general argument about the importance of understanding how we frame our knowl-edge of both past and present in time, since such knowledge is our invaluable collective resource for living in time. The overall argument focuses upon the multi-dimensional shape of history. But the linkages in my view flow both ways. Thus my final speculation is that the shape of history, viewed 'long', also throws light upon the shape of time – not only in its synchronic meshing but also in its diachronic power.

CHAPTER 1

History in Time

To situate history in the long term entails having a view upon time. Its dynamic force provides the unfolding framework within which things both continue from the past and also change. Time's three perspectival states of past, present, and potential future remain fixed in their successive sequencing. Yet the eras to which they apply are always being updated. As that happens, more history is generated daily for humans to consider.

This consistent temporal flux means too that interpretations are perennially liable to adaptation in the light of altered circumstances. The here-and-now, poised at the fulcrum of retrospection and anticipation, changes all the time, whilst always remaining Now. 'And do not call it fixity,/Where past and future are gathered', as T. S. Eliot, the twentieth century's most famed poet of temporality advised in his elegiac *Four Quartets*.[1] The immense power of the present, however intensely felt – 'quick now, here, now, always' – does not erase the mental awareness of 'before' and 'after': 'Only through time time is conquered.'

So history's complex unfolding has to be understood within an even more complex temporal process that ceaselessly welds duration and change, persistence and flux. Pervading this universe, it is known as cosmic time. And it has – uniquely – the capacity for auto-renewal, as each present moment both lives and dies simultaneously.

Assumptions about the shape of the past are therefore linked with assumptions about time as the framework power. One striking visual representation of this is seen, for example, in the Aztec calendrical map of the Five World Regions (*see* illustration 1). It was devised in fifteenth-century Mexico to provide a summary of cosmic history. The designs at the four cardinal points, N, S, E and W, indicate four past eras (N is located on the left, E at the top). Each time zone is protected by two tutelary gods standing by an emblematic tree, topped with a great perching bird.[2] At the centre is the fifth era, which represents the present. Here dwells the celestial fire-god, sustained at the heart

1 The fifteenth-century Aztec calendrical map shows the present, sustained at the heart of Five World Regions of Time, each with its own tree of life and tutelary gods.

of all that has gone before. So a complex and dynamic past is rendered as also orderly and explicable, leading from then to now, via the patterned dots that mark the days.

Of course, not all communities by any means visualise history within such a structured plan. Nonetheless, the challenge to find some way of understanding time, and the past in relation to time, is one that confronts all who live within unfolding temporality. So there has emerged a global case history of approaches and problems, which are ripe for re-examination.

History and Defining Time

In the first place, it is right to consider whether it is possible for humans stuck in the here-and-now to investigate something as vast and strange as cosmic time. The Scottish philosopher and famed sceptic David Hume once warned sharply that it is hard to range mentally beyond our immediate sense-data: 'Let us fix our attention out of ourselves as much as possible: Let us chase our imaginations to the heavens, or to the utmost limits of the universe; we never really advance a step beyond ourselves.'[3] How, then, can any one generation of humans, limited in time and place, make any valid comment about times past and long ago?

However, Hume's prohibition is not as limiting as it might at first seem. As creatures of the universe, we are ourselves temporal as well as spatial beings. Time is therefore not a purely external phenomenon that is completely 'beyond' us.

Humans have access to the workings of temporality in many ways. Time not only surrounds us, as something that can be studied, measured and debated, but it also inheres within us, in the form of our subconscious body clocks, our genetic timetabling and our capacity to live in time. Accordingly, we recognise temporality de facto, even without having an agreed explanation or full definition. Even young children can be taught to 'tell' the time, without any special lessons in science, philosophy or the study of history being undertaken either by the learners or the teachers.

Such a state of familiar-unfamiliarity was noted long ago, in one of the most celebrated comments ever made on this subject. The fourth-century Christian theologian St Augustine asked himself rhetorically: 'What then is time?' And he answered with a paradox: 'Provided that no one asks me, I know. [But] if I want to explain it to an enquirer, I do not know.'[4]

For most ordinary purposes, an Augustinian intuitive response is quite sufficient. In fact, it is notable that people very rarely express anxiety about 'what is time?' (as opposed to the more common 'where are things going?') even though it might be thought worrying not to know about the essential medium in which we live. But it is so basic that it readily appears as a 'given'. Nonetheless, that has not stopped people from also cogitating about the subject. And there are plentiful external clues, as well as our internal time signals. For example, the light of the stars sends visual messages about their own past via long trajectories of sparkling luminosity.[5] While we see these in the present, we can calculate their earlier history. So our own sense-data, plus the effort of thought, can move us mentally beyond our own eras. Within planet earth's immediate vicinity, meanwhile, the sun is another marker of longevity. It is calculated to be approximately halfway through its life cycle, with sufficient power to last for at least another five billion years before it evolves into a red dwarf. By careful study and calculation of such stellar evidence, astronomers can apply a range of data to the complex task of telling the age of the universe.

Another signal of its long history comes, uncannily, from the residual electro-magnetic 'noise' or reverberation, known as cosmic background radiation, which is faintly detectable in the here-and-now by sophisticated radio-scanners. This sound, scientists argue, is a 'ghostly remnant' from an original Big Bang that in all probability formed this universe some 13 to 15 billion years ago.[6]

Meanwhile, closer to home, the restless power of temporality is also detectable through its effect upon the interacting processes of creation and decay, decay and creation, in the animate and inanimate worlds all around. Early in the twentieth century the economist Maynard Keynes, living up to his profession's reputation for ironic gloom, propounded the classic dictum that '*In the long run* we are all dead'.[7] Yet he might have added too that destruction is counterbalanced by renewal. In the long run, the dead are replaced by the living, if not always of the same species. As a result, any point on earth, viewed attentively, contains evidence of time's longitudinal dynamics, with signs of both endings and beginnings.

Given many clues, therefore, and the will to analyse them, it is possible to discuss the history of the cosmos, in terms of its origins, its age, its effects, and its future prospects.

Since all the observations and interpretations of such evidence are made by conscious humans, however, the argument is sometimes brought round once more to the sceptical position of David Hume, in this permutation to argue that the very concept of time is nothing but a human invention. Far from temporality being 'beyond' us, this viewpoint considers it to be purely 'within' our minds. Time is thus presented as a sensory illusion, although even the sternest theorists who reject the externality of time do concede that it is an extremely potent illusion that is found among all human communities. (This argument, by the way, intends to refute the 'existence' of a persistent temporality. It differs subtly therefore from (say) those Buddhist teachings which urge people to live 'as though' time is an illusion. That is a different proposition.)

Anti-persistent-time theories, that accept at best a fragmented temporality of the moment, emerge in time studies as classic heresies, propounded by a minority of physicists and philosophers. The recurrence of such sceptical viewpoints demonstrates the difficulty of finding a definition and explanation with which all agree. Nonetheless, the continuing 'illusion' of a connected temporality, if no more, indicates the converse difficulty of abolishing the concept.

Were there no persistent duration, then there would be no past that had happened and that could be recollected in the present. Instead there would be only a happenstance of sundered instants. Thus, leading the case for a theory of fragmented time, Julian Barbour argues that each nanosecond (a billionth of a second) or even each atto-second (an infinitesimal billionth of a billionth of a second) frames its own separate universe, each one being the outcome of a different quantum probability. With such a splintering, humans would have no possibility of a through-time identity. They would scarcely have time to draw breath, let alone to ponder their thoughts and feelings about the process. It would mean, speculates Barbour, that 'All the instants we have experienced are other worlds, for they are not the one we are in now.'[8]

Yet this remarkable formulation has quietly smuggled some through-time phenomena back into the picture. If 'we' are able to experience many worlds, some before others, then some durable beings must have persisted across the notionally divided micro-moments to have such different experiences. By contrast, any atemporal beings, who truly live instant by instant, would know only their own instant, which would appear timeless. They would not be able to experience many separate worlds because, if they could leap across from one quantum-world to another, the micro-moments would no longer be entirely separate.

Moreover, any atemporal beings that do manage to live exclusively within a single atto-second would have to signal any instant reactions to their condition instantaneously, because they would be debarred from any through-time modes of communication, such as speech. But, in fact, sequential sounds are regularly joined together by many living species to convey comprehensible messages that unfold as they are conveyed. In addition, humans have also invented communication via written words that are read in a specified order and via moving pictures that have to be viewed in specific sequence. These through-time messages would make no sense if the successive moments are entirely fragmented and dissociated. Thus Barbour is obliged to use consecutive language to present his case against consecutive time. Moreover, he fills his preface with autobiographical information about his own intellectual history and his text with details from past scientific debates, presenting these antecedents not as occurring in separate para-worlds but within this one.

Indeed, it might be speculated, in reverse-Barbour, that only in a time-bound cosmos is it possible to argue about the nature and meaning of time. By contrast, within the endless present of an atemporal and unattached atto-second, there would be nothing to suggest even the remotest possibility of something as strange as alternative temporal states, whether anything as remote as a past or as subversive as a potentially different future.

Be that as it may, the fragmentary-time arguments, while repeatedly stimulating good scientific and philosophical debates, tend not to attract majority support. There is no generally agreed formula for temporality in the guise of $T =$. Nonetheless, that it has some characteristic persistence is generally accepted, or simply taken for granted, as befits something that is familiar as well as strange. Some binding agency, whether it be viewed as a divine or cosmic power or both, therefore links the micro-moments together.[9] The process survives, even if human understanding of that process is only imperfect. In traditional Islamic thought, then, it is the unifying force of divine providence that compassionately holds the cosmos together, while enabling individuals to participate in the immediate moment: 'now' thus intersects with eternity.[10]

Among physicists, there are analytical tensions between those who favour insights from quantum physics, which stress the jagged and restless toing and froing of subatomic particles at micro-level, and those like Roger Penrose, who stress countervailingly the cohesive power of the forces of gravity at macro-level.[11] These scientific debates are currently subjects of much research and argument. To a historian, however, it appears plausible to accept that some high-level balance between steady persistence and rapid turnover is consistently in operation, in order to sustain something as remarkable as long duration and, within long duration, continuously unfolding change. In other words, there is a prevalent meshing between the quantum micro-cosmos and the gravitational macro-cosmos.

Certainly, it is within this ordered time frame, that is both coherent and dynamic, that through-time humans have and sustain valid through-time knowledge. The present links to the past, rather than opposes or excludes it, just as the past blends into the present, rather than halts before it. On those grounds, humans generate interpretations of the shape of history that stretch through time. With no impermeable barriers between past and present, furthermore, our verdicts or statements about things long gone may be as potentially true – or as untrue – as are verdicts or statements about the current moment.[12] Thus we operate routinely within a time-infused cosmos. And temporality forms a prime subject for our study, not because we have invented it, but because it is simultaneously all-important and completely beyond our control.

History and Time's Arrow

Not only do we live in time, but we can strive to identify time's particular characteristics. Throughout the long temporal progression, the regularity of the process is apparent from the fact that humans are able to measure it systematically. Conversely, were there a fragmentary-time of purely sundered micro-moments, there would be no way of quantifying duration.[13] Being able to measure time means too that we can date historical events and processes by situating them within specified calendars. However, a human capacity for temporal awareness historically preceded the development of formal measurements. As a result, our awareness of past and present does not depend upon absolute precision in such matters. It is highly characteristic, indeed, to combine a sense of 'before' and 'after', 'then' and 'now', with considerable haziness about precise dates.

Crucial to the entire process of time measurement, and the consequent framework for history, is the special characteristic of time in that it is unidirectional. Moments run onwards and never go into reverse. A favoured metaphor, often used to describe this feature of temporal progression, is time's arrow. It points poetically to momentum in one single direction. So there is a coherent process that links the past to the present and that heralds the potential future, on the strength of what has gone before. This was noted long ago by St Augustine. 'But no time is wholly present,' he wrote, '. . . all past time is driven backwards by the future, and all future time is the consequent of the past.'[14]

Another term for this unidirectionality is temporal asymmetry. Again physicists are uncertain as to why time has this property. Logically, some argue that a case could be made for temporal momentum to run either onwards or in reverse. On the other hand, other scientists are currently investigating the singularities in the cosmos and its physical contours – singularities that inhibit time from either splitting into multiple directions or from backtracking. And those constraints must pertain universally, commencing with temporal origins and persisting thereafter – or, if temporality has no specific origin, then simply persisting.

From the point of view of an imaginary archer, it does not matter whether the arrow is considered as being flighted upwards, downwards, forwards, backwards, from left to right, from right to left, or in any direction of the compass. The only proviso, and it is a major one, is that, once it has left the bow, the arrow never reverses itself in time to retract into the archer's bow *at the moment it left*. On film, it is true, the reel can be rewound to make the action seemingly run backwards. However, as that happens, time's arrow still moves onwards. It does not reverse itself with the film but continues unabated, just as it does when a clock's hands are moved backwards. We cannot thus stand outside time to alter its direction, as all changes to representations of time are undertaken within time.

The metaphor from archery, however, is incomplete as a full explanation. It is not just time's arrow that moves from the bow of an imaginary archer, but the notional archer and the bow, with everything else within the cosmos, must share in the universal momentum too. Accordingly, speaking is always undertaken 'onwards', just as listeners understand in the same sequence. Even when recollecting (say) sentences from the past, we do not mentally spool them in reverse. Instead, we recall them in the 'onwards' order that made them comprehensible in the first place.

Nonetheless, the principle of unidirectionality requires only that cosmic time unfolds in one direction. It does not further insist that the links between past and present within such a framework should be considered as travelling exclusively in straight lines. Indeed, as will be discussed in subsequent chapters, there are plentiful alternatives that have been envisaged historically, such as circles, spirals, waves, zigzags and random pathways.

It is, however, the unshakeable asymmetry of time's arrow that makes it possible to analyse the past retrospectively, as we investigate evidence of things that have gone before from the ever-changing perspective of the unfolding present. By contrast, we can anticipate and try to forecast the future, but we cannot study its workings in the same way. Its relationship with the present is asymmetrically different from the relationship of the past to the present. Time's arrow therefore specifies something significant about the operation of time's combination of momentum and duration; and it is within this 'onwards' framework that history is dynamically shaped.

History and Relative Time

All approaches to these themes were radically transformed in the early twentieth century by Einstein's new theories of relativity. He specified that time measurements, when made at vastly different speeds, will not appear constant but instead will vary in relation to the differential mobility of the observing agent.[15] Thus a notional traveller through space at high velocity would experience a counter-intuitive but nevertheless detectable slowing of the still unbroken temporal unfolding. This 'stretching' phenomenon is known as time dilation.

Nothing like this has ever been experienced by humans and there are no immediate possibilities of our doing so in the future. Nevertheless, the technological innovations that speeded methods of travel and communications in the nineteenth and twentieth centuries have made people increasingly aware that we can experience our relationship to time and space in ways that are not immediately obvious to our sense-data. The physical universe cannot be squashed. Yet we can, with technological aids, greatly speed human movement and, above all, the sending of messages around our own local planet, making the distances immensely faster to bridge, so that the effect seems like compressing space. Already in 1850, Prince Albert, the well-informed consort of Queen Victoria, had expressed his delight in the new electric telegraph. He reported triumphantly that 'The distances which separated the different . . .

parts of the globe are rapidly vanishing ... and we can traverse them with incredible ease.'[16]

Einsteinian physics sprang from the scientific and technological culture of the later nineteenth century that was busily investigating radio communications, powered flight, the internal combustion engine and the mysteries within matter. Impossible things began to seem possible; and previously 'fixed' things became ripe for reconsideration. The subject of time was a classic challenge. The existing scientific view was derived from Isaac Newton's synthesis in the later seventeenth century. This stated unequivocally that 'Absolute, True, and Mathematical Time, of itself, and from its own nature flows equably without regard to any thing external, and by another name is called Duration.'[17] It seemed an unassailable bedrock. True, Newton did distinguish this formulation from mere 'Relative, Apparent, and Common Time', which was locally applicable. Yet it was the absolute principle that really counted.

By establishing the relativity of time measurement, Einstein was taken as dethroning the core of Newton's physics. The understanding of temporality was taken into a new level of sophistication. Einstein's revision did not, however, reject time's unidirectionality. Nor indeed did he offer any simple formula for T. Yet the implications of relativity clearly indicated that time could no longer be regarded as a separate quantity. Instead, its measurement varies with movement in space, into which it elides to form a continuum. The significance of this formulation was quickly appreciated by Hermann Minkowski, the mathematician who had once taught Einstein. Old mental maps needed to be drastically overhauled. 'Henceforth space by itself, and time by itself, are doomed to fade away into mere shadows, and only a kind of union of the two will preserve an independent reality,' Minkowski announced, naming the composite as space-time.[18] And Einstein agreed. 'Time is no longer absolute,' he stated. The new theory he introduced as 'special relativity' and then general 'relativity'.

Such an intellectual recasting had significant implications for interpretations not only of physics but also of history, which is framed within time. It took some years, and extensive debates and experimentation, before Einstein's analysis became accepted. Gradually, however, first physicists and then others began to accept the concept of 'space-time'. And new suggestions for its shape and structure were canvassed. Thus if space-time in certain circumstances is curved or warped, as relativity specifies,[19] then the history it frames may not run along perennially straight lines as some popular models of history as 'progress' had implied.

Fresh thinking about these possibilities was encouraged among intellectual circles not only by the gradual impact of Einsteinian relativity but also through the unfolding conundrums of quantum physics, the other great new development of twentieth-century physics, whose implications were repeatedly puzzled over by Einstein himself. Few among the wider public delved into the details of the scientific arguments. However, again there was a wider circulation of new ideas in summary form. Hence Heisenberg's famous 1927 postulate of the 'uncertainty principle', which indicated the probabilistic nature of measuring the simultaneous position and momentum of subatomic particles,[20] appeared also to shake confidence in a settled cosmos. The unfolding framework for history, and indeed for historical causation through time, thus began to seem much more wobbly and uncertain than had previously been imagined.

One creative response was to abandon absolutes and to cultivate instead diversity and plurality. The range of human interpretations of time, and history within time, can be celebrated without having to declare one to be more 'right' than another. So the different and even conflicting perspectives are simultaneously accommodated. While history may appear as undeniable 'progress' to some, the same developments may indicate an obnoxious 'degeneration' to others. Or a completely different shape – such as steady-state – might be detected instead of either of these interpretations of change. The possibilities become multiple.

Thus a form of cultural relativism has emerged to fit alongside scientific relativity, encouraged also by anthropological studies that approach all communities equally seriously, without elevating one above another. As an approach to global history, this even-handedness has proved highly fruitful and indeed, in many ways, necessary.

Nevertheless, cultural relativism, or multiculturalism as it is also known, has also been in some cases enthusiastically exaggerated beyond its core remit. At its most extreme it implies not only that there can be no universal values but also that there is no possible way of judging between one viewpoint and another. One famous catchphrase states boldly that 'everything is relative'. Nothing is excluded from this summary dictum. So all forms of knowledge and morality are considered as equally meaningful – or meaningless. A cheerful slogan provides a pop summary as 'anything goes'. In that vein, an advertisement in *Time* magazine in 1979 (celebrating the centenary of Einstein's birth) felt able to declare that 'In the cool, beautiful language of mathematics, Einstein demonstrates that we live in a world of relative values',[21] even though Einstein himself opposed such a conclusion. His work had nonetheless contributed to an influential cultural pluralism as well as launched a new scientific theory. So it was not without good justification that Einstein was eulogised in December 1999 by the appropriately named *Time* magazine as the outstanding 'person of the twentieth century'.[22]

Logical as well as practical difficulties, however, follow from elevating the proposition that 'everything is relative' into the status of a new absolute. These difficulties were already demonstrated in the pre-Einsteinian history of relativity as a cultural concept. The first person to use the phrase was the indefatigable social theorist Auguste Comte in mid-nineteenth-century France, when offering his synthesis of world history past and future. He argued that the basis of all knowledge was shifting away from 'irrational' beliefs, based upon religious dogma, and moving towards rational or 'positive' enquiry, based upon experimental science. History would see an 'inevitable passage from the absolute to the relative', he declared, almost as though predicting the advent of Einsteinian physics.[23] More particularly, the readiness of scientists to challenge old ways underpinned for Comte a new philosophic truth. Thus he declared that 'everything is relative' constitutes 'the only absolute principle'. However, there is an inner contradiction within Comte's claim. If relativity itself is an 'absolute' principle, then not *everything* can be relative after all.

That central conundrum was immediately noted when Einstein's work began to be accepted, uncritically, as a slogan with universal application. For example, in 1924 Max Planck, the founding parent of quantum physics, expostulated that absolutes had not been banished from scientific knowledge. And another colleague, concerned at confusions within the terminology, argued that 'co-variance' would be a better name for relativity theory, as better signalling the mutual variability between spatial and temporal measurements.[24] Einstein was not unsympathetic to the suggestion. It was too late, however, to change a terminology that was already becoming world famous.

What Einstein had brilliantly done was to dethrone an 'absolute time' that is divorced from absolute space. However, he had left behind not a void but instead the space-time continuum.[25] The old process of temporal succession remains still detectable and still measurable. Indeed, Einstein's formulation makes its calibration better understood, not less so. Moreover, the measurement of time requires some stable points of reference, for otherwise the task cannot be done. One cosmic factor that is 'given' is the speed of light in a vacuum, defined as $= c$ (*celeritas*, Latin for speed) and measured at just under 300,000 kilometres per second. Accordingly this fixed feature appears within Einstein's most celebrated equation $E=mc^2$, so that the energy content (E) of a mass at rest is calculated in terms of its mass (m) multiplied by the speed of light (c) squared. Hence his physics is one of relationality, allowing the calculation and measurement of different variables against each other – which is very far from being the physics of a cosmos without absolutes.

When considering the shape of history within the complexities of the temporal process, this latter point is of considerable relevance (and it is further discussed in the next chapter). At the very least it indicates that the cosmos is not completely indeterminate. There are, after all, some constants and fixed elements, which interact with the dynamic forces of change. That combination is one that lends itself to historical as well as scientific examination, without having to declare either that everything is absolute or that nothing is.[26] Moreover, it may be remarked that there are notable elements of convergence as well as differences within the rich global array of cultural interpretations of time and history. So the flux is not limitless.

Talking about Time

How people address the temporal process is a matter of some variegation. Certainly, not all linguistic communities have one specific word for the one central phenomenon of 'Time'. Yet all people have some means of expressing the basic temporal concepts of 'before' and 'after'/'earlier' and 'later'/'then', 'now', and 'next' – whether that is done by tensed verbs or by other means such as changeable word endings and different vocal inflections (the latter being particularly hard to transfer into written systems).[27]

Viewed in the abstract, time is notoriously hard to depict. One way is by showing its effects. Another is to humanise the process by giving it a personal imagery. Traditionally in Chinese popular culture, for instance, figurines of Shou Lao or 'Old Longevity' represent the power of time. He appears as a venerable old man with a high-domed forehead, wearing a robe of stars and carrying a scroll that records the date of everyone's death. With such ominous knowledge, his good favour is auspicious.

A vivid mythology derived from ancient Greece, by contrast, depicts time in two distinctive forms. One is *Kairos*, a winged youth representing the power of choice in the immediate moment. He carries a pair of scales, indicating that fortunes always hang in the balance. The other figure is that of Chronos or Saturn, the father of the gods, representing the long term. Mighty and pitiless, he devours everything – even his own children.

Brueghel's 1574 woodcut *The Triumph of Time* places Chronos centrally amidst the multifarious symbols of his power (*see* detail in illustration). The maestro of temporality sits upon an hourglass as he travels in a chariot rolled by the wheels of fortune. These are mandala, or traditional Hindu representations of completeness. Behind him is the earth, decked with the signs of the zodiac (including Gemini – the twins – who are embracing amorously), while a tree of life grows upwards bearing Libra (the scales of judgement) and a clock that is about to strike the hour. Chronos simultaneously holds aloft an entwined serpent biting its own tail, as an ancient symbol of the cycle of death and renewal. Meanwhile, crushed to the ground beneath his chariot wheels are

2 Brueghel's *Triumph of Time* (1574) reveals the power of Chronos/Time amidst cross-cultural symbols, including wheels of fate, zodiac signs and a pendulum clock.

miscellaneous emblems indicating the vanity of human endeavour, such as swords, helmets, work tools and a battered crown.

Traditional incarnations of time as an all-powerful parent figure also recur in the mythology of Chronos as Old Father Time. As the reaper of death, this figure often holds a scythe. Or he consults an hourglass, to indicate that the sands have almost run. And he has a special role in traditional end-of-year festivities, when the venerable figure of Old Father Time disappears at midnight, to be replaced by a newborn baby or very young child. Here is a countervailing sign of renovation and the eventual coming of spring. So time also brings mercy and creativity, as well as doom and death.

Metaphorical representations of temporality very often incorporate movement. So time fires its arrows, unidirectionally. It flies, it hurries. Or it rides through the skies in a wingèd chariot, on high like the sun. Or, in ancient Hindu cosmology, time is itself a fiery galloping steed, 'with seven reins, thousand-eyed, ageless'. Or it may flow onwards steadily like 'an ever-rolling stream'. Or it overwhelms and devours. Or else it lurks everywhere, like a brooding 'vast shadow', tugging the world through the bright light of Eternity, as poetically imagined by Henry Vaughan in mid-seventeenth-century England.[28]

Time may, upon due occasion, also take its time. And, by notorious repute, it can dawdle, crawl and drag. It does that especially when people are stuck in boring circumstances, or when they are waiting for a longed-for development that never seems to arrive. Rarely, too, in breathless moments of crisis, time appears to 'stand still' or 'hang in the balance'.

Visual messages alert attentive observers to these changing tempos. Traditionally, the Inuit people read the time from the state of the stars and the Arctic seasons.[29] Humans have also invented a remarkable array of time markers, from ancient stones and sundials to ringing bells, running water, burning incense, and many mechanical devices, not excluding the latest digital displays and electronic pulsation. While the updating is often completely silent, like sands running sleekly through an hourglass, the rhythmic tick-tocking of a clock gives an audible sound to temporal procession. Furthermore, once time is routinely measured, then the days, years, centuries and millennia can be named and numbered.

Immediate or *synchronic* time has a brisk vocabulary of the present, the instant, the second, the split second, the here-and-now, a point in time, a jiffy, a tick, a trice, a moment, a 'mo' – or even, in a nice English colloquialism, 'half a mo'. Such a brief window of opportunity equates to the 'point of no return', 'the crisis', 'the crunch'. Classically, the immediate moment is always brief, as time speeds past in a veritable 'blinking' or 'twinkling of an eye'. Many languages have idiomatic phrases to note this high-speed transition. So things happen 'faster than words can leave the mouth' or before a particular sound or phrase can be articulated. In an English popular song of the 1930s the passing moment comes and goes 'quicker than you can say Jack Robinson'.

Diachronic perspectives, meanwhile, are longitudinal, through time, across time, 'ringing down the ages'. This long-term framework embraces all the passing moments. But there are no rules that stipulate how lengthy a diachronic process must be in order to qualify as truly longitudinal: the synchronic insensibly extends into the diachronic. Islamic thought makes the subtle distinction between duration without end (*Abad*) and duration without beginning (*Azal*). And other phrases invoke *deep time* or *time immemorial* or *world without end*. Prosaic is *the duration*, which becomes more emphatic in the variant used by the historian Fernand Braudel.[30] For him, it was *la longue durée* or the long duration that constitutes the foundation of all history and historical studies. Or an alternative phrase for the diachronic comes from the Russian cultural theorist Mikhael Bakhtin, who saw the cumulative years as offering a chance for long-term vindication. No cause, however defeated in the short term, is 'absolutely dead', he insisted. Accordingly Bakhtin labelled the redemptive force of temporality as *Great Time*, indicating the proverbial message that 'Time will tell'.[31]

Alternatives are also available for those who seek to reject/adapt or go beyond the temporal cosmos. So *non-Time* is cultivated by Buddhist techniques of living serenely through the moment, as though time is an illusion.[32] Or faith casts its hopes beyond the constraints of this world. *Beyond-Time* thus contains the vision of a timeless, changeless and endless eternity.

And there are analysts of discontinuity, as has already been acknowledged. From such a perspective, *fragmentary-Time* is a splintered affair that lacks any long-term coherence. A suggestive reference is to '*chronoschisms*'.[33] And if one immediate moment were never to melt into its successor, then Time would remain in an endless present. For that, an old Platonic term has been revived by Jacques Derrida, the French philosopher of anti-philosophy. Rejecting any long-term temporality as a purely 'metaphysical' concept, he offers instead the notion of *chora* or *khōra*, to signify an atemporal spatiality that subsists not 'in the long' but 'in the round'.[34] However, this specialist term, which downplays the scientific insight that space is intrinsically yoked to time, does not seem to be gaining many converts, even among the time-doubters.

Practically, after all, there is no cosmic option of choosing between either temporality or spatiality. So they are known together, in Minkowski's summary of Einstein, as the *space-time* continuum. In physics, this is given the numerical signature of 3,1. The simple formula indicates the conjoining of space, with its three dimensions of latitude, longitude, altitude, with time. They cannot be sundered, so that the one is as real as the other. It means, in effect, that depictions of anything in space are also depictions of the workings of time.

Currently, there are exciting discussions that potentially extend the 3,1 formula into new terrain. Some physicists and cosmologists are debating whether there may be a number of dimensions within the temporal component of space-time. The theoretical postulates of string-theory refer to foundational moments at the start of this cosmos. Perhaps, it is conjectured, time then contained tiny 'curled up' dimensions – perhaps as many as eleven – where infinitesimal particles of matter interacted with infinitesimal particles of force. Such a *hyper-space-time* might have obtained briefly at the Big Bang, before the unfurling of the classic 3,1 of space-time.[35] The question of inner dimensionality within a singular process is certainly one that is relevant for historical exploration – and these are themes for later discussion in this book.

An older definitional variant, meanwhile, is tending to fade. In the early twentieth century, time itself was sometimes known as the *fourth dimension*, adding one onto the three of space. The swashbuckling time-travel fiction of H. G. Wells in 1895 gave the term wide circulation, well before the sober calculations of Einstein.[36] Meanwhile, writers about spirituality and the occult also augmented the sum. References are made to other-worldly dimensions – the 'second', 'fourth' or 'fifth' – to suggest transcendental realms that pervade and surround this one.[37] Such visions have not in themselves disappeared. Nonetheless, the specific language of dimensionality is now tending to be captured for potential dimensions within time rather than for alternative realms of the spirit.

Collectively, the many options indicate the protean qualities of *temporality*. This term, while lacking in any proverbial glamour, still remains the abstract noun for the process of through-time duration plus change/progression.

Furthermore, there is one new change in terminology adopted here that needs a comment. When the German-speaking Minkowski named the continuum as space-time (*Raumzeit*), he did so by inverting the established Teutonic compound noun *Zeitraum*, which means a significant stretch or period of time. The resulting formula gives the verbal priority to space. After all, time is measured within its contours. On the other hand, there is a good case for reconsidering the sequence of the nouns. While 'space' acts as the locational sheet-anchor and realisation of the pairing, it is 'time' that establishes onwards momentum. Perhaps ideally, the two terms should be spoken together: 'Sptimace'. But, short of that, the continuum is here signified not as space-time but as *time-space* (*Zeit-Raum*), in tribute to time's dynamic role. The reversed term is a variant that has been adopted so far by only a tiny minority.[38] Yet it serves to signal the concern of this study with longitudinal time or, more properly, with longitudinal time-space and the shape of history.

History in Time-space

Here the chosen methodology is to examine in turn the major patterns and shapes that emerge again and again from human explorations of these themes. In that way, the spotlight falls directly upon models of the diachronic and how they can be examined/critiqued and combined.

Rich evidence for this sort of thematic analysis comes from comparative cultural attitudes to time and history – attitudes whose gestation and evolution in themselves form part of the history of time.[39] When considering such material, it is important to avoid simple stereotypes. For example, the world is sometimes divided into 'the West' where history is seen as running along a straight line, and 'the East' where cyclical models are preferred. But that sort of crude dichotomy is unconvincing, because, quite apart from excluding the 'north', the 'south', and central Eurasia, it ignores internal debates within cultural traditions, and also changes that take place over time. So any unalloyed belief in history-as-linear-progress-on-assumed-western-models, as touted in the nineteenth century, has long been under challenge in the twentieth century, being battered intellectually by Einsteinian curved space-time and by cultural relativism, as well as by the bitter evidence of world wars and genocides. All this means that cultural attitudes are themselves never static, even within traditional expectations.

Further interesting evidence comes from subjective human responses, both individual and collective, to history and/or time. Again, however, it is worth noting that personal assessments often differ. Individual pronouncements are therefore thought-provoking but, on their own, are not conclusive. One bold summary in this vein, which is often quoted respectfully, came from the Russian cultural thinker Nikolai Berdyaev in the mid twentieth century. He found three different levels of time, nested within one another. The first is measured by scientists as cosmic time. (Berdyaev saw this as a circle.) The second informs the history books and is known to collective memory as historical time. (For Berdyaev, it was represented as a line stretching into the future.) And the third is experienced individually as existential or psychological time. (Berdyaev proposed a dot or point.)[40] This immediate moment contains the concentrated 'buzz' of an individual's instantaneous time consciousness, which has been much studied by philosophers of phenomenology, with their stress upon delving inwards.[41]

There is no reason, however, to assume that Berdyaev's own classification of mental attitudes, ingenious as it is, applies universally. Far from all people view historic time as running along a line. Nor, even more importantly, do all communities or individuals share his three-tier consciousness. Other theorists have suggested different alternatives, such as metaphysical time (as in

philosophy and religion) or socio-cultural time (allowing for cultural variation), making four or five complex levels. The quest for a finite number of
subjective temporalities is, however, something of a will-o'-the-wisp, which is
ultimately distracting rather than enlightening.

Instead, it is enough to assume that there is one cosmic time-space that
provides the ambit within which people strive to interpret history (and not
just human history). After previewing many options, this study accordingly
presents three longitudinal themes for consideration. Following the idea of
possible dimensions within time, the focus here falls upon detectable dimensions within history. These are shaped by firstly, deep continuity; secondly,
gradual (evolutionary) change; and, thirdly, discontinuous or 'lumpy' (revolutionary) change. Defined in more abstract terms, they form a longitudinal
triad that can also be summarised as persistence/momentum/and turbulence
in history. They cohere seamlessly very much as do latitude/longitude/altitude
to form space.

World-watching in order to understand our environment is something that
is undertaken by every generation of humans. Daily we witness and have
witnessed the earth, sun, moon and stars. Their evidence spurs our repeated
attempts at measuring time and interpreting both the past and the present.
And it is an immensely long legacy. Above all, the light from far distant stars
takes millions of years to reach us, making the stars into primordial time
markers. They are powerful prompts for thought and wonder. In that context,
astronomers and environmental planners are now rightly campaigning to
reduce the artificial light pollution of the night skies, in order to improve
people's access to this primordial scene. It is this universal legacy of the stars
that has been evocatively hymned by the Indonesian poet W. S. Rendra, when
imagining 'The World's First Face':[42]

> . . . So, in all beginnings
> The world is bare
> Empty, free of lies,
> Dark with silence –
>
> . . .
> Then comes light,
> Existence,
> . . . Millions of stars in the sky.
> This is their [the first humans'] inheritance;
> Stars and more stars,
> More than could ever blink and go out.

Shaping History – Time Travel

Shaping and reshaping history is a retrospective art, performed after the event. Communal and individual interpretations of the vast and complex past are, however, perennially open to debate – which has spawned the intriguing thought of sending not merely the mind travelling to other epochs but living people to do likewise. If such voyages were to become feasible, then the shape of history could be viewed from both far away and close at hand. And epoch jumpers could not only witness past events to provide a trans-time commentary but they might even, so it is speculated, be able to change things that have once happened in the past. That would give not historians but successful time travellers the notional power to rewrite history at will.

Such stirring and disconcerting possibilities have spawned countless imaginative visions, theories, calculations, beliefs, representations, dreams, fictions, films and fables both old and new. All tales of strange escapes from the here-and-now envisage the transportation through time of one or more sentient individuals who are extracted from their own present to reappear, unchanged – without any significant physical, mental or emotional damage – in another epoch. That is a considerable set of assumptions. In addition, in many though not all versions of temporal transitioning, the travellers are then allowed to return home safely and to tell their tales, which may well be disbelieved. Sometimes the journey back is a relief. But, in other variants, the intrepid travellers regret leaving their new time zone, or feel torn between the two different eras which they have experienced.

These fictional travels outside time differ markedly from reincarnation beliefs, which are found in a number of religious traditions. From such perspectives, humans can certainly transcend the constraints of temporality – but only after their deaths. Either people are reborn spiritually within this world but in a later era and in a different physical form (not necessarily a human one); or people are resurrected as the same being, physically and spiritually, but within the afterlife in the next world. The concept of time travel, by contrast, focuses not upon reincarnation of the dead into a different form but retemporalisation of the living into a different epoch.

One of the simplest imagined mechanisms for achieving such a transition has a dreamlike quality. Individuals, or more rarely groups of individuals, fall deeply asleep in their own era and then awaken seamlessly in another, to everyone's surprise. Or people lose consciousness, perhaps with a stunning blow on the head, to find that they have been precipitated, rather groggily, into another epoch. Such imaginary time-dislocations are reminiscent of the sense of momentary disorientation that is sometimes felt upon awakening from deep sleep. The experience provides a pertinent reminder that the human awareness of being-in-time is by no means automatically geared to precise chronological reckonings. Our ancestry as temporal creatures is much older and more instinctive even than our ancestry as inventors and sharers of calendars.

Another imagined mechanism for leaving one's own time is also deceptively simple. It entails stepping or jumping through a sudden warp or rent in the fabric of daily reality into an alternative cosmos, with its own temporal and spatial rules. A classic example in this genre is Lewis Carroll's *Alice*, who falls headlong down a rabbit hole and, later, climbs painlessly through a huge looking-glass. The implication here is that the alternative world is close at hand, like a secret room or garden, locked away but potentially attainable. As a result, strange discoveries are always possible even in the midst of dull routines. Any humdrum box or container may have a secret power. So a prosaic police telephone-kiosk eerily transports Dr Who from one time zone to another, while appearing outwardly as nothing more than an ordinary item of street furniture.

In fact, those theorists who speculate about the possible existence of parallel universes, outside our own, generally conclude that any such parallel worlds must normally remain sealed within their separate temporal and spatial systems.[1] Nonetheless, the concept of a sideways jump to explore a new place and time celebrates the sudden drama of a mind-opening insight or experience. Incidentally, the general quest in time travel narratives tends rather to romance and high adventure than to raw carnality, although there is a hint of erotic possibilities in the theme of going through a secret door to reveal new worlds.

Meanwhile, no realistic mechanism has yet been invented that will enable living people to 'conquer time' either by departing for a far distant epoch or by getting calendrically younger in our own era. Nor are there any plans for such a machine. Theoretically, an enterprise to escape the constraints of time might perhaps be undertaken by entering a giant collapsed star or black hole – a singularity in the cosmos – with its hypothetical string-like gap or tunnel, which is termed, prosaically, a 'wormhole'.[2] Yet even such staggeringly momentous hyper-travel, which is far beyond the technologically achievable let alone the physically survivable, would still only lead 'beyond' the time-space continuum. It would not lead retrogressively into our past nor onwards into the future of this cosmos. Things that have happened and will happen are not like fixed places, which are eternally available for us to visit if only we can find the means of transport to get there. Instead, as time passes, so does time-space as a whole, absorbing elements from the past and creating the potentiality of the future.

Nonetheless, the prospect of escaping the bounds of the here-and-now has continued to inspire the technological imagination. In particular, theoretical devices for time travel encourage thoughts of streamlining the available transport technologies, assisting the quest for speed. A famous prototype was the *Time Machine* as imagined by H. G. Wells in 1895, shortly after the invention of the internal combustion engine: 'There in the flickering light of the lamp was the Machine, sure enough, squat, ugly, and askew; a thing of brass, ebony, ivory, and translucent glimmering quartz.' Its dials could be set for distant centuries, refusing to accept any limitation to the power of travel. And since then, indeed, technological innovations have greatly speeded transport possibilities in every medium: by land or sea, in the air and outer space. More than that, the sensation of travelling into other temporal universes can be imagined by all viewers of science fiction films, as different temporal eras are juxtaposed seamlessly by the techniques of flashback and flash-forward.[3]

Within these fables, however, 'normal' time is always allowed to resume once the momentous time-jump has occurred. So people, who notionally travel backwards, do not then continue to talk backwards. For example, one time-challenged character in Alice's looking-glass world is the White chess-Queen, who at moments experiences time in reverse. She screams first, and then pricks her finger on a pin. However, even in her distress the Queen cries 'Oh, oh, oh' in the normal way, and not 'Ho, ho, ho', as her cry would appear if uttered *sdrawkcab*.

This indicates that even imagined alternative worlds generally share the common expectation about time's 'onwards' unidirectionality. Mental maps that shed such an expectation cannot be processed and become gibberish. Lewis Carroll's vivid imagination envisaged another time-alternative that makes the same point, via the case of the Red chess-Queen in the looking-glass world. At given moments, she runs fast-forwards furiously, taking with her the startled Alice, their feet not touching the ground (see illustration 3). Yet all this effort leaves them just where they began. The imagined drama of dislocated time (a wonderful symbol of stress) subsides

3 Tenniel's illustration for *Through the Looking Glass* (1872), provides a humorous proxy for the dream of time travel – that runs faster than time but ends where it began.

back into the here-and-now. After rushing outside the normal rules, Alice and the Red Queen are quietly reclaimed by 'ordinary' life. Time-space and its routine conditions remain at the start- and end-points of all these mental journeyings.

Travelling notionally into the past allows for much amusing by-play with the shock of anachronism. In the first episode of Steven Spielberg's film trilogy *Back to the Future*, a teenage hero from 1985 returns to his hometown in 1955. At the high-school dance, he gives an exuberant guitar-smashing performance of a popular hit. Both the music and the stage style, however, date recognisably not from the 1950s but from later times. The viewers of the film can thus smile knowingly when the young hero assures his high-school audience, who include his own parents as teenagers: 'I guess you guys are not ready for that yet – but your kids are going to love it'.

However, the protagonist of the first *Back to the Future* also has a serious problem on his hands. Arriving in 1955, he finds that his future parents show no signs of falling in love with each other. History will not unfold in the 'correct' sequence unless he reshapes events that happen before he is born. He therefore contrives a situation at the school dance that will enable his parents to fall in love, so ensuring his own later existence. As a bonus, when the hero rematerialises in

1985, he finds that his formerly sad and dysfunctional family has become a pleasant and successful one.

Back to the Future is a light-hearted transformation story with a happy ending. But it highlights the conundrum that ensues when time travellers intervene in the past to which they have journeyed. In this case, the parents cannot fall in love without the help of their son, who will not be born unless they do. So the consequence of their affections would have to become the cause.

By intervening in this way, the imaginary traveller manages to 'save' the known historical outcome. But the situation becomes even more complicated when the unfolding of past events, as they must have happened, is disrupted or halted by a stray visitor from a later era. For example, a time traveller who returns to an epoch before his or her own birth may destroy, either accidentally or deliberately, a bloodline ancestor before that ancestor has produced any offspring. An entire genealogical sequence has thus been derailed. The notional time traveller has destroyed the specific version of the past that leads to his or her own existence. Put simply, the result has killed the cause.

Such paradoxical reshapings of history by unwary time travellers do, however, ultimately indicate that there is a regular time-sequencing that is built into the cosmos by the unidirectionality of time-space. Whether the route from past to present is envisaged in the form of a line or a circle (these are particularly common images) or any other contouring, there must be at least one strand of uninterrupted history that has simultaneously produced the time traveller and all his or her living contemporaries. Speciality keeps temporality coherent, and vice versa.

Alternative sequences, if any there be, cannot have disrupted that particular sequence. The notional worlds must unfold separately, without disturbing the ground rules. As a result, even cross-time visitations from people, who wish merely to observe another epoch without meddling, are theoretically and practically prohibited within this cosmos, because merely the presence of an outside observer has an influence, however minor. Just by being there, he or she causes a disruption in the seamlessness of time-space. And through such a rent in normality, anything or everything might fly in too – or fly out.

Time-space thus appears to have its own 'Chronology Protection Agency', as hypothesised by physicist Stephen Hawking.[4] It is a safeguard that works longitudinally so that, while we are synchromeshed in our own time (and thus able to live in the present), we are simultaneously diachromeshed into an unfolding history (and thus enabled to remember elements of the past and to anticipate facets of the future). There is more latitude for movement in space, but even spatial mobility, within the time-space continuum, is ultimately confined by the constraints of temporality.

Not only does the Chronology Protection Agency debar time travel in bodily form but it also forbids interactive long-distance communications between speakers existing in different periods of time. A caller today cannot telephone people living in another era – not even the many who have lived within the past 130-plus years of the 'telephone age'. Thus the new technologies of communication that are 'shrinking the globe' spatially are not displacing the sequencing of time, on whose synchronic coordination such worldwide communications in fact depend.

If jumping into the past is prohibited, what about moving rapidly onwards, jumping ahead into the far-distant future? Imaginatively, that offers excellent scope, because such visions are offset against potential states to come rather than referred backwards to a logically deducible past. Many are the futuristic epics, therefore, that preview the rise and fall of empires, the clash of civilisations, the turmoil of wars, adventures, and cross-time love affairs, as well as ambitious dreams of better worlds that might one day be.[5]

A number of celebrated political warnings have also used the genre of time travel to make their point. Futuristic masterworks that denounce twentieth-century totalitarianism include, classically, Yevgeny Zamyatin's *We* (written in 1920), Aldous Huxley's *Brave New World* (1932) and George Orwell's *1984* (first published in 1949). In all these writings, the author's current concerns are projected onto the future, with the implicit message that, if people will take appropriate precautions in the here-and-now, such dire outcomes can be avoided.

H. G. Wells's classic *Time Machine* was another pioneer of this genre of social warnings. He envisaged a future society that is divided between the effete if charming people of the 'upper world' and the sinister tribe of their predators, the Morlocks who dwell in the dark 'underworld'. His hero is drawn into their struggle after he arrives accidentally in his self-built time machine. In this way, Wells transformed his youthful memories of the country house ethos at aristocratic Uppark, where his mother had been employed as housekeeper and where the servants ran through a dank network of underground passages. And his message warned of stark social dangers to come, if the toiling 'downstairs' world forever remains excluded from the gracious 'upstairs' world of leisure and cultivation.

Theoretical travels into the future such as these run parallel to the debates among scientists about the practicalities of any such potential exercise. An experiment in October 1971 provided some thought-provoking evidence, when the astrophysicists Joseph Hafele and Richard Keating arranged for four ultra-precise atomic clocks to be flown at supersonic speeds around the world, firstly east-wards and then westwards. Their aim was to assess the effect of very rapid motion upon time measurement. In fact, because planes fly at only a tiny fraction of the speed of light, the recorded variation was tiny (and furthermore was not absolutely consistent from clock to clock). Nonetheless, once allowances were made for the effect of the earth's own rotation, it was clear that motion at high speed did have an impact. The clocks flying eastwards lagged behind the control clocks in the home observatory by an average of 59 nanoseconds (billionths of a second), while those flying westwards were on average 273 nanoseconds fast.[6] Temporal succession (time's arrow) is not abolished but its measurement, at ultra-high speed, is altered, as temporal relativity specifies.

Building upon that, it can be hypothesised that people on a manned space flight moving at ultra-high speeds would therefore live within a separate timetable. An intrepid twin, dispatched far from earth in a super-accelerated capsule close to the speed of light, would experience time dilation which would slow things down. He or she would not have escaped from the constraints of temporality. But, if enabled to return to earth unharmed – a problematic exercise in itself – the travelling twin would find, after coping with astonishingly horrendous jet lag, that significantly more moments, perhaps years, depending upon the length of the trip, had been measured on earth than in the travel capsule, so that the earthbound twin would be older in terms of measured time.

Significant discrepancies such as these might initially suggest that the sundered siblings have diverged into different eras. However, the twins reunite simultane-ously in the earth's present. It is true that they travel by different routes through the time-space continuum, taking different times to get there. In other words, the twins are not having symmetrical experiences. They nonetheless remain in the same cosmos, so that, were a reunion technically achievable, they would meet in the same time. Similarly, on a very much more restricted scale, the atomic clocks in the 1971 round-the-world fast-flying marathon all landed in the then earth's present – and not in a separate future or past.

So we collectively abide in a secure location within time-space. We are locked into our temporal frame. Yet the experience is so normal that it generally does not seem like a constriction. Meanwhile, we can test the boundaries mentally and imaginatively by every means at our disposal. Thoughts in the here-and-now can be directed both prospectively and retrospectively to contemplate other times. In that way, we can undertake and share thought experiments that imagine the future and give shape to the past.

CHAPTER 2

Deep Continuities

Persistence or continuity in history is an underrated and often overlooked factor. It lacks the high drama of mutability, and it is at variance with the everyday awareness of diurnal changes – from day to night, and on to day again. In the phraseology of Henri Bergson, the fertile French philosopher–psychologist who probed the human sense of temporal flux: 'Being is always Becoming' and 'Becoming is infinitely varied.'[1] Yet to be able to measure change, whether at macro- or micro-level, there must be some constant factors to act as benchmarks.

As a result, it is possible to formulate some propositions that appear timeless and changeless. For example, many (though not all) of the laws of physics are formulated in a manner that is indifferent to temporality, in the sense that such laws operate in the same way today as they did yesterday. As a result, when scientific experiments are validated by repetition in laboratory conditions, the passage of time is factored out, because its effect is taken as neutral. The laws of physics do indeed conceal a silent proviso that such laws are co-extensive with the timespan of this cosmos. But that framing duration is so immensely great that it rarely needs mentioning. There is thus a marked contrast between the 'timelessness' of the laws of physics as they are expressed and the intrinsic temporality of the human experience of formulating, testing, contesting and reformulating such laws.

Another example of deep continuity can be seen in the staple rules of mathematics. At an absolutely basic level, the sum of one plus one always makes two in all regular numbering systems.[2] Even the most simple known notations count 'one-two-many', while most proceed successively from one to mathematical infinity. As far back as the historical evidence goes, moreover, the original concept of basic quantification is indicated by displaying fingers to indicate quantity – a technique that is still used today between people who have otherwise no spoken language in common.

Of course, the constancy of simple numbers in no way implies that the philosophical and cultural frameworks of numbering and calculating systems are always and universally the same. On the contrary, the study of 'ethnomathematics' offers a pertinent reminder that both the role and expression of mathematical ideas show an impressive range of historical variations over time.[3] The renowned sailors from the Caroline atolls of Micronesia in the western Pacific, for example, traditionally use a unique navigational system, which is based upon the assumption that the ship remains still while the star compass and adjacent islands move around it. Theirs is a subtle geometry not of static lines but of celestial motion.

Nonetheless, there are common principles of calculation, which remain accessible across all human cultures. Over time, many dextrous manual and verbal counting systems have been developed.[4] And, above all, the spread of written notations eventually provided the basis for a shared language and philosophy of mathematics that could be developed and ultimately communicated worldwide. One notable innovation in this long story came in the fourth century CE, with the Indian adoption of an operational zero – the perfect circle. The usefulness of this device for purposes of numbering and calculation was such that its usage gradually spread, via commercial contacts, to encourage the flowering of Arab mathematics, which in turn transmitted the innovation, from the twelfth century onwards, to transform European mathematics, so that ultimately this indispensable notation was conveyed by multiple routes to become adopted worldwide.[5]

How the use of zero was diffused is a fascinating process that indicates both a capacity for adaptation and a common sharing of a time-invariant concept of number.[6] As a result, while humans have generated thousands of word-based languages, there has been, alongside that, a worldwide consolidation of only one single symbolic and highly precise 'language' of calculation – as expressed in mathematics. It is certainly true that the subject is always open to refinement and further sophistication among what is today a worldwide community of mathematicians. Nonetheless, the basic rules of the subject remain diachronically valid – and indeed many problems are discussed and eventually resolved by several generations of scholars. In the case of solving Fermat's 'Last Theorem' (propounded in 1637), it was not achieved until 1994, while the quest for 'Sophie German primes', defined by this pioneering woman mathematician when analysing Fermat's theorem in 1825, still continues. Consequently, extending the same principle, if some numerate Sumerians from the world's first literate culture could jump unscathed from 3000 BCE into the present day, they would recognise the basic exercises of addition today, just as they themselves might have executed similar sums with the aid of pebble counters or an abacus.[7]

Furthermore, because the principles of mathematics are timelessly valid, the language of mathematics can be successfully used to describe the 'through-time' (and simultaneously through-space) properties of the physical universe.[8] Again, it is important to note that the human understanding of these subjects is always liable to revision. That there are some identifiably persistent and calculable time-invariant factors, however, makes it possible for a mathematicised science (as in, for example, physics, engineering and computer technology) to be applied not only theoretically but additionally for a great array of practical purposes with operational success.

Beneath the outward flux, therefore, there are various deep continuities in history, which need due acknowledgement and understanding. As will be seen, these persistent elements are not isolated from other mutable factors but overlap, to a greater or lesser extent. So there is always scope for debate and disagreement as to what is 'given' and what is liable to change.

These tensions apply equally to the human experience. As living creatures of the cosmos, people share common elements not only of change but also of long-term persistence. Numerous philosophical beliefs accordingly stress the importance of fundamental continuities within the apparent turbulence. Thus Heraclitus of Ephesus, in the classical world of the first century BCE, argued: 'This world [is] the same for all; . . . it always was, and is, and shall be, an ever-living fire . . .'. Hence all people 'living and dead, awake and asleep, young and old, are the same'.[9] Another much quoted dictum comes from the Biblical preacher Ecclesiastes: 'There is no new thing under the sun.' Variants of this formula recur in many cultural expressions. 'Nothing is New: we walk where others went,' sang the plangent poet Robert Herrick in seventeenth-century England.[10] It is a viewpoint that signals a refusal to be impressed by apparent novelties. They are trivial compared with the immanence associated with the concept of perennial order. So Ecclesiastes succinctly emphasised that true values are everlasting, in comparison with the superficiality and frivolity of merely ephemeral changes: 'Vanity of vanities; all is vanity.'[11]

Deep Structures

Even in human technology, which is often taken to constitute the heartland of innovation, there are persistent elements both in design and usage. For example, some inventions, once made, have not been significantly amended for millennia. Staple utensils such as bowls, plates, chisels, hammers and needles are recognisable across the centuries in their basic design for everyday use, even while there have been many refinements of style and changes in the preferred construction materials.

The same is true of the wheel. A simple and beautiful invention without a known inventor, it has endless practical ramifications as well as immense symbolic power. Many adaptations have been incorporated, such as spokes, hubs, rims, tyres, teeth and ratchets, since the earliest surviving wooden exemplar which dates back to at least 2500 BCE.[12] Yet its core principle of operation remains unchanged. Moreover, the wheel is far from technically outmoded, remaining a component of many later inventions such as the mechanical clock, the mill, the train, the bicycle, the motor car, the aeroplane and the moon buggy (three of which wheeled vehicles are still resting quietly on the lunar surface, demonstrating the continuing fusion of technology old and new).

In fact, even the most apparently dramatic innovations continue to incorporate elements of older technologies. Not only is it impossible to invent absolutely everything from scratch, so that producers create by building upon as well as revising earlier knowledge, but users also appreciate elements of continuity to promote familiarisation. For that reason, the designers of the path-breaking electronic computers in the mid twentieth century retained, for English-language keyboards, the familiar QWERTYUIOP layout of letters and numbers from the old typewriter days. This 'continuity' tactic eased the shock of the new. In fact, various rival English-language keyboard layouts have been invented, but such alternatives are so far losing the battle to gain acceptance, being unable to undermine the appeal of familiarity.

However, technology is not the most obvious area to search for deep continuities. Instead, attention is often directed to the world's spatial and geographical configuration. The broad configuration of the world generally appears, from moment to moment, as reassuringly stable. It is true that mountains do slowly crumble; riverbeds are scoured or silted; coastlines erode; continents slowly drift apart; and dust blows in the wind. But major geophysical adaptations, short of exceptional upheavals and catastrophes, often take a very long time to have a major impact, especially when contrasted with the relatively limited human lifespan. (Fears that current climate changes are accelerating rather than developing gradually are the more destabilising because such a scenario conflicts with 'normal' expectations.)

A 'semi-immobile' geohistory was positively identified as the central force underpinning historical continuity by Fernand Braudel, France's pre-eminent historian–theorist of the long term. He argued that the framing of the physical world is innately calibrated to an unhurried temporality, with 'a slower tempo, which sometimes almost borders on the motionless'.[13]

It is noticeable, too, that patterns of human settlement often display great longevity, as they respond to long-term features of climate, terrain and environment. Mountains and inhospitable landscapes act as barriers. By contrast, indented coastlines with safe harbours and interiors with long, deep rivers encourage traffic and communications. Historic trackways survive for long periods of time. Old building materials are recycled: in one striking example, stretches of the nineteenth-century rail-track from Lahore to Karachi are built on foundations made from 3,600-year-old bricks from the ancient city of Harappa.[14] Often, too, venerable plot boundaries are still detectable beneath later developments. Some village settlements do disappear, but many persist for centuries, throughout changing times.

And vanished great cities are rarer still. It takes something as drastic as the collapse of a political system or major climatic change to consign whole urban networks to oblivion. Ancient Ur of the Chaldees has disappeared beneath the sands of Iraq; the ruins of Chichen-Izta are covered in jungle on Mexico's Yucatan; and the toppled statues of Herakleion lie under the Mediterranean, offshore from the Egyptian port of Alexandria. Nonetheless, great cities frequently demonstrate great resilience, as their inhabitants rebuild on or near devastated sites, after even the severest disasters. Post-1944 Hiroshima, rising from the nuclear ashes, is but one urban phoenix among many. And now it is New Orleans that is facing the challenge of recovery from an entire urban drowning.

Such continuities and renewals of continuity in human settlements act as a form of collective conservation of effort within established networks, just as an element of locational stability provides some communal ballast against the perennial mobility of individuals. These sorts of linkages are not immune to change, it should be stressed, but they mesh human endeavours into the long term of Braudelian 'geohistory'.

Capital cities in particular display great tenacity in retaining their primacy. Within established states it is unusual, though not unknown, for the seat of government to be moved.[15] But such changes, if made once, do not occur frequently. A time traveller from today who returned to Europe in (say) 1600 would have no trouble in recognising the core role of Vienna in Austria, London in England, Paris in France, Dublin in Ireland, Stockholm in Sweden, or the nascent Madrid in Spain, although he or she would then seek in vain for a great metropolitan Berlin among the German principalities.

Many examples of great urban longevity, stretching over thousands of years, indicate how a human-lived geography may reinforce its own perdurance in history. The city of Jericho is one of the oldest continuously inhabited places in the world, with evidence of settlements dating back to *c.* 5000 BCE. Another lengthy saga is that of Beijing. Once a small border encampment, it grew as Yanjing, the 'city of swallows', long before being confirmed as one of several capitals from the twelfth century onwards and eventually China's sole capital, its hegemony varying as the imperial boundaries expanded and contracted under different imperial dynasties.[16] To the north-west of Beijing, there persist too China's formidable outer fortifications, constructed as great earthworks from *c.* 220 BCE onwards, and later upgraded by the Ming emperors in the fifteenth century. This is the Great Wall, stretching for a startling distance of three thousand kilometres (2,150 miles) to constitute a veritable part of the mountainous landscape.[17]

Western Europe meanwhile has a parallel example of longevity in the case of 'eternal' Rome. It too has grown, via many fluctuations, from a small river-side settlement to play a fulcrum role as the capital of, variously, an empire, an international religion and, since 1870, a nation-state. Its palimpsest of buildings, the new built upon and among the old, reveals its long history. Some of the city's present-day water supply, for example, comes through channels that originally supplied the aqueducts of imperial Rome. And, close to the city centre, the elliptical Piazza Navona, once an emperor's stadium, has been used at different times for games, tournaments, water festivals, fairs, markets, religious ceremonials, street entertainments and the social parade. To gather there on a summer evening, among the throng of residents and tourists, is to experience the living history of an urban meeting place that is more than two thousand years old.[18]

Given the force of continuity, underlying and commingling with the rival pressures of change, it can be hard to decide which is the more powerful. Which constitutes the default system: persistence or mutability? This problem recurs again and again when trying to disentangle the permanent from the evanescent, showing how closely intertwined they habitually become.

For the pioneering world historian H. T. Buckle in the mid-nineteenth century, it was physical geography (the climate, food, soil and environment) that provided the decisive framework for all human affairs. This approach extended Montesquieu's influential analysis of comparative constitutions, as formulated in the mid eighteenth century. He too had stressed the importance of climate and environment as framing factors, while allowing scope also for the role of different customs, laws and cultural traditions.[19] Buckle, however, hoped to establish geography as an unchallenged scientific rule. All 'changing phenomena have unchanging laws',[20] he declared, seeking a general basis to explain surface variations. This would transform history-writing and rescue the subject from the obsessions with passing trivia that were displayed by mere 'biographers, genealogists, collectors of anecdotes, [and] chroniclers of courts, of princes, and of nobles – those babblers of vain things' – the reference to 'babblers of vain things' echoing the Biblical refrain 'all is vanity'.

Buckle's emphasis upon geography in many ways foreshadowed the historical approach of Fernand Braudel, who has already been introduced as the twentieth century's foremost theorist of historical continuity. Short-term events he dismissed as 'capricious'. That made them 'delusive' as guides to understanding history.[21] They were 'vain things' on a par with the trivia that Buckle had also sought to discard.

When, therefore, Braudel posed the question: what factors make France so identifiably 'French'? he answered himself by reference to the country's enduring geohistory.[22] In fact, its environment has not always been so completely stable. France was contiguous with Britain until some six to seven thousand years ago, when rising sea levels from melting glaciers inserted a deep-sea channel between them. However, Braudel was thinking of more recent centuries. And he was particularly alert to the sheer physicality of human existence. Each event occurs 'on a particular site and on no other', he once remarked. He admired the 'fixing' power of place – and especially of rural place – in cementing individual and collective identity. There were clear echoes in this of his personal recollections of a happy country childhood in Lorraine, on the contested borderland between France and Germany where locational identity remains a classic preoccupation.

Indeed, the enduring power of spatiality can be seen in the way that many others besides Braudel experience a link between personal memories and specific locations.[23] Conversely, people who are abruptly uprooted from familiar surroundings may feel physically or psychologically unwell, with sensations of 'homesickness' and disorientation when their habitual bearings are disrupted. So effective are the organising powers of mental mapping, indeed, that many traditional mnemonic systems use the technique of spatial imaging as a way of 'storing' items in an invented location for later retrieval and remembrance.[24]

Yet it should be noted that not all individuals respond so strongly to place. Many intangibles of human thought, like communicated ideas and beliefs, can and do transcend the immediate vicinity of the thinker.

Nevertheless, underlying geographical factors do exert a strong 'framing' influence which is often, though not invariably, tilted on the side of historical continuity.

Following upon this, one obvious and long-running constant for humanity is the importance of the fate of the earth itself. The ecosystem to which we are adapted is that of the solar system's beautiful 'blue planet' – its colouring when viewed from space imaginatively foretold as predominantly blue-green by Jules Verne, in his 1865 adventure tale of moon-travel, and strikingly confirmed by the cosmonauts' eye-witness testimony just over one hundred years later.[25] This planetary attachment is a deep structure that not only endures but has to endure for our survival.

Cultural Continuities

Grids of cultural connections further help to create inter-generational continuities in human history across the generations. Such linkages are particularly enhanced among people who stay put within a shared location over many years. Yet culture, here used in its very broadest sense as a communal set of ideas, values and shared 'way of life', is a protean force, constantly subject to shifts and adaptations – not least because migration and the meeting of cultures have long been a feature of the human experience too. Elements of continuity are therefore buffeted by change, but changes are simultaneously absorbed into pre-existing ways, whether consciously or unconsciously. In Mexico under the colonial rule of Spain, for example, many cultural traditions of the defeated Aztecs were smuggled unofficially into the newly imposed Catholic religion. (*See* illustrations 4 and 5 for a sixteenth-century visual symbol of the epic Spanish–Mexican cultural encounter.)

Continuing ideas, information and social attitudes are regularly transmitted through the efforts that each generation devotes to the education and upbringing of the highly dependent human young. A huge stock of collective know-how is constantly conveyed, both informally and formally, as well as regularly updated. Babies acquire the language (or the plural languages) of the host communities in which they are nurtured and, with languages, a range of cultural assumptions. It is true, needless to say, that there is often friction between the generations. If adults complain about the unruliness and ingratitude of their children, the young in turn deplore the oppressive control or, alternatively, the tired inertia of their seniors. Such habitual rufflings of feathers do not, however, halt the constant interplay between the different age groups as vectors for cultural transmission.

Living languages provide particularly fascinating examples of the welding of continuity and changes. New words are coined; new idioms become diffused; and from time to time new linguistic conventions about sentence construction emerge. Yet many of the basic rules of grammar and syntax, as well as a core stock of terminology, show great stability over time. To make sense, new components must dovetail with the 'vast, unchanging areas' that persist within languages.[26]

An English speaker from today who suddenly returns to England in 1600 could converse with Shakespeare and his contemporaries with tolerable success, although the differing accents and nuances of word use would at first be somewhat bewildering.

After a longer retro-journey to talk to Geoffrey Chaucer in the 1380s, when he was writing *The Canterbury Tales*, conversation would be much more stilted. But it would still be possible, with enough common ground to improvise.

4 The Catholic Mission Church of San Agustín at Acolman, near Mexico City, quietly incorporates a traditional Aztec place-sculpture on its façade.

5 [Detail of façade] The traditional Aztec place-sculpture records the Aztec creation myth which saw Acolman as the place where fruitful life began.

Some of Chaucer's vocabulary would be incomprehensible. On the other hand, his translation of a familiar Latin tag such as 'womman is mannes joye and al his blis'[27] could be understood well enough, even though his turn of phrase might seem archaic.

Going further back in time, however, would render communication ever more risky. Returning to speak to the eighth-century author of *Beowulf* would require the help of translators for more than basic exchanges. Various pithy 'Anglo-Saxon' nouns and verbs that remain in the language today would be recognisable; but the inflected dialects of Old English, prior to the post-1066 infusion of Norman French, would sound highly Germanic and hard to comprehend. Nonetheless, there would be still some elements of familiarity, underneath the variations in pronunciation. A notional twenty-first-century time traveller to eighth-century England could pose the deceptively simple query: 'to be or not to be?' and expect to be understood. Without the benefit of knowing *Hamlet*, the startled speakers of Old English would not cap the quotation by responding: 'That is the question', because anyway the Latinate noun 'question' did not feature in their vocabulary. They might, however, declare '*Thæt is the thyngge*' and be understood in return, though all would still be left to ponder the ultimate answer to Shakespeare's timeless meditation.

Long-surviving linkages of this sort indicate that some elements of linguistic patterning do persist within the structure of languages across very long eras, even though languages are simultaneously updated and adapted – sometimes quite substantially, as in the well-known case of the fusion of Old English with Norman French after the Norman Conquest in 1066. It is these persistent features that enable linguists to construct (and to argue about) systems of classification. Thus Old English is a Germanic variant within the Indo-European 'family' of languages. The structural prototype for this linguistic grouping, which probably always contained a variegated cluster of dialects, dates back to *c.* 4000 BCE or even earlier. And from this source has sprung an immensely complex linguistic inheritance, persisting through many millennia and still today underpinning a multitude of tongues spoken globally by more than two thousand million people.[28]

To that, it may be added that one great constant in human history, ever since the epochal advent of speech, is the universal capacity for verbal communication.[29] Whether there is anything as systematic as a universal grammar – and, if so, what such a grammar contains – remains disputed. That there is a generic human capacity for language, including the ability to create and to understand linguistic structures, is not, however, in doubt. It remains an unchanging skill across the generations.

Furthermore, pre-linguistic sounds (screams, yelps, grunts, laughter, sobs, sighs, yawns), which have even more historic origins, also survive as significant modes of communication, as do facial and corporeal gestures, though the specific meanings of these vary greatly according to different cultural codes.

Key framing elements thus often persist for very long periods of time, despite frequent adaptations in detail. For example, different peoples have long-standing conventions about foodstuffs (what can or cannot be acceptably eaten) and about clothing (how much or how little it is acceptable to wear in given circumstances). These are societal norms. They can, of course, be challenged openly and/or adapted quietly. But such social conventions provide a shared framework for routine living, saving time and effort without the need to reinvent everything daily.

'Custom, then, is the great guide of human life,' observed David Hume philosophically in 1749.[30] Established habits frame normal experiences and provide a routine and settled template against which to test novelties. Young children, who are absorbing a lot of new information all the time, have a particularly strong need for such stable frameworks. Socially learned and culturally ingrained habits and expectations exert considerable influence, the more so for generally being taken completely for granted. Indeed, custom amounts to an 'unwritten Law', as the Restoration poet Charles Davenant proclaimed in 1677, 'by which the People keep even Kings in awe'.[31]

Rulers, no matter how powerful, should therefore think twice before attempting to override the routines of daily life. These form grids of cultural expectations and unwritten social rules, which are constantly adopted and adapted. Collectively, such daily patterns establish what is defined by the French sociologist Pierre Bourdieu as the human *habitus*, or basic lifestyle.[32]

Among local customary usages, dress codes do appear to be relatively adaptable. As clothing materials are relatively easy to transport over long distances, people can and do adopt fabrics and styles from other cultural traditions. That can be seen today in the spread of western dress, such as the ubiquitous blue jeans and casual sportswear, as showcased by images in films, television and magazines. Nonetheless, marked regional differences in dress codes still persist around the world. Within those, it also remains hard for individuals in ordinary circumstances to deviate *too* far from the self-presentational norms of the local communities in which they live.

Eating practices, by contrast, seem relatively more resistant to change. That is partly because many foodstuffs are perishable and costly to move over long distances but also because culinary tastes are deeply internalised. For example, since the Second World War the people of Japan have abandoned the kimono in favour of western dress for ordinary wear, but they generally retain as standard foodstuffs their customary high-protein, rice-based diet, eaten with traditional chopsticks. There is thus a continuing dialectic or contest between continuity and change. And even when eating habits change, as they may well do, the new cuisine often continues to incorporate elements that acknowledge traditional taste preferences.

Cultural continuities on great matters, such as religious faith and belief systems, are particularly deeply ingrained. Popular convictions and observances are buttressed not just by habit but by institutional powers, such as those of religious and political organisations. As a result, whole communities collectively change their official faith only rarely in history. On the other hand, the details of doctrine and ritual may well be liable to modification, just as the intensity of belief and formal religious observance is proving to be far from static over time.

All these traditional customs and expectations are transmitted by inter-generational communication by gregarious humans. Social information is circulated not only between old and young but also, interestingly, between young and younger. Some traditional children's songs and games survive essentially through playground transmission, without adult intervention,[33] although, when such traditions are perceived as lapsing, adults sometimes intervene to record and even to retrieve them.

Belief in the existence of a tradition also constitutes a form of continuity, even if the details of the tradition in practice vary. 'National' identities between people who share a common history and geography often contain a mythic element but simultaneously provide a way of recording collective survival 'through time'. One French ethnographer once claimed, in a mood of enthusiasm, that France's neolithic civilisation from the Stone Age era did not finally vanish until the 1970s. 'That is perhaps putting it rather strongly,' commented Fernand Braudel, conceding rather regretfully that continuity sometimes yields to change.[34] But the sense of a 'primordial' France acquires a traditional force among its adherents – and the same applies to any group's determined belief in its own age-old history that stretches 'time out of mind'.

Healthy individuals ordinarily generate their own personal versions of diachromeshed self-identity as well. A 'through-time' consciousness survives within us, despite the constant process of cell renewal/decay that leads to physical growth and eventual ageing. Indeed, an individual's self-awareness 'as a homogeneous entity in time, a blend of past and present' is well noted by Salman Rushdie, the Bombay-born novelist of questing identity, as consti-tuting the veritable 'glue of personality, holding together our then and our now'.[35] Conversely, a disordered or missing sense of temporal identity is a mark of mental ill-health and, in its most extreme manifestations, of a sad incapacity for living independently.

So important is the sense of consciousness through-time that it also forms the basis of moral judgements. These depend crucially upon the ability to appreciate the longitudinal linkages of cause and effect over time, as well as upon an immediate environmental awareness.

Socio/Cultural Biology

Collectively, humans as a species constitute a subset of the ape family who are relatively recent arrivals in world history. The oldest direct evidence of bipedal hominids, walking fully upright, survives in the remarkable Laetoli footprints (*see* illustration 15), dating from some 3.6 million years ago. But those unknown beings, who trod in the volcanic mud of northern Tanzania, were no more than distant precursors of *Homo sapiens*.[36] There were several distinct variants of walking apes, long before the successful emergence, some two hundred thousand years ago, of our own direct ancestors in genetic terms. Their original homeland was Africa, which continues to store the most varied gene pool of any global region. But by the time of the so-called Cro-Magnon era, some 35,000–40,000 years ago, the human species had spread worldwide. Meanwhile, a genetically distinct branch of apemen and -women, the Neanderthals, quietly disappeared.[37]

Based upon this common ancestry, a collective human kinship persists through time. In some cultures it is acknowledged in modes of address, as when, in India today, complete strangers are greeted as 'cousin'. And, whether welcomed or not, we share a set of broadly defining species characteristics as gregarious, large-brained, mind-conscious, language-speaking, tool-wielding, rule-making (as well as rule-breaking), versatile, omnivorous, restless, bipedal mammalians, complete with a common stock of blood groups and a universal complex of genetic codings, known as the human genome.

Were some time travellers from today permitted to return to the Cro-Magnon era, conversation between humans across the temporal divide would be tricky at the very least. Nonetheless, despite some major differences in clothing and presentational styles, there would be an element of biological recognition. If very ancient and ultra-today men and women could (impossibly) meet, they could also mate.

Fundamental processes of waking, sleeping, eating, drinking, excreting, living, procreating and eventually dying remain unchanged. Historians can therefore make various plausible assumptions about past communities that go beyond any direct testimony. For instance, it is highly probable that the biology of sexual pleasure has remained a constant feature throughout the generations, even if cultural attitudes towards sex vary considerably between cultures and over time. An orgasm in one era thus resembles, physiologically, an orgasm in any other (that is, excluding varieties of the faked version).

Additionally, there are mental as well as physical continuities. Humans display a recognisable combination of instincts, emotions, rational faculties and a species-unique capacity for laughter and joking. These permutations, between them, produce a versatile set of culturally sanctioned behavioural patterns, but the variety, although great, is not limitless. Hence the famous observation by the historian–philosopher Giambattista Vico, that anything done by humans can eventually be understood (though not necessarily endorsed) by other humans.[38] An older version of this capacity for mutual comprehension came too in an admired dictum from a play by Terence in classical Rome. One character accordingly declares: 'I regard nothing that is human as alien to me: *Humani nil a me alienum puto*'.[39]

Substantial arguments have also followed in the wake of this sense of common biological identity. Not content with accepting that there is a broad-based and versatile 'human nature', some analysts insist that it be defined exclusively in terms of one leading characteristic. A 'competitive' interpretation, for example, stresses rivalry and aggression,[40] while a rival 'cooperative' version detects sociability and altruism. Or some genetic determinists consider that our disposition is genetically pre-programmed. Thus 'we are born selfish', states biologist Richard Dawkins. According to this view, our genes seek constantly to replicate themselves, rendering humans essentially into gene 'survival machines'.[41] Consequently, all behaviour should be single-mindedly directed towards one goal, which translates, on this view, into the urge for genetic reproduction. Attention would be lavished upon offspring or, failing them, upon close blood relatives with a similar genetic inheritance. And the alleged reproductive imperative should also cause people to recoil instinctively from all forms of non-reproductive sex, including same-sex love affairs; and certainly no contraceptive devices would be either invented or utilised, if there was a universally shared preoccupation with transmitting genes to the next generation.

Reductive interpretations such as these are substantiated by some people's observable behaviour but easily refuted by the many exceptions to the claimed rule. Among other things, genes do not operate in isolation but act as building blocks in interlocking clusters to sustain complex and varied people, who live in complex and varied societies too.

Repeated attempts at providing summary generalisations nonetheless indicate a recurrent interest in understanding and classifying our own species. From this concern comes a clutch of verdicts, not only about all humans but also about various intermediate groupings. These claims, often provocative, then provide a basis for popular myths and folk stereotypes. They offer a comforting hope that there is a simple 'clue' behind apparent diversity. For example, 'the Spaniards have always been cruel, the French boastful, the

Italians crafty and cunning, [and] the English lovers of fair play', stated a Victorian anthropologist named Dr John Beddoe at a public lecture in 1891, confident that at least his English audience would cheer.[42] Such portrayals, however flawed, had deep historical roots which made them deeply reassuring.

While rejecting such crude caricatures, later analysts can identify the social and cultural role played by such attitudes. They propose a shape for studying history by casting it in terms of a morality contest. The admirable qualities of the home team are boosted in contrast to the unworthy qualities of the 'other', whether the rival team or teams be feared or hated or despised or all of those. It is not uncommon, moreover, for such popular stereotypings to persist for lengthy periods of time. They are generally expressed with heightened intensity during eras of conflict. But these attitudes may also linger long afterwards in a shadowy half-life, recurring in traditional jokes and sayings – and sometimes reviving suddenly in moments of crisis – well after the immediate rivalries have abated and the grossest nationalist prejudices have been generally disowned.

Needing to find forms of group identity has also led to another set of arguments about the notional division of the human species into separate 'races'. In fact, geneticists confirm that there is a globally prevalent mix of genotypes within all communities, which has been produced by our long history of repeated demographic migrations and intermarryings from the earliest times.[43] There are therefore not separate 'races', as some of the pioneering anthropologists mistakenly thought, but one continuing human race. That is confirmed by the perennial capacity of people from all areas to interbreed. Accordingly, the sequencing of the human genome applies to all, not just to some, allowing the complexities of genetic inheritance both globally and in its local variations to be studied systematically.

Past attempts at finding a scientific basis for biologically separate 'races' thus proved to be problematic. The many different criteria that were proposed – from skin colour and hair texture, to average heights, cranial (skull) formation, nose shapes, and testable intelligence – yielded different and inconsistent answers.[44] Estimates of the number of different human 'races' within the human race ranged from as low as two to as high as sixty-three, with no consensus emerging. For example, the many subtle variations in the spectrum of skin colours, from lily to ebony, make drawing up hard-and-fast divisions based upon colour a subjective and fallible exercise.

Unlike (say) an agreed classification of botanic specimens, the sub-classification of humans into genetically and perennially separate 'races' or 'tribes' has remained a shifting terrain of rival assertions and counter-assertions. Hence those theories that shape history into a continual struggle between permanently sundered biological rivals have rightly been discarded. Even the comte de Gobineau, whose confident 1854 tract on the *Inequality of*

Human Races helped to popularise this approach, regretfully acknowledged that his proposed three groupings, the 'white' (European), the 'yellow' (Asian), and the 'black' (African), had all lost their original 'purity' through intermarriage.[45] Meanwhile, the fact that his tripartite global model in fact excluded the people from large swathes of central Eurasia, the Indian subcontinent, south-east Asia, north Africa, indigenous America, Australia and the Pacific islands, went entirely unmentioned by Gobineau.

Notwithstanding such difficulties of drawing boundaries, it does remain the case that strong communal beliefs in communal identity, among rival groups of humans, exist and are historically persistent. But the criteria for such clan attachments are commonly selected from amongst a wide range of characteristics. These include options in any combination potentially based upon shared appearance, cultural or 'ethnic' tradition, homeland, religion, language, historical experience, political allegiance, or any other emotionally powerful identifier.[46] Moreover, it is very common for individuals to have more than one group allegiance at the same time (such as a national and a local identity, or a religious and a linguistic affiliation).

At a guess, therefore, the still-surviving terminologies that refer to biologically separate 'races' among the human population will soon be discarded, as scientifically invalid and as proposing a false model of separated continuities in history. However, other intermediate group designators, such as those based upon origins or residence by world regions for example, are likely to continue.

Testing all forms of generalised assertions about innate human characteristics, whether applying to all humans or to separate groups of humans, clearly remains both a fascinating and a problematic exercise. People cannot be investigated in the abstract since all are located within specific times and places.[47] Individuals learn socially and culturally as they grow biologically, while biological processes are simultaneously sensitive to the micro-environment in which growth occurs.[48] Hence all the many arguments about the separate and rival importance of nature or nurture rather miss the point: one constant for the human species as a whole, with its infant offspring entirely dependent on adult care, has always been that human nature positively requires nurture to survive.

Individuals thus find their lifestyles are perennially defined between biology and cultural history. Nowhere is that more pronounced than in the case of the gender roles of men and women. Not only are there continuing physical differences but these are also framed and reframed by changeable expectations. Dogmatic statements abound. One patriarchal model of society sees men as typically strong, bold, rational and intelligent leaders, while women are supposedly warm, nurturing, intuitive and emotional camp-followers.

Hence the predominance of the male principle over the female one would be based upon biology: 'There is no alternative; this is simply the way it [nature] is,' remarks one male professor,[49] alarmed at the failure of feminists (of both sexes) to accept what seems obvious to him.

On the other hand, the historical ranges of behaviour patterns and individual characteristics among both sexes suggest that gender roles in practice have the potential for considerable plasticity. At one point, it was feared that too much mental endeavour would masculinise the female body. Intellectual women should thus develop the secondary physical characteristics of men (beards, bald heads, deep voices). Yet female participants in tournaments of chess, the most cerebral of games, have succeeded without sparking a physiological crisis.[50] A more plausible formulation is that all human thought processes retain the capacity to combine logic/rationality and intuition/empathy, while individuals display a spectrum of mentalities, some being more logical (the so-called 'male' brain), some more empathetic (the so-called 'female' brain), and a considerable group uniting both logic and intuition (the so-called 'balanced' brain).[51] But since these different mentalities do not correlate at all exactly with the two biological sexes, it is likely – again at a guess – that the distractingly gendered terminology for mental profiling will gradually, though not immediately, be dropped.

Pairing and comparing men with women, however, has not ceased to be a matter of intense interest. A recent school of thought focuses not upon claims to differential brainpower but upon rival sexual strategies. Known as Evolutionary Psychology, this approach in fact endorses a rigid continuity rather than a flexible evolution, on the grounds that the human species is a recent arrival, biologically speaking, and has not had time to evolve substantially. 'We carry around a stone-aged brain in a modern environment,' stresses American social psychologist David Buss.[52] All actions are thus modelled upon the presumed behaviour of our ancestors in hunter–gatherer societies. Sexual activity is simultaneously envisaged as a matter of rational calculus. On this basis, all women supposedly seek to mate with high-status, economically successful males, who will provide resources and 'good' genes for future offspring. Men, by contrast, are viewed as promiscuous sperm-scatterers. They should seek to father as many children as possible, in order to maximise their genetic transmission to the next generation. An ultra-version of this 'Stone Age' theory warns that all men are naturally rapists, if thwarted in their reproductive drive.[53]

Again, the outward promise of such generalisations is that they can both detect and explain history's immutable patterning. There are problems, however, when activities that are observable in some people for some of the time (or even in many people for much of the time) are turned into universal rules, whilst other orientations such as homosexuality, bisexuality and asexuality, which do not fit the basic model, are entirely excluded. Because there is no direct evidence of the sexual philosophy of the Stone Age population, Buss instituted instead an international survey of a thousand young people from thirty-seven different countries, on the grounds that attitudes in these matters are timeless.[54] The results, however, indicated an intriguing cross-cultural spectrum of viewpoints. While there were differences between gendered responses, there were also variations within and across the gender groupings, with a spectrum of responses variously influenced by personal, cultural and biological factors.[55] There was no automatic bipolar split between all men and all women, as there should be if an automatic division in attitudes to sexuality had been biologically hard-wired into the human psyche.

Moreover, Buss did not check that the actions of his respondents matched their stated preferences. Sexual behaviour is not mediated purely or even chiefly in terms of rational calculus. It is not uncommon therefore for sexual desire to lead people to behave in previously unintended ways. As C. P. Cavafy, Greek poet of sensual longing, once wrote:

> Night comes with its own counsel
> Its own compromises and prospects –
> . . . night comes with its own power,
> of a body that needs and demands . . .[56]

It would be more plausible, therefore, to argue that biology has endowed humans with an intense interest in matters of sex, and a less universally intense but nonetheless serious interest in reproduction, and that these concerns are expressed in distinctly polymorphous ways, both within and outside the socially acceptable frameworks that different local customs and legal systems permit.

Because human behaviour does not invariably follow in one groove, people habitually scrutinise one another closely, in order to decipher intentions and attitudes, which cannot be automatically assumed on the grounds of biology alone. We are sufficiently alike with our common template that we can seek to understand on the basis of shared species sympathy. Yet we are also sufficiently variegated within that to evade simple categorisations, even while often seeking to find them. The 'stone-aged brain' thus does indeed survive, but by dint of displaying an impressive flexibility, which includes a capacity both to generalise and to challenge generalisations.

Talking about Tradition

Continuity in history, though less discussed than change in history, has nonetheless been saluted with a nuanced vocabulary. 'Standstill' refers to geological eras that remain unchanged over long epochs. And other bedrock terms include steady-state, sameness, stasis, perpetuity, immanence, permanence, and the rarely used perdurance. There is also the state of poised equilibrium – homeostasis – when the balance of countervailing forces holds things in a stable state. Or the diachronic perspective may focus attention upon *la longue durée* (long duration) or outright immobility: *l'histoire immobile*, the 'history that stands still'.

Those who praise ancient ways can welcome continuity as longevity, survival, endurance, stability, constancy, the comfort of routines. There are virtues in things that have happened 'time out of mind' or since 'time immemorial'. Novelty is discounted: 'seen it all before'; 'nothing new under the sun'; 'history as usual'. Even after great crises, it becomes apparent that 'life goes on'. Respect is paid to 'tradition', 'custom', 'antiquity', 'venerability'. Proposed innovations can be rejected with the Mexican phrase *No es Costumbre* – 'it is not the custom'. The 'force of habit' is admired; and ancestral 'wisdom and prudence' extolled. An ambitious representation of continuity in three dimensions – *Unique Forms of Continuity in Space*, as sculpted in Milan in 1913 (*see* illustration 6) – presents a stalwart striding figure, with bulging muscles, hard angles, sensuous curves, and flying draperies within one energetic form, armless, featureless, sexless, the whole radiating intense biological vitality fused with a semi-mechanical strength. As a vision of powerful persistence, it is not what everyone would invent. On the other hand, the three-pronged figure invokes well an elemental microcosm, inhabiting confidently its unique place in macro-space.

Policy applications of continuity also have a positive phraseology. In ecology, preservation is lauded as 'conservation'; in politics, it is defined as 'conservatism'; in morality, 'constancy' and faithfulness unto death; in religion, obedience to 'the chain of traditions' and the spiritual immanence associated with the divine. Traditionalists try to 'hold the line'; to respect the 'established order'. Or, more proactively, they seek to reverse changes in order to bring back the 'good old days', when mythically people were ever merry, food cheap and summers golden.

Critics simultaneously have a fine choice of value-laden terms to denounce the 'dead hand' of ancient ways. Inertia and stagnation are condemned as are monotony, torpor, vegetation, backwardness, inflexibility, 'stick-in-the-mud' and even paralysis. One person's venerated tradition may be another's hated incubus from the 'bad old days'. It was in this mood that the revolutionary

6 Boccioni's *Unique Forms of Continuity in Space* fuses classical drapery with three-dimensional cubism to imagine continuity striding through space and time.

activist and theorist Karl Marx, already in 1852 well aware that fundamental transformations are not easy to achieve, passionately denounced 'the tradition of all the dead generations [that] weighs like a nightmare on the brains of the living'.[57]

Upon close inspection, however, the relationship of continuity and change is not one of total opposition. While stern 'diehards' may oppose every innovation, flexible conservatives often argue for accepting some adaptations in response to different times. In 1790 the Anglo-Irish pundit Edmund Burke offered the apparent paradox that: 'A state without the means of some change is without the means of its conservation.'[58] He was thinking specifically of political reform. The principle, however, remains applicable more widely. Another version of the same paradox appears in *The Leopard*, a tale of pragmatic nostalgia by Sicily's Giuseppe di Lampedusa. As the novel unfolds, the 'progressive' young aristocrat argues subtly that, in turbulent times: 'If we want things to stay as they are, things will have to change.'[59] The noble leopard will outwardly adapt his spots but will remain a leopard, so retaining power.

Herein, however, there lies a perennial problem. Once the old ways begin to be abandoned, it often becomes difficult to draw the line. Is a proposed innovation a necessary adjustment to preserve a genuine tradition or is it instead the 'thin end of the wedge' that opens the floodgates to change? There is no general rule for deciding. If the noble leopard changes its nature *too* much then it will no longer be a genuine leopard.

Confusingly, too, even the most apparently long-standing traditions can turn out to be deceptive. Some things, that seem ancient and are venerated as such, may not truly be so. Such revelations tend to provoke anger from true believers. Nonetheless, various 'historic' customs and rituals were after all 'invented' or, if not completely invented, then substantially updated, often more than once.[60] To take one example from many, the European gypsy travellers' brightly painted caravans are not constructed along the lines of ancient designs, complete with occult symbolism, as rumour once suggested; but instead these sturdy wooden conveyances were first built in the nineteenth century, when the ritual of burning the vehicle on the death of its owner also began.[61] Yet, as this case also shows, an innovation could in turn establish the basis for a new tradition. Thus, while many apparently time-honoured practices do in fact incorporate later changes, so too various forms of change may be consolidated into later rituals and continuities.

The Power of Continuity

Everywhere, then, there are marks of persistence through time. Not only the landscape but all buildings other than those actually under construction are visible reminders of 'the presence of the past', as observes I.M. Pei, the Japanese architect responsible for renovating France's palace-museum the Louvre.[62] Individuals meanwhile continue as 'walking archives'[63] of their own genetic histories. And our automatic reflexes provide a reminder of our far-distant ancestral origins, as in the case of the sudden frisson in times of fright or tension – the *heiliger Schauer* or 'holy shiver' of the German poets – which is a biological inheritance from a pre-human bristling of fur.[64]

Amidst the continuities that persist despite outward changes there is also an underlying paradox. The role of many frequent mutations and adaptations may itself be part of a deep structure. Thus an element of change itself can be considered to be one of life's great constants. Such a paradox was cheerfully invoked by an English poet of the seventeenth century, who realised that this inversion of the expected could be interpreted as a philanderer's charter. If change is perennial, then to be faithful in love is unnatural, sang Abraham Cowley: 'The *World's* a *Scene* of *Changes*, and to be / *Constant*, in *Nature*, were *Inconstancie*.'[65] This argument suits roving lovers rather than settled pairings, so does not cover the whole panorama of human sexual attachments. Nonetheless, the paradox highlights the point that macro-continuity may well be able to incorporate a range of micro-changes.

More too. Continuity may lurk disguised within even major transformations. This perception was pithily summarised in another paradox from Alphonse Karr, a French critic and journalist best known for his world-weary dictum in 1849 (just after Europe's failed 'year of revolutions'). He quipped: '*Plus ça change – plus c'est la même chose*' – '*The more things change, the more they remain the same*.'[66] The maxim is certainly open to challenge, in that some mega-changes are not just more of the same (as will be discussed in the following chapters). Nonetheless, the apparent paradox acts as a potent reminder that deep continuities are not so easily dislodged. In politics, for example, it takes more than a mere declaration of reform or even a wholesale turnover of personnel at the top to produce a truly fundamental governmental and social metamorphosis.

Differentiating the ephemeral from the long-lasting thus remains a perennial challenge. Throughout the cosmos there is a mixture of indeterminacy and constancy; and it is the 'universal constants', like the measurable strengths of gravitational forces, that provide the standards against which the extent of variations can be calibrated.[67] Even at the microscopic level of calibrating subatomic particles, there is a tiny invariant element (h) within the definition of turbulent energy. Discovered at the start of the twentieth century by Max Planck, it is known as 'Planck's constant' (h) and the notation is inscribed on his simple gravestone at Göttingen in Germany. That microscopic value, calculated at *c.* 4.2 thousand-trillionths of an electron-volt second, remains detectably stable amidst the seething quantum variability.[68]

Little wonder, then, that Planck denied that Einsteinian relativity had killed all absolutes. Moreover, Einstein himself believed that there were some cosmic 'holding' factors that work to counteract a post-Big Bang runaway inflation of the universe.[69] He accordingly speculated for many years about the existence of a 'cosmological constant', expressed in his equations by the Greek letter lambda (Λ).[70] While the scientific arguments remain to be clarified, some foundational role for continuity remains intrinsic, not least as the contrasting basis against which change can be identified.

Deepest of deep persistence relates to all factors that are coextensive with time and accordingly appear 'timeless'. There are also other structural continuities that change so very slowly, especially in comparison with the limited human lifespan, that they also seem 'age-old'. These include features of the cosmos, like the sun and other stars, which appear to us virtually timeless. In addition, there are very many other elements in our local environment that are slow to change and either are or seem to be repositories of continuity. Additionally, we can ourselves enhance the emphasis upon through-time survival by cultivating traditions, practising repetitions and encouraging replication. All efforts at natural and wildlife conservation pay tribute to the appeal of continuity, which becomes especially poignant when under siege. Nor are the campaigns confined to the 'wild': the asphalt jungles within cities can be greened by planting trees and using latticed concrete with space for grass to grow, adopting the pre-urban within the urban. How all these elements of persistence, both mental and material, then interact with the countervailing forces of change constitutes the very stuff of existence.

Shaping History – Time Cycles

The round wheel turning full circle embodies movement but allows for a return to the starting point, or at least to somewhere close to that. Thus the cycle is commonly invoked as a powerful symbol in all interpretations that stress regularity, recurrence and familiar patterning.

Such shapings draw from the human awareness of routine cyclicalities in everyday experience, as in the rotation of the hours of the day, the seasons of the year, the phases of the moon, the menstrual cycles of fertile women, and the circadian biorhythms of wakefulness – sleep – and wakening again. Visually, the round O of the sun and the full moon are familiar to all. And the earth has long been depicted as a circle, whether as a disc (in much traditional thought) or as a sphere (by some thinkers from at least the time of Pythagoras in Greece of the sixth century BCE).

Practically, too, the circle is the basis of one of the world's oldest and most successful technological inventions. An ancient survival from c. 2500 BCE, an oakwood wheel (see illustration 7), which has been worked with stone or flint tools, features a double circle, in which the outer one rims the disc, while the inner one surrounds the hollowed nave that holds the axle of the turning wheel.

Circular completeness readily carries symbolic meanings too. The form recurs in many religious iconographies. So Buddhists, for instance, push great prayer wheels to symbolise the turning wheel of existence or rotate small hand-held wheels. Illustration 7 shows a renowned Tibetan *Dharma*. It is the golden wheel of life and enlightenment that glistens over the entrance to the Jokhang Temple in central Lhasa. At the hub are symbols of worldly views to be overcome (ignorance, lust, anger), while leading to the rim are the eight spokes representing the eightfold pathways to spiritual betterment. Two attentive golden deer flank the wheel, as a reminder that Buddha's first teachings were issued in a deer park. The tensions and strivings of life are held in serene balance.

7 The wheel as ancient technology is represented here by an oak cart-wheel, dating from c. 2500 BCE, found in a Dutch peat-bog in 1960.

Recurrent cycles thus often convey a reassuring sense of closure and fulfilment.[1] Even death, as the culmination of an individual lifespan, comes as a form of completion – 'the wheel has turned full circle'. 'Home is the sailor, home from the sea, / And the hunter home from the hill,' as proclaimed in the simple *Requiem* by Robert Louis Stevenson, the novelist wanderer from Edinburgh who died in Western Samoa, far from his birthplace. In his case it is these poetic lines that are engraved on his tombstone on Upolu island, signalling that there he had finally found his place of rest.

One form in which historical cycles can be envisaged is in the complete repetition of one era in another. The contentious German sage Friedrich Nietzsche was one who speculated about such possibilities. Anxious and ill, he derided the view that history had a purposeful direction. Instead, he detected a perennial human will-to-power, which would lead not to progress but instead 'the eternal return of the same'. He did not, however, expect this to happen via bodily reincarnation. It was the principle of 'return' rather than the practicalities that he stressed,

8 The wheel as symbol is the golden Wheel of Life, encircling the pathways to enlightenment, from the Buddhist Jokhang Temple at Lhasa, Tibet.

proclaiming the relative unimportance of individuals before the dark forces of reit-
eration: 'the eternal hourglass of existence is turned upside down again and again,
and you with it, a speck of dust'. History in action was thus for him a repetitious
process of growth–decay–renewal–decay, and nothing more.

Furthermore, without actually travelling to other times, people do from time to
time record an expected sense of repetition, even in apparently new circumstances. Things have been experienced before or seen before: *déjà vu*. This has
good dramatic possibilities. The Yorkshire author J.B. Priestley developed the
concept in *I Have Been Here Before*, a play in which the characters suddenly realise
that they are reliving a past that they cannot quite remember. In their case,
however, the repetition is merciful. As things are rerun, old bad decisions can be
changed into new and better ones.

Recycling history would therefore offer a chance of redemption, rather as
though the past is a reel of film that can be spooled backwards and forwards to
relive at will. Here Priestley was influenced by the ideas of a bold aeronautical engi-
neer and self-taught philosopher named J.W. Dunne.[2] In his *Experiment with Time*
(1927), he advanced his own theory of precognition based on dreams. Buttressed
with claimed case histories, Dunne's analysis was presented in quasi-mathematical
style to affirm his scientific credentials, although his later writings were more
overtly mystical. His theories attracted much attention, in the post-Einsteinian

climate of rethinking ideas about time; and fresh interest accordingly was directed to the role of dreaming as a subconscious means of assimilating and sifting past experiences and immediate preoccupations. However, dream-messages turn out to be much less literal than Dunne suggested; and the technical means of rerunning the past remain obstinately unavailable.

Indeed, while the idea of repeating history again and again might have some initial attractions, it becomes frustrating when the repetition never ends. Being stuck in a baffling labyrinth of recycling time, with no way out, has haunting possibilities. One fantasy that circles around this theme is recounted in the *Manuscript Found in Saragossa*. Written in the early nineteenth century by the Polish count Jan Potocki, a noted traveller, linguist and occultist, the text is formed of interlocking stories within stories, later edited into a circular story in a 1960s cult film of suitably surreal humour. The setting is southern Spain, on the old cultural frontier between the Christian and Moorish worlds. And the invoked theme is disorientation – personal, temporal, mental, spiritual and sexual. Voluptuous encounters with two exotic and beautiful sisters end in shock awakenings among rotting cadavers and feasting vultures. Pleasures oscillate with penance. And the stories have no real ending, leaving the hero within the tales (like later readers) continually bewitched 'with mysteries, which at one moment I think I understand in part, only to be plunged back the next moment into the blackest doubts'.[3]

Repetitive accounts and tales of recurrence throw suggestive light on experiences within the psychology of obsession and/or acute anxiety or any form of persistent over-concentration. Minds become fixed upon one theme, 'circling' and 'recircling' around the same point, as though trapped in time. So the repetitious melancholia of a thwarted life is presented in one Dutch fantasy tale, which depicts a solitary male who sees visions of a misty female wraith. She is his incomplete 'other' and she too is sad: 'always yearning, always hearing the crying, crying here, crying there, crying within my innermost being'. Such regretful craving for something unattained can gnaw into the consciousness, like the hypnotic persistence of a haunting love in the 1968 ballad to the *Windmills of Your Mind*:[4]

> A circle in a spiral, a wheel within a wheel,
> Never ending, no beginning,
> On an ever-spinning reel.

To escape, if escape is required, and to 'move on', as the familiar therapeutic mantra requires, it follows that the image of the unbreakable cycle needs to be sundered and a fresh 'way out' envisaged into a new time.

For historians, such imaginings show the power that visions of the shape of history exert upon patterns of individual behaviour and expectations. Cyclical theories in particular may lead either to fatalism – with no means of escape from the enclosing wheel – or to the possibility of redemption with another chance, as the wheel of fortune turns. Rings of destiny – potent circles that can be won and worn – are thus often taken to symbolise such choices, whether carried on the fingers of gods or mortals.

Another vision of recurrence in history argues not that history recurs but that individuals do so, being reincarnated in changed physical forms that live again in other eras. Hindu and Buddhist teachings thus envisage a prolonged spiritual pilgrimage, as each person's consciousness migrates through time. Individuals are not expected to remember their previous lives – although some do claim this power – but they should endeavour always to live worthily.[5] Every moral decision has potential ramifications that ricochet down many centuries, as each time cycle returns into a seed-state to await its next creation: 'dissolving with the dark, and with day returning / Back to the new birth, new death . . .', in the majestic words of the Hindu sacred book *The Bhagavad-Gita* (c. 500 BCE).

A number of thinkers in the West, from Pythagoras onwards, have also believed in cyclical rebirth, although this remains heresy within the Christian tradition. The Italian philosopher Giordano Bruno was one who argued that every soul both pre-exists and survives each bodily manifestation. In support of his view, he cited Ecclesiastes: 'There is no new thing under the sun.' But the Catholic Inquisition, unimpressed, burnt him at the stake as a heretic in 1600: a statue in Rome's Piazza di Campo dei Fiori today marks the location of the funeral pyre.

In Bruno's case, his philosophy was based upon theological reasoning. For others, meanwhile, the theory of reincarnation can offer a historical reassurance. One somewhat surprising tract, published by an unnamed group of feminists in Oxford in 1978, was entitled *Breaking the Time Barrier*. It announced briskly that 'We do not only live once.' Believers were encouraged to reconstruct their previous incarnations as peace-loving matriarchs who ruled benignly in ancient times, before power was rudely seized by aggressive men. This was a form of current consciousness-raising as apparently endorsed by historical therapy. Not all the group's adherents, however, reported happy memories from their mental trips into the past; and most feminists were unconvinced by the tactic of appealing to a theoretical matriarchy, which had lost once and thus might lose again.

Theories of cyclical recurrence indeed run into problems if the return is taken too literally. What they do helpfully highlight, however, are patterns and similarities between past and present. One classic cyclical model focuses upon forms of government. The Greek historian Polybius, for example, explained his view that every political system was liable to degenerate into its worst aspect; but then each degenerated regime would be opposed and replaced by a new one, in a continuing cycle of renovation and degeneration. An anonymous English commentator, much later in 1689, gave a standard summary of the resulting merry-go-round:

> from Monarchy [rule by one] to Tyranny, from Tyranny to Aristocracy [rule by the few], from Aristocracy to Oligarchy, from Oligarchy to Democracy [rule by the many], from Democracy to the Rule of the Rabble, and thence back to Monarchy. This is the round that all Governments run; this is the course, the order, and economy of Nature.

People living in agrarian societies, close to the cyclical rhythms of the farming year, have often, though not invariably, favoured such assumptions. The idea that success is followed by decadence which leads anew to rebirth is thus very deep-rooted. It was in that spirit that the humanist scholars in sixteenth-century Italy, who were not country dwellers, described their recovery of the classical learning of Greece and Rome, which they were then updating for a new era, as a 'rebirth' or 'Renaissance'. They were culturally 'reinventing the wheel' but moving it onwards at the same time.

Cyclical models, when applied to history as a whole, mark a perception of familiar patterns in past events. In fourteenth-century north Africa, Ibn Khaldūn, for example, famously built social and economic change into the heart of the cycle. He saw human development in terms of a transition from nomadic husbandry into settled urban cultures, on which were founded great empires, which in turn contain the possibility of their own decline by becoming too corrupt and decadent. The epic ebb and flow of contrasting experiences had also prompted China's foundational historian Sima Qian to enunciate in the second century BCE a similar principle of history:

> When a thing has reached its height, it must begin to decay, and when an age has gone to one extreme it must turn again in the opposite direction; therefore we find periods of rude simplicity and periods of refinement alternating with each other endlessly.

Linking transience with repetition means that history, however complicated, need not seem inexplicable. And if closed cycles seem too rigid, then circling spirals will supply the imagery instead.

Giambattista Vico in the early seventeenth century suggested another variant too. In his *Principles of a New Science* (1725), he noted that history's stages of development were not straightforward. Any one sequence (*corso*) could eventually lead to a return (*ricorso*), but in the form of a cultural 'echo' from an earlier and different epoch. That added scope for variation within the idea of recurrence. Or the repetition might be inverted. So the German philosopher G. W. F. Hegel speculated that some great 'world-historical' events might happen twice but in an opposite format. 'He forgot to add: the first time as tragedy, the second as farce,' commented Karl Marx a generation later, supplying a sardonic edge to the original maxim.

While it is often claimed that cyclical models are particularly characteristic within 'eastern' cultures, there have in fact been notable attempts in the West at synthesising world history into great cycles. Oswald Spengler in Germany tried that sensationally in the 1920s. His *Decline of the West* was influenced by Nietzsche in rejecting all ideas of 'progress'. Instead, Spengler declared that entire cultures have organic life cycles, matching human life cyles, from birth to maturity to senescence and eventual death. For him, the decadence of the 'West-European–American' way of life signalled a system in terminal decline.

Other scholars also vied to calculate the periodicity of cyclical change. One obscure but learned English scholar named Alfred Bradley Gough sought to chart the 'rhythmic waves of human energy' that powered history. He mapped them as tides, moving through time in a process that he saw as wrapping around the globe from north-east to south-west. Each world-cycle, Gough calculated, took 850 years to unfold, publishing his results in the 1936 *Sociological Review*. Later, he changed his mind and declared that the answer was 743. This attempt at an improbable precision, however, ran into the sands, and the remaining calculations were left obscurely in Gough's unpublished notebooks.

Central to the problem remains the subjectivity of the criteria for defining a completed historical cycle. What seems like 'decadence' to one historian may be 'improvement' to another. This challenge was confronted once more in the massive *Study of History* in twelve volumes (1934–61) by the British historian Arnold Toynbee. He was no Spenglerian pessimist. Instead, he praised the ambition of those, like Ibn Khaldūn, who sought a synthesis of history worldwide. For his own version, Toynbee identified twenty-one historic civilisations (later increased to thirty-one) as well as eight 'abortive' or 'arrested' civilisations and at least 650 'primitive' societies. Their rise and fall was then charted as a process of challenge–response–challenge, each cycle ending in either demise or renewal. In a fanciful moment, Toynbee further announced that the death of a civilisation has its own 'signature' rhythm, being 'apt to take a run of three and a half beats – rout, rally, relapse, rally, relapse, rally, relapse' . . .

Yet, upon close inspection, this bold intellectual edifice also ran into familiar problems. Toynbee's classification of 'advanced' and 'primitive' societies was disputed, as was his specification of the timing of historical cycles, while his 'challenge-and-response' mechanism is portentous yet elusive in application. At times, an entire way of life may disappear abruptly, such as after massive military annihilation. Yet 'decline' may also be lengthy, circuitous and hard to determine: a matter of subjective opinion rather than scientific law. In particular, the extent of chronic overlapping, borrowing and fusion between world cultures makes it difficult to allot them separated life cycles with clearly defined start and end dates. Accordingly, Toynbee's reputation, like that of Spengler before him, at first soared and then plummeted.

Since then, analysis generally tends towards caution. Global patterns and rhythms in history are modelled, when they are so proposed, over shorter spans of time. And closed cycles tend to be modified into more open-ended 'waves'. But here too variation always remains to be incorporated. Thus the 'trade cycles' in industrialised economies are presented graphically as fluctuating waves, of non-constant dimensions. The same applies to long-term economic analysis. The sequences of booms and slumps do not exhibit an agreed periodicity. Thus neither Simon Kuznets' proposed twenty-year 'long swings' nor Nikolai Kondratiev's fifty-year 'long cycles' are being precisely upheld by the unfolding experience of industrial economies.[6]

Too much literality in historical application therefore tends to render cyclical models open to challenge. As metaphors, however, the image of the closed cycle, the wheel, the ring – and variant shapes in the form of the open-ended spiral and the variable wave – retain their power to invoke an awareness of significant patterns, parallels, similarities and recognition across time. And from these we can learn, whether to avoid or to imitate.

CHAPTER 3

Micro-change

Restless 'change' accompanies and intrudes upon continuity, which it helps to define by offering a contrast. However, it is misleading to think solely in terms of a binary divide between two forces. While history is often said to contain a mixture of 'continuity and change', the formulation needs radical amendment to recognise significantly different sorts of 'change'. Otherwise the breadth of just one concept of non-continuity is so great that it loses any real explanatory force.

'Change' embraces everything from the smallest adaptation to the very greatest upheavals.[1] In historical application, however, it is helpful to distinguish between, on the one hand, slow, adaptational 'micro-change', summarised as evolution or gradualism and, on the other hand, rapid, drastic and fundamental 'macro-change', summarised as revolution or structural discontinuity.

Certainly, there is no automatic demarcation point between these polarities. Very slow change at one end of the spectrum becomes close to stasis, while a massive acceleration of multiplying micro-changes eventually generates macro-change. Nevertheless, these two dimensions within 'change' can be distinguished one from the other. That applies both to their characteristics and to their historical impact, as 'evolution' and 'revolution' work sometimes in conjunction together but sometimes too in opposition and contradistinction.

A significant element of regular, gradual micro-change is everywhere detectable in the steady progression of measured time, as viewed by humans from our fixed location upon planet earth. Days and nights succeed each other routinely, unaffected by any local upheavals. Years pass. And irregular, gradual changes are visible in countless imperceptible forms of slow transformation, which occur, for example, as rocks erode, rivers silt up, or living creatures grow and wither over time.

One key proposition that is fundamental to all discussions of cosmic change is the second law of thermodynamics, which states that, in every process of energy exchange, there is some fractional, even infinitesimal, heat loss. It means that there is an ultimate penalty built into the operation of any energised system over time.[2] Matter, which constitutes a form of more or less stably stored energy, changes its nature as it expends energy and thus loses heat. In the process, structures ultimately mutate from an orderly into a less ordered condition. This is known as 'entropy' or thermodynamic transformability. It does not mean, as it is sometimes loosely taken to mean, that no immediate processes of change can ever be reversed. Milk poured into hot tea cannot be extracted as milk again; but water that has been frozen into ice can be unfrozen (although still not without some thermodynamic consequences). Entropy applies to all mutations, whether from simple to complex or back again, over the long term. Hence there is a dynamic of heat loss, which affects the state of all cosmic matter diachronically, until the universe itself ends through heat death – or, alternatively perhaps, re-energises itself into a new start and a new trajectory.

Gradual change is integral in this way not only to the temporal process but, in a linked way, to all cosmic energy structures. All actions that are repeated, whether by living creatures or by machines, are never exactly replicated, no matter how faithful the attempt, because the infinitesimal changes of time and heat change are integrally part of the process. This links back to long-standing philosophic perceptions of flux as part of the cosmic order. So the same Heraclitus who endorsed deep continuities also detected micro-change as a component of the whole: 'Into the same river you could not step twice.'[3] Both the walker and the river alter from moment to moment, just as things consciously repeated vary, however fractionally, from repetition to repetition.

Admittedly, for some purposes of abstract analysis, the pulse of time is factored out of the equation. In such circumstances, the incessant micro-changes that accompany the temporal process are assumed to be operationally neutral in their impact. For example, economists in their mathematical models and theoretical explanations of economic activity generally use time to provide a date line but they do not expect the regular diachronic updating to reshape the basic framework.[4] However, the abstraction of this approach on occasions finds itself seriously outdated. From time to time, there are significant changes, often presenting themselves in the form of unpalatable new problems. In such cases, the mathematical models and their underlying assumptions are disrupted and need to be reformulated. Timeful history thus often challenges 'timeless' theory, as economic historians and geographers are increasingly prone to warn insouciant economists.[5]

The concept of gradual change does not, however, require or expect that everything must be changing slowly all the time. Nor indeed does it imply that the pace and direction of transformation are identical in all cases and in all circumstances. On the contrary, micro-change is itself mutable. It is quite possible to detect several different or even directly contradictory trends at once. And, above all, the process of gradual change over time does not imply that everything in history is invariably moving along a single straight line from the deep past to the present and on into the future. This version, which is summarised as 'linearity', is but one possible directional pathway for gradualism among many options.

Slow incremental change has acquired a number of names, as the concept plays a role in many systems of thought. Thus 'evolution' as a concept can be applied generically but has its greatest resonance in application to accounts of biological development. 'Progress' is a version of cultural faith that assumes gradual change as a motor force in history, moving living systems from a state of primitivism to maturity or 'civilisation'. But there is also an obverse view, which is much less euphoric. 'Change and decay in all around I see', as one sonorous Victorian hymn declared. Theories of 'degeneration', such as those that underpin many current warnings of ecological deterioration, see collapse and disorder as the outcome rather than progress and improvement. In both cases, the cumulative impact is achieved as micro-change follows upon micro-change. Thus, alongside the undoubted power of persistence, there is also another significant force, often concealed within outward continuities, which can be identified as gradual variation produced by many 'micro-changes'.

Incremental Adaptation

Incremental adaptation is characterised by many small-scale changes over long periods of time, taking a multiplicity of forms – like the slow unfurling of many forms of vegetation. Notable examples of leisurely growth, taking thousands of years to reach maturity, can be appreciated today in the living wood of very ancient pines, yews, redwoods, giant sequoias and spiny baobabs, as well as in the contours of the globally endangered *Ginkgo biloba*, the 'dinosaur tree' whose earliest ancestors predate those of all other arboreal rivals.[6]

As species flourish over the long term, so too gradual and unplanned changes may slowly appear within their ranks. This is the process of biological evolution, as living organisms adapt to their environment, which is itself liable to change over time. Rates of mutation are very variable. The ginkgo tree, for example, has not been much modified over 200 million years; and the oyster of 150 million years ago looked very like an oyster today. But changes among geographically mobile mammalian species are more conspicuous. Humans have not only evolved from ape-ancestors but we have also generated a considerable, though far from unlimited, spectrum of external appearances amongst ourselves. One example can be seen in the handsome range of skin pigmentations that has developed from an original brown or dark-toned epidermis, once the dense body hair of the earlier hominids was lost. These variations represent historic melanin-adaptations in response to differential levels of ultra-violet radiation as experienced by peoples living at different global latitudes,[7] although the effects of such differentiation are being constantly modified in every generation by population migrations to new climes and by intermarrying.

Another very gradual change is affecting the anatomy of the human jaw. A substantial minority of people congenitally produce fewer than the standard thirty-two adult teeth. Thus, in some parts of the world, over 33 per cent of the local population constitutionally lack third molars (wisdom teeth). This hereditable condition, known as hypodontia, is conjectured as an evolutionary response to dental overcrowding, which has become intensified as the human jaw size has diminished over time in comparison with the detectably larger jaws of the early hominids.[8] Certainly, the condition of having fewer than the standard number of teeth is much more common among humans today than having an excess number of teeth. However, as biological adaptations occur gradually over millennia, the hazards of dental overcrowding are not likely to disappear tomorrow.

There are other anatomical reminders of even older past changes, as seen in the bodily persistence of vestigial features which have almost entirely atrophied through disuse. Charles Darwin was one of the first to note this process.[9] To take one example from the human skeleton, the short bony extension, or coccyx, at the base of the spine is a biological reminder of a very far-distant ancestral tail.

Such adaptive changes to form and function over time supplied the evidential basis for Darwin's account of diachronic change. In his *Origin of Species* (1859), he identified biological evolution as a process of 'natural selection' whereby living creatures struggle for survival within a competitive environment. Those that flourish do so by virtue of an unplanned sequence of micro-changes, which adapt the different species over very long spans of time. As the hereditary factors handed on from generation to generation slowly mutate, so advantageous features survive over the long term, and disadvantageous ones are shed. Darwin was not alone in this insight. It was his detailed account, however, that focused both scholarly and public attention. Thereupon 'Darwinism' not only founded evolutionary biology as a subject but has also encouraged a range of 'neo-Darwinist' speculations about the role of competitive struggle in human social behaviour and human psychology.

His work was thus controversial from the start. However, Darwin carefully based his biology upon a scrupulous array of field observations. Parallel evidence for human evolution was soon forthcoming in the fossil record too, as palaeontologists extended their quarrying for 'old bones'. Geologists too had already drawn attention to the great antiquity of the earth's crust. The planet itself is a veritable 'theatre of reiterated change'. So Charles Lyell, the geologist friend and mentor of Darwin, wrote in 1830, stressing that such a state of affairs had lasted for 'myriads of ages' over an 'immensity of time'.[10] Over such great spans, the slow forces of wind- and water-erosion are able literally to move mountains,[11] carrying them away grain by grain. The illustration below provides an imaginative reconstruction of one of the world's most famous landscapes *before* such inexorable processes began: where now there are weathered and much eroded rocks beside the deep fissure of Arizona's Grand Canyon, there once loomed the peaks of a massive mountain range, some 1,700 million years ago.

Arguments about the role of long-term incremental change in both biology and geology faced (and continue to face) some opposition from Christians

9 Artist's reconstruction of Arizona's Grand Canyon some 1,700 million years ago, with peaked mountains before their long, slow erosion by wind, water and possibly ice during the snowball earth period 700–800 million years ago.

with a literalist rather than metaphorical belief in the Biblical account of the seven-day Creation. However, after an initial fuss, the views of Lyell and Darwin were assimilated relatively quickly. One reason lay in the prior acceptance, in European intellectual circles especially, of the view that nature, which they generally agreed to be divinely sanctioned, tends to proceed in an orderly and gradual fashion. A Latin tag provided a crisp summary. '*Natura non facit saltum* – nature does not make leaps'.[12] In Britain, this assumption was particularly popular with supporters of political gradualism, who believed accordingly that the concept of 'revolution' was positively unnatural. For example, in 1858 (a year before Darwin published) the legal reformer Lord Brougham referred unhesitatingly to 'the law [of nature] which forbids a sudden and rapid leaping forward, and decrees that each successive step, prepared by the last, shall facilitate the next.'[13]

Intellectual authority for this view can be traced, in European thought, at least back to Aristotle in the Greece of the fourth century BCE. He considered regular, uniform and continuous movement to be the defining characteristic of nature, dismissing irregular events as merely accidental.[14] The Roman jurist Cicero, summarising the accepted cosmology of his day, later concurred that rational order was the norm: 'The heavens contain no chance or random element, no erratic or pointless movement.'[15] If so, then change must be regular too. In the first century CE, the theory of the orderly cosmos was crystallised by the renowned educator Quintilian. His maxim stated unequivocally that 'Nature itself does not seek to effect great things rapidly'[16] – a view that still consoles harassed teachers today if their recalcitrant students prove slow to learn.

Notions of an orderly cosmos were also absorbed by numerous Christian and Jewish theologians, who identified divine power as the 'unmoved mover' sustaining the whole. God, after all, was habitually described as the 'author of Nature'. The dramatic scientific discoveries in the seventeenth century, which calculated and explained the regular workings of the sun-centred planetary system, also gave this harmonious model a further intellectual boost. By 1704 G.W. Leibniz, the Leipzig-born philosopher and mathematician, felt able to applaud the dictum '*la nature ne fait jamais des sauts*' (nature does not make leaps) as not only 'one of the greatest' of maxims but also one of the 'best verified'.[17]

Confidence in nature's gradualism was additionally merged with a trust that nature's secrets, once revealed, must be open to simple explanation. This conjunction was expressed in a remarkable 1709 tract by an obscure English Protestant clergyman named Thomas Robinson. Although a keen geologist, he was no scientific innovator and he still doubted the new heliocentric model of the planetary system. Yet Parson Robinson was sure about the natural order, listing its key principles as the conventional scientific maxims of his day:

- Nature's Productions are never in vain.
- Nature's Productions are not by blind Chance.
- Nature never works in haste.
- Nature's Productions are not by precipitous Leaps, but by gradual Motions.
- Nature never does that by Much, that may be done by Less.[18]

Philosophically, the final point expresses a conceptual trust in the natural economy of explanation. It means that, if two rival accounts of a given phenomenon are offered, then the least complicated is always taken as preferable.[19] 'Nature is pleas'd with Simplicity', concurred Isaac Newton.[20] Such an attitude was and is encouraging to the quest for the concealed oneness at the heart of complexity. It does, however, contain a further risk not just of simplicity but of oversimplification, although such an outcome tends to occur not so much in new scientific studies as such but rather in popularising summaries that try to elevate new scientific theories into universal formulae.

'Darwinism' as a corpus of ideas faced something of that paradox. Darwin, though a cautious innovator, found that he was pushing at an open door. Despite initial scandal and controversy, his synthesis gained mainstream acceptance with notable speed. Moreover, evolutionary ideas were applied not only to biology but also to many other fields of study. Darwin himself accepted that there is much trial and error in the process of natural selection. However, upon occasion he did express some diachronic optimism about the long-term target of biological change. Ultimately 'all corporeal and mental endowments will tend to progress towards perfection', Darwin suggested; and, among human societies, he added that 'progress has been much more general than retrogression'.[21] It was a viewpoint that could easily be taken as applying evolution not just to a long-term instinctual biology but to immediate thoughts and actions as well.

Hence neo-Darwinist social theorists invoke the case for untrammelled competition to achieve 'progress' in social or political life; or neo-Darwinist psychologists endorse a universal sex-specific calculus, allegedly designed to advance the successful reproduction not just of the human species as a whole but of individual genetic inheritance within that.

Among the following generations of biologists, however, the research and discussions have become more technical. They focus, for example, upon the genetic mechanisms of change, especially once the Japanese biologist Motoo Kimura in 1983 proposed that random genetic drift at molecular level constitutes a more plausible agent of change than a Darwinian process of sexual selection.[22] Or the debates review whether evolutionary adaptation occurs optimally or otherwise.[23] And research probes too the basic physics and biochemistry that produce the notable extent of patterning and orderly systems within nature. With all this, a substantial majority among biologists accept the prevalence of an in-built process of slow, incremental change, although a minority (as discussed later) prefer to stress episodes of sudden biological upheaval.

Meanwhile, it has already been noted that an alternative minority world view, known as 'creationism', determinedly rejects all evolutionary explanations whether in biology, astronomy, cosmology, geology, archaeology or any other long-run study, preferring instead a literal interpretation of biblical genesis. In this scenario, the world is divinely created in a short timespan, and that event is deemed to have happened comparatively recently, some six thousand years ago. If the globe seems older, that is taken to be so only in appearance and by divine decree.

Most Christians tend to reject this anti-science timetable, not least because the hypothetically recent date for the world's creation comes from fallible scholars and not from a specific biblical text. The debates, however, serve to highlight the spiritual as well as intellectual issues that are involved in beliefs about how the world began and then evolved.[24]

Awareness of the impact of small imperceptible adaptations certainly informs the scientific study of human demography. Small changes in individual levels of fertility and mortality can eventually generate a dramatic cumulative outcome, by increasing or decreasing aggregate pressure upon the resources needed for survival. Thomas Malthus, another Protestant clergyman, was the first to stress this point, writing at the end of the eighteenth century when food prices in England were reaching unprecedented levels. His fearful sense of life as a struggle for scarce resources greatly influenced Darwin.[25] In fact, there turned out to be more demographic options than Malthus initially envisaged. Many countries have experienced falling rates of natural reproduction, while global food supply has expanded. Nonetheless, at the heart of Malthus's theory there remains a valid observation: that great demographic outcomes are affected by the gradually accumulating impact of many individual micro-actions, as well as by collective policy decisions.

Humans also face endemic confrontations with an invisible array of microbes. Thus, as well as frequent contests between people, there are many frequently renewed struggles between people on the one hand and countless bacteria, viruses and micro-organisms on the other.[26] Yet the relationship is not exclusively one of pitched battle. Some bacteria are favourable and outright essential to human life, while others are neutral. Moreover, these micro-organisms are themselves constantly mutating in suitably micro-ways. Hence the story is one of slow mutual adaptation, punctuated admittedly with occasional episodes of crisis and maladaptation.

Genetic evolution among humans is thus influenced by prolonged exposure, generation by generation, to the stealthy presence of all these micro-organisms. Microbiological adaptation can be seen, for example, when communities gradually acquire a 'natural' immunity to infectious diseases, although the beneficent trend, without medical intervention, may be painfully slow. Or, conversely, potential genetic problems also appear among human populations who are exposed for long periods to biologically hostile environments. For example, there is a high incidence of thalassaemia and related immune-system disorders among peoples whose ancestors lived in areas of the world – such as Sardinia – where they were exposed to endemic malaria, which is a disease that triggers such adverse responses.[27] The local microbiological environment thus regularly intervenes to produce variants within species-level evolution. And it is likely that the rate and range of these potential epidemiological confrontations will increase, as increased global mobility speeds people's exposure to unaccustomed hazards for which they have no habitual immunity, as well as accelerating the transmission of disease.[28]

Nonetheless, because small cumulative changes take a long time to achieve their impact, it remains hard to tell in any particular case whether a minor adaptation is merely a surface blip or part of a significant trend. Hence the often very slow pace of diachronic unfolding: 'Only time will tell.'

Uncertainties about the nature of micro-changes also underpin the well-known experience that it is much more difficult to arouse public anxiety about potential long-term problems than it is to get action in response to an immediate crisis. However, some multiplying troubles eventually become too great to ignore. A thoughtful novel by Meja Mwangi, entitled *The Last Plague* (2000) explores the gradual devastation of a dusty Kenyan township by the Aids epidemic. The young adults are dying and the graves are fast growing: 'Where there was one today, there would be two tomorrow. Two would become four and four would become eight. They would mutate and multiply . . .'. But perhaps as the deaths accumulate, people will overthrow existing expectations and adjust their sexual behaviour. 'Taboos and tradition had to go, they had to be eliminated, to make way for meaningful progress,' the novelist muses.[29] Without a 'quick fix', however, the answer requires many micro-changes, daily sustained by countless individuals. Such adaptive behaviour, in response to a new medical threat, does not occur instantly by automatic biological reflex but takes much social effort, over time.

Innovation and Communication

Flexible communication systems, meanwhile, provide humans with crucial mechanisms for transmitting information about such changing circumstances. Here there is always a fine balance between continuity/conformism and adaptation/nonconformism.[30] While communication systems operate within formal and informal parameters that retain considerable stability, as has already been noted, such systems are also adapted incrementally and fine-tuned in their 'running' performance from day to day.

No doubt numerous micro-variations in behaviour, speech and thought are quickly done and as quickly forgotten. Yet the existence and adaptability of language, both spoken and unspoken, among all known human communities indicates a species that survives and flourishes on the strength of a complex exchange of information and ideas, and by an equally complex process of acceptance/rejection/modification/recyling/updating/repetition and renovation. Many individual decisions converge to produce a common outcome. One biological term for such a process is 'teleonomy' or directional co-organisation (as opposed to a teleological movement towards a specified end). The experience of sharing is an intensely social one, so that, except in the very rarest of circumstances, no person 'is an island, entire of itself' – each is 'part of the main'.

Adaptive changes are habitually transmitted in all social directions: not only horizontally among similar age cohorts but also vertically between different age groups.[31] Inter-generational change, when young people start to do things differently from their elders, is particularly noticeable in social terms and may prove a source of friction. Thus traditional sayings chastise the fecklessness of the young and, simultaneously, mock the torpor and resistance to change of the old. 'No sooner does wisdom grow, than man becomes senile', as a Korean proverb quips.[32] Yet mature adults prove upon occasion quite capable of adapting their views and behaviour, sometimes in surprising ways.

Once a new development has gained critical mass by widespread adoption, it becomes hard for even the most determined objectors to resist the tide for a lengthy period. There are cultural pressures, silent and not so silent, to conform, which help not only to preserve old ways but also to assimilate innovations. For example, in the case of something as intensely reciprocal as speech, it is virtually impossible to ignore the currency of the surrounding linguistic community in one's own time. So a speaker today who wanted to converse in (say) the English spoken when Shakespeare died or (say) the Spanish spoken when Cervantes died would struggle to identify, let alone to purge, all the intervening changes that have been imperceptibly incorporated into the respective languages since 1616.[33]

From time to time, some historians express a pious wish to explain the past entirely in terminologies known to the past, in order to avoid all anachronistic references. But the task is impeded by the perennial process of language mutation. Moreover, all 'words are slippery' even in their own day, as Henry Adams, doyen of American historians, specified pointedly.[34] Instead, the challenge when studying the lives of past communities remains that of explaining one era in the terminology of another, later one.

Linguistic changes emerge from the play of creative intervention by current speakers and writers, while unused or 'dead' languages remain in an arrested form. Such 'live' innovations occur frequently but often take time to gain general adoption, although they can, upon occasion, spread very rapidly. As a result, the diachronic fortunes of specific languages exhibit considerable fluctuations. They wax, wane, compete, coexist, subdivide, arrive, depart and, exceptionally, are returned from near-abeyance into active use.[35] Moreover, even 'dead' or, more properly, dormant languages, like classical Latin, may retain a muted semi-life. They are thus still comprehended by specialist scholars but no longer communally used, except ritually. Over time, some twenty thousand separate spoken tongues have been identified historically, of which some 4,500, with many variant dialects, are currently 'live'.[36] However, the very large extent of overlapping and borrowing between languages makes such calculations only very approximate. Overall, there is a clear contrast between the plurality of linguistic forms and the universality of number. On the other hand, numbering systems also lend themselves to the generation of many different computer languages, each based upon its own defined string or combination of letters, numbers, and/or symbols.[37]

To explain the luxuriant process of linguistic adaptation and innovation, Charles Darwin suggested that it is a human characteristic to have 'a strong love for slight changes in all things' – neatly encapsulating his own gradualist credo.[38] That would produce an evolution of languages on a par with biological evolution, he further argued. So words and grammatical forms might be seen as engaged in their own struggle for survival. However, the parallel between linguistic history and organic biology is not a precise one. Languages are not living organisms but instead constitute the interpersonal communication systems of a live species that, most unusually, has the capacity to vary the form of its communications. It is thus not biological struggle but human history which frames the fortunes of the different human languages.

Variations occur in the meanings, spellings and sounds of words; in the number and popularity of words; in grammatical usages; and in linguistic conventions, such as how to address other people. Such cumulative alterations change entire languages over hundreds of years – a relatively rapid process in comparison with the thousands of years needed for structural genetic changes.

But there is no standard 'pace' of linguistic change. Indeed, it is possible that the advent of printing (which helps to standardise languages by facilitating the circulation of dictionaries, grammars and stock texts),[39] and the gradual spread of literacy (which spreads awareness of 'correct' usages), are between them tending to slow the rate of structural transformations in written languages, even while facilitating an increasingly rapid dissemination and high turnover of novel words, phrases and idioms in spoken versions.

Nor is there any pre-set direction to linguistic change.[40] Optimists once argued that all languages evolved from barbaric plainness to cultivated beauty, while pessimists detected a process of degeneration from original purity instead. 'Every *change* is a *gradual corruption*,' fretted one anxious commentator in seventeenth-century England.[41] Meanwhile, other analysts proposed that languages become streamlined over time, changing from an original prolixity into a 'modern' brevity and clarity – a theory with which Darwin felt some sympathy. However, usages are more variegated than that suggests. Different linguistic registers are often found within one generic tradition. Thus a terse street slang coexists in many languages with a rotund diction for formal occasions, and plain speaking is heard alongside abstruse technical jargons.

Over the very long term, there have been some cumulative developments. Written languages, for example, tend to be much more highly codified than are purely spoken languages, and all extensively used languages are much better documented than are rare ones. In terms of scripted representation, the Roman alphabet, notably aided by the first generation of electronic keyboards, is today the most widely deployed on a daily basis, although there is a global array of well-used alternatives.

Something like 130-plus leading world languages have emerged and continue to flourish, each with over one million regular speakers. At the same time, the total number of separate tongues is historically falling. However, attrition is not inevitable. New languages and cross-language inventions (known as 'creoles') emerge from time to time, while fading languages sometimes recover with suitable support from their relevant linguistic communities. In addition, there is also a varying history of bilingualism and multilingualism.[42] Speaking more than one language extends linguistic communities, which can become very large or even global if one language is adopted, officially or unofficially, as an international standby or *lingua franca* for people with otherwise no languages in common.

All these permutations indicate the force of human creativity, and the ways in which countless small changes are shuffled, and a proportion then become accepted and culturally diffused. Language is particularly prominent as an example of shared social endeavour, because languages always involve more than one participant. But the same processes apply in many other areas of human life, as gradualism works in harness with framework continuities. Musical traditions, for example, display considerable variegation alongside persistence, as seen in many small changes to instrumentation, orchestration, notation, repertoires and performance styles. Here creativity and copying intermesh dynamically. And indeed music is notable for the ease with which borrowings, sharings and 'crossovers' occur within and between the different musical traditions.

Imitation is thus one integral element in the process of diffusing change. Not all are equally creative but the human capacity to imitate new forms of behaviour and to copy new attitudes is very widespread.

Indeed, another neo-Darwinist explanation of cultural change has recently been proposed on precisely this basis. It argues controversially that there is a raw struggle for survival, not between living organisms or even between 'living' languages, but between mentalistic idea-units that are single components of human thought and behaviour. These have been termed 'memes' as conduits of cultural imitation (mimetics), by analogy with biological 'genes' which frame physical growth (genetics). The human mind then becomes the arena for struggle. Successful memes 'leap from brain to brain', replicating themselves automatically as happens when people hear a 'catchy' tune that they cannot forget. According to this theory, ideas that have universal value will spread quickly and persist, while those that do not will tend to disappear.[43] As the carriers of these contending idea-units, people are regarded effectively as 'meme machines' or, in a phrase that makes us sound less like automata, as 'meme constructs'.

Here is another remarkable tribute to the appeal of Darwin's model of evolution through micro-struggle. And 'meme' theory also observes the quest for simplicity in nature. However, it is not hard to detect that, in this case, one factor – the human capacity for imitation – has been pushed too far, into gross oversimplification. Even at the very simplest level, far from all behaviour is copied from others. A very young child having its first tantrum is not in thrall to imitative 'memes'.

Moreover, people do not formulate complex new ideas and theories or accept them, once formulated, solely through an unconscious process of imitation. Thought and practical applications, including trial and error, and intentional communications are also centrally involved. Indeed, the theory of self-copying 'memes' is not really a valid way of describing the structure of complex ideas, let alone why they flourish in some circumstances and not in others. To say that successfully replicated ideas – like belief in a divine power – are evidence of 'memes' that have psychological value to humans amounts to little more than a truism about the appeal of religion, in the case of those to whom it does appeal.

Single-factor explanations like 'memes' also face problems in accounting not only for the changing forms of intelligently constructed ideas but also for the specifics of their historical timing. For example, it is not at all clear how theories of replicating memes could account (say) for the spread of European fascism in the 1930s while simultaneously accounting for its defeat in 1945. To say that one political ideology successfully invaded people's minds 'like a virus' in one era while anti-fascism recolonised their minds a decade later is not so much an explanation as a (highly incomplete) description of change.

Theories such as 'meme-infection' do, however, show the efforts being made to understand how ideas inform human consciousness and how such ideas are gradually spread. The debates also provide a reminder of flux. Views and accepted codes of behaviour change over time. Consequently, people in the past should not be chided as foolish or ignorant simply because their ideas and practices seem 'outdated' to later generations. 'After all,' as E. P. Thompson, the analyst of Britain's industrial transformation, commented firmly, 'we are not at the end of social evolution ourselves.'[44] A degree of cultural humility is required when studying the past. Yesterday's trends will not continue for ever. Today's ideas, and the language in which they are expressed, will change too. 'Tomorrow is another day.' So 'now' is always in momentous transit, as hymned by Norway's Rolf Jacobsen:

A microsecond
Slips through your hands, through your eyes . . .
The cutting edge of all that's been
and has never happened before.[45]

Invention and Accumulation

Diversity is particularly characteristic among human societies, whether viewed diachronically or synchronically. By contrast, animals in the wild broadly maintain their traditional ways of life from generation to generation, subject to appropriate adaptations to changing environmental conditions. 'There are no innovations amongst the instinct part of her [nature's] forma-tion: birds sing, cocks crow, asses bray, and horses neigh in the old primitive way,' as an eighteenth-century observer proclaimed, rather gleefully.[46]

Communicative humans are, however, the world's foremost species at both problem-creating and problem-solving (not always in synchronisation). Economic life is one of the key arenas where, for practical reasons, experience is often shared. Great amounts of time and effort are collectively invested by all generations in the production and distribution of food, raw materials and other goods and services. Consequently, basic economic know-how is a central component of information exchange. Techniques of production and construction, for example, are spread both by example and by instruction. While such educational effort by no means ensures the universal adoption of 'best practice', it does encourage the spread of 'common practice', which helps to systematise economic life.

Shared know-how includes too a range of mechanisms for coping with change, although such communal resources can be overwhelmed by major disasters. Even the most outwardly traditional economies undergo constant micro-adaptations and fluctuations. In agrarian communities, for example, land is regularly taken into or out of cultivation, in response to changing climatic and demographic circumstances. As a result, many so-called 'backward' peoples, whose way of life may remain traditional, have a reservoir of flexibility that provides some cushioning in hard times.[47]

Communal adaptiveness is particularly marked in the circulation of information about technical innovations that are practical but not too costly or complicated. The use of the wheel, for instance, spread within a few centuries from c. 3500 BCE Sumeria to all the contiguous communities across Eurasia which kept draught-animals capable of pulling wheeled vehicles.[48] Admittedly, information networks are never perfect. People sometimes waste time in resolving problems that have already been solved: the state of affairs famously known as 'reinventing the wheel'. Furthermore, the history of technology incorporates disuse as well as use. In the regions of north Africa where the hardy camel became the staple pack-animal after the third century CE, the use of older wheeled carts drawn by oxen or horses was discontinued.[49] Yet the technology itself was not discarded. The basic usefulness of the wheel meant that it was deployed in many different ways, such as in potting, milling, horology and hydraulics.[50]

Invention followed by subsequent refinement and sometimes discarding is particularly common in the history of applied technology 'from stone tools to micro-chips'. The same also applies to the long history of producing ornamental items for decoration and delight, as well as items for practical purposes. In some cases, credit for innovation is attributed to a single pioneer. But in very many cases the application and development of inventions remain a communal process, frequently involving more than one generation of people. For that reason it is often difficult to date the introduction of a specific new item or manufacturing process or design modification. While the fundamental concept of a hammer has not changed over time, there have been numerous uncharted variants in its form: for example,

Birmingham manufacturers in the 1860s were selling hammers that were designed to over five hundred different specifications.[51] None of these varieties was credited to a special inventor; but the diversity had emerged within a common production culture of experimental modifications.

Tool-making humanity has thus garnered and developed an enormous stock of technical know-how over time. If there were no improvements from generation to generation, then 'we should still sail on rafts', as Quintilian the orator declared triumphantly. Ingenuity and adaptability, in the light of local circumstances, are widespread features of a long process of trial and error. Eventual technological successes are often preceded or 'shadowed' by earlier failures and blunders.[52] The creative process is marked by many hit or miss efforts.

Collectively, the state of technical skills at any given time is closely allied to the nature of economic production, which in turn influences the nature of social and cultural life. For that reason, the linked processes of invention and innovation (referring to the subsequent adoption/adaptation of invention) are often taken as major indicators of change over time. Thus whole eras are identified diachronically by their material tool culture: from the prolonged 'Stone Age' of early humanity to today's 'Microchip World'.

In biological terms, 'Man [sic] began his career as a rare animal', with small numbers living in fugitive settlements.[53] With time, however, improved production techniques made it possible for larger communities to congregate in towns and cities, and they could in turn share new ideas and inventions. The process of mechanisation in the eighteenth and nineteenth centuries, following the introduction of steam power, is the best known example of technological acceleration in human history. Yet there have been other earlier cases of notable innovation-based growth. The relatively affluent and sophisticated economy of Sung dynasty China in the eleventh and twelfth centuries, for example, was prosaically based upon successful new techniques of iron smelting and of water-powered milling.[54] Such growth processes often direct attention to the distribution of the fruits of growth. By the twenty-first century, the entire global family 'business' has been massively expanded, as ideas and innovations are spreading worldwide. A population of over six billion people thus provides not only a record number of mouths to feed but additionally sets new challenges in terms of how to eradicate systemic poverty amidst the areas of wealth.

How growth is in practice generated and sustained remains debated. For Adam Smith, who founded the subject of economics from his base in the prospering Edinburgh of the eighteenth century, there was 'an invisible hand'[55] – also known as the 'hidden hand' – that produced a favourable outcome from a great miscellany of private transactions. This ultimately harmonious model assumed that the market process remains orderly and non-chaotic. Changes were also thought likely to occur gradually, within a self-equilibriating system, on a par with eighteenth-century ideas about an orderly nature. Smith's model did not cover all eventualities, therefore, but it paid significant attention to the role of micro-change, with many small adjustments continually reconfiguring market conditions.

More aggressive interpretations of technological innovation, however, stress instead the contribution of competition and 'struggle' on neo-Darwinian lines. Natural selection in economics has been claimed to operate as a form of 'organisational genetics', promoting the successful and dumping the rest. And the 'jungle' in which this process occurs is the competitive market.[56] However, it is not clear in this model who or what might qualify as the unconscious biological agency to promote technological evolution. The various inventors, technicians, entrepreneurs and firms who contribute to the process of economic change are operating collectively within complex societies, and learning from each other, not responding individually to imperceptible environmental changes in the wild.

Or could it even be the newly invented machines that are themselves evolving? That teasing possibility was raised by Samuel Butler in 1863. As each invention is a selective improvement upon the one before, the mechanical servants will eventually triumph over their human masters: 'The upshot is simply a question of time', he wrote.[57] However, Butler's fable was intended not as a forecast but as a satire upon misapplications of Darwinism. Machines are not organic beings, evolving freely. Nonetheless, some argue that an ultra-new process in world history has just begun. A novel breed of techno-humans, hand in socket with their computerised thinking machines, may be about to co-evolve, it is maintained – either in hope or in fear.[58]

Thus neo-Darwinian gradualism, with or without competitive struggle as the mechanism for transformation, remains a popular model of micro-change in many fields of analysis. However, Darwin studied an unconscious process of biological adaptation to environment over millennia. Once conscious intentionality is included, the processes of change are rendered very much more complex. Human creativity – itself a biologically adaptive trait – is now intervening directly to alter both the species and the environment. To take a common example, people with defective eyesight are not now weeded out by natural selection but are aided by artificial eyeglasses or by optical surgery. As Darwin's friendly rival Alfred Russel Wallace rightly observed, humans adapt the environment as well as adapt to it.[59]

On the strength of that, it has further been claimed that the old instinctual organic evolution has ended and an interventionist 'cultural' evolution has usurped it. That alternative, however, goes too far in corralling biology, whose power has by no means been terminated. It has just become more complicated, incorporating linkages and feedbacks between the untrammelled forces of 'nature' and the activities of its brainiest progeny, the meddling *Homo sapiens*, whose impact upon the global environment is daily increasing as human numbers continue to multiply.

With the common experience of micro-change, there has also developed, particularly since the eighteenth century, a significant cultural strand of confidence in long-term processes. This attitude, while emphatically not shared by all, was based upon admiration for the consolidation and continual updating of the human stock of knowledge in accessible forms. Theory and practice would alike benefit, gaining from the accumulated wisdom of time. So things would 'progress'. Classical Greece and Rome might be ancient in history, wrote the scientist and lawyer Francis Bacon in the early seventeenth century, but they were young in experience. Later generations had the advantage of a much larger stock of knowledge, observations and experimentation.[60] The achievements of one age would assist the next. So when publishing the world's most famous encylopaedia in mid-eighteenth-century France, Denis Diderot declared nonchalantly that his aim was to systematise the entire global range of knowledge and to transmit it 'to those who will come after us, so that the work of past centuries may be useful to the following centuries'.[61] It is true that he was not as open to absolutely all thought-systems as he believed himself to be. His compilation was inevitably selective and skewed towards European culture. Yet the aim was clearly universalist and indelibly optimistic.

Thinking 'long' encouraged a willingness to make plans for incremental change over long spans of time. For instance, eighteenth-century medicine in Europe was not too proud to borrow and then to dream. The technique of inoculation against the disease of smallpox, which severely scarred those victims it did not kill, was imported, at first controversially, from Turkey in the 1720s. Within a few years, surgeons in England and France were experimenting with different methodologies and inoculating large numbers.[62] The possibilities of preventive medicine began to be canvassed. Already by 1784, one visionary proposed plans for the complete eradication of smallpox, long before Edward Jenner discovered the successor technique of vaccination.[63]

Since then, the history of medicine has hardly been error-free. Yet a worldwide programme of public healthcare has been formulated and to a large extent adopted. This was one important factor in helping to sustain the global population growth of the last two centuries via the gradual 'mortality transition' to lower death rates and lengthened average life expectancy.[64] Many small changes, planned generally but undertaken locally, have helped not to eradicate all infectious disease but to reduce the ferocity of many.

Sadly for simple theories of 'progress', it must be conceded that human population growth on a massive scale around the globe is proving far from optimal in ecological terms. A new set of demographic pressures is calling for new micro-responses, already to be seen in policies and practices that are reducing global reproduction rates. However, there are many other daunting environmental challenges that are not (yet) resolved, and the solutions may in themselves generate new difficulties.

Belief in the human capacity to respond, however, remains one of the products of confidence in the accumulation of theoretical and practical know-how. The importance of building his science upon historic foundations was once noted by Isaac Newton, who was much praised for his own originality. 'If I have seen further,' he wrote graciously in 1676, 'it is by standing on the shoulders of giants.'[65] He was using a traditional metaphor, which contains some mock-modesty. Moreover, it remains open to parody. Thus Sigmund Freud later issued a diatribe against a rival psychologist, with the crushing comment that a louse on the head of a philosopher cannot surpass the original vision of the philosopher.

It is not necessary, however, to assert that all change is for the better in order to note the process of human knowledge accumulation over time. That there is such a process, often eclectic and unsystematic, means that, as the philosopher Karl Popper argued,[66] there is a cumulative and evolving human cultural input, which operates alongside biological evolution, especially now that there are abundant means of storing and preserving know-how, as part of long-term global history.

Talking about Micro-change

Many see micro-change and incessant novelty rather than continuity as the norm, so there are plenty of ways of talking about change. 'Always something new out of Africa' ('*ex Africa semper aliquid novi*') ran a popular saying in ancient Greece and Rome, as reported by Pliny the Elder. It is an evocative dictum, particularly as that continent provided the first home for the *Homo sapiens* branch of the many earlier upright hominid species.[67]

Talking of gradual change in the hybrid English language – itself a classic example of linguistic accumulation – offers many choices. There are rotund Latinate terms for: alteration, adaptation, acceleration, amendment, innovation, progression, refinement, revision, transformation, transfiguration, transmogrification, transition, mutation, modification, modulation, differentiation, diversification, variation, procession, fluctuation, flux, vicissitudes. Borrowed from Latin, there is the terse *paulatim* or 'little by little'. And the Greek heritage is nuanced too. *Dynamics* refers to the forces of action;

entropy to thermodynamic transformability; *metastasis* to the process of transformation from one state into another, as when ice melts into water; and *metamorphosis* to significant amendments in shape or substance (as when mythic Zeus turned himself into a swan to seduce the entranced Leda).

'Reform' or 'reformation' signals measured changes to affairs of church and state. One version of an unrushed and gradual history is dubbed 'the Whig interpretation' after England's nineteenth-century Whig politicians who favoured moderate, discreet and gentlemanly change. 'Expansion', 'growth' and, more neutrally, 'development' refer also to cumulative changes in economic affairs. But 'modernisation', which was used in the 1950s with generally favourable connotations, has now become more controversial and more opaque.

'Improvement' meanwhile conveys the eighteenth-century Enlightenment trust in change for the better. It was followed by 'progress', which held extensive conceptual sway, in many but not all circles, until the First World War. Benevolent change was held by enthusiasts to be embedded in nature. 'Progress . . . is not an accident, but a necessity,' explained the Victorian guru of social statistics Herbert Spencer, 'a law underlying the whole organic creation.'[68] Many other terms have positive connotations too. Advance, ascent, rise, regeneration, renovation, renaissance, amelioration, betterment, all lead 'onwards and upwards'. Things are said to be 'on the move' or 'on the go'. And a sense of the inexorability of change is still expressed in the mantra 'you can't stop progress', which is often intoned solemnly rather than defined, especially in debates about new technologies. So we are enjoined to 'move with the times'.

Opposing this, there is at the same time an alternative lexicon. It deplores ruination, retrogression, corrosion, corruption, worsening, weakening, dissolution, decay, deterioration, degeneration, dilapidation, decadence, descent, decline and, ultimately, fall. The tone is melancholy. Terms with the initial letter 'D' have sad affinities with: dismay, discontent, dejection, demoralisation, depression, despondency, discouragement, defeat, darkness and despair. 'Things fall apart; the centre cannot hold', ran a celebrated line of Yeats's poetry. Colloquially, matters are always 'going to the dogs', a destination reserved for the whole country in bad times and/or for young people at any time. Hence, in cockney verse, "fings ain't what they used to be'. And there is always more to deplore. As a wisecracking American journalist once advised: 'Cheer up – the worst is yet to come.'

Supporters of gradual change, however, are not easily discouraged. The tactical advantage of incremental reform lies in its gentle, step-by-step nature. Philosophically, Immanuel Kant defined attempts at human betterment as 'eudaemonism', or being 'a good angel'. No need to rush. Opponents need time to assimilate the shock of the new. Discretion advises not a quick sprint but a 'long march'. 'Softly, softly, catchee monkey.' 'Slow but sure.' A classical adage counsels *festina lente* – 'make haste slowly'. Patience is, after all, a virtue. The wise tortoise defeats the impetuous hare. Only '*Fools* rush in where *Angels* fear to tread', proclaimed Alexander Pope. Divine powers, being eternal, certainly have absolutely no need for haste. 'The mills of God grind slowly.'

Gradualism as a conscious tactic, however, is not problem free. It can seem too tame and cautious. The celebrated Roman consul Fabius Maximus, whose name became synonymous with delay as he avoided open battle with the marauding Carthaginians in the third century BCE, was often unpopular with the people; and later 'Fabian' advocates of gradualism, taking their name from his, are often criticised for timidity too. Indeed, if slow change takes too long to arrive, it may ultimately be hard to distinguish from continuity.

If nonetheless cumulative micro-changes do combine together, then the outcomes of such slow transformations, whether for good or ill, are usefully described as 'trends'. But these results are not inevitable. Thus it is always necessary to establish whether any given micro-change is either a proverbial 'flash in the pan', with no subsequent significance, or the 'thin end of the wedge', which becomes a portent of 'things to come'.

Above all, incremental adaptation, once cumulatively unfolding, is hard to undo, as it depends upon gradual micro-changes that are insidious, each relatively minor in itself and difficult to detect. Such a process is sometimes termed 'drift'. Yet 'evolution' remains the descriptive term par excellence, being boosted in circulation not only by post-Darwinian biology but also by 'neo-Darwinist' ideas in other disciplines. The illustration below shows the distant

10 Post-Darwinian line-drawing (1863) of the skeletal cousinhood of the ape family, with the gibbon (twice life-size), the orang, the chimpanzee, the gorilla, and, in the lead, the upright human.

cousinhood of humans with the gibbon (drawn at twice life size), the orang, the chimpanzee and the gorilla, as skeletally revealed for startled public inspection in mid-Victorian times. And the genetic linkages have been confirmed subsequently by studies of comparative DNA. The similarities *and* the differences provide a classic indication of the cumulative power of micro-change to effect a branching transformation within the ape species over long spans of time.

Interpreting Micro-change

Putting precise dates to slow change is often difficult, because the processes are slow and insidious. Micro-changes after all can be noted at any point from their first arrival through to their accumulated outcome in macro-change. Thus a gradual trend may be plausibly dated either by its first appearance, or by its accelerating mass, or by its majority success, or, later, by its complete achievement. It is always helpful, then, to specify what stages of micro-change or cumulative trend are under discussion.

Furthermore, to avoid the nebulousness that comes with loose talk of 'change' without any further qualification, it is constructive to specify *what sort of change?* and/or *change from what to what?* Otherwise, the term, as already noted, can apply to everything and nothing. Surprisingly little theory assesses gradual change in human affairs, other than in biology. That contrasts with extensive discussions of the origin and meaning of 'revolution'. No doubt, the old assumption that gradual change was an intrinsic part of 'nature' meant that no special explanation seemed necessary. Among philosophers who have considered the question, Leibniz argued that there was a veritable 'law of continuity'. He meant by that, however, *not* stasis, but a steady process of unbroken change.[69] But, because he took this continuous transformation to be entirely natural, he gave no further explanation. Similarly an expert on technological invention attributed this process to a positive 'law of [technological] evolution'.[70] Yet it is hard to see how that can be a general proposition that is true for all time. There have been many long periods without great or frequent technological innovations, just as we are also living now in a period when technological changes are accelerating and also diffusing widely.

Historians would therefore note that it is not so much the general principle of change that needs explanation but rather its specific forms, as and when they occur in and through time. And the answers are not always simple. There is often more than one micro-change in play at any given time. So a development in one direction may be cancelled out by contrary forces. The same applies to trends, which are not required by history or nature to run along straight lines in a linear fashion; and which are sometimes contradicted or complicated by countervailing trends. The overall power of slow transformation, based upon many micro-changes, is undoubtedly very considerable. Like continuity, it is everywhere to be found. But, unlike continuity, it leads in surprising directions.

Micro-change thus shows its insidious power at macro-level in the visible cosmos, and additionally can be analysed at micro-level in the invisible quantum state of subatomic particles. These processes of infinitesimal adaptation occur both with and without friction. And the specific forms of micro-change are themselves very sensitive to micro-variations in the context of changing circumstances, so multiplying micro-unpredictability. Hence for humans, while there is always scope for detection and prediction of trends, there is also much speculation and uncertainty about the long-term direction of history's pathways.

Shaping History – Time Lines

Thinking of history as travelling along a line, rather than round in a completed circle, is an alternative way of interpreting the experience of time. The seasons go round; but each spring is a new one, not an old spring revived. Life is viewed as a journey from youth to old age, which is halted only at the 'journey's end' by death. 'An individual is a four-dimensional object of greatly elongated form. In ordinary language, we say that he [or she] has considerable extension in time and insignificant extension in space,' explained physicist Arthur Eddington kindly. Not all, of course, live long. Too many die young, taken 'before their time' as the regretful phrase declares. But the linear vision looks beyond the moment, envisioning that individuals, families and communities form part of a longitudinal process as they travel along history's trackways.

Such diachronic perspectives direct attention either backwards or onwards across the centuries. An unfolding narration is generated that commences with 'once upon a time' and marches to its conclusion. Historical or personal accounts also intersect with religious teachings, which stress the centrality of the spiritual quest or journey.

Looking backwards along past linear trackways offers a perspective that tends to stress continuity, tradition and family ties. In traditional Chinese culture, for example, the generations are felt to be bonded by a temporal thread or filament (*ji*) that links the past to the present. Ancestors who have gone before are reverenced, as the custodians of historic values. They act as benign family guardians, although, if neglected, they may become restless or angry spirits that plague rather than aid their descendants. Linear elements of history, such as this, coexist happily with the alternative tradition that views time as a revolving path (*li*), which runs in sixty-year cycles. Family lines could thus outlast the passing turmoil of events, and cyclicality entwine with linearity.

Ancestor ceremonies, sometimes misleadingly known as ancestor 'worship', recur in many areas of the globe, notably in west Africa and large swathes of Asia. Rituals are embedded in local cultures. So there are intricate conventions to regulate which family ancestors (whether on the paternal or maternal side) are to be reverenced and which family member (often the oldest son) has the main responsibility for the ceremonials.

Belonging to a 'line' that stretches far back into the past gives people a clear place in the world. Individuals who study their personal antecedents can reconstruct a family 'tree' as a personalised tree of knowledge. Particularly in oral cultures, the communal understanding of both past and present is often centred upon such awareness. For example, village memory men in traditional west African culture act as 'living libraries', storing and recounting family histories and imparting this key information to the next generation.

The massive importance of ancestor-ties becomes apparent in the profound and prolonged cultural dislocation that follows when they are disrupted, not by chosen migration but by enforced exodus. It amounts to an 'uprooting' not just of people but also of their knowledge systems, history and language. The trauma of the west Africans from ancestor-reverencing societies, who were forcibly taken to the Americas as slaves, especially during the harsh mass transits in the eighteenth and early nineteenth centuries, still ricochets down the centuries. In homage to that crisis, the later success of the American writer Alex Haley's account of his reconstructed African family *Roots* (1976) indicated the strength of hopes that old, severed linkages might be reconnected as he travelled to the ancestral homeland to hear a recital of ancient clan lineages by a Gambian *griot* or village memory man.

'Placing' people diachronically thus has immense cultural importance. Linkages are not only heard but witnessed, as in the case of visible funerary monuments. Their format varies greatly from culture to culture, depending upon beliefs about what happens to individuals after death. And the monuments themselves range from the grandest to the simplest. Nonetheless, they convey both an acknowledgement of mortality and a sense of linkages across the generations. With a mystic belief in the possibilities of transmission across time, indeed, some of the world's grandest funerary monuments from the far-distant past, like the Egyptian Sphinx and the great pyramids, are repeatedly rumoured to hold potent 'secrets' – or equally potent curses – that are still 'alive' today.

Sequentiality also underpins political as well as personal legitimacy. Some of the oldest ever written sources contain the ancient Sumerian 'king lists', dating back to the third millennium BCE, which confirmed the ruler's ancestry by naming them turn by turn. These sources were prototypes of later annalistic histories, which recorded the chronological sequence of years and great events. A striving for a known temporal framework is similarly conveyed by tribal genealogies in the Bible. Litanies such as 'Hezron begat Ram, and Ram begat Amminadab' are not obviously inspirational. But such details, included in both Old and New Testaments, root the spiritual message within the framework of a specified human history.

Interest in such Biblical genealogies has subsequently spurred numerous feats of ingenuity. More than one Christian scholar, for example, has provided a bloodline attempting to show how Jesus Christ was descended from King David and, further back in time, from Abraham and thence from Adam and Eve. And this interest in lineage is projected onwards too. Mythic accounts search for the putative descendants of Christ today, assuming that he married Mary Magdalene and became a father. To add to the romance, the divine inheritance is also linked to royalty. Thus one publication in 1996 declares that Prince Michael Stewart, 7th Count of Albany, is not only the lineal descendant of Christ but also the 'true' heir to the British throne, as a scion of the long-exiled Stuart kings. This is supposedly history's 'Holy Grail', long hidden by the malign powers of church and state. A rival website, unamused, counters by 'outing' the current claimant as a non-royal Belgian-born impostor.[1]

So riveting are the possibilities that mythic tales of fabulous but hidden lineages frequently recur in fiction. The best-selling novel on the *Da Vinci Code*, for example, identifies the lineal descendant of Christ and Mary Magdalene as an enterprising young woman who also turns out to be the last representative of the traditional Merovingian rulers of France after Charlemagne.[2] Again an ancient 'secret', both royal and divine, is unlocked, as the true heir struggles against wicked enemies to discover her historic lineage. The fact that several changes of dynasty and the French republic have intervened since the Merovingians is not important for the story. It ends not with a political or spiritual restoration but with personal recognition: the finding of family roots. So the narrative thrust is based upon unravelling the secret, and the tales of those who have guarded it, rather than what happens once elements of the mystery are revealed. The high melodrama thus ends tamely, almost cosily: with homecomings, tranquillity and echoes of the timeless (feminine) 'wisdom of the ages' which still awaits true human recognition.

Powerful and widespread as is the retrospective gaze at traditional time lines, it is partnered by an equally insistent prospective view that seeks to envisage or even to predict future trends. The two perspectives are sometimes understood as alternatives. But they can also cohere, as when time lines from the past are held to stretch unbrokenly not only up to the present but also onwards into the projected future.

A forwards linearity tends to become relatively prevalent as an attitude in mobile urban/industrial societies, where most people are free from close acquaintance with the cyclical rhythms of the agricultural year, where many families are not in continual touch with older generations, and where lifestyles are especially open to variation. Care for the individual and collective futures can be seen, for example, in personal savings, in insurance schemes and in civic exercises in long-term planning.

Yet such a linear perspective is not by any means purely a recent invention. A future-oriented pattern of thinking is a particularly prominent element in the theologies of the three major prophetic and monotheistic religions – Judaism, Christianity, Islam – which all initially developed within communities living in the disputed terrain at the crossroads of great Eurasia. The historical sense of flux and the pivotal movement of peoples in the 'holy land' between east and west fostered a set of spiritual teachings that see life as a journey through an always hazardous world. One much later nonconformist Protestant allegory of the quest for salvation has become world famous as *The Pilgrim's Progress* (1678). In it, Bunyan depicts the temptations along the route and warns all travellers that, even at the very gates of heaven, there is still an apparently enticing pathway nearby that leads straight to hell.[3]

For the people within the historic Jewish tradition, the world's story stretches unbrokenly from the Creation to the expected arrival of the Redeemer. There is one God, who decrees a single destiny. Accordingly, the faithful continue to look ahead, awaiting the day. This longitudinal history furnishes the Jewish cultural tradition with an exceptionally resilient sense of continuation, looking both backwards and forwards. Such a rooted perspective provides the possibility of coping with adversities, while still hoping for better to come. Moreover, the inscribing of the faith in a portable holy book means that Jewish beliefs are capable of being retained and adjusted even throughout the diaspora of communities of the faithful.

Christian teaching, augmenting the Old Testament with the New, similarly identifies a unique sequence of events: the creation, the fall, the first coming of Christ the Redeemer, the crucifixion, the resurrection, the second coming of Christ, the rule of the saints and the final day of judgement. Here is a single pathway through history. It is summed in Christ's remark that 'I am the way'. Accordingly, influential Christian theologians like St Augustine of Hippo denied utterly that the maxim 'there is no new thing under the sun' could ever apply to momentous events like the coming of the Redeemer. While other historical changes, like the rise and fall of governments, can still be discussed in cyclical or any other terms, these are mere local vicissitudes within a greater spiritual saga.

Islamic thought, which acknowledges both Abraham (Ibrahim) and Christ as holy teachers, distils linearity still more strongly. All true believers are wayfarers, in a religion of pilgrimage. The prophet Muhammad's emigration from Mecca to Medina (the *Hijra*, Latinised *Hegira*), in 622 CE – the first year in the Muslim calendar – symbolises the quest, just as Muhammad's return to Mecca, before his death in 632 CE, marks its fulfilment. Current affairs are always full of turmoil, warns the Qur'ān, but there is a spiritual destination beyond such relative ephemera. The holy book, whose name means 'reading', facilitates the transmission of the message to different parts of the world. And, throughout the centuries, distinctive schools of thought within Islam canvass and debate the rightful pathway.

Spiritual linearity, however, does not preclude considerable elements of cyclicality within the forms of religious worship. All these faiths have their own liturgical calendars, with prescribed sequences for prayer, services and celebrations. For active believers, these rituals give 'shape' to the day, the week and the year. In that way, the regular cycles of religious duties provide reassuring way-markers during the lifetime's long pilgrimage, showing again that ideas of directional change can coexist readily enough with ideas of recurrence.

It was, however, particularly in eighteenth-century Europe and North America that linearity gained a new cultural potency, when the view of life as a journey, both for communities and individuals, took on a new resonance and a specifically secular guise. The pilgrim's progress gradually merged into anticipations of social progress for all. Models of individual self-improvement mesh with hopes for universal betterment. 'Forward march!' as the slogan proclaims, urging people to get in step with the trend. Ultra-optimists dream of a new 'heaven on earth'.

High hopes were increasingly voiced, controversially in the seventeenth century, more strongly in the eighteenth century, and ebulliently in the nineteenth and early twentieth centuries, before they were eventually discouraged by the disasters of mass warfare in 1914–18.[4] Even before then, however, it is important to note that there were plenty of critics and doubters, including those who favoured cyclical models of history. Nonetheless, the advent of mass urban/industrial societies, already succoured by historic traditions of linear religion, has tended to produce a new, highly influential and secularised version of 'forward thinking', initially in the West but, latterly, far from confined to western cultures.

One much-favoured metaphor depicted humanity as engaged in a progressive long march from darkness into light. The direction also went from low to high: 'onwards and upwards', towards a secular version of the spiritual haven atop Mount Zion. One English schoolmaster in 1795 depicted the slow climb with unabashed good cheer:

Man [sic] is a progressive animal, and his advance towards improvement is a pleasurable state. Hope cheers his path as he toils up the hill that leads him to something better than he has yet experienced, on its gay summit gilded with sunshine.

Condorcet, the eminent *philosophe* in neighbouring France, was even more of an enthusiast's enthusiast. Writing just before his execution in a French revolutionary purge in 1795, his testament to the *Progrès de l'esprit humain* (*Progress of the Human Spirit*) affirmed an unshaken faith in the march towards knowledge and happiness. It might sometimes falter, Condorcet accepted ruefully, but would never seriously retreat. So the destined outcome remains the 'perfectibility of man [sic]' in this world, not in the next. Not only would political freedoms follow for all but even endemic poverty would be abolished worldwide.[5]

No specific rituals buttressed this secular faith in progress. However, it was associated with confidence in science and the hope that human reason would swiftly uncover all the secrets of the cosmos. Indeed, since authorities like Descartes and Newton showed that unfettered motion travelled in a straight line, it was not implausible to assume that history might progress similarly. Pioneers on the route thus become 'ahead of their time' while laggards are 'behind the times'. When Darwin's model of leisurely evolution in biology was published in the mid nineteenth century, the case for the gradualist model appeared to be clinched. Everything seemed to fit. One keen Darwinist was euphoric: 'Progress – or what is the same thing, Evolution – is her [Nature's] religion'.

Applied technology in particular seemed to offer practical proofs. In the nineteenth century, the new railway trains, travelling of course along straight lines, became noisy but potent signifiers of 'forward movement'. The synchronisation of their timetables promoted fresh attention to the synchronisation of clocks and time zones. And they resonated a message of unstoppable high-speed change. The enthused French anarchist Pierre-Joseph Proudhon applied the metaphor to history itself. Individual liberation was arriving, he wrote, on a veritable 'freedom railway': *le chemin de fer de la liberté*. Illustration 11 demonstrates the looming impact of a legendary Australian express locomotive named *Spirit of Progress*: it

11 Australia's *Spirit of Progress* locomotive – built 1928–30, streamlined 1937, scrapped 1954 – demonstrated the pace of techno-fame followed by techno-obsolescence within thirty years as steam gave way to diesel.

is massive, purposive, steely, with a huge circular lamp to illuminate the straight route ahead. Now scrapped, it nonetheless represented in its day the latest human technology at the 'cutting edge'.

Not all welcomed such stark intrusions into the landscape. Innovations, which to some constitute 'progress', to others represent 'degeneration'. Expressing doubts in the mid-nineteenth century, the Catholic Pope Pius IX feared that, if human history and biology were seen as acquiring a mantle of inevitability, then all scope for divine intervention would be lost. In 1864, he issued an across-the-board rejection of 'progress, liberalism, and civilisation as lately introduced'. Interestingly, too, similar debates are now occurring within early twenty-first-century Islam. Traditionalist imams in Iran issue religious edicts against 'liberalism, secularism and pluralism'. Yet trends of cultural transformation, if deep-rooted, are not easily halted by diktats, no matter how determined. Rival views often remain locked in competition for long periods. Meanwhile, one of the chief factors to curb, not social change, but beliefs in an infallible human progress has come from history's capacity to spring unwelcome surprises. Innovations that have solved some problems have turned out to create new ones. And, above all, the repeated horrors perpetrated by humanity against humanity in the twentieth century, from world wars to genocides, have induced a justifiable element of disillusionment with the most rose-tinted scenarios.

Universalist claims for the inevitability of 'progress' on all fronts are thus generally eclipsed. Some things do get better – like, for example, techniques of dentistry in the later twentieth century – but not everything does. Beliefs in the benefits of technological change, which still persist quite widely, are made more cautious by a rival techno-suspicion. And there were and are continuing strands of pessimism, now especially fuelling ecological activism. In this context, the name of Parson Malthus is often invoked for his warnings of the dangers of human overpopulation.

Nonetheless, while models of an inevitable linearity in history have generally disappeared, it is notable that many if not most historical narratives are now couched within secular frameworks. And thoughts of both past and future are framed, without apology, within long timespans and wide horizons. But inexorable pathways are more likely to be interpreted these days as 'trends'. This shift still acknowledges that micro-changes do accumulate, in certain circumstances, to produce long-term outcomes. But time's unidirectionality does not require that all trends must be purely singular or unbrokenly linear. In each synchronic moment, there are multiple legacies from the past and more than one option for the future. Similarly, historical epics do not have to be conveyed always in straightforward chronological accounts that run without a narrative break from start to finish.[6] Lines, like cycles, both develop *and* rupture. As a Russian proverb sapiently warns, the unexpected is always possible: 'You go up the hill and the devil grabs your foot.'

CHAPTER 4

Radical Discontinuity

Drama, novelty, friction, irregularity, upheaval, radical discontinuity, abrupt metamorphosis, revolutionary transformations – these also occur, in nature as well as in human affairs. For that reason, the old twofold distinction between 'continuity' and 'change' is inadequate to 'shape' the whole of history. Instead, the different forms of transformation need to be assessed separately. 'Change', which sounds unitary, is in reality highly diversified, as the previous chapter has argued. There are many forms of transformation, from the micro-changes that form 'evolution' to the macro-changes that form 'revolution'.

Radical discontinuity is the generic term for all forms of drastic upheaval that are both significant in their actual happening and/or fundamental in their long-term impact. They are different in kind from slow, gradual adaptation, though, just to complicate the picture, many small micro-changes, when accumulating together, may also combine to produce macro-change. Such big 'breaks' with historical continuity are manifold. They are just as 'natural' as micro-change, but they tend to appear on an irregular basis and with irregular effects. The role of radical discontinuity therefore needs to be factored into the long-term dynamics of continuity and 'change'.

For living beings, birth and death constitute the most fundamental discontinuities, no matter what, if anything, happens after death or might have happened before birth, in another life. Each specific life cycle is finite. Such organic processes of birth and death provide a reminder of the wider forces of creation and destruction that are found throughout the cosmos. At the most extreme, macro-change is entailed in the start of the universe and the possibility of its ending. And at the micro-level, physicists since Max Planck's pioneering work in 1900 reveal a restless microcosm of subatomic particles that unleash and absorb energy not in a regular flow but in discrete bursts. Hence some levels of instability are integral to the complex dynamics of the 'non-sleeping universe'.[1]

Natural disasters on planet earth provide local examples of events that have sufficient randomness and force to disrupt orderly patterns. Progressive opinion in eighteenth-century Europe was for that reason shaken in its trust in a benign 'Mother Nature' by the great Lisbon earthquake of 1 November 1755.[2] The sudden destruction of an opulent capital city, and the loss of some sixty thousand people in Iberia and north Africa as a result of the disaster and its accompanying fires and tidal waves, was startling as well as horrific in a region that was wholly unprepared for such an eventuality. The force of the quake (later calculated as 8.5 on the Richter scale) remains one of the most violent in recorded experience. It indicated an untamed energy, deep within an outwardly stable physical world. 'How can wretched man find security anywhere if the strong earth itself no longer offers security?' agonised the writer Pina e Mello in northern Portugal, where he experienced the repeated aftershocks from the Lisbon jolt.

Viewing the catastrophe from further afield, another contemporary, Voltaire, was galvanised into a wholesale philosophic assault upon complacency. He presented this in his satirical novel *Candide* (1759), which recounts the wanderings of an artless youth in a dangerous world.[3] The journey is a satiric pilgrim's progress, leading not to salvation in the next world but to sober wisdom in this one. Candide's tutor, the irrepressible Dr Pangloss, constantly repeats the optimistic mantra – that all is for the best, 'in this best of all possible worlds' – while Candide and his friends face endless adversities, both major and minor, ranging from warfare, religious persecution, slavery, violence, mutilation, rape and physical decay, through to greed, corruption, snobbery, disappointment in love and boredom. In this playful guise, Voltaire's study of history warns of disasters and disharmony rather than of enlightenment and progress. Blind optimists, who don't see disasters, are duly mocked as 'Panglossians'.

In fact, there is no automatic requirement that all shocks to the system must be unpleasant ones, just as the systems that they disrupt are not invariably benevolent ones. But, for good or ill, elements of disharmony, radical discontinuity and fundamental transformation also intrude to shape and reshape history. All great upheavals have an immediate, synchronic impact and, in specific circumstances, some have long-term effects that last for centuries.

As macro-shocks to the system are irregular and unexpected, so too are their results. To those in the thick of a crisis, the urgency is undeniable. Yet it not infrequently happens that, when the dust settles, the consequences are not always so very immense after all, as continuity and gradual change reassert themselves to repair the damage. An earthquake may destroy a city; but levelled cities are also rebuilt. Radical shocks to the system thus have notably diverse outcomes, whose full significance becomes apparent only over time.

Natural Cataclysms

Discontinuities as well as continuities within the wider cosmos are now understood to be 'normal'. The harmonious Newtonian model has given way to one that has many regular features but that simultaneously incorporates instability and restlessness. Accordingly, the scientific vocabulary refers readily to natural upheavals, turbulence, disequilibria, chaos and discontinuity.[4] This terminology bypasses the ambiguities that attend the word 'revolution', which in physics refers not to confrontation and fundamental change but instead to the established cycles of planetary bodies as they revolve steadily in their orbits.

Historically, the earth itself has experienced one absolutely major discontinuity to its local environment that has occurred since its own origins. That macro-change occurred some 4.5 billion years ago, when the moon was created, almost certainly as the result of a collision with a massive planetoid which dislodged from both bodies the materials that then coalesced into a satellite. This development had a highly significant effect upon the earth's local environment, conferring moonlight at night, augmenting the tidal rise and fall and, by its co-gravitational interaction with the earth, slowing the earth's previously much more rapid rotational pace to a more measured rate.

Nothing since then has remotely approached that scale of drama. Yet planetary turbulence continues unabated, with clashing tectonic plates, volcanic action, earthquakes, the huge tidal waves known as *tsunamis*, storms of varying degrees of violence, blizzards, avalanches, floods, fires, droughts, pests, crop blights and the danger of meteoric impacts large and small.

Cataclysms play a role in natural processes of destruction and also renewal, as in the case (say) of forest fires that create space for new growth. Yet the random violence of such radical discontinuities causes humans to classify them all as 'disasters', even if they are not all equally disastrous. At one extreme, for example, the Tambora volcanic eruption in April 1815 remains one of the most deadly in recorded history. Not only did its immediate impact kill many thousands in the populous Indonesian archipelago but its aftermath in the form of ash and gases in the earth's upper atmosphere reduced levels of sunshine for months, depleting harvests and causing famines in several parts of the world.[5] By contrast, the much less ferocious 1980 explosion of Mount St Helens in the sparsely populated Cascade Mountains in the north-west USA took the lives of fifty-seven people, although still blasting an entire local landscape within a 13-kilometre (8-mile) radius.

These sorts of cataclysmic upheaval do not at first glance fit well into regular cyclical models of history. Yet an accommodation can be made, by assuming that disasters and crises function as turning points. In that case, they are taken as signals or stimuli that inaugurate some new phase in the cycle.

Or, since communal memories of even the greatest disasters eventually fade after the immediate terror lessens, the role of cataclysms can be recalled indirectly rather than directly. These dramas may thus form the basis of ancient legends of loss and transience. In c. 1640 BCE, for example, there were repeated volcanic explosions within the Santorini crater in the mid-Aegean. Some land entirely disappeared, and the old port of Akrotiri on the rim of the crater was completely smothered, its fossilised fate foreshadowing that of Pompeii under the ash of Vesuvius. Direct knowledge of this dramatic disappearance was lost for over a millennium, until recovered, unexpectedly, in the 1860s. Yet the erasure of an entire seafaring community may have been one of the generic sources for continuing Egyptian and Greek legends of a lost island of Atlantis. Such tales were later adapted by Plato in the fourth century BCE to incorporate instability into his cosmic history. 'Many and divers are the destructions of mankind that have been and shall yet be', warns his text: and 'the greatest are wrought by fire and water'. He gave details of his imaginary island and then noted that: 'In one terrible day and night of storm . . . Atlantis . . . sank into the sea and vanished.'[6] Plato's account was left incomplete at his death; but its moral plainly indicated that all history was hazardous, combining episodes of advancement with those of great loss.

At the other end of the spectrum, optimistic views of history are particularly challenged by random disasters. Even the most determined Panglossians are troubled by nature's apparently wanton savagery. Nonetheless, there is still scope for a suitably modified optimism that responds positively to the possibility of disaster, as seen in efforts at providing better warning systems, better systems of disaster-proofing (for example, constructing quake-resistant buildings) and better ways of coping with the aftermath of crises. And recovery can be particularly rapid when impelled by urgent economic necessity and collective will. In 1976, for example, the deadly Tangshan earthquake (7.8 on the Richter scale, with a massive 7.1 aftershock as well) flattened one of China's leading industrial cities, killing over 240,000 people and injuring almost 750,000 others.[7] Nonetheless, the urban area and its industries, though not the lost lives, have been rebuilt.

Attempts at modelling the incidence of natural cataclysms deal in statistical probabilities (often with a wide margin of error) rather than with firm predictions, because such events, although natural in themselves, count as 'stochastic' processes or random external shocks to the routine functioning of the system.[8] While calculating the odds, therefore, humans are always aware that the unexpected often is truly unexpected. To produce that element of genuine surprise in 'stochastic music', for example, electronic compositions build dissonance and shock into the programme. Within a preset range of options, the components are selected randomly, either by the composer or by a computer, so producing the jangling, splintering, banging, crashing, reverberating sounds of the unexpected.[9] (Interestingly, however, the harsh and dissonant noises, when listened to for long periods at a stretch, can become, after some time, almost soothingly hypnotic, as the ear adjusts to the medley.)

Random shocks in the physical world have also prompted debates among biologists about the role of the random in organic change. Perhaps nature *does* make leaps after all. Before Darwinian evolution appeared to sweep the field, Baron Georges Cuvier in 1812 had already argued that there were intermittent catastrophes or 'revolutions' that transformed the global development of all living species.[10] The story of Noah's Flood, he suggested, was a prototype saga of such a cataclysm, envisaging the experience of devastation and recovery. This theory of sudden change, known as 'saltation' from the Latin *saltus* or leap, focused upon the relatively sudden disappearance of entire species, like the dinosaurs, for which it offered a better explanation than did theories of evolution. Thus T. H. Huxley, who was one of Darwin's first and closest supporters, warned his mentor that 'you have loaded yourself with an unnecessary difficulty in adopting *Natura non facit saltum* so unreservedly'.[11]

One alternative is known as the theory of 'punctuated equilibrium', following the phraseology first proposed in 1972 by the American fossil expert Stephen J. Gould.[12] This viewpoint reinstates deep continuity as the natural template, but argues that continuity is overthrown from time to time by occasional, large-scale transformations. It showed Gould, the child of Marxist parents, as sympathetic to the idea of drastic breaks in history, although far from endorsing the orthodox Marxist theories of revolutionary upheaval which are discussed below.

Evidence for biological 'catastrophism' depends upon taking a very long time frame indeed. Two great discontinuities in the fossil record do then suggest the possibility of mass extinctions.[13] The first indicates that, at the end of the Permian period in geological history, some 245 million years ago, as many as 95 per cent of all invertebrate marine species disappeared. This remarkably high rate of loss is attributed to very significant alterations in the global land mass, with correspondingly severe climatic and ecological effects. The other notable case is the disappearance of the dinosaurs, in the late Cretaceous period, some 65 million years ago. A high percentage of other animal species also became extinct, although plant species remained considerably more resilient. This macro-change was probably also provoked by climate degeneration, either after the impact of a huge meteorite landing – most probably in what is now the Gulf of Mexico – or from intensified volcanic emissions or both. It may be noted that the mass extinction of the dinosaurs did not happen overnight but took anything from five thousand to fifty thousand years to be completed. It was therefore not literally one sudden event. The extent of the transformation, however, marked an abrupt transition, not a gradual evolution.

Discrete upheavals, even if infrequent and irregular in their timing, are by this means restored to the picture. Those early critics of universal Darwinism, who had complained that evolutionary biology underplayed 'events' and history,[14] felt themselves, after all, to be justified. Structural changes in the earth's climate are one obvious example of macro-change, especially as climatic conditions set the bounds for subsequent biological developments. Some experts even seek to find a regular periodicity for global upheavals. Perhaps climatic coolings and species extinctions recur in cycles of some 26 or 32 million years. But the empirical data are too scanty to confirm even that very limited degree of regularity,[15] and there is no guarantee that past climatic periodicities will continue into the future.

Among other things, the activities of humans are now impacting upon the global ecology, in unprecedented ways. The first emergence of *Homo sapiens*, from among many hominid variants, was one historic discontinuity in itself; and our mass multiplication since the end of the most recent Ice Age, sometime around 10,000 BCE, is another. And today the biological success of the world's most ecologically meddlesome species to date is impacting upon the whole planet. Hence the verdict from one eminent biologist that 'human cultural evolution' marks 'a change in the earth's history as drastic as, if not more than, any that has taken place on the earth since the appearance of cellular life'.[16] And that realisation in turn leads to predictions that the current predominance of *Homo sapiens* will one day be ended by another extinction, quite possibly following a mega-disaster of our own making.

Major cataclysms do not appear or strike in a vacuum but their impact is alleviated or worsened by different human actions. That can be seen particularly in the case of the silent mass killers in the form of epidemics and famines, which often appear together. In the case of infectious disease, the impact varies with the ferocity of the contagion *and* with the nature of medical and public health intervention. When cholera, which was endemic in northeastern India, swept around the world in 1830/3 and again in 1848/9, it killed millions. By the mid 1850s, however, experts in public sanitation were learning how to reduce very substantially, though not to eliminate entirely, the incidence of the water-borne disease. Even more dramatically, the killing and disfiguring scourge of smallpox has been combated by worldwide healthcare programmes. Eventually in 1979, after years of effort, it was eradicated.[17] It is true, meanwhile, that there remain many other major epidemiological hazards and that viruses are notoriously prone to micro-mutation which means that new ones appear even while old ones are combated. Yet there is now a track record of countervailing human effort, shared worldwide, which is likely to be expanded, if not always to succeed.

For this reason, the impact of natural cataclysms cannot be modelled purely in isolation. A clear example of the role of human action or inaction is seen in the history of droughts, crop blight and consequent famines. On more than one occasion in the nineteenth century, responsible governments reacted to the natural onset of disastrous food shortages by relying upon laissez-faire doctrines. They believed that, in a harmonious world, unfettered markets would resolve the problem optimally. But the unplanned 'solution' of matching demand to a suddenly limited food supply too often took the 'natural' form of cutting demand by a surge in premature deaths or by mass migrations of starving families.[18] Eventually, policy attitudes, confronted with disasters made worse by official inaction, began to shift in favour of intervention or even prevention.

Paradoxically, however, various government actions in the twentieth century, which were intended to boost food output permanently, have also triggered devastation, as when Marxist governments pushed their agricultural populations into badly planned farm collectivisations. The harsh evidence of Ukrainian famine under Stalin in the 1930s, the 1959–61 famine in Mao's China after the Great Leap Forward policy had failed to leap, and the 1975–8 famine in Pol Pot's Cambodia/Kampuchea, all demonstrate that harmful actions, as well as harmful inactions, can cause or exacerbate disaster on a scale fully as great as the depredations caused by unfettered 'nature', aided and abetted by negligent governments.[19] Applying dogma to agriculture has a poor record, as examples today continue to reveal. Thus, while 'something should be done', the nature of that 'something' needs careful planning with and not against the grain of nature (including humans within that formula).

Disequilibria of all sorts occur often enough to challenge interpretations that stress either pure continuity or pure gradualism. Disruptions are therefore also part of normality. They bring upheaval and yet the possibility too of fundamental change. Scholarly attention has thus been turned instead to analysing 'non-linear dynamics', although so many are the variant possibilities of radical discontinuities that they do not fall into one simple formula. Chaos theory, as it is known, provides a probabilistic analysis of irregular processes, which are repeated with many tiny variations – like the twisting and winding plumes of smoke issuing from a burning cigarette.[20] This type of explanation assumes not complete randomness but an element of underlying patterning. Accordingly 'chaotic' models are useful for explaining repeated features that recur with considerable local variety within a comprehensible order. Changes within weather systems are a paramount example, as these tend, in the short and medium term at least, to be 'globally stable, but locally unstable'.

Abrupt discontinuities, meanwhile, are also modelled by an alternative approach, known as catastrophe theory. This focuses upon exceptional events, such as unusually violent tempests, that constitute 'bifurcations' from everyday experience. The model shows how an initial small deviation from the norm may become magnified into something exceptional.[21] Here the much-quoted butterfly beating its wings in (say) China is said to 'cause' a hurricane in (say) North America, via initially tiny and then compound alternations to the atmospheric flow. However, this metaphor for the macro-impact of a micro-event only operates in certain climatic conditions. Otherwise, since Chinese butterflies are numerous, America would never be free of hurricanes.

Repeatedly, these approaches seek to understand how discontinuities and disjunctures fit into the wider picture. In the field of economics, for example, such ideas are now gaining fresh attention from analysts who reject the assumptions of equilibrium that underpin neoclassical economic theory. The old theories, influenced by Darwinian evolution, were formulated expressly by Alfred Marshall, the high-Victorian doyen of the gloomy science, when he identified what he termed a gradual 'Principle of Continuity' (meaning unbroken development) that precluded any possibility of sudden ruptures.[22] As against that, chaos and catastrophe theories are now being used, given suitable data with a settled baseline, to model field dynamics within economic systems. However, the new models of cataclysm and chaos will in turn become restrictive if applied too rigidly to all situations regardless of circumstances. Not everything in life is randomised. Indeed, there has to be some routine framework that can be calibrated in order for some eventualities to be perceived as genuinely unexpected. And then, when the normal order breaks down, sudden new possibilities are revealed, both for good or ill. So the febrile beauty that can be found even in chaos is caught in an old Japanese handscroll illustration of a twelfth-century battle amidst the dancing tongues of fire (*see* illustration 12).

Upheaval and Revolution

Within all human societies, the existence of friction and conflict is so common that it hardly counts as a 'surprise' factor. Impulsions of rivalry and enmity are as widely observed as are the countervailing impulsions of cooperation and alliance. All communities thus have systems of rule, whether formal or informal, to hold these tensions at bay; and settled communities generally manage to do so, unless overcome by internal crisis, warfare, or an exceptional external challenge. Traditionally, one of the chief means of accounting for the social and political upheavals that followed upon

12 This thirteenth-century Japanese depiction of the *Night Attack on the Sanjo Palace* (Kyoto, 1159) shows the dynamic disaster of both fire and warfare.

conflict was by appeal to cyclical models of history, turning with time's own 'revolutions'.

Interestingly, however, this latter word was itself to be revolutionised in meaning. By the nineteenth century, models of 'evolution' were challenged by a rival vision of 'revolution'. This term came to refer to a historic disjuncture – a challenge to the smooth progression of history – in the form of mass political action, usually but not invariably accompanied by violence, with the aim of not only overthrowing an established government but also transforming the entire social and political order. By contrast, the mere violent ousting of a set of rulers remains a *coup d'état*.

New usages of the term 'revolution' emerged in seventeenth-century England, though it took some time for it to gain its later connotations of bloodshed and thunder. One early use of the word came from the devout Oliver Cromwell in 1655. As a mere commoner raised to rule as Lord Protector of England, Scotland and Ireland, he commented on God's power to achieve 'His revolutions', specifying that 'The Lord hath done such things amongst us as have not been known in the world these thousand years.'[23] Here the term was losing its old sense of cyclicality and was pointing instead to truly exceptional events. By 1689, the constitutional upheaval that replaced the

Catholic James II by the Protestant William of Orange was greeted by supporters as the 'Great Revolution' (1689), the 'Happy Revolution' (1690), the 'Wonderful Revolution' (1693), and – the name that eventually stuck – the 'Glorious Revolution' (1715).[24] Later, it was the revolt of the American colonies against Britain that gave the term new impetus in the years 1776–83. The 'rebels', as they were seen from London, saw themselves as zestful revolutionaries. Hence 'revolution' became so well known that by 1790, within a year of the fall of the Bastille and the unfolding crisis in France, the process was being described, in both French and English, as '*the* French Revolution'.[25] Its further unfolding then crystallised the concept and produced its classic political exemplar.

A massive and unexpected people-quake, leading to the execution of a king and the creation of a new republic, fully deserved a new name. The notion of revolution also encouraged new interpretations of history to incorporate such dramas. Commentators across Europe were galvanised, particularly in early nineteenth-century France which reverberated with the complex lessons of 1789 and its aftermath. One new philosophy of drastic change, for instance, came from the socialist Charles Fourier. In 1808, he declared that human history went through different stages, propelled by distinctive laws of social development. At first, societies were tolerably peaceful but, even so, there was still much turmoil. However, there were possibilities of gain as well as loss. Close at hand was the cheering prospect of the 'Apogee of Happiness', at the height of history's unfolding trajectory. 'Wretched nations, you are very close to the great metamorphosis', Fourier claimed, prophesying that, in the new era, family units would be transformed into local communes (*phalanges*). By that means, the human passions, once a source of friction, would mesh constructively. Work will become a pleasure and sex lives will be liberated too, creating a harmonious new utopia of well-being.[26]

To assist this, Fourier sought to establish a novel system of psycho-physics that would accommodate the variety of human erotic needs. For good measure, he also believed in reincarnation, so that people from unhappy past eras could live again in future happy ones. Even the earth will survive, after its eventual death, via repeated recreations. It was an optimistic vision that attracted enthusiasts to establish Fourierist communes in mid-nineteenth-century France and America. Nonetheless, even with the promise of improved sex, these groups struggled economically and did not long survive.[27]

Another advocate of revolutionary change in France was Henri de Saint-Simon. He too had faith in progress: 'The golden age of the human race is not behind, but before us,' he specified in 1814.[28] But the route was circuitous, proceeding in spirals. An 'organic' epoch of construction would be followed by a 'critical' one of opposition or revolution. Historically, Saint-Simon saw such a change in his own day. He considered that the intellectual authority of traditional Christianity was being superseded by the new claims of science – an idea that he shared with Comte. But, the next age would reconcile faith with technology, added Saint-Simon. There would be a new socialist system of industrial production, with a new religion of science, sanctified by a new ceremony of 'Newtonian baptism'. Again, various eager young Saint-Simonians attempted to translate these teachings into practice, again ultimately unsuccessfully.

Societies were increasingly seen as mobile, rather than static, and thus potentially ready for transformative change. Pierre-Joseph Proudhon, the admirer of steam power and the railway, paraphrased an Old Testament text, 'I destroy and I will rebuild', to identify a divine law of permanent revolution. Hence drastic change was natural. 'Stop a revolution . . . the greatest absurdity imaginable!' snorted Proudhon in 1851: 'Stop matter from falling, flame from burning, the sun from shining!'[29] As a radical and an artisan individualist, his own targets to oppose were manifold: not only old kings and nobles, but also new industrial bosses *and* new workers' organisations such as trade unions *and*, for good measure, uppity women. Proudhon thus promoted his own model of anti-centralism, buoyed by the conviction that he and his ideas of radical (male) individualism represented an unstoppable trend: 'I am one of the incarnations of the nineteenth century.'

Dynamic new interpretations of history such as these sprang from the seedbed of cultural change in eighteenth- and nineteenth-century Europe, at the hub of expanding world trade, competing empires and rapid technological innovation, just as, much earlier, the cultural crossroads of the 'holy lands' at the meeting of Europe and Asia had generated a series of powerful new religions. Not only was 'evolution' given its synthesis by Darwin in the mid nineteenth century but, in the same era, 'revolution' was invoked as an alternative theory of macro-change.

'Without Contraries is no progression' was one pithy dictum that welded together the language of conflict and progress. It came from the practical–mystical poet–artist William Blake in 1793,[30] then a little-known artisan toiling in south London. His metaphysical poems breathed his concern to understand how historical conflict could be satisfactorily resolved. Disorder and antagonism were themselves natural, Immanuel Kant had already decided, when locating his philosophy historically. His *Idea for a Universal History* (1794) impressed readers not only in Germany but throughout Europe. It was precisely the friction of people's 'unsocial sociability' that stimulated new thought, Kant decided: 'Man [humanity] wishes concord, but nature, knowing better what is good for his species, wishes discord.'[31]

Very notably, the new theories of change-through-conflict were secular in their general expression and assumptions. As these were developed, however, these ideas did have some parallels with a covert strain of apocalyptic fervour. Both the Old and New Testaments refer to the power of faith to turn the 'world upside down'. Now things would be fundamentally changed by a new twist to history, in a secularised vision of instant religious transformationism.

'Revolution' as a philosophy of world metamorphosis gained by far its most influential form in Marxism, which doubles both as a theory of human development in the past and as a programme for political action in both present and future. This interpretation was first formulated in the turmoil of nineteenth-century Europe and adapted for global export in the turbulent twentieth century. Marxism's remarkable trajectory shows the supreme confidence conferred upon its supporters by the belief that they are part of a 'winning' history, which simultaneously explains past conflicts and confers success in future ones.

Highly significant for Marx's whole approach was his grounding in the conflict-based historical philosophy of Hegel. In the 1820s, Berlin's lecture halls were packed by students keen to hear this new approach. Building upon Kantian insights about the normality of friction, Hegel defined 'contradiction' as the core mechanism for historical change, for which he used the Greek term 'dialectic', meaning argument by opposition. He argued that ordinary nature (which, in his usage, excluded humans) has no capacity to innovate and thus moves in cycles. But people are not so constrained. They do argue, they do innovate, and their history therefore changes dialectically. Each stage 'negates' or contradicts the one that went before. The ultimate pattern, for Hegel, is progressive. The diachronic process, however, emerges not through regularity but from conflict: 'Time entails the property of negativity', as he commented. Furthermore, the arena is truly global. Hegel's lectures depicted an unfolding 'Idea' of freedom, which began with China in the East, and then swept historically westwards across Eurasia to Europe (excluding Africa, about which he knew little), and was ultimately heading for the Americas, where there was likely to be a future contest between North and South America for final success.[32]

It was heady stuff. For the young Karl Marx, one of the rapt students in Berlin in the 1830s where Hegelian ideas were hotly discussed, the details were less important than the perception that conflict could power history through time. Neither he nor Hegel ever applied the dialectic rigidly. But a standardised view was circulated, depicting change as a three-stage process: firstly, the thesis; secondly, a countervailing antithesis; and, ultimately, the fusion of the best qualities of both thesis and antithesis to create a new synthesis.[33] In this model, history incorporated upheaval without losing shape.

Marx, who was also debating with advocates of Saint-Simonian socialism, and his philosophical/political alter ego Friedrich Engels, a businessman who had seen at first-hand the social hardship within industrial society, together fused the dialectic not with conflict based on abstract ideals but with conflict that emerged from the daily economic frictions between rival groups of humans as they strove for material resources. 'The history of all hitherto existing society *is* the history of class struggles,' ran their *Manifesto* declaration in 1848.[34]

Furthermore, Marx and Engels specified revolutionary upheaval as the mechanism that would represent each dialectical turning point. Whenever the 'contradictions' within a particular stage of economic development become intolerable, a wholesale social-cum-political conflagration follows and, if successful in ending old ways, then inaugurates a new political era. For both Marx and Engels, the process was ultimately progressive. The rule of the few would be replaced by the rule of the masses. If properly instituted, people's power would put an end to old class antagonisms and economic exploitation, and institute a communist system of sharing. As Engels later summarised it, social inequalities, however widespread, are not destined to last for ever. Instead, revolutionary upheavals will lift humanity 'from the Kingdom of Necessity into the Kingdom of Freedom'.[35]

With their base firmly in economics, Marxist theories could be applied to many different circumstances. This approach was defined as 'dialectical materialism' or even '*diamat*' to convinced communists in the USSR.[36] Everything was included. Engels's speech at Marx's graveside in 1883 expressed full confidence that: 'Just as Darwin discovered the law of development of organic nature, so Marx discovered the law of development of human history.'[37] Marx's supporters were convinced and 'Marxism' began to take on some of the qualities of a new secular faith. Over time it acquired a highly developed corpus of theoretical analysis as well as political parties dedicated to pursuing its aims. The ideology appealed not only to workers but also to intellectuals, including a number of academics. And it had a founding figure who was not a martyr or a saint but a teacher and organiser. Indeed, Marx 'was the real Pope of the Socialist world', as one reluctantly impressed critic noted appositely in 1879.[38]

Only after 1917, however, did Marxism gain the allure of political success and a testing-ground for an entire theory of history when applied to running a state machine and creating a new communist society. Supporters of the cause were as aware of the high stakes as were their political opponents. So the Russian revolution would herald no less than the 'general psychological transformation of twentieth-century humanity', specified Li Ta-chao, China's leading Marxist intellectual who went on to found the Chinese communist party and to mentor the youthful Mao Zedong.[39] While each struggle was local, therefore, the perceived scope of potential change, for convinced Marxists, was global – and rooted within a universal saga of oppression and resistance to oppression.

Marxism as a historical schema was meanwhile adapted into a political machine in the writings, and even more the practice, of Lenin. He allotted to the Russian communist party cadres a vanguard role, to rule on behalf of the masses, under the banner of the people's *soviets* (workers' councils).[40] Thus Marxist-Leninism gained not only an analysis of exploitation and a call for revolution, but also a disciplined form of political organisation. Throughout the twentieth century, these elements, variously adapted in different countries, proved able to sustain peasant guerilla warfare in Mao Zedong's China; *and* to strengthen nationalist resistance to colonial powers in Ho Chi Minh's Vietnam; *and* to underpin the aggressive policies of ruralisation and anti-intellectualism in Pol Pot's Cambodia; *and* to encourage a quest for a different socialism based upon village community (*ujamaa*, or familyhood) in Julius Nyerere's Tanzania;[41] *and* to oppose American political, economic and cultural might in the name of an attempted egalitarianism in Castro's Cuba; *and* to employ revolutionary violence, including against rival Marxist groups, during Abimael Guzmán's *sendero luminoso* (Shining Path to the Future) guerrilla campaign in Peru in the 1980s and after;[42] *and* to try, with variegated success, to rally industrial workers' resistance against economic exploitation in Europe and North America; *and* to inspire a lively and diversified intellectual tradition, which proved, however, notably more productive outside rather than inside the official Marxist states.

How and why these political movements subsequently evolved – a question not considered by Marx – has now become a matter for historical study. And there are arguments, especially on the left, about the extent to which the different leaders espoused or betrayed a 'true' version of Marxism.[43] All made serious attempts at turning a theory of history into history-making in practice. However, the 'dictatorship of the proletariat', by which the Communist Party leads the way in the name of the people, too easily degenerates into dictatorship over the people. Policy-making also becomes brutalised by the perceived need to 'hurry' history on its pathway. And the 'correct' Marxist route to an egalitarian destination was interpreted in diametrically opposite ways. So while seeking to end the old 'opposition' between town and country, in some countries (China, Cambodia) unwilling bureaucrats and 'bourgeois' intellectuals were forcibly sent into the countryside to ruralise,[44] while conversely in others (Russia, Romania) unwilling countrypeople were sent into planned towns to industrialise.[45] Either way, Utopia remained elusive.

Applying Marxist policies in so many different contexts managed ultimately to splinter the doctrine, just as practical problems within Saint-Simonianism and Fourierism were revealed in the mid nineteenth century by the operation of their back-to-the-land communes. Moreover, the Marxist model focused too much upon economic injustices, which anyway proved hard to resolve, and took insufficient notice of other, non-economic, factors.

History's inner dynamic refuses repeatedly to be narrowed to just one explanatory factor and to just one mechanism for change. Mass 'revolutions' do indeed remain an essential subject for analysis.[46] But there are other forms of epidemic conflict too, ranging from counter-revolutions, warfare, civil war, inter-communal violence, to outright genocidal attacks. None of these take one single form or spring from a single source. All indicate history's capacity to surprise. And, ironically, it was established Marxism in Russia and eastern Europe that faced such an unexpected outcome in 1989–91. Under the combined pressures of internal dissent, political atrophy and economic underperformance, the communist regimes crumbled, providing a further instance of drastic metamorphosis in history – but not as anticipated within their own ideology of drastic transformation.

Turning Points and Transformations

Seismic change, furthermore, does not occur exclusively as the result of conflict. For that reason, it is also helpful to retain the terminology of 'turning points' and 'watersheds'. These refer to fundamental macro-changes in history that are not necessarily perceived as crises when they occur – and indeed may be positively ignored or underestimated – but which come to be seen as constituting significant switch-points in historical pathways.

Verdicts in such instances depend upon the subsequent outcomes and are therefore judgements of time. By contrast, notable achievements at any synchronic moment are easily underestimated – or indeed overestimated. When on 20 July 1969 Neil Armstrong became the first human to walk on the moon, he called it a walk with destiny: 'That's one small step for [a] man – one giant leap for mankind.'[47] His lunar capsule was carrying pieces of the Wright brother's first powered aircraft from 1903, in conscious homage to aviation progress. So Armstrong's footsteps were presented as the techno-version of a revolutionary 'great leap forward'. The moon walk 'opens the next chapter of evolution', argued a commentator in 1970.[48] 'Apollo [the American lunar programme] may be the only achievement by which our age is remembered a thousand years from now,' agreed the science fiction guru Arthur C. Clarke.

However, the long-term implications are far from clear. Rocket science remains a very costly and specialist enterprise. While air travel through the earth's local atmosphere became routine within thirty years of the first flight, the same has not happened to human movement through outer space. There has been no further lunar promenade since Apollo 17 in 1972 – now well over a generation ago. The enterprise is decidedly risky, and no great power wants to be the first to leave unburied corpses on the moon, in nightly reproach. By the early twenty-first century, the lunar landings by six teams of astronauts often seem 'unreal'; and 'deniers' publicly doubt whether they happened at all. The excited predictions that all earthlings would forever remember the date of Armstrong's 'giant leap' have not come true – very few can even recall correctly the year, despite the fact that an estimated 700 million people watched the event on television broadcasts. Moreover, since the space programme is tending to switch from manned to unmanned probes, the lunar walk may prove to be no more than a spectacular diversion. In that case, the date of 4 October 1957 could become regarded as the pivotal 'turning point' instead. It was then that the first Soviet *Sputnik* (meaning Companion) was launched into earth orbit, with a jubilant salutation from Sergei Korolev, the programme director: 'The conquering of space has begun'. But, in either case, it is too soon to be sure. And indeed the vast reaches of space may well prove resistant to anything like 'conquest' from one small planet.

Nonetheless, such rhetoric offers a reminder that human explorations have often led to historic turning points, as voyagers to the frontiers of the unknown then find new resources and meet new cultures. The subsequent encounters between previously sundered peoples are the human equivalents of the clashing of global tectonic plates: the results are powerful but unpredictable. Because of such historical experiences, there are many speculations in film, fiction and ufology (the study of 'unidentified flying objects') that we may next encounter alien civilisations in outer space. If so, that would undoubtedly constitute a cosmic turning point, for us at least.

Unexpected cultural encounters, however, do not always lead to an immediate outcome of constructive mingling. A famous example is the case of Japan from the 1600s to the 1850s. During those years, a policy of seclusion (*sakoku*) was maintained by the Tokugawa shoguns or military commanders. Contacts with the wider world, and especially with traders from the West, were kept to a minimum. Furthermore, in a historically rare example of conscious technological discontinuance, the craft of gun-making, that had been imported from Europe and skilfully developed by Japanese gunsmiths, was largely halted.[49]

Eventually, however, the *sakoku* system foundered before both internal and external pressures. In 1853, an American squadron of 'black ships' arrived uninvited in Edo (Tokyo) bay, demanding access for trade. This sudden meeting paved the way not for renewed seclusion but instead for the collapse of the Tokugawa regime in 1868. After that, Japan launched a selective programme of 'westernisation', undertaken in a mood of mixed admiration and anxiety. Thus sudden contacts with strangers had a dramatic impact upon Japanese history on two separate occasions, but with diametrically opposite results: the first leading to attempted rigorous closure, the second to the exact reverse.

When considering the global implications of all these examples of exploration, a good case can certainly be made for viewing the summary date '1492' as a major turning point – a classic bifurcation or changing of the ways, in chaos theory terms. That is not because the arrival of a Genoan traveller in North America achieved an immediate revolution. Christopher Columbus may not even have been the first to sail there successfully. But his voyage was followed relentlessly by those of many more explorers, traders, soldiers, settlers and missionaries, under the flags of European powers and the banners of their own religions. Travelling with them, too, came an array of Old World killer diseases that were unknown in the New.[50] Smallpox in particular devastated millions of indigenous Americans, who had no acquired immunity to this virulent contagion. 'Great was the stench of the dead . . .' remembered a Mayan chieftain, writing about the 1521 epidemic in what is now Guatemala: 'The dogs and vultures devoured the bodies. The mortality was terrible. . . . So it was that we became orphans, oh, my sons!'[51] How people coped with this sequence of bruising encounters – and what happened thereafter – continues to propel America's long and complex saga to this day. So 1492 marks the significant moment that brought a massive continent with its own historic cultures into regular contact with the rest of the world, ending the isolation that had persisted – how completely is still debated – since the migration surge of the first human settlers across the Bering Strait from Asia some 15,000–35,000 years ago.[52]

Patterns of population movements took on new forms. Europe provided numbers of voluntary migrants to the colonial and then post-colonial settlements in what was dubbed the 'New World', while west Africa between the sixteenth and nineteenth centuries lost some ten million enforced migrants who were traded into slavery there.[53] The Americas then became described not as part of 'the East' – across the unpacific Pacific – but as part of 'the West', being linked by the Atlantic trade winds and by new history to the western end of the Eurasian land mass. Later were to follow extensive American contacts with China and Japan in the nineteenth and, especially, the twentieth centuries. But the terminology, dictated by history rather than by global contours, had by then become established and is now taken for granted.

Of course, even seismic encounters, like those of 1492, have their own prior context. Columbus did not sail to America from a void. He came from a seafaring culture with expansionist dreams of trade and gold. Moreover, he himself saw his journey as part of a divine plan.[54] Without faith as well as his nautical know-how, he and his sailors would not have risked the unknown so readily. Nonetheless, their journey did lead to macro-change: a genuinely 'new thing under the sun'.

Meanwhile, not everything was changed in and by 1492 alone. Continuities sustained elements of the contending cultures, in defeat as well as in victory. For example, the descendants of the Maya were able to incorporate more or less surreptitiously numerous traditional beliefs and customs into the newly imported Catholicism, despite official church disapproval; and in Guatemala today popular interest in Mayan languages, calendars and ancient cosmologies is spreading.[55] Aggressively, too, in the 1980s the Marxist–Maoist guerrilla leader Abimael Guzmán invoked ancient Inca symbolism to attract initial support in the 1980s and he learned Quechua, the language descended from the Incas which is widely spoken by the descendants of Peru's indigenous population. Furthermore, the migrants to the Americas from Europe and Africa also brought their own cultural traditions. Even the harshly uprooted people who were sold into slavery managed to retain through adversity some traditional ways which were fused into the New World mix.[56] And in particular, popular music in both North and South America beats with an eclectic fusion of ancestral rhythms from Africa, Europe and the indigenous societies of pre-Colomban times.[57]

Complex turning points on the geohistorical scale of 1492 and its aftermath are very rare. The concept of a non-violent macro-change within as well as between cultural traditions remains, however, a useful one. A weaker variant of the 'turning point' phraseology is simply a 'turn', following an expression coined by the American philosopher Richard Rorty. In 1967, he declared his conviction that western thought in the later twentieth century was changing its basis. There was a 'linguistic turn'.[58] Not everyone agreed with this analysis; but the terminology was catchy. Accordingly, others have claimed to detect, variously, an 'anthropological turn', a 'cultural turn', a 'psychological turn', a 'biographical turn', a 'pragmatic turn', an 'aesthetic turn', an 'ethical turn', and a 'global turn'. The entire lack of agreement between these claims certainly suggests that the phrase is becoming overused and thus losing its specificity. Furthermore, shifts in cultural and intellectual attitudes are often nebulous and hard to pin down in their direction and timing, not all following an orderly and clearly signalled pathway.

From time to time, however, there are major intellectual upheavals. These are sometimes signalled as 'paradigm shifts', referring to the rare moments when there are discontinuities not just in traditional ideas but in the entire framework of ideas. The terminology was first applied to intellectual breakthroughs in the sciences by Thomas Kuhn (himself a trained physicist). He argues that there is often a preliminary period of doubt, while new data fail to match existing theories. Then, a real innovator arrives – a Newton, an Einstein

– and provides a better solution. This then constitutes, after further research and argument, the new paradigm.[59] Kuhn's model has some parallels with Hegel's dialectic, which also depicted idea-systems as generating inner 'contradictions' that could only be resolved by revolutionary change. Another variant expression for the same moment of fundamental transition is that of an epistemological 'break' – a terminology used by the French social philosopher, Michel Foucault. In all cases, these are helpful formulations, provided that it is not assumed that all ideas and idea-systems inevitably change in this manner.[60]

Knowledge also mutates through accumulation; through cross-fertilisation with interpretations borrowed from other disciplines; through collective debates; and/or, as Karl Popper has emphasised, as the result of attempts at disproof. This he called the technique of falsification.[61] Moreover, pluralistic knowledge systems often contain more than one competing paradigm at the same time. Political thought in the nineteenth-century West, for example, contained imperialism and anti-imperialism, pro-progress beliefs and anti-progress alternatives, faith in laissez-faire economics and denunciations of the same, to name but some of the major debates. In such circumstances, there are frequent shifts, cross-currents and diversities within the history of ideas, rather than the formulation of one paradigm followed, after a break, with another.

Given these complexities, it is often difficult to date major changes that have compound roots. In the case of technological innovations, for example, there are genuine breakthroughs and surprise inventions. Yet such developments depend, far more often than is usually realised, upon repeated efforts of trial and error. For instance, it was only after years of experimentation that the Wright brothers in the USA turned the theory of powered flight into reality on 17 December 1903. It was a genuine moment of historical drama. Yet the Wrights drew upon a long-generated international corpus of scientific knowledge. Their breakthrough produced the propeller/piston engine, which was in turn overtaken in the 1930s by the 'turbojet revolution', developed by Frank Whittle in the UK. And he too relied upon others, particularly to provide the engineering capacity to build a heavy engine that would have crippled the Wrights' lightweight aircraft.[62] Accordingly, the history of powered flight is not best described as a single revolution, or even a series of discrete revolutions. Instead, it was a prolonged and complex transformation along a critical developmental pathway.

Social, cultural and economic changes are particularly likely to see moments of radical transformation that both jostle and interlock with evolutionary change. Hence very many claimed 'revolutions' are hotly debated. Historians argue about their timing, their causation and their meaning. One long-running debate focuses upon the so-called 'Industrial Revolution'. There is no dispute that James Watt's steam engine was patented in Britain in 1769 and that it was, over time, applied to transform industrial production by reliance upon a tireless non-human source of power. Hence for the doyen of British Marxist historians Eric Hobsbawm, this technological breakthrough, plus all its wider economic, social, cultural and political ramifications, constitutes 'the most fundamental transformation of human life in the history of the world recorded in written documents' – a true mega-change on a par with the distant era when organised agriculture, towns, metallurgy and writing were first invented.[63] Yet for others, the basic concept of 'Industrial Revolution' is nothing but a 'myth', a 'fiction'. At most, these 'deniers' do generally concede that a long-term economic evolution or 'industrialisation' did eventually occur; but a few would not even go so far.

Such an extreme divergence of views, about an era of history for which ample evidence survives, indicates the difficulty of applying the concept of 'revolution' to long-span socio-economic-cultural change. Particularly in its general usages, the term is losing its Marxist connotations of conflagration and confrontation. So today there are casual references to the 'internet revolution', the 'green revolution' and the ever-absorbing variants of 'sexual revolution', while cautious political reformers thus dream of a 'quiet revolution'; and French feminist Luce Irigaray calls for new women and new men to generate together a 'peaceful revolution'.[64] In that latter case, then, the term has come to be applied, in a paradoxical turn of the circle, to mean something close to a dosage of pacific evolution.

Nevertheless, history does reveal radical discontinuities in the past and always contains the possibility for more in the future. Other significant instances of upheaval are major economic disasters, mass demographic crises and destructive wars, particularly when losses are heavy and/or when at least one of the combatant groups is severely defeated and cannot rally to fight again. Such massive failures often bring profound cultural changes in their wake.

Everything is thus potentially open to drastic discontinuity, although some aspects of history are more so than others. Even linguistic usages, which are very commonly framed by continuity and tempered by slow change, can show rapid and drastic change on rare occasions. New tongues are invented, such as Esperanto – a hybrid of various European tongues, with its first dictionary published in 1887. Or virtually extinct languages have been revived. The paradigm case here is traditional Hebrew, which had lapsed colloquially, albeit still remaining in use liturgically. In the course of the twentieth century, a version has been regenerated and is now spoken by well over three million people. This feat was considered impossible by linguistic experts. Critics of the planned revival claimed that such an action would amount to reversing evolution. However, with a determined community of speakers, aided by educational resources and considerable linguistic creativity, the task is not impossible.

Admittedly, the process includes adaptation and updating for a different world. Thus contemporary Hebrew meshes its biblical inheritance with the Slavic framing of the pioneers of its linguistic revival, as well as input from many other migrants to contemporary Israel. The outcome is a composite whose precise status is debated by scholars.[65] Nonetheless, the result is a signal success for a willed discontinuity in language history, which indicates that the forecast 'deaths' of currently threatened languages, even if dismayingly likely, are not inevitable.[66]

Talking about Radical Discontinuity

Multiple terms describe macro-change, just as radical discontinuities themselves take many forms. 'Revolution', which has become rather confusing and debatable when applied to long-span economic transformations, still works well for great socio-political confrontations. Since 1789, France offers the prototype case. 'All history is full of revolutions', warned the historian Lord Macaulay in a speech to the British Parliament in 1831. He argued that, if gradual change was not accepted, then greater and worse upheavals might follow (a classic argument for moderate reform). It was intended to alarm his listeners – and it probably did.

Other words and phrases for upheaval retain the note of drama: from 'the world turned upside down' to rapid metamorphosis, clean sweep (*tabula rasa*), radical disjuncture, break point, take-off, dialectical transition, 'revolution within the revolution', or Chairman Mao's 'great leap forward'.

Popular uprisings have another roll-call, which embraces revolts, rebellions, wars of liberation, insurrections, insurgency, and *jacqueries* or militant peasant protests. These are clear signs for social scientists of 'dysfunctionality' and structural breakdown. Meanwhile, the violent seizure of the levers of power by a small group of activists is a 'putsch' or a *coup d'état*.

Moments of potential macro-change are signalled by crises, crossroads, conjunctures, watersheds, 'broken symmetry', 'broken lines', step-changes, sea-changes, phase transitions, pathway shifts, significant bifurcations, 'turns', turning points or 'tipping points' when the balance finally plunges into a new configuration. 'Double-loop' transformations bring not just novelty within the loop but a switch into a new loop. 'Diagenesis' is a different process, meaning a dissolution and recombination of elements. 'Qualitative' change then records a fundamental alteration in kind, as contrasted with 'quantitative' change, which refers to changes in scale. Even at microscopic level, there are irregular 'quantum leaps' in energy levels, as electrons emit and absorb radiation in uneven bursts. Other discontinuities bring schism, caesura, rupture, hiatus, breakdown, dissolution, disaster, convulsion, seismic shock, cataclysm and catastrophe. And non-linear dynamics feature uncertainty, perturbation, incoherence, 'strangeness', fuzziness, indeterminacy, randomness, anarchy and chaos. In such shattered circumstances, the times are truly 'out of joint'.

'Deep change' then signifies a truly fundamental transformation while, mathematically, it means a rate of change in rates of change. Amorously, a sudden falling in love may happen like a 'bolt from the blue' or a *coup de foudre* (lightning strike). Intellectually, a 'paradigm shift' or an 'epistemological break' signifies the breakthrough advent of an entirely novel theoretical framework. Individually, a drastic change of mind marks a 'dialectical leap'. Or a change of faith parallels a 'conversion on the road to Damascus', alluding to St Paul's epic saltation from persecuting Christians to preaching Christianity.

Enthusiasts revel in the exhilarating shock of the new. 'All that is solid melts into air, all that is holy is profaned', in the gleeful words of the *Communist Manifesto*.[67] 'New' is the modal adjective. Renovation is beautiful: 'let a hundred flowers bloom'. Amidst the ancient griefs in Shakespeare's *Tempest*, the young lovers rejoice: 'O brave new world!'[68] Radical discontinuity has a symbolic colouring too, from the *bonnets rouges* of the Parisian crowds in 1789: bright, fiery red, signalled emblematically by the red tulip or the red rose. And, by liberating the masses, a beckoning new force begins to reshape history, as graphically displayed in a 1925 Russian poster for Sergei Eisenstein's epic film *Battleship Potemkin* (*see* illustration 13). The whistling sailor is everyman, rising up against tyranny – and he has the firepower of the fleet behind him – as the abortive 1905 uprising in Russia is taken symbolically to herald the new dawn.

But great transformations can bring great troubles too. The beauty that is born may yet be Yeats's 'terrible beauty'.[69] Crises produce unexpected outcomes. 'The revolution brings forth monsters.' 'Burn, baby, burn.' Ambitious policies that 'force' humanity to be free may just achieve force without freedom – producing terror but not the expected kingdom of freedom. In that case, 'darkness at noon' replaces the hoped-for brightness. Rosy dreams may turn to horror.[70] 'In this night of awful darkness, / Who can say in what state we will be / When dawn breaks?' asked Nimâ Yushij, the Iranian bard, when contemplating in 'Cold Ashes' the human resistance to tyranny/darkness. Anguish, injustice, violence, hope and beauty dwell together, uncertain. So the African American poet Dudley Randall wrote in 1968, amidst urban-political turmoil:

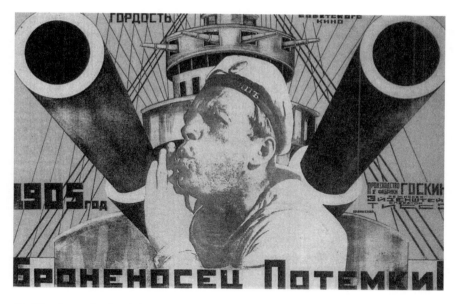

13 Film Poster for *Battleship Potemkin* (Eisenstein, USSR: 1925) – showing Russia's 1905 uprising and a revolutionary faith in the masses with history's big guns on their side.

> Musing on roses and revolutions,
> I saw night close down on the earth like a great dark wing, . . .
> and I heard the lamentations of a million hearts.

Meanings of Macro-Change

Great revolutions, both 'natural and human-made', in obvious ways find themselves in conflict with continuity and with gradual change. Those provide countervailing forces that muffle or deflect the impact of great upheavals. Hence one signification of revolution is an assault on all 'old ways'.

Yet the passage of time produces another paradox. Great changes, once successfully introduced, establish a new basis and then become sustained rather than undermined by continuity. Hence consciously directed revolutions, if not defeated by counter-revolution, eventually turn from permanent revolution into consolidation. Viewed over the very long term, even the greatest of upheavals thus appear subtly 'flattened' by the passage of time.

Ultimate convergences of this sort mean that explosive discontinuities are not 'separate' factors within the cosmos but are part and parcel of the familiar state of play, both in human and non-human affairs. Transformations and turning points are particularly difficult to classify, precisely because they are variegated and non-standard in their origins and characteristics. But major breaks with continuity can be considered along a spectrum, in part differing substantially from micro-change, and in part overlapping, as when a long sequence of micro-changes eventually turns quantitative change into qualitative transformation, which can in turn become the basis for a new tradition.

Radical discontinuities are endemically possible in a cosmos that has experienced at least one dramatic singularity, in the crisis of its own formation. And that potential for macro-change remains the case whether or not there were worlds before this one, of which we know nothing. There are degrees, moreover, even in mega-upheavals, some transformations being more unusual and dramatic than others. Often, they are characterised in terms of disasters and cataclysms, both natural and human-made; but revolutionary outcomes and turning points can also be favourable ones, though judgements in such matters are always open to dispute. The upshot of all such upheavals is that many forms of macro-change constantly interlock and wrestle with continuities and gradual change. Thus it should not be a matter of surprise that history retains its capacity to surprise . . .

Shaping History – Time Ends

Paramount among the cataclysmic surprises that history might spring is the possibility of the imminent end of the world. After all, stylistically, an abrupt, transformational finale to any story remains one of the leading alternatives to the slow, gradual fade-out.[1] So perhaps the world will conclude not with a whimper after all, but instead with a bang. Fears and hopes about cosmic endings lead some to intense experiences of 'time anxiety' – although for all who worry there are others who scoff at the prospect and others still who just decide to wait and see.

Scientists who research the future of the entire cosmos are themselves not agreed about the long-term outcome.[2] Perhaps there will be a 'big crunch', ending everything dramatically in some multi-million years' time, as a reverse of the original 'Big Bang'. Or instead there may be a continuing expansion of an accelerating universe, perhaps rebounding with a renewed 'big bounce' or perhaps instead thinning the cosmos to induce a gradual freezing into a 'big chill'. Such outcomes represent the range of revolutionary or evolutionary options which constitute alternative models of 'change'. Yet it is also possible that deep continuity may prevail after all. The 'steady-state' theory sees the cosmic forces of creation and destruction as evenly balanced. Hence, while galaxies have distinct life cycles, new ones are always in formation. This minority view among today's cosmologists harks back to the words of a Scottish pioneer of geology, James Hutton, who in 1785 profoundly shocked the conventional religious teaching of his day, by recording that his own studies of the earth's crust led him to see 'no vestige of a beginning – no prospect of an end'.

Most people in their daily lives ignore these uncertainties, especially when the conjectured timetable is set in the far-distant future. However, responses are altered for those who become convinced that the end is very close at hand. Here religious beliefs play a crucial role, though secular issues – for example, anxiety about the state of planet earth – also generate strong concerns. In the case of people who expect an imminent doomsday of divine judgement, their focus is intensely personal and spiritual, awaiting either eternal paradise or eternal damnation.

Mainstream religious teachings discourage individuals from speculating about the timetable for this epic event, leaving to theologians the study of death and the end, a subject known as eschatology. Nonetheless, believers repeatedly attempt the exercise, particularly in times of turmoil, as a way of pre-empting history and preparing for the ultimate crisis.[3]

Preoccupations with 'cataclysmic' endings are particularly common in 'linear' religions, because life's journey implies not only a start but a finish. However, even in cyclical philosophies there is room for titanic upheaval, marking the end of one great cycle of history. And other cosmological systems, that seek messages in the stars, can also detect dramatic messages in rare but significant conjunctions of the planets or in any other unusual manifestations of moon, stars or comets.

Among the prophetic religions, Islam determinedly shuns all attempts at fore-telling the Last Judgement, as the Qu'rān (7:187) specifies that the moment will come as a surprise, quite unexpectedly. Signs may be vouchsafed – but fallible humans should not rush to judge these too hastily. In the early history of the faith, some Muslims had expected that the world would end exactly five hundred years after the first revelations to Muhammad but, as Ibn Khaldūn later reported, this belief was not upheld by experience. Different communities within Islam now sustain special expectations as, for example, the 'Twelver' Shi'ite Muslims. They follow the teachings of the long-departed Twelfth Imam, who is now, in theological terms, deep in 'occultation' (concealment). His eventual return will signal the end. However, it is not the task of believers to calculate when that will be. Instead, they wait, living worthily and handing on the message to future generations.

There are some parallels here with secular beliefs in a lost or 'sleeping' leader who will return in times of trial, to lead the people again. In such popular mythologies, the 'revisiting' tradition is not attached to a set of moral and religious teachings, but it carries the same ultimate hope that, despite the vicissitudes of fortune, history will bring an eventual redemption or salvation.

One sign of the Mahdì, or the divinely guided one, returning as the 'messenger of the latter days', will be turmoil. Hence in troubled times various Muslim spiritual leaders have been saluted with that title. Egypt and Sudan, in particular, have seen several. All are associated with resistance against oppressors. One was an ascetic holy man, Wad al-Turabi, who protected the poor against the harsh tax collectors of the Funj Sultanate in later seventeenth-century Sudan. Another appeared in Egypt in 1799 to oppose Napoleon and the invading French army. And the best known Mahdì challenged the British and Egyptian forces in Sudan in the 1880s. He was Muhammad Ahmad ibn Abdullah, who besieged and took Khartoum in 1885, killing the British commander General Gordon in the process. The Mahdist uprising was defeated militarily, in the short term, but the Mahdist tradition continued strongly within the region, where both the *Mahdi*'s youngest son and grandson later played significant roles in twentieth-century Sudanese politics. So the linking of actions to remedy practical grievances with sincere spiritual hopes, vested in a charismatic leader, have often contributed to shaping immediate political outcomes as well as anticipating history's eventual end.

Abrupt finales are similarly envisaged within Jewish and Christian thought. In the Old Testament, the prophetic books of Isaiah and Daniel are central as, in the New Testament, is the Revelation of St John the Divine – known in Greek as the 'Apocalypse' or the unveiling of secrets. The texts are evocative yet cryptic. What did Daniel and Revelation mean by 'a time, and times, and half a time'? Among the scholars who puzzled over such cryptic messages was Sir Isaac Newton who, like many in the later seventeenth century, believed that the world was old and that the end was therefore nigh. However, his painstaking eschatology did not match the originality of his physics. So Newton too endorsed the biblical warning that the actual date of doomsday remains 'closed up and sealed till the time of the end'.

Whenever that occurs, however, Jewish and Christian teaching expects the advent of the Messiah or 'Shiloh', the redeemer who will inaugurate god's heavenly kingdom of Zion. In Judaism, this event has yet to occur; and attempts at guessing it are discouraged. 'Do not calculate the date of redemption, wait patiently . . .' the poet-philosopher, Rabbi Jehudah Halevi, advised unequivocally in the twelfth century. Nonetheless, there was a semi-secret tradition of cabbalistic writings on the theme; and from time to time, imminent claims were made. In eighth-century Persia (now Iran), for example, an unpretentious tailor named Abu-Isa ben Ishak identified himself as the Messiah's messenger and led an unsuccessful Jewish revolt against Muslim rule. He himself died in battle and most supporters were disillusioned. But a handful of Isavites adjusted the prophecy to a longer timescale. They left Persia for Damascus, where a small sect survived for the following two hundred years, handing on the faith among families and close associates. Thus one alternative outcome of a failed end-of-the-world crisis is a process, even if only in a tiny minority, of 'dogged waiting' for the Messiah's return.

The same result followed again in the mid seventeenth century, when international Judaism faced another great schism. It began in 1665 when a mystic named Sabbatai Zevi, from Izmir (Smyrna) in Turkey, was acknowledged as Messiah by his chief lieutenant, one Nathan of Gaza, who began to organise a new sect.

Followers arrived from all over Europe. Moreover, even the shock conversion of Sabbatai to Islam, after his capture by the Ottoman Turks in 1666, was not enough to deter a minority of the faithful. His actions were given an occult interpretation, as part of a secret mission. During the following centuries, two different groups of believers handed on Sabbatai's teachings in semi-secrecy to their descendants – the Sabbatianist/Muslim *Dönme* surviving in Turkey to this day. The vanished leader's return remained continually expected. However, those claiming to be either Sabbatai or his son were in turn denounced as 'false messiahs'. The saga demonstrated once more the potential appeal of subversive theology, when doomsday is believed to be imminent. And elements of Sabbatai's cabbalistic teachings, which challenged the traditional religious laws in order to release the inner 'divine spark', continued to be circulated, complete with rumours of scandal, within some liberal Jewish circles in eighteenth-century Europe.

Mindful of the controversial nature of dramatic end-of-the-world prognostications such as these, the Jewish leaders of the programme of secular Zionism in the twentieth century were careful not to link the creation of an independent state of Israel with any explicit intimation of the 'last days'. However, not all appreciated their caution. For example, in 1940–2 the militant Abraham Stern and his confederates broke with secular Zionism to launch a violent campaign against the British mandate in Palestine, hoping to 'force the end' as soldiers for 'king Messiah'. In their case, the response remained a minority one. The Stern Gang's immediate uprising was quashed and its leaders condemned to death. Nevertheless, it may be noted that the potential role of a restored Israel, as prophetic of imminent doomsday, remains much debated within some fundamentalist strands of both Jewish and Christian thought today.

Amidst life's continual uncertainties, there is clearly consolation in knowing how the story will unfold. Christianity is particularly prone to recurrences of end-of-the-world prophesying, because its theology teaches that Christ the Messiah has already appeared once, so giving the authority of experience to expectations of his second coming. Furthermore, the verses of Revelation are intensely evocative as well as darkly mysterious.[4] The pathway to the end is far from straightforward but it has some signature moments: the four horsemen of the Apocalypse – pestilence, warfare, famine, and death (see illustration 14) – ride out. Christ's second coming will launch the last great battle of Armageddon against Antichrist ('the Beast') and all sinners bearing 'the mark of the Beast'. Another foe to be defeated is the 'scarlet woman', the 'great whore' named Babylon. (In the sixteenth and seventeenth centuries, zealous Protestants were prone to identify this dread

14 Detail of the Four Horsemen in Albrecht Dürer's *Apocalypse* (1498), riding forth at the end of the world and trampling all before them.

female as the Catholic Church of Rome, which clothes its cardinals in deep crimson vestments.) After defeating these enemies, Christ will triumph and rule with his saints for one thousand years – the long-awaited millennium. Then the Last Judgement pronounces a final verdict. And 'a new heaven and a new earth' follows, lasting for all eternity.

From the start, the Christian Church strove to prevent undue chiliastic speculation about this stirring but undeniably complex end-saga. However, within Christianity worldwide there have been many millenarian movements, anticipating Christ's kingdom. Often, the stimulus comes from a charismatic Messiah figure or, alternatively, from firm predictions of the saviour's imminent advent. In Samoa in the 1830s, for example, the Siovili 'cargo' cult believed that Jesus would come 'walking over the sea', bringing coveted consumer goods for his people. He did not arrive but a small group continued to wait, vainly, for some years. Another example comes from the 'Christ craze' in Georgia, USA, in 1889. Numerous African Americans, struggling economically, were enthused by prophecies that on a specified day they would be taken to Canaan, the promised land, thus gaining the spiritual rewards that the abolition of slavery had failed to deliver in practice. They left their fields and gathered in prayer. Three messianic leaders appeared in turn, the last claiming to be the returned King Solomon, being attended by his Queen of Sheba. But all three claimants were arrested and, on the appointed day, nothing happened.

In episodes such as these, it is clear that hopes for a dramatic change in life's circumstances have a special appeal for those who feel themselves to be socially marginal or otherwise wronged. And there is a piercing sadness in the frustration of their expectations, as in the case also of the ecstatic Ghost Dances of the American Sioux in 1890. They dreamed not only of meeting their returned Christian saviour but also of resuscitating their departed ancestors and of restoring the exterminated buffalo.

While waiting for the end, an alternative tactic is to establish a settlement of millenarian believers with their own separate lifestyle. Such schemes rely upon the charismatic 'pull' of the leader – and also upon the willingness of followers to accept privations. That applies currently, for example, to the Church of the Last Testament, whose members live in rudimentary comfort in a remote Siberian commune, gathered around 'Vissarion Christ', formerly named Sergei Torop, an unemployed factory worker and later a traffic policeman. In 1989, a year of political upheaval, he introduced himself as the reincarnated son of God; and, since then, a self-selected band of followers have left their old lives to join him.

Both men and women are attracted to such Messiah claimants. And, although the allotted female role within millenarian groups tends to be subordinate, the millenarian challenge to convention offers scope for female initiative too. In 1810, for example, Lady Hester Stanhope, an aristocratic Englishwoman, left her home and family in order to settle in the Lebanon to witness Christ's second coming in the biblical holy lands. Donning eastern dress, she waited there, at first in eccentric splendour and later in dire poverty, until her death twenty-nine years later. Stanhope developed her own mystic philosophy, with a hybrid of occult claims; and, in a zany touch, she kept in a special paddock two 'sacred' Arabian mares, ready to be ridden by herself and the expected Messiah.

A variant role invoked female leadership directly via a special millenarian wedlock and/or millenarian maternalism. Thus the founder of the Shaker end-of-the-world community in America in 1774 was Ann Lee, who called herself both 'bride of Christ' and the 'first Mother', or spiritual parent, of her flock. An alternative divine message was proclaimed in 1814 by Joanna Southcott, an Englishwoman of modest social status who had already written numerous prophetic tracts. At the age of sixty-four she announced that she was pregnant with the new Messiah. Her supporters funded a beautiful 'celestial bed' for the coming 'Shiloh'. And Southcott herself issued handwritten 'seals' guaranteeing heavenly salvation to those she deemed worthy. But she died, childless. Most of her following disappeared. Again, however, a small and semi-clandestine Southcottian movement continued into the twentieth century, with later Joanna claimants from time to time emerging to contend (unsuccessfully) for her dwindling legacy.

Not only Messiah figures but also cataclysmic events may suggest a sign or an 'alarm to a careless world'. Violent natural disasters such as volcanic eruptions and earthquakes are particularly ominous. 'Wo unto thee Britain; wo unto thee Ireland; wo unto thee London; wo unto thee Liverpool', began a preacher uncompromisingly to his Liverpool flock in 1756. Unless they repented speedily, he warned that they would face divine wrath on an even greater scale than the massive Lisbon earthquake which had already erased the Portuguese capital. Similarly, violent military and political confrontations lend themselves to apocalyptic interpretation, as though signalling the onset of Armageddon, the last battle. Moreover, interestingly, the biblical imagery is available not only to those seeking change but also to those opposing it. Thus in 1812, when Napoleon marched upon Moscow with his *Grande Armée*, the Russian Orthodox Church quickly identified him as the 'Beast' or Antichrist. For all true believers, resistance to the French invaders became a Christian crusade as well as a patriotic duty. And the Russian people responded with the famous 'scorched earth' policy, denying food and resources to the devilish intruders, whose defeat had become a spiritual as well as practical necessity.

Another very different possibility, however, implies that the end will arrive without fanfare, since Christ remarks that his return will be stealthy: 'Behold, I come as a thief.' An alternative method of predicting the end therefore relies not upon assessing public turmoil but upon decoding hints within the Bible. This is particularly common in the literalist strand within Protestantism, which values close knowledge of the holy text. Many biblical scholars agreed that the world will last for six thousand years, each thousand years matching one day of the creation. The seventh would then equate to the final thousand-year rule of Christ. Finding the correct dates, however, generated many controversies. In early Christianity, canvassed dates for the end were either 1000 or 1033, constituting the millennial anniversaries of Christ's birth and crucifixion. And, much more recently, a flurry of millenarian excitement also attended the year 2000 which, if the world began in 4000 BCE, would have completed the required six thousand years.

Apocalyptic excitement around specified dates generally rises steeply before the due date but then is doused when nothing happens. However, there is always scope for reinterpretation. That happened after William Miller, a Vermont farmer and lay preacher, announced 22 October 1844 as the coming doomsday. As the date neared, an estimated hundred thousand Protestants in the USA and Britain stopped work and made ready. However, there followed the 'Great Disappointment'. 'Still in the cold world! No deliverance – the Lord not come!' sighed one disillusioned believer on 23 October. Nevertheless, some of the most ardently faithful were not deterred. They reasoned that the 1844 debacle was but a stage in an unfolding prophecy and refounded the Millerite church as the Seventh-Day Adventists, now a thriving Christian denomination with an international following.

Intense millenarian anxiety has, however, on occasions curdled into outright 'catastrophism'. That happened in 1978 with mass deaths in the isolated settlement at Jonestown (Guyana), when 913 followers of James Warren Jones, the man they trusted as a Christian prophet, died in a collective ceremony of self-killings and child-murders. The few young men who managed to escape report a shared delusion among an embattled community. Alternatively, the emotional violence is turned outwards. In later twentieth-century Japan, the Aum Shinrikyo sect fused an apocalyptic Buddhism with Egyptian occultism, Christian millennialism and the prophecies of Nostradamus, the sixteenth-century French astrologer. The leader Shoko Asahara declared himself as the 'last Messiah of the last century'. His own critics within the sect were poisoned as were in 1995 a number of innocent travellers on the Tokyo subway system. It was a shared criminal frenzy, at which former disciples of Asahara, now freed from the secretive cult identity, express amazement as well as remorse.

Rhetorically, the language of imminent endings is thrilling. It puts listeners at the urgent denouement of history. Not surprisingly, therefore, endgame religious terminology is borrowed for secular usage too. Sombre environmentalists, worried not about cosmic death but about the degradation of our local habitat on planet earth, speak warningly of coming ecological or environmental apocalypse, unless policies are changed. So Our Final Century: A Scientist's Warning was published in 2003, and book titles had already proclaimed The End of History (1992); The End of the Future (1995); The End of Time (1999; 2002); indeed, the end of everything from The End of Agriculture to The End of Masculinity (both 1998), as well as The End of Modernity (1988); and, naturally, numerous texts on The End of the World, these being particularly frequent in the later 1990s, before the new millennium.

Total apocalyptic excitement, however, is hard to sustain for long periods, particularly when the expected crisis does not materialise or when human effort is applied to remove its source. So the obverse of initial fame for prophetic inspiration may be subsequent ridicule for prophetic failure.[5] That was the fate of the English Protestant clergyman Thomas Beverley. He predicted Christ's second coming to occur in 1697, but wrongly. Cynical laughter ensued. Resenting this, Beverley rallied in 1698, explaining that the end really had come but so quietly that no one had noticed.

Joking and humour, as Beverley's critics showed, remain an alternative means of coping with chrono-anxiety and excess prophetic angst. 'Time alone will tell.' One immediate antidote to long-term worries is to concentrate upon the synchronic moment. 'Eat, drink, and be merry, for tomorrow we die.' So one fictional character, travelling through the cosmos in order to dine at the spoof Restaurant at the End of the Universe (1980) and to watch the non-stop end-of-the-world show, suggests hopefully that not just history, à la Henry Ford, but even 'Time is bunk'.[6]

CHAPTER 5

Mutable Modernity

As fast as time and history are rejected from the analysis, however, they immediately smuggle themselves back into the picture. Everything within the cosmos occurs within the temporal–spatial process that frames it. Thus, explicitly or implicitly, we seek ways of accommodating ourselves in time and of understanding the trajectory of history.

From the multiple examples that have already been discussed, it is apparent that the challenge derives not so much from a lack of meanings but from almost too many possible interpretations. Everything that has happened, great and small, has potential significance. The result is a clear risk of historical overload *and* the converse danger of opting for simplified single trackways through history at the expense of complexity.

The best way of proceeding, therefore, is not by adding another single-track explanation to those already available, nor by opting for just one or another theory of history, but by considering instead how the core elements, which persistently emerge and re-emerge from amongst the variety of competing interpretations, can be reconciled. Under the surface confusion, the picture is not as chaotic as it seems at first or even at second sight. There are overlaps in all directions, as macro-changes and micro-changes both collide and interlock, and as the two interacting forms of change simultaneously interact with deep continuities as well.

Such a compound history, with three rather than two longitudinal dimensions in play simultaneously, may be termed a threefold dynamic, summed as 'trialectical'. It incorporates the principle of plurality but within a shape that is not so complex as to defy all interpretation in terms of its components. As a general analogy of simultaneous pluralism, it may be noted that light is studied by physicists as a phenomenon that not only appears stably coherent, refracting into its customary prism, but which also behaves, electro-magnetically, like waves in space and like discrete light particles, known as photons, when interacting with matter.[1] All these properties apply at once, even while they can be studied separately.

Whole history is similarly a coherent composite of complexity: the outcome of the ever-interlocking and ever-variant forces of continuity; micro-change; and macro-change. Notionally, their proportional input is summed as *one third; one third; one third.* But in practice, the balance keeps shifting, sometimes considerably. Continuity provides ballast to the system. It also provides a benchmark against which other variations can be assessed. Micro-change, being gradual and incremental, represents the process of slow adaptation. It adds its own gentle dynamism and prevents the system from clogging. Meanwhile, radical transformation gives sharp impetus as well as turmoil. It may release one set of tensions but equally generate new ones, as when subterranean tectonic plates abruptly shift and resettle. But radical discontinuity is also assimilated by the forces of micro-change and continuity; and indeed radical discontinuity can then become the basis of a new continuity. Hence, at no time does the potential for any one feature disappear. Drastic revolutionary change, as befits its episodic nature, is the most irregular in its incidence and the most dramatic or notorious in its impact. Yet all three dimensions are simultaneously possible, as they pull and tug at one another, aiding and abetting, but also acting as countervailing forces.

With such intricate inputs, the study of history lends itself equally to summary interpretations and to disputation. Things do appear to make sense, once they happen. People very characteristically chat daily about recent events, and sometimes about those from the more remote past, as a way of meshing them into experience and formulating a message that can be conveyed to others. Nevertheless, the repeated mixings and remixings of continuity, slow changes and revolutionary changes mean that historical interpretations that do not sufficiently incorporate the trialectical process can always be disputed.

Thus arguments that point chiefly to revolutionary change, for example, are undercut by pointing to countervailing elements of continuity. And vice versa. Arguments about continuity are similarly subverted by reference to historical alterations, large or small. Moments that seem like great turning points to some are negated – or just ignored – by others. Perspectives are also amended over time, as evidence for deep continuities tends to resurface only when/if the turmoil of great upheavals abates.

In later twentieth-century history, for example, the fall of the Berlin Wall in November 1989 seemed epic when it happened – and it is unlikely to disappear from the history books. But just how and how importantly will it be rated by future historians? Furthermore, ask those who heard the news in November 1989 whether they now (over fifteen years later) think it more or less historically significant than they did then. At a guess, most will reply *less*. Others will say *the same*; and, in my experience, only a minority though not a negligible one say *more*.

These difficulties in finding generally agreed turning points, even among people who have themselves all witnessed upheavals, point to the problems of finding agreed answers to questions like: Where are we now, historically, and how did we get here?

One influential answer has been traditionally formulated in terms of a long narrative of 'modernity'. This view, first framed in the West, initially ran, apparently self-evidently, from 'ancient' to 'modern' times. It offers a strong story of ultimate improvement over long spans of time. Recently, 'modernity' has become further embroidered to refer also to a prolonged period of 'premodernity' before it, and a highly contentious state of 'postmodernity' thereafter. But none of these categories remains historically stable. The contradictory usages stem from the fact that the rival pulls of continuity and of the different sorts of change are not analysed together. Summary statements that pick up on one aspect, but ignore countervailing factors, are then readily open to critical attack. These problems are all revealed when probing current and past usages of 'modernity' and its mutable variants for what apparently comes before and after.

It is the argument of the rest of this chapter that these period divisions no longer shape a significant history but have become overstretched. The terms 'ancient' 'medieval' 'modern' and even 'postmodern' have not yet vanished into oblivion – indeed, in default of alternatives, they remain extensively in circulation – but they are disappearing into terminal uncertainty as to what they actually mean, through overuse and under-specification.

Uncertain Postmodernity

Tracking human history as a collective experience requires some means of summarising the many tiny moments. One method is to give period-names to distinctive eras, grouping the years into significant sets of centuries or, going further back into the long geological past, grouping them into long geological eras that stretch over millennia. However, old labels and key dates for change regularly become outworn, especially as the accumulating evidence of history changes perspectives upon the past. Thus the later twentieth century saw a series of possible 'names' come and go. These range from 'New Age' to 'post-modernity', and are equally uncertain in their application. At this point, then, the gradual emergence of alternatives to simple 'modernity' began.

Witnesses to events certainly provide an interesting preliminary draft of impressions that contribute towards the eventual long-term assessment.

Nonetheless, because contemporaries frequently disagree, there are always multiple options available for the historians' retrospective view. By the mid twentieth century there were many who had come to doubt the picture of history as 'the march of progress'. After the experience of global warfare and new technologies of mass killing, there were many sober warnings of peril. 'Since Hiroshima we know that we live on the rim of disaster, and that we shall stay there till the end of history,' warned a commentator in 1956. The era is an unpleasant 'totalitarian, mass-producing, conscripted age', another glumly claimed in 1947. Continuing geopolitical tensions saw further alarmist prophecies in every generation: so after a review of the world's current problems in 1980, one best-selling Christian tract *Countdown to Armageddon* advised, classically but entirely without irony, that 'The decade of the 1980s could very well be the last decade of history as we know it'.[2]

Others, meanwhile, took quite a different stance. They saw not fraught endings but joyous beginnings. Particularly in the 1960s and 1970s, an American alternative youth culture borrowed an eclectic mix of ideas from Zen Buddhism, hippy astrology and Christian millenarianism, to proclaim an optimistic 'New Age'.[3] A contributing strand of support for this cultural medley came too from Victorian occultism, via the international Theosophical Society (founded 1875), with its quest for universal fellowship and the welding of eastern and western spiritual values. As the world wars receded into history, optimism revived, particularly among liberal circles in the affluent West. Some indeed were positively euphoric. Thus a 'Revelation for the New Age' (1967) foresaw – wrongly, as it transpired – an imminent 'breakthrough of spiritual values, which will sweep us all into a worldwide co-operative community'.

To explain the *Zeitgeist* change, an inventive astrological-cum-Christian timetable was suggestively incorporated within the 'New Age' rhetoric. Never precise in its chronology, the zodiac history instead added an epic significance to current changes. Thus there was supposedly a shift from a departing 'Age of Pisces' (dating from the birth of Christ, the 'fisher of men') to an incoming 'Age of Aquarius' (the water-carrier, signifying universal plenitude and peace). It was a sunny model of friction-less change. However, experts disagreed about its due date. One zodiac history began the new age in 1929; two more in 1943 and 1948; the song to the Age of Aquarius in the hippy musical *Hair* dates from 1967; and the new era was still described as 'emerging' in publications in 1977, 1981, 1990 and 1996 respectively. *Now You See It, Now You Don't*, as one Aquarian sage jested, truthfully enough.[4] The epic change did not seem so well named after all; and world peace repeatedly failed to materialise. Quietly, then, the aquarian terminology, which was never in majority usage, lapsed in popularity and has now almost disappeared into oblivion.

Another timetabled prediction was supposedly derived from the traditional Mayan calendar. A great 'Harmonic Convergence' of interplanetary energies was foretold for August 1987, when the new era would be launched. Crowds assembled at the Niagara Falls (the predicted hub of the drama) but . . . were disappointed. Or there were possibilities in traditional Hindu teachings, which focus upon grand cycles of history. Some New Age theories thus predicted the imminent end of the *Kali Yuga*, the present dark era of destruction, which would restore the *Krita Yuga* or the vanished age of perfection. This transformative scenario offered a sense of momentous destiny, as traditional teachings allot over four million years for the entire revolution of a grand cycle.[5] Nonetheless, the actual date of this transformation remained uncertain too.

All these invented histories-cum-theology were controversial, playing with both linear and cyclical models of change. Christian fundamentalists were particularly hostile, rejecting all New Age teachings as the work of Antichrist. However, these alternative schemas marked both a belief and a hope that things were changing in some fundamental way, for individual lifestyles as well as for the deep forces of history. 'New Age' books about personal transformation had eye-catching titles like the over-hyped *Zen and the Art of Motorcycle Maintenance: An Inquiry into Values* (1974).[6] And enthusiasts experimented with various lifestyle alternatives to conventional 'bourgeois' materialism, trying options such as communal living, yoga, meditation, soft or hard drugs, sexual permissiveness and, in some cases, witchcraft revival and neo-paganism.

None of the terminologies for the supposed new era of history, however, coalesced into a generally accepted formula. Old 'modernity' did not seem quite enough. But what did the 'new' portend? Many onlookers remained doubtful, because the extent of change seemed oversold and its nature uncertain. Instead, rhetorical claims of New Ageism, especially when augmented by a politicised student radicalism in the later 1960s and early 1970s, triggered a strong conservative counter-response, especially in the West, where much of the New Age rhetoric had been invented. By the 1980s there were unofficial 'culture wars' between rival interpretations of 'modern times'. The rhetoric of Thatcher in the UK and of Reagan in the USA, far from marking the end of bourgeois materialism, encouraged an aggressive blend of free-market liberalisation with neo-conservative politics to extend an unbridled consumerism. 'New Age' attitudes did not disappear entirely. Individualist intentions ('do your own thing') merged well enough into consumerism, while elements of alternative activism fuelled the new ecological movements, as in *The Future will be Green: Guidelines for the New Age* (1996). However, on all sides by the 1980s there were fewer serious claims that an epoch of hippy communalism had arrived or even was imminently due.

Uncertainties about the new encouraged an intensified fashion of identifying late-twentieth-century trends in terms not of inaugurations but of 'aftermaths'. 'Modernity' still seemed muddled, and alternatives still required. A new terminology particularly favoured the 'post' mode, as in 'postmodernism'. It allowed that things had changed, without needing to specify the precise form of the new. The 'post' mode is not strictly the same as being 'anti', so that, for example, some former communist sympathisers in the 1990s described themselves as being 'post-communist' rather than 'anti-communist'. However, there is often a subtle disparagement within the 'aftermath' terminology, or at least a downplaying, of what has gone before. In particular, 'postmodernist' attitudes to 'modernity' were often hostile ones of rejection.

Examples of the 'post' style reveal simultaneously the sense of change and disagreement about what exactly has changed. A plethora of lifestyles and ideologies are summarily waved goodbye. Thus 'post-industrialism' and 'post-Fordism' (the end of the factory assembly line) are discussed by economists; and 'post-structuralism' is debated by cultural theorists, while the times are also dubbed, with varying degrees of wishful thinking, post-imperial and post-colonial, as well as post-communist, post-Marxist, post-Leninist, post-socialist, post-fascist, post-totalitarian, post-nationalist, post-Zionist, post-Christian, post-conservative, post-capitalist, post-liberal, post-feminist, post-Freudian, post-punk, post-gay, post-ethnic, post-racial, post-tribal, post-genomic, post-biological (robots), post-work (cybernetics), post-mathematics (cheering for the numerically challenged), post-history and even post-human (artificial intelligence). Yet sweeping labels such as these, which are all culled from the titles of recent publications, are temptingly easy to assert, while being much harder to prove. Some of them seem more plausible; others much less so.

'Postmodernity' has, among these inventive concepts, been the most influential and the most theoretically sophisticated. As developed in the 1980s and 1990s, it proposes an alternative intellectual philosophy.[7] And, for its most convinced protagonists, it defines not only a set of ideas but a new era of history which has allegedly just arrived. For that, it bases its 'infrastructural' claim upon the economic analysis of post-industrialism; and its visual claim upon the evidence of 'postmodernist' architecture, as 'old hat' high-rise buildings in steel-and-concrete are shunned in favour of low-rise vernacular-influenced styles, employing wit and whimsy.

Particularly crucial to postmodernist thought is the rejection of what is perceived as the false optimism underpinning two of the twentieth century's 'grand narratives' within the exposition of history: namely, evolutionary progress and revolutionary Marxism. The brief flourishing of youth culture hopes for a new world has also been sidetracked since their heyday in the

1960s. Moreover, fascism, once a strongly contending mantra, was defeated militarily in the Second World War and discredited at the Nuremberg Trials. Its historic dismissal is thus taken for granted in these discussions, even though fascist ideas have far from disappeared.

Postmodernist theories prefer to stress, in lieu of ideology and grand trends, the role of chance and contingency. These chaotic elements, which undeniably contribute to the historical whole, are thus elevated into its sole motors. As a corollary, the apparent linkages of 'cause plus effect' through time are rejected in postmodern theory, as being no more than story-telling mirages.[8] The tone is determinedly sceptical and disillusioned. Thus, while inheriting some of the 'alternative' attitudes of New Ageism, postmodernists disdain New Age euphoria.

Change in the twentieth century is seen as a switch from one binary opposite to another, with experts listing in two columns the rival qualities of the eras. Thus alterations are acknowledged, in a decidedly sweeping style. 'Modernity' (or sometimes the 'Enlightenment project') is taken to represent a past era of abstract Reason, totalising science, intellectual arrogance, mass industrial production, giant techno-projects, imperialist power, and the dominance of man (specifically) over nature. Its architecture is characterised as internationally austere in steel and concrete, ignoring and crushing local vernacular styles. Ultimately, by this definition (in schematic summary), the *Zeitgeist* of old-style 'modernity' is defined as linear, stern, inflexible, elitist, male, aggressive and, in a word, *bad*.

Its claimed historical successor, 'postmodernity', is represented conversely as valuing subjective feelings, intuition, scepticism, consumerism rather than producerism, cottage industry, local democracy, feminism and small-scale projects generally ('small is beautiful'), while being suspicious of 'big' science and seeking harmony with unfettered nature. 'Postmodern' architecture is eclectic, favouring the vernacular. It mixes materials and styles with self-admired humour and idiosyncrasy.[9] The new 'postmodernist' *Zeitgeist* is (again in schematic summary) non-linear, playful, flexible, inclusive, female, peaceable and, in a word, *good*.

Binary contrasts are extended even to love-making. 'Bad' modern sex, old-style, is depicted as a quasi-rape, with the dominant, thrusting, phallo-centred male penetrating the passive, recumbent and unaroused female. Postmodern love-making, by contrast, is supposed to be warm, playful, 'touchy-feely', with lots of foreplay and gentle entwining, celebrating all aspects of humanity's variable sexuality.[10] This echoes some of the New Age experimentalism, which fostered not so much the practice of sexual unorthodoxy as the habit of talking publicly about it. Diverse options are freely canvassed. For example, manuals advise on the slow, voluptuous techniques of tantric sex, spiced with a hint of eastern mystery. All unrecon-structed macho males are especially the subjects of criticism. Instead, 'new' man is encouraged to discover his 'inner woman' (while apparently it is not considered either necessary or advisable for 'new' woman to locate her 'inner man').

Diversity, pluralism and consumer choice, in both material goods and personal beliefs, can accordingly be advocated as desirable and specifically as 'postmodernist' social goals. Such teachings when first encountered could have a wonderfully liberating effect, especially for people living in politically enclosed and repressive societies. The Romanian poet Andrei Codrescu, for instance, was exhilarated to learn about the postmodernist challenge to stale communist orthodoxies. In 1986, he confided that: 'the great discovery of my thirties is plurality / . . . not just the tolerance / of difference, but the joyful welcoming of differences / into one's heart . . .'.[11] However, it may be noted that Codrescu's optimistic response to the new social liberalism was far from the playful irony or cool scepticism that protagonists of postmodernism claim as a leading characteristic of the new ethos.

Dramatic confirmation of the end of history's 'grand narratives' seemed in 1991 to be placed beyond all doubt by the fall of the Soviet system and the collapse of communism in its first state bastion. 'Postmodernity is not an ideology or position we can choose to subscribe to or not – postmodernity is precisely our condition,' remarks Keith Jenkins, a leading British advocate of 'new times'. And he adds a millennial hint that, having rejected old-style modernity, humans may learn to live unburdened by the past, thus getting ready to liberate 'the pure humanity of man [sic]'.[12] It is a philosophy that rejects diachronic history and, consequently, history-writing as well. At the same time, however, events like the collapse of Soviet communism can be interpreted in markedly different ways. For American conservative ideologues, the events of 1989–91 marked not the end of history's grand narratives, but the confirmation of a 'new world order', led by US-style political freedoms and the market economy. But, as time goes by, that picture too is becoming complicated by later events. Future historians are likely to have other, different views, seeking especially more globalised and less exclusively westernised interpretations than either postmodern (Europeanised) doubt or late-modern (Americanised) euphoria.

Paradoxically, in attacking an exhausted 'modernity' and lauding the new 'improved' state of postmodernity, the postmodernist theorists are themselves using a tactic that is often considered as notably 'modern'. Boasting about representing the winning tide of 'new times' is a historical narrative in itself. Indeed, 'once the "modern" becomes tradition, the "postmodern" can play the modern', a commentator quips.[13]

But history, particularly on a global scale, resists being simply explained by a binary change from state A to state B. Thus the claimed polarity between 'Modernity/Postmodernity' greatly underestimates diversity within the former concept and equally overestimates novelty within the latter.[14] Developments like the growing public roles played by women, for example, are based upon very long-term trends that began in the allegedly macho era of 'modernity' and are by no means completed in the supposedly female era of 'postmodernity'. Feminist theorists, who remain aware that gender inequalities have by no means disappeared, are accordingly cautious about the new rhetoric. To say, in post-ideological, world-weary 'postmodernist' terms, that 'nothing matters' is not a recipe that commends itself to those who believe in causes, both past and yet to come.[15]

Difficulties in pinning down super-binary changes are particularly seen in disagreements over the significant chronology of postmodernity. As already noted, the fall of the Berlin Wall in 1989 or the ending of the USSR in 1991 are now favoured dates. Yet, initially, a much earlier period, centring upon the 1970s, was specified, being particularly linked with the architectural revolt against high-rise buildings. Jean-François Lyotard's pivotal analysis of the *Postmodern Condition* (published in France in 1979) identified what he saw as an already-arrived cultural pattern, reflecting an already-achieved post-industrial economy. And, even before then, there were English references to 'postmodernism' in the 1950s; and Spanish ones in 1934, when an analyst of poetic *modernismo* in the early twentieth century saw the next stages as *post-modernismo*, followed by *ultramodernismo*.[16] As one commentator noted in 1988: 'It becomes more and more difficult as the 1980s wear on to specify exactly what it is that "postmodernism" is supposed to refer to as the term gets stretched in all directions . . .'.[17] The hazy terminology, once a modish register for a fluctuating cultural mood among western liberals, has thus quickly faltered. There are now references to 'beyond' or 'post-postmodernism'. Indeed, the *End of Postmodernity* (2001) has already been announced: it is 'slipping into the strange history of those futures that did not materialise'.[18]

Yet, after all, were there significant changes in the later twentieth century? Yes, and still continuing. Have these changes been well named? So far, no. What's in a name? Plenty, but it must be the right one. And, if the times are to be labelled globally, then the label should be one that has meaning for all global cultures. The historian Eric Hobsbawm suggests instead that the 'short' twentieth century from 1914 to 1991 constitutes one collective 'age of extremes'.[19] Its horrors, its warfare, its successes, its prosperity, were all on an outsize scale. So other options for the post-1945 era might be 'extreme-' or 'hyper-modernity' – or 'ultra-modernity' – or perhaps, more tamely, just 'late modernity'.

Even these rival formulations, however, do not escape one further problem. Everything depends upon what is taken as quintessentially 'modern'. For the global historian Arnold Toynbee, that concept referred to relative social harmony, economic betterment, scientific advance and progressive culture. Logically for him, therefore, the First World War, with its huge loss of life for an inch of Flanders mud, was the end of an era. In 1939 he declared retrospectively that 'our own "Post-Modern" age' had begun in 1914.[20] Subsequently, he pushed the start date back to c. 1875, with the advent of mass culture in Victorian Britain. Consequently, 'postmodernity' as a suggested era of history is highly elastic and its provenance unstable. Its suggested birth-dates retrospectively stretch for over a hundred years, from 1875 to 1991; and the term has been used in contemporary application for fully seventy years, from the early 1930s to the early 2000s.

And a similar haziness applies to 'modernity', only more so. The phrase 'all that is solid melts into air', which might seem like a slogan of the post-modernists, was in fact first applied by Karl Marx to describe the tradition-shattering impact of modern bourgeois industrialism.[21] But when did that emerge and have its impact? As the next section shows, historical 'modernity' is just as hard to define. Given that some of its birth-dates are actually later than those proposed for the advent of 'postmodernity', it could be that a post-modernist Oedipus, arriving to slay the modernist father, might find that the hapless victim has yet to be born.

Mutable Modernity

Immediately, there are problems in conceptualising humanity's trackway through history as a single journey that moves from prehistory to antiquity to modernity and beyond, with the unstated implication that eventually everyone everywhere will sooner or later have to catch up with the latest version. New Age and postmodernist ideas originated in the West, even though both viewpoints in their different ways made some acknowledgement of global changes. But the trends of history can be understood differently in other climes and from different cultural perspectives. Postmodernist theorists, however left-leaning in their own estimation, have thus been criticised in turn as neo-imperialist in their totalising vision and Eurocentric in their presentational style.

History instead has multiple trackways, that criss-cross between different cultures, but do not all follow the same route, even while they are all located within the common framework of persistence/adaptation/turbulence. The art of the tracker is to understand differences as well as similarities, changes as well as continuities. Two contrasting sets of footprints, from the early hominids and the 1969 lunar spacewalkers (juxtaposed in the illustrations overleaf) highlight

15 Surviving trackways form historic markers, like the 3.6 million-year-old Laetoli foot-prints, made by pre-human hominids walking across volcanic mud in northern Tanzania.

16 Twentieth-century trackways add a new pattern to human wanderings: a compacted human footprint in the lunar dust, from the first moon walk on 20 July 1969.

both the similar tread and the contextual variation in where and how the steps are made.

Choosing 'modernity' as the core nomenclature for a notional trackway through time creates particular confusion, because 'modernity' refers not only to the specific qualities of a specific era, deemed to be 'modern', but to everything that is part of the contemporary 'now', which is the other meaning of 'modernity'. In this simplest sense, it embraces everything that is current. So by that definition, everyone alive today – including all postmodern theorists – exists in today's modernity. And the same applies retrospectively. Past people had their own 'modern' times. Thus the Carolingian churchman Rhabanus Maurus, writing in the mid ninth century CE, referred to himself and his peers as living in *tempore moderno*, their own era, in contrast with the olden days of 'Antiquity'.[22]

According to this straightforward usage, then, 'modernity' is an ever-moving target, constituting a swathe of time around 'now', which is constantly updated with time itself. In that sense, the term remains a useful one. However, that does not exhaust its historical variations. 'Modernity' may also refer to an era of history (with disputed dates, as will be seen); or to a set of historical trends ('modernisation'); and/or to a specific literary and artistic movement ('modernism'), whose dates are also disputed. As a result of this conceptual overload, the term is expiring through exhaustion.

Look, for example, at 'modernity' as a period of time, established retrospectively. Historians conspicuously differ about the relevant chronology. Books with titles like 'the birth of the modern' or the 'making of modernity' refer between them to a timespan of some eight hundred years, from the thirteenth to the twentieth centuries. Are all these historians wrong? (No profession is perfect.) Or did 'modernity' have a remarkable series of multiple births over a prolonged span of time, as a gynaecological freak? That is a possible defence of the profusion of start dates. However, if 'modernity' is turned into multiple modernities, then the concept loses specificity and it certainly turns the exercise of historical periodisation into a highly malleable process.

Over time, more and more options have been proposed. For a true return to cultural roots, *The Genesis of Modernity* returns the concept back to 'ancient' times, with classical Greece and Rome.[23] That is at the extreme end of the spectrum. But a long-ago gestation is also suggested in *The Birth of the Modern Mind* (1989). This account, by a literary expert, focuses upon early thirteenth-century Europe and defines the key moment by the invention of the sonnet.[24] This form of poetry – introspective, personal, written in the vernacular, initially for silent reading rather than for musical performance – expresses an individual self-consciousness that is held to be distinctly 'modern'. Only a short 'Middle Ages', then, for the poetic pioneers, with a correspondingly early start for Modernity. That matched the arguments of the American historian Charles Homer Haskins for whom 'modern' learning and science began in the twelfth century. He saw the process as an early 'Renaissance', complete with Europe's first universities and their habitual ranks of impoverished students.

Very few historians go so far back to find the elusive 'modernity'. But another group settle for the fifteenth and sixteenth centuries instead. The epic journey of Columbus was once a popular birth-date and is still invoked, as in *1492: The Decline of Medievalism and the Rise of the Modern Age* (1991). Or there is the Italian Renaissance, when the revival of classical learning fostered intellectual innovation. 'The human spirit could not be forever held in bondage', enthused a historian in 1910. Hence, unfettered, it launched the *Transition to Modern Times*, while others dubbed the Renaissance *The Dawn of Modern Civilisation*; *The Birth of Modern Europe*; or as laying *The Foundations of Modern Political Thought*.

Unsurprisingly, however, a familiar problem looms. There is no agreement about defining and dating the Renaissance. Some historians refer to *c.* 1500, roughly matching Columbus's 1492 American expedition. Yet others push the classical Renaissance back into the fourteenth century, almost meeting the high tide of Haskins's twelfth- and thirteenth-century early Renaissance. Or were these changes really not so epochal after all? Historians thus debate *The Renaissance – Medieval or Modern?* with no sign of consensus in reply.

Disagreements are often productive. So, by that criterion, the concept of 'modernity' is very successful. But the outcome is also confusion, as the term is often used as a known name, without any attempt at definition. Perhaps 'modernity' did not after all arrive with the Renaissance (whenever that was) but was spawned by the sixteenth-century Protestant Reformation and *The Faith that Helped to Make the Modern World*, as a 1926 tome announced? Or perhaps something much less high-minded applied? A book on *Obscenity and the Origins of Modernity, 1500–1800* argues that the advent of commercialised pornography marks the true start point, catering for the allegedly 'modern' needs of an individualised sexuality.[25] Nor is gender confusion ever far away. Thus one study argues that a masculine identity crisis – also considered symptomatic of late twentieth-century 'postmodernity' – was already worrying men in Shakespeare's England.

Options crowd in thick and fast. The seventeenth-century 'Scientific Revolution' is sometimes praised as launching 'modernity', as new ideas were circulated between Europe's thinkers and experimenters. But did things change so rapidly? Or was there instead a slower process of evolution? Two centuries divide Copernicus's pioneering astronomy from Isaac Newton's celebrated synthesis. Meanwhile, France's René Descartes provides another date, as his mid-seventeenth-century mathematised philosophy of science is also heralded as originating modernity.[26]

Or there are strong claims for the rationalist teachings of Baruch Spinoza in Holland as the source of *Radical Enlightenment . . . and the Making of Modernity, 1650–1750*. This view chimes with those economic historians who nominate the Dutch Republic (as it became in the 1580s) as *The First Modern Economy.* [27] Or were things happening faster across the Channel? British historian Roy Porter points to the creativity of the empirical tradition, leading to *Enlightenment: Britain and the Making of the Modern World* – matched by a number of social historians who denote eighteenth-century Britain as *The First Modern Society*. But Arthur Herman reserves the accolade for those living north of the Border. So the *Scots' Invention of the Modern World* really led the way.[28] Meanwhile, the philosophy of Immanuel Kant ('Dare to think!' is his famous maxim) in later eighteenth-century Germany is also credited with primacy.[29] Perhaps, however, it is more justifiable to think transatlantically. So Gertrude Himmelfarb's *Roads to Modernity* sees change as inaugurated not just via Britain and France but, especially, via the liberal constitution of the newly republican USA[30] – the intensification of

African-American slavery after American independence in 1776 being, in this case, overlooked.

On the other hand, it is far from clear that all these scintillating new ideas were widely circulated or understood in the eighteenth century. An alternative historical interpretation accordingly depicts Europe in this period not as the hub of Enlightenment modernity but as representing the traditional world of the *ancien régime*, so-named after the pre-revolutionary government in France before 1789. When extended to Britain, this conservative interpretation agrees with those economic historians who debunk its 'classic' Industrial Revolution.[31] So the survival of continuity is used to out-trump the birth of 'modernity'. And, not surprisingly, attempts at discovering other, earlier 'industrial revolutions' in the thirteenth and fourteenth centuries are rebuffed unhesitatingly too.

Nevertheless, the terminologies have their own history to contribute. In seventeenth- and especially in eighteenth-century Europe, the concept of the 'modern' began to acquire positive connotations, alongside its established meaning as the 'contemporary'. Scholars debated the point. Were they, as 'moderns', superior in knowledge to the much-praised 'ancients' of classical Greece and Rome? Increasingly, the answer seemed clear. The 'moderns' were sure that they had won, as witness, typically among many similar effusions, the boast of English astronomer Jeremy Shakerley, when addressing the 'ancients' rhetorically in 1649:

> Heaven and Stars! How much hath our age triumphed over you! Neither doth our victory end here, still new miracles adde to the number of the old, and no day passeth without a triumph.[32]

Ebullient confidence on that scale did not pass without criticism, both at the time and later. Thus, for example, a critic like Reinhart Koselleck in the postwar Germany of the 1950s stressed the dangers inherent in radical dogmas of modernist change, in his *Enlightenment and the Pathogenesis of Modern Society*.[33] And postmodernists consider too that the eighteenth century marks the onset of western hubris, in the form of excess confidence in both scientific rationalism and its application in 'giant' schemes to 'master' the untrammelled forces of nature.

However, the 'birth of modernity' is too tempting a title to have been corralled even into the eighteenth century. More and more eras and events are increasingly cited. Thus Ferenc Fehér looks to political upheaval with the *French Revolution and the Birth of Modernity*. And 1789 remains a popular choice when people are invited to pick one single date. But Paul Johnson prefers the era *after* Napoleon, with the postwar Congress of Europe and the slow steps towards a system of international law. Hence his *Birth of the Modern World* looks at 1815–30, although C. A. Bayly's rival account takes a longer evolutionary timespan with *The Birth of the Modern World, 1780–1914.*

Cultural consciousness, meanwhile, suggests a different criterion, focusing upon people's own sense of change. A study of *Freud and the Construction of Modernity* cues Freud's notorious 1900 interpretation of dreams and the subconscious as providing the real breakthrough.[34] Here the advent of an allegedly novel awareness of human psychological complexity highlights neither intellectual trends nor political events but transformations within private realms of feeling. Yet Peter Mandler's probing analysis of the liberal elite in later nineteenth-century England, who lived supposedly at the height of 'modernity', finds that their beliefs fluctuated between confidence and doubt. So they did not display a general rush to embrace 'the modern' or history-as-unbroken-progress.[35]

Big events, however, continue to provide alternative possibilities. Could it be that the radical discontinuity of the First World War was not the offspring of the new but its midwife? Modris Eksteins argues for such a scenario. His *Great War and the Birth of the Modern Age* gives it a gloomy start in 1914, even while Alice Marquis goes later still with *The Birth of Modern Times, 1929–39.* Such a delayed date certainly suits historian Arno Mayer. He argues that Europe's economic system remained predominantly pre-industrial and its politics traditional throughout the nineteenth century. Hence, for him, *The Persistence of the Old Regime* lasted until global warfare in 1914 introduced a harsh new world of modernity. Yet it may be recalled that this date is also the one selected by Arnold Toynbee as starting the 'postmodern' era. Thus, if he and Mayer are simultaneously correct, 'modernity' was born and as promptly died at Sarajevo in August 1914.

Different national traditions of usage complicate the issue still more. In France, the conventional (but also disputed) view decrees that 'modern history' starts with the sixteenth-century Renaissance and ends with the French Revolution of 1789. Everything after that is 'contemporary' – a period whose validity is becoming increasingly overstretched as more and more years have elapsed since the fall of the Bastille. At the same time, theorists of cultural 'modernism' in France also identify a moment of modernity in the mid nineteenth-century role of Charles Baudelaire. He is the prototype of bohemian revolt against bourgeois complacency and one of many poets (since Sappho) to be unofficially dubbed 'the parent of modern poetry'.[36] Hence Baudelaire's cultural modernism features within an elongated contemporary France, in complete detachment from the country's 'modern' history that apparently ended in 1789.

Every nation is, of course, free to define its own trajectory or trajectories, all being open to debate. One expert sees modern Mexico as emerging in 1821, with independence from Spain; two others equate Mexican modernity with the Mexican 'Revolution' of 1910–17, almost a full century later; and one more attributes it to avant-garde art in the twentieth century.[37] It all depends upon the criteria selected. In German philosophy, the notion of 'modern' thought is closely linked with Kant and the eighteenth-century Enlightenment, as noted above. Yet political timetables suggest an alternative chronology. Thus a study of modern Berlin commences only in 1871, when the city became the national capital. And every country multiplies the variants. So in Egyptian history, contradictory dates propose the start of 'modernity' in 1517, in 1798, and in the mid twentieth century, while in contiguous Libya, 'modern times' have been variously attributed to: changes in the 1830s; to direct rule by the Ottoman Turks; to 1951 with independent statehood; or to the Gaddafi coup in 1969 under the banner of 'Islamic socialism'.[38]

One-off political dramas at least provide precise markers, while 'loose' trends of cultural change are more difficult to specify. Thus 'modern times' in Japan, for example, are normally dated from the Meiji emperor's resumption of power in 1868. Nonetheless, the 'modernisation' programme that followed was not only selective in its aims – borrowing from the West but retaining many features of traditional Japanese culture – but it was also slow and patchy in its implementation.[39] The result was a distinctive adaptation process, and not a wholesale cultural transfer.

Reviewing all these variants of 'modernity' indicates that the terminology is still popular. But it is also fast losing its specificity. In acknowledgement of that, temporal subdivisions are often applied to European history. An 'early modern' period, sometimes also called the 'baroque era', runs from approximately the sixteenth to the eighteenth centuries;[40] while full modernity then applies from (approximately) the eighteenth to the twentieth centuries. These subdivisions, whose distinctive dates are naturally open to dispute, in effect dilute the concept of an unbroken modernity. And they raise new debates in turn. For example, should the eighteenth century in Europe be best regarded as the tail-end of an earlier path-breaking Renaissance; or as the real key to modern Enlightenment in its own right; or as a deeply traditional precursor period to a much later modernity? All three cases are argued by different historians.

Retrospectively, then, 'modernity' has been applied to diverse swathes of time over the past two thousand years, from classical Greece and Rome at one extreme, via the early thirteenth to the twentieth centuries in between, with no consensus; and numerous individuals have also, at various times in the last 350 years, since at least the mid seventeenth century, identified their own eras as 'modern', in the sense of being 'up-to-date' and embodying the coming trend.

So much variety makes it hard to undertake good comparative studies and even harder to get agreement upon global or regional periodisation. Sometimes similar changes are being considered under different names, while at other times different things are being analysed but under similar names.[41] 'The old star departs / Leaving us here on the shore / Gazing heavenwards for a new star approaching; / The new star appears, foreshadows its going . . .' as Christopher Okigbo wrote in 1967, at a time of bittersweet hope and turmoil, not only in Nigeria but in many countries around the world.[42] And, for a while, 1967–8 was heralded as one of global history's 'modern' turning points. In effect, however, the extent of continuous overlapping and exchange between different eras, and the different rates and types of change among different cultures, means that crude either/or terminologies end by creating as many problems as they attempt to solve. So when Antoine Compagnon dissects *Five Paradoxes of Modernity*, it is hard not to respond that five is too modest a number.[43]

Unstable Modernism

An awareness of problems within the concept of the modern and modernity is hardly new. These terms continue to be used because they are resonant of 'change over time' and – chiefly too – because there is no agreement on acceptable alternatives.

Much the same point applies again to modernity's supposedly quintessential cultural formation, which is known as 'modernism'. This term is also unstable both in concept and in chronology.[44] Loosely defined, it refers to the culture of 'modern times', whenever they are deemed to be. Yet it also has a more specific meaning, as Modernism, a multi-faceted artistic and architectural style. It is this cultural programme that many postmodernists reject – as keenly as they reject so-called Enlightenment rationalism and belief in science. But while the critique is sincere, the chronology is distinctly hazy. Thus Charles Jencks, doyen of American postmodernist interpreters, condenses many eras of history in a trice to claim breezily another elongated gestation: 'Modernity, as a condition, grew out of the Renaissance until, in the nineteenth century, it gave birth to cultural modernism.'[45]

Given the uncertainties of definition, there are many other variants on offer too. While Jencks allows a multi-century gap between the first onset of modern times with the Renaissance and the later nineteenth-century emergence of a characteristic modernism, other experts are somewhat less expansive. The majority focus upon the artists, musicians and writers of the very early twentieth century, especially upon the avant-gardists who revelled in abstractions, playful invention and the 'shock of the new'.[46] Yet even then the suggested starting points go back to the mid seventeenth century; or to 1793;[47] or to a range of dates in the nineteenth century; or specifically to Baudelaire; or to the advent of impressionist art in the 1870s, led by *Cézanne: Pioneer of Modernism*;[48] as well as to the years 1900–20; and, artistically, to the young Pablo Picasso, cubism, and post-impressionist art more generally, which gave London a celebrated 'artquake' when the new works were first displayed there, to much fuss and attention, in November 1910.[49]

Alternatively, architectural history may suggest a somewhat later date. Hence modernism does not arrive until the first year of peace in 1919, according to a study of *Bauhaus: Crucible of Modernism*.[50] This particularly highlights the moment when Walter Gropius's streamlined new building in steel and concrete launched his techno-art academy (1919–33) in Dessau, the small town in the heart of Germany where Gropius and his fellow teachers encouraged his students to liberate art and architecture from the trammels of outmoded tradition.

Hence the concept of 'modernism' also lacks stability. The repeated changes in art and architecture were never as completely divorced from the past as their creators liked to think; and 'shock' new styles quickly tended to become mannered and repetitive.[51] Furthermore, innovations that are considered radical in one generation often become standard in the next. As commercialised and consumerist societies readily absorb change, the self-defined avant-garde is regularly conscripted into the mainstream, in a process that eventually turns one-time *enfants terribles* into venerated figures. No doubt for that reason, therefore, the multiple changes in western culture in the early twentieth century, known as Modernism, have been variously portrayed, either as a powerful revolt against bourgeois materialism *or* as a quintessential characteristic of the same bourgeois society.[52]

Consumerist cultures tend to be notably eclectic in their styles and cultural practices. As a result, there are often plural usages – innovation *and* reaction; classical form *and* romantic anti-form; realism *and* abstraction – at the same time. Creative artists continually look for inspiration both forwards *and* backwards; and consumers respond both to the 'shock of the new' *and* the 'shock of the (rediscovered) old'. The characteristic ferment was once named dialectically by the English poet Stephen Spender as *The Struggle of the Modern*.[53]

Frequent overlappings and cultural fluctuations, which began before the early twentieth century and continue still today, thus make it equally difficult to detect not only when 'Modernism' began but also when it came to an end, if it has ended. One German text in fact discussed the exit of the modern as early as 1909.[54] In general, however, postmodern theorists point to the 1950s as a fulcrum decade of change; or, more determinedly, to the 1960s and 1970s.

This latter periodisation applies particularly in architectural history, with the onset of a revolt against 'soulless' high-rise steel and concrete buildings. But many individual artists and works of art remain disputed. Thus James Joyce's florid 'fourdimmansional' wordplay in *Finnegans Wake* (1922–39) has been hailed as both modernist *and* postmodernist.[55] As has the bleak humour of Samuel Beckett's terse anti-Joycean dramas;[56] *and* the electronic music of John Cage;[57] *and* the surrealist art of Salvador Dalí,[58] who continued throughout a long lifetime to depict quixotic visions of melting clocks and swooning memories. His oeuvre can equally be interpreted as 'modernly' Einsteinian, in its dislocation of absolutes, or as 'postmodernly' playful, in its intuitive rejection of 'cold' science and abstract logic.

Considering such complexities of dating and defining the intricate cultural fluctuations within commercialised societies (ever avid for the 'shock of the new'), there is a manifest need for a better vocabulary to describe the heightened mixture of changes and continuities. Rather than just one turning point, there are many, some being more major than others. And rather than alternate cultural styles, there may be overlapping and competing fashions, competing for their market niche. Rightly thus does art historian Lisa Tickner comment that 'There is more than one kind of modernism (and modernity) at stake'.[59]

Architecture in consumer societies in particular is characteristically too variegated to provide either/or turning points. The favoured 'postmodernist' building style, with its preference for low-rise 'vernacular' shopping malls in lieu of 'international' tower blocks, was not the only style in use even in the 1970s, when high-rise was relatively out of favour. Nor has there been a design consensus since then. High-rise constructions have certainly not disappeared. And various individual architects borrow eclectically from different styles as fashions change.[60] It may be, speculates Charles Jencks, that 'new' postmodernism has begun to merge with 'late modernism' in the later twentieth century, producing a yet-newer architectural style to be known as 'modern Baroque'.[61] However, that ingenious term, with one more eclectic crossover between times and concepts, seems more likely to confuse than to clarify.

Long before the twentieth century, architecture that had abandoned a purely vernacular style became prone to zigzag between many alternatives at the same time, rather than to move dialectically from one design consensus to another.[62] And eclectic revivals or updatings of old forms are not just a feature of a so-called 'postmodernity'. For example, in early Victorian London, Britain's Houses of Parliament already offered a striking example of a design created in homage to much earlier times. The construction of this monument to 'Gothic' revivalism was begun in 1840, while the interior was hung with pictures commemorating British military successes over the French in the eighteenth century. And this occurred at the height of Britain's imperial and 'modern' success.

Collectively and individually, all these twists and turns of history and cultural trends are fascinating in their own right. The question is whether some better terminologies would be more helpful for studying them.

A further reminder of the multifarious chronologies attached to these contemporary usages comes when considering theological debates. Within international Catholicism, 'modernism' became the codeword not for an artistic or architectural style but for a package of proposed doctrinal and liturgical changes that would allow congregations a greater role in church services and simultaneously liberalise the church's social teachings. As such, the programme was highly controversial and much denounced.[63] The modernising campaign was not just confined to the early twentieth century, when it was first debated; nor did it end then. Its most successful moment followed at the Second Vatican Council in 1962; and its legacy is still today a contentious issue within worldwide Catholicism.

Implicitly and explicitly, all long-lasting religious movements both generate and respond to social changes. The use of the term 'modern' indicates those interactions to be part of contemporary life – as in the recent and variegated studies: *Confucianism and Modernisation*; *The Tao of Modern Living*; *Modern Buddhism*; *Hinduism and Modernity*; *Islam and Modernity*; *Al-Qaeda and What it Means to be Modern*; and even *Modern Pagan Witchcraft*.[64] In all these cases it can be seen that there is no common chronology other than a general reference to recent experience. Meanwhile, 'postmodernity', which does not feature in the discussions just cited, returns for debate in a parallel literature, also relating to contemporary times, but questioning instead *Religion and its Relevance in Postmodernism*. The free-for-all is complete.

How versatile is the terminology becomes further revealed in interpretations of the history of music and dance. The human ear and eye, soothed by repetition, is often startled by sudden change. So innovations in dance are greeted as 'modern' dance in the 1890s and again in their subsequent revival in the 1950s.[65] A new 'jazz modernism' causes a stir in the 1900s but soon becomes 'traditional' jazz. It is then disrupted by the invention of 'modern' jazz in the mid twentieth century.[66] Little wonder that the deliberate atonality of Arnold Schönberg's *Pierrot Lunaire* in 1912 was immediately controversial. It too was heralded as a new 'modern' or 'ultra-modern' music although, ironically enough, the classical compositions of Claudio Monteverdi had long ago been savaged by an Italian critic for the faults of *Moderna Musica*, published three centuries earlier in 1600.[67]

Gender relations, being also contentious and often held to be on the brink of upheaval, attract both the vocabulary and the same chronological uncertainty.

For example, the *Emergence of Modern Marriage* has been detected in the years 1550–1800, while other experts find *The Creation of Modern Masculinity* in the later eighteenth century; but *The Making of the Modern Body* not until the nineteenth century. Every permutation finds a sponsor. A study of *Modernist Sexualities* refers emphatically to the early twentieth century when polymorphous sexualities were cheerfully celebrated by bohemians in the West. This was long before 'New Age' experimentalism and/or the later 'postmodernist' praise of 'difference'. A guide to *Modern Woman – and How to Manage Her* appeared in 1909. But other liberation narratives detected a longer process. The 'modern' *Sexual Revolution* either began in the 1920s, encouraged by Marie Stopes's 1918 advocacy of birth control and sexual ecstasy or, alternatively, in the 'swinging' 1960s, following the advent of the contraceptive pill. It all depends on the criteria. So which era sees *The Transformation of Intimacy . . . in Modern Societies?* Sociologist Anthony Giddens detects this process only in the later decades of the twentieth century. In so doing he ignores entirely the putative claims of 'postmodernity' to be the key agent of change in the years from 1970 to the 1990s; and the term is not even listed in his index.

If, then, 'modernity' is viewed as a period of time, it incorporates everything that happens within that temporal embrace. Its range is thus global and eclectic. Alternatively, if 'modernity' is viewed as a set of specific trends then its characteristics are specific to time and place. They need not constitute universal destiny.

'Modernism' is similarly either general or specific. And the same applies to 'modernisation'. This abstract term, not surprisingly, is also described as 'an elusive one', which is hard to define.[68] Its qualities are often taken as derived from the economic and social experiences of the West. But 'modernisation' and 'westernisation' are not automatically the same, even though they may be denounced together as such.

Among the long-term trends that can be observed widely but not universally in the twentieth century are urbanisation; the demographic surge; the spread of consumerism; global commercialisation; the speeding of transport and communication networks; industrialisation; attempts (far from successful) at alleviating structural poverty; the adoption of science and applied technology; interventionist medicine, the diffusion of mass literacy and mass media; the internationalisation of scholarship; an extension of secularisation and religious pluralism; the creation of international institutions and attempts at conflict resolution; the ending of formal empire; the impact of mass democracy; an emphasis upon individual rights; changing gender roles; increased ecological problems and (not in synchronisation) growing ecological awareness; familiarity with closely structured time; 'forward' thinking; and the 'cult of the new'.[69] Upon inspection, however, these developments are not all the same and they certainly do not all occur simultaneously. For example, many poorer countries that have shared the twentieth century's experience of urban growth have not experienced concomitant industrial take-off: 'modernisation' may well include urbanisation but not industrialisation.

Similarly, the global meeting of people and ideas leads to convergence in some respects but also to differentiation and to outright resistance in others. Thus there are multiple modernities, and pluralist modernisms too, with 'many gods and many voices'.[70] The powerful vision of the 'new' appears in George Grosz's 'modern' metropolis of Berlin: it signals excitement, crowds, stimulus and danger, all intimately spliced together (*see* illustration 17). It is no surprise, however, to find that experts differ about the real-life chronology of urban transformation. For some, the twentieth century was the real moment of the 'modern metropolis' but, for others, it had already arrived long before, with the growth of London either in the Victorian era, or under the Hanoverians, or in the later seventeenth century, as rival studies proclaim.[71] Thus significant urbanism may apparently recur in different times and places.

Still embracing the cultural tradition of the German Enlightenment and the ideal of universalist values, philosopher Jürgen Habermas underwrites a dynamic vision of change. Arguing that 'postmodernist' philosophy constitutes a neo-conservative snare, he stresses the continuance of 'Modernity: An Unfinished Project'.[72] And many, who still reject the marked Eurocentrism within much of this terminology, also retain similar hopes for unfolding efforts to find common values. So Asian architect William Lim discusses an *Alternative Post(Modernity)* which rejects exclusive 'Western' modernities but ultimately values inclusive alternatives that will perhaps generate a 'more humane modernity'.[73]

Generally, however, all these points of reference have now become very diffuse. Irked by so much confusion and by the apparent 'modern' neglect of the important role of continuities in history, anthropologist Bruno Latour stands aside to protest that *We Have Never Been Modern!*[74] He then adds, somewhat paradoxically, that 'We have all become premodern again'. That does imply that there was once a modern moment. Yet, anyway, he concludes open-endedly that 'It is up to us to change our ways of changing'.

Elastic Premodernity

Putting all these alternative usages together has demonstrated the need for a better vocabulary of historical transformations than references that circle around a vague and contested 'modernity'. The same point applies to all its other variants too. Stretching backwards in time to cover everything before

17 George Grosz's *Berlin* (1918) captures the chaotic allure and danger of big city life – which is commonly taken to represent 'Modernity'.

'modernity', 'premodernity' becomes a huge and amorphous residual category. It is obviously not a term that sprang from contemporary applications but is bestowed retrospectively. It therefore shares to the full the elastic definitional problems of 'modernity'. For example, two recent studies, investigating respectively *Trade in the Premodern Era* and *Premodern Sexualities*, locate these experiences within Europe in the years *c.* 1500–1800. But this timespan and location, of course, is already typically 'modern' for other historians.

Premodernity, indeed, has become super-elastic. Differing accounts project its birth backwards to the Stone Age, and postpone its death-rattle until relatively recently. One account of China, for example, sees the premodern world as ending with the abdication of the last Manchu emperor in 1912, while another sees its demise only in the 1980s with the commercialised expansion of the Chinese economy.

Britain's own social evolution has led to similar disagreements. The historian Peter Laslett once declared that its 'modern times' did not commence until the 1950s, when women were no longer willing to work as live-in domestic servants. But 'that was revolution as seen from suburban Cambridge', the Marxist Christopher Hill countered. For him, the end of premodernity came two hundred years earlier, with the execution of the king in 1649 and the proclamation of a republic.[75]

Following the miring of 'modernity' and 'premodernity', so the 'Middle Ages' also run into definitional difficulties. These are the 'intervening' years, so named by eighteenth-century commentators. They are assumed to divide the 'ancient' world of classical Greece and Rome from 'modern times'. Dignified by Latin-speakers as the *medium aevum*, the Middle Ages become adjectivally 'medieval'. The effect seems admirably authoritative. But, as the onset of 'modernity' glides up and down the centuries, so too does the demise of the Middle Ages. It may thus occur at any point between the thirteenth and twentieth centuries, according to taste.[76]

Moreover, its own birth-date is equally fluid. In general, a slab of European history between (say) 1100 and 1450 is often specified as a core of medievalism, but the start of the era may be located anywhere between 1100 and the fifth-century fall of the Roman Empire in the West. Indeed, one pious *Universal History*, published in 1786, argued with a certain Christian logic that the true middle period began with the birth of Christ.[77]

Suggested chronological subdivisions within the timespan add further complications. A range of eight hundred plus years are cited as possible start dates for the 'early Middle Ages' (anywhere between 200 and 1066), while another three hundred plus years allow for the onset of the 'late Middle Ages' (anywhere between 1100 and 1417). Meanwhile, art historian Arnold Hauser preferred three stages. For him, the 'early' and 'late' medieval periods were sundered by a middle or 'high' Middle Ages in the twelfth and thirteenth centuries.[78] But this interpolation did not settle matters either. The 'high' medieval period is variously cited as occurring in the years from 900–1200 *or* from 1200–1550. The only consensus seems to be that there was no 'low' version. It is true that Enlightenment thinkers in the eighteenth century, when looking backwards, were generally hostile to the epoch that preceded their own 'light'. Accordingly, they named the 'Middle Ages' as the 'gothic' and barbaric 'Dark Ages'. But historians who today study this once despised period reject this interpretation and the hostile nomenclature. Some do, however, refer still to an earlier 'Dark Age', which refers to an intermediary period between the fifth-century fall of the Roman Empire and the 'true' Middle Ages, sometime in *c.* 1000.

Mix-and-match history allows every permutation. Biographies thus proclaim *The Modernity of St Augustine*,[79] who lived in the fifth century CE. Hybrids make particularly stimulating titles too. So a study of *The Postcolonial Middle Ages*[80] yokes a postmodernist concept with a premodern timetable. And surely 'Medieval Modernity' or 'Postmodernist Antiquity' cannot be far behind . . . .

Quixotic time reversals have certainly been posited by the quixotic French cultural theorist Jean Baudrillard.[81] He declared that time passed its apogee at some point in the 1980s and is now running backwards (but, alas, none of us is getting any younger). His dictum specifically invoked the polemical attraction/repulsion of returning events to a lost past. For that role, the 'Middle Ages' are sufficiently far away to be notable. Often they are invoked in warnings against a descent into 'medieval barbarism'. Or sometimes in ardent hope for a return to a religious world view. So, in 1933, the Christian philosopher Nicolas Berdyaev predicted that, after the coming darkness, a respiritualised 'new Middle Ages' would revive.[82] He added too that the rhetoric of 'the modern' would soon become obsolete.

Historians, when confronted with such diverse claims and usages, tend to reply that turning-point dates are mere conventions; and that period 'meanings' are ideal types that are useful for teaching purposes. The force of habit also inhibits any potential momentum for change. Over fifty years have passed since the historian Geoffrey Barraclough launched a swashbuckling critique of '*the* Middle Ages';[83] and his call for a new periodisation for a truly global study of history has not yet been answered. Nonetheless, there are signs that the trio of Ancient/Medieval/Modern, with added Postmodern, is beginning to lose ground. Long-span histories are now written without using those labels at all. And, having battled successfully to shed his first identification as a 'medievalist', the Italian historian Massimo Montanari comments simply: 'In the end, I felt freed as from a restrictive and artificial scaffolding . . .'.[84]

'Antiquity', as containing its own internal tensions and dynamics, is rightly now being reconsidered. Instead of being encapsulated from afar as an idealised and homogeneous Greece-and-Rome, constituting the joint cradle of European or even world culture, the people of these societies stand revealed as diversely living in time and holding their own complex debates on the nature of temporality and their place in it. Undoubtedly, there are fascinating linkages as well as disjunctures to be studied between 'then' and 'now'. There have been, however, many other historic cultures around the globe, some of them much older and subsequently lost in the sands and jungles of history, but all now subject to active debate and research.[85] Reconsidering the 'antique' or 'ancient', *and* what came before and after, is just as liberating as reconsidering the 'modern'. In all these cases, too, there is much to be said for a new and more expressive vocabulary.

Human lives in even more distant times, before the advent of writing and settled farming communities, are now being investigated in novel ways too. It is therefore becoming less and less appropriate to talk of one vast 'prehistoric' era that precedes a 'proper' history. Instead, the entire human experience is open for exploration and re-periodisation – not only with its debated continuities from the 'Stone Age' but also with its remarkable global array of micro- and macro-changes since then.

The Length of History

Challenges and problems spring alike from the great scope and ambition of human history. 'How can you gather together / the thousand fragments / of each person?'[86] And now there are and have been so many people. Not only is new archaeological research stretching the record backwards but the passage of time continually adds new data in the contemporary world. Already by 1860 – almost 150 years ago – one historian was fretting about the sheer scope of the subject:

> The extent of time, over which it has stretched its range, is appalling . . ..
> And as History is growing every day, and every nation is engaged in the manufacture of memorable events, it is pitiable to contemplate the fate of the historic [*sic*] student one hundred years hence.[87]

Nonetheless, the subject flourishes more vigorously than ever. Old issues are continually reassessed; and many 'lost' histories that were once thought impossible to retrieve are now being investigated in new ways.

At the same time, as the framework timespan becomes ever more immense, so does the concomitant uncertainty of how to weld so many things together.

At one time, scholars hoped at least to have a clear start date for the origin of the world; and very many calculations have been proposed.[88] So the orthodox Jewish calendar settled upon 6 October 3761 BCE as the date of creation. Christians meanwhile were divided on the issue, but the most influential verdict eventually came from Ireland's Protestant Archbishop James Ussher in the mid seventeenth century. His calculations showed the creation as occurring on 22 October 4004 BCE.[89] That gave Adam (and humanity) a birth-date on the sixth full day afterwards – at nine in the morning, as another scholar helpfully explained. It was these meticulous calculations that made 22 October a recurrently favoured day for end-of-the-world predictions. However, in general such certainties, of both start dates and endings, have been abandoned.

Welding the whole thus sets the challenge of finding significant patterns in an immense timespan, without forcing history into too rigid a formula; and of acknowledging diversity, while avoiding a collapse into meaninglessness. Some sense of how things cohere is certainly necessary, as the German theologian Karl Jaspers remarked, when himself proposing a spiritualised schema of world history. Otherwise humans remain diachronically in limbo. Understanding thus remains still the goal, to avoid fragmentation into 'the pathlessness of many sham paths'.[90]

Shaping History – Time Names

Naming the age is one important way in which people respond to collective experience. On the debit side there are 'hard times', 'times of trouble', 'ages of iron';
on the credit side, 'good times', 'years of plenty', 'days of wine and roses' and,
retrospectively, 'golden ages'. These enter into songs, sayings, mythologies. They
send messages about the past, and prepare people for emotions to come: 'Come
listen a while, I'll sing you a song / Concerning the times – it will not be long . . .'.

Particularly in times of transition, contemporary verdicts become more specific
and discussions more intense. 'Do we at present live in an *enlightened age?*'
pondered Immanuel Kant, writing in Germany, in a spirit of philosophical enquiry,
in 1784. His personal answer was: No. But he then conceded that: 'We do live in
an age of *enlightenment*'. This summary then became a cliché of educated opinion,
though there were always some prepared to disagree. Yet the very habit of
defining the age precisely was a mark of change, added the liberal philosopher
John Stuart Mill in Britain in 1831. Accordingly, he declared his own era to be an
'Age of Transition', thus coining another much-repeated dictum.[1] 'A change has
taken place in the human mind,' he further explained: 'A change which, being
effected by insensible gradations, and without noise, had already proceeded far
before it was generally perceived'.

Societies with linear models of history, progressing along a single pathway, are
particularly prone to examine the trends, searching for the nature of the new. But
the future often remains misty. So the critic and author Matthew Arnold in mid
nineteenth-century England expressed, in a poetic outburst, the classic *angst* of
uncertainty: 'Wandering between two worlds, one dead, / The other powerless
to be born, / With nowhere yet to rest my head . . .'.[2] Others, however, were
less solemn. Britain was living in an 'age of soapsuds', an observer suggested
brightly in 1839. No, it was instead a frippery 'age of tinsel', scolded another in
1843.

Many of these definitions circle around assessments of the public mood. References to an 'Age of Uncertainty' or one of 'Anxiety' recur frequently, voiced by those in the Arnoldian tradition of cautious doubt. A tract entitled *Worry* even decided in 1907 that 'worry is pre-eminently the disease of this age and of this civilisation, and perhaps of the English-speaking race in particular'. Certainly, plentiful examples can be found without difficulty. For example, an American mystery novel in 1954 contained a fictional exchange for pessimists. One character names the age as one of anxiety, while a second responds that 'Every age that people live in is an age of anxiety.' Instead, he prefers to call the era one of violence. But then a compromise is reached. 'Well, maybe we live in an age of anxiety *and* violence. . . . Now, that sounds more like it. Come to think about it, I guess that's what our age is really like.'

Whether real conversations took quite that form is a matter for speculation. The imaginary exchange, however, shows how 'naming' might be improvised between individuals, and it also suggests that countries and epochs which seem relatively placid in retrospect (like the USA in the 1950s) might well seem more problematic to people at the time. 'Mood' assessments are therefore very personal and subjective – interesting as evidence for later historians, but not conclusive proof of collective cultural attitudes across the board.

Specific evidence of the mutability of individual verdicts can be found in the private opinions of individuals who live for a long time and who repeatedly change their minds. One example was Horace Walpole, famed in the eighteenth century as an art-connoisseur and Gothic novelist. On occasions, he was complacent. In 1746, he admired 'this wise age'; in 1757, 'the times are very entertaining'; and in 1778, it was a 'sublime age'. On the other hand, he also grumbled. In 1748, the current era was 'so barbarous an age'; in 1750, it was 'a dull age'; in 1769, 'these are melancholy times'; in 1774, 'it is an insipid age'; and, in the same year, 'the age is as dull as I am!' In all this, there was no clear trend over time. Walpole did not decline from cheerful youth into melancholic old age; nor did he mellow from juvenile criticism into benign venerability. 'Is this a consistent age?' he wondered in 1764. He himself was not; but contemporaries reacting to daily experiences have no obligation to be so.

Less subjective, although still open to dispute, are identifications that take their reference from some new product or technology. An anonymous pamphleteer in Shakespeare's London in 1591 announced in mock-lament: 'it is a printing age'. And the end-result? 'Every red-nosed rhymester is an author, every drunken man's dream is a book. . . .' That was exaggerated, as a literal statement. Yet it correctly caught the growing adoption of the new media of communication, with a consequent growth too in the number of readers, authors and would-be authors.

Certainly, by the nineteenth century, the pace of technological change was hard to ignore. Listing the *Signs of the Times* in 1829, the Scottish historian Thomas Carlyle declared impressively: 'It is the age of machinery, in every outward and inward sense of that word.' And the effect was seen not only in industrial production but in the speeding of travel and communications. 'We must remember,' observed an onlooker in 1855, 'that this is the age of the rail, electric telegraph, and a general desire for everybody to be everywhere.' In the 1880s, the sense of dizzying rush was much repeated. 'We have almost annihilated time and space,' was one comment in 1888. The German philosopher Friedrich Nietzsche was lofty in his disdain for all the fuss. In 1886, he decided that it was an era 'of indecent and perspiring haste'.

References to speed and to accelerated time recur throughout the twentieth century too. Thus 'we have reached the epoch of the nanosecond', announced a gleeful 1999 study entitled *Faster*.[3] 'This is the heyday of speed,' added the author, forgetting not only those stuck in urban traffic jams and clogged airport terminals, but all those without access to the latest technologies of transport and communication.

Trends of change, often hyped with enthusiasm, provide a particularly frequent source of comment, thereby giving a shape to the world's past and, by implication, its future too. These may be highly clichéd. It is 'an age, wherein every part of Science is advancing to perfection', an English merchant serenely declared in 1772. Enlightenment rhetoric habitually praised the march of reason and progress, even if satirists frequently mocked such claims.

It was a style, moreover, that lent itself to cultural embellishment when wishing to make a case. Thus 'we live presently in the era of civilization and enlightenment . . .' wrote a group of Osaka merchants in Meiji Japan, when petitioning the newly empowered emperor in 1872 for permission to start a bank. Whatever their private thoughts, they calculated that such a declaration would help their cause, and they calculated correctly. As a result, their proposal matched the official expectations of how things should be 'in this day and age . . .'.

Again, however, not all welcome trends that others praise. One of the most famous howls of anguish came from Edmund Burke in 1790, his rhetoric at full pitch while viewing from Britain the early unfolding of the French Revolution. Well before the proclamation of the new republic, he was eloquent in his disapproval: 'The age of chivalry is gone. That of sophisters [tricky debaters], economists and calculators, has succeeded; and the glory of Europe is extinguished for ever!' And this comment was immediately prescient in forecasting the trend towards a culture of audit and business calculation. Britain's own first national census followed in 1801.

Yet Burke's generalised lament for the end of civilisation was clearly exaggerated, as such laments generally are. Europe, although buffeted by warfare and complexly stirred by the ramifications of the French Revolution, not only survived the 1790s but emerged to global eminence in the nineteenth century. One hundred years after Burke's prediction of decay, the imperial reach of the European powers was at its greatest extent. On the other hand, the ideas of the French Revolution also spoke of freeing all peoples from oppression. In 1822 the exuberant Shelley prophetically dreamed of the future birth of liberty amidst the turmoil of immediate defeats: 'The world's great age begins anew, / The golden years return, / The earth doth like a snake renew / Her winter weeds outworn.'[4]

Diversities in contemporary reactions on this scale indicate that historians cannot simply accept every dictum as the final verdict upon the events through which people live, even though their responses are undoubtedly authentic expressions of their personal hopes and fears. An epoch in history, as the novelist Tolstoy once remarked, may seem static for many long years 'till suddenly . . . it is finished, it is out-of-date'. On the strength of that, he predicted in 1905 'the age that is ending is the age of Empires' – and the fall of the Russian Tsars and the Austrian Hapsburgs duly followed, with, later, the ending of the European colonial empires, though not the termination of all 'empires' of power politics or of ideas.

Ultimately, long-term interpretations require long-term evidence, which takes into account 'what happens next'. A joking reminder of that process occurs in a much-repeated anecdote about assessing 1789 and the French Revolution. When asked if it 'succeeded', a wily twentieth-century politician (often in anecdote Charles de Gaulle; sometimes Ho Chi Minh) replies: 'It's far too soon to say.' A mere two hundred years is only a moment. Historians do not usually hesitate for quite so long a time. But the point remains that contemporary opinions are preliminary draft assessments, which await long-term confirmation or refutation in the light of diachronic evidence and reinterpretations.

This proposition about the contingent nature of people's immediate assessments is particularly important to recall when considering their comments about trends in personal, familial and sexual matters. Here it is strikingly easy to pronounce but very much more difficult to know with certainty. A pamphlet in 1727, for example, bemoaned the decline in social deference, denouncing *The Brutality of the Present Age, Particularly the Pertness and Insolence of our Youth to Aged Persons* (see illustration 18). In fact, there is no special evidence for any extra

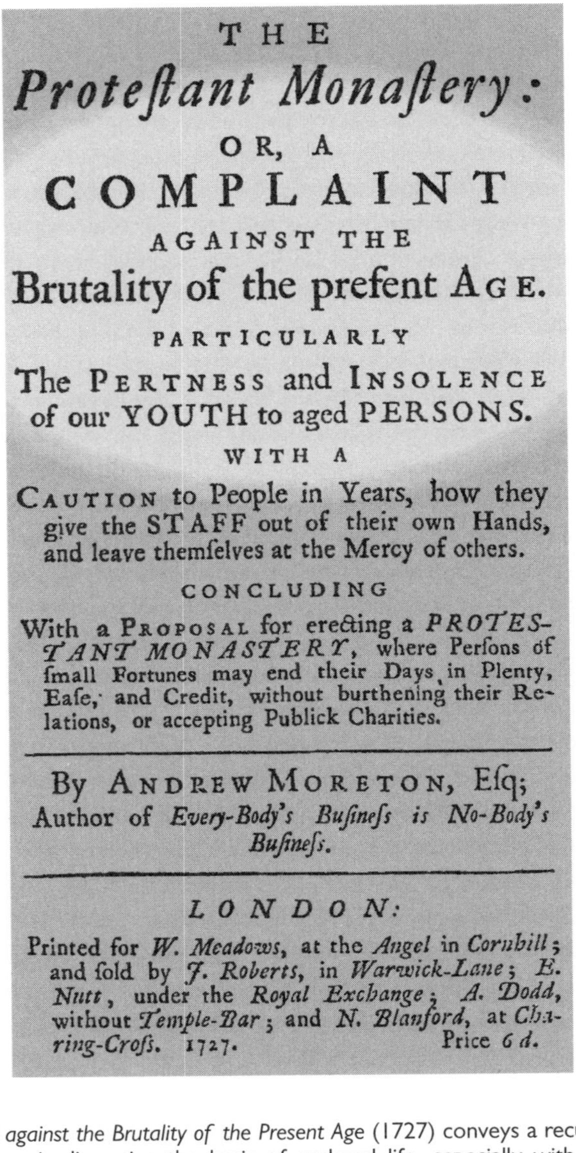

THE

Proteſtant Monaſtery:

OR, A

COMPLAINT

AGAINST THE

Brutality of the preſent AGE.

PARTICULARLY

The PERTNESS and INSOLENCE
of our YOUTH to aged PERSONS.

WITH A

CAUTION to People in Years, how they
give the STAFF out of their own Hands,
and leave themſelves at the Mercy of others.

CONCLUDING

With a PROPOSAL for erecting a *PROTES-
TANT MONASTERY*, where Perſons of
ſmall Fortunes may end their Days in Plenty,
Eaſe, and Credit, without burthening their Relations, or accepting Publick Charities.

By ANDREW MORETON, Eſq;
Author of *Every-Body's Buſineſs is No-Body's
Buſineſs.*

LONDON:

Printed for *W. Meadows*, at the *Angel* in *Cornbill*;
and ſold by *J. Roberts*, in *Warwick-Lane*; *E.
Nutt*, under the *Royal Exchange*; *A. Dodd*,
without *Temple-Bar*; and *N. Blanford*, at *Cha-
ring-Croſs.* 1727.   Price 6 d.

18 *A Complaint against the Brutality of the Present Age* (1727) conveys a recurrent anxiety
that social change is disrupting the basis of ordered life, especially with reference to
insubordinate youth.

tensions between the different age groups in English history during that particular decade. But the headline undeniably made for good journalistic copy.

Another frequent comment on 'decadence' refers to the uppishness of house-hold servants. Arnold Bennett's novel *The Old Wives' Tale* (1908) gives a fictionalised version. His two elderly heroines appear, 'their faces gravely troubled, aghast, as though they had glimpsed the end of civilized society – as though . . . they had lived too long into an age of decadence and open shame'. And what has provoked this agony? Pert, disobedient servants are the cause. But eager complaints on that score recur in many different generations. As a result, it is much harder for historians to detect fluctuations in the nature of master/servant relationships *en masse* than it is to assess overall changes in the numbers engaged in domestic service.

Gender relationships are particularly likely to prompt grand assertions that are difficult to test historically. Did the later twentieth century really belong to women, as more than one cultural theorist suggests? An American guru of revivalist masculinity, Robert Bly, sees the advent of a new and dispiriting 'age of the sanitized, hairless, shallow man' (1991). The old-style macho male has apparently been cowed out of existence. And a professional career woman is also on record as demanding triumphantly: 'Who would choose to be a man in this century of women?' Not only access to jobs but sex lives are widely believed to have changed. So one female student, when asked to define the past hundred years, declared it to be 'the century of the female orgasm'. Yet experiences differ from case to case, and also from culture to culture around the globe, making it hard to disentangle typicality from polemics in these intimate matters.

For historians, therefore, people's expressions of change always need evaluation in their context. Consider the following fictional exchange:

'SOMETHING NEW!' . . . [says] a worthy disciple of the old school . . . 'that is impossible. "*There is nothing new under the sun,*" . . .' 'Nothing *New!*' [retorts his sister] . . . 'What can you mean, brother? Why everything is new: we are alto-gether a new race of beings . . . . *New* doctrines, *new* ideas, *new* language, *new* manners, *new* habits, *new* style, *new* schools, *new* studies, *new* inventions, *new* fashions, and even *new* religions, mark the novelty of the age we live in. In short, as I said before, everything is *new.*'

When was that written? It might almost have been penned at any time between 1700 (or even earlier) and 2000. But, in fact, it comes from a satire, published in England in 1828. The old-fashioned brother – a 'disciple of the old school' – quotes the famous tag from Ecclesiastes, which is so often used when people wish to deny the existence of change. Meanwhile, the rhapsodic sister claims that everything is being transformed, from biology to religious faith. But the satire is no proof that things were actually changing as she alleges – merely that such 'New Age' assertions were 'in the air' and thus available as subjects for humour.

A particularly famous witness claim to social transformation came almost a century after this parody. The English novelist Virginia Woolf felt that she and her network of fellow intellectuals and artists, later known as the 'Bloomsbury Group', represented a cultural avant-garde. And, looking back in later life, she gave destiny a date:

> In or about December, 1910, human character changed. . . . The change was not sudden and definite . . . . But a change there was nevertheless; and, since one must be arbitrary, let us date it about the year 1910. . . . All human relations have shifted – those between masters and servants, husbands and wives, parents and children. And when human relations change there is at the same time a change in religion, conduct, politics, and literature.[5]

Woolf's statement (frequently misquoted as 'human *nature* changed') parallels the earlier remark by Mill that the 'human mind' had changed. In both cases, their sensitive awareness of cultural transition was heightened by personal liberation in their twenties from the weighty influence of their intellectually dominant fathers. Woolf's comment was clearly not meant literally, but rhetorically, since she noted that changes were actually taking time to spread. Nonetheless, the date was a significant marker. It is often held to refer to the big London exhibition of post-impressionist art in November 1910, thus turning her remark into a contemporary accolade for 'modernist' art. But Woolf was not herself overly impressed with the show. It was rather literary and cultural change that she emphasised. And in her own private life, she recalled too an earlier evening (in c. 1906–7) that marked a 'great advance in civilisation' when she and her close friends began to talk frankly amongst themselves about all forms of human sexuality. And in that regard, the Bloomsbury Group certainly was pioneering, not for being interested in the subject but for talking and writing about it, publicly, without leering or sniggering.

Interesting as it is, that people tend to generalise on the basis of their own life experiences, 'age namings' characteristically over-claim immediate traits and underestimate the extent of diversity. 'The world broke in two in 1922 – or thereabouts,' remarked Willa Cather from America, proposing another date that does not now seem so conclusively divisive. Historians should take these rhetorical dicta seriously, as evidence of people's beliefs, but not literally, as incontestable verdicts. So while some later commentators agreed with Woolf in seeing progressive social changes in the course of the twentieth century, there were also many sceptics. Other summary statements derided the era, variously, as 'an age of chaos', 'an age of folly', 'an age of thunder', 'a tormented age', while George Orwell provided the most famous single dictum to warn against the dangers of state-brainwashing in the 'Age of Big Brother'.

Or, too, there are harsh perceptions of binary conflict. 'The Euro-Ameri-Zionist age and the age of Islam are two opposite ages: antagonists,' writes Safinaz Qazim in 1986. Her viewpoint is that of an Egyptian woman who seeks changes in gender relationships while still rejecting western lifestyle and feminisms. 'It is impossible to combine the ages, impossible to be neutral among them . . .', she adds. This sort of dichotomous vision of irreconcilable conflict retains its currency today, even while there is an alternative that stresses the potential for convergence, tolerance and reconciliation. Moreover, there are more than just two rival world views on offer. It is 'the age of creolisation', argues a Japanese study of migrations and intermixing, adapting the term 'creolisation' (initially one of disparagement) to refer positively to the creative encounters of many global languages, lineages and lifestyles.

Collectively, all these inventive 'namings' of their own eras by the people who live in them provide immediate assessments of history as it is experienced. Their dicta make wonderful book titles. And, as evidence for historians to assess, they are invaluable.[6] Accordingly, an era cannot be defined plausibly as one of tranquil continuity if every contemporary sees it as a time of turmoil; and, conversely, too an era cannot be convincingly named as one of epic upheaval, if all contemporaries maintain unhesitatingly instead that 'there is no new thing under the sun'.

However, given that verdicts so often differ, that leaves historians with considerable scope. 'It was the best of times, it was the worst of times, it was the age of wisdom, it was the age of foolishness, it was the epoch of belief, it was the epoch of incredulity, . . . it was the spring of hope, it was the winter of despair'; in short, it was 'an age like any other', wrote Charles Dickens, with a binary humour that was appropriate for his *Tale of Two Cities*. His jibe was friendly but sharp about the confusions of immediate responses. Assessing the ages and stages of history is ultimately a retrospective art that waits upon the passing of time.

CHAPTER 6

Variable Stages

Distinctive epochs in history do not automatically follow in known sequences. So when the novelist F. Scott Fitzgerald, ever sensitive to the mood of his times, described the liberated postwar youth of 1920s America as living in a new 'Jazz Age',[1] he did not mean that it followed the 'age of Classical Music' and even less did he predict an ensuing 'age of Rock 'n' Roll'. It was enough for Fitzgerald to invoke a frenetic, jazzy alternative to what seemed to him, in retrospect, to be the staider, calmer world that existed before the First World War, even though those years had not seemed particularly calm to those who lived through them. Virginia Woolf's rival dating of change, after all, fixed upon the prewar year of 1910 as a revolutionary year in human relationships and in politics, religion and literary culture to boot.

Putting an age into a grander sequence of historical change invests the identification with a greater authority. Each epoch becomes but a stage in a larger picture. And the most influential of these interpretations contain within them not only a description of fundamental changes, but an account of how and why things change from stage to stage. This chapter is concerned with such interpretations – and with their merits and weaknesses in explaining the 'shapes' of history over the long term.

Sometimes the models are generated by hope rather than experience. In 1895, for instance, an ardent Methodist minister in the USA announced publicly that there are three great stages in humanity's historic struggle against evil, as each 'race advances from barbarism to civilisation'. Firstly, immoral habits are socially tolerated; then, they become controlled by law; and, thirdly, they are freely rejected by the people. For the Methodist minister, the true evil was the consumption of alcohol. Given his confidence that American society was on the verge of Stage Three, he argued that an official ban on producing and selling intoxicating liquor was bound to succeed. But, when Prohibition was adopted in 1919, the case proved otherwise.[2] On the other hand, the minister's model of how social attitudes change does work in some circumstances. A shift from communal acceptance, to legal restrictions, to public rejection *is* very gradually happening with reference to smoking tobacco, with strong encouragement from the medical profession, although the change is occurring at very different rates in different countries.

Explaining history in terms of contrasting stages has a double appeal, not only explaining past transformations but also providing a basis for predicting future stages. Another example comes from the French Enlightenment reformer Condorcet, who has already been mentioned as an optimist's optimist. He identified ten 'grand epochs' in humanity's progress towards universal truth and happiness. Nine had already passed. Hence the tenth – a future age of liberal world civilisation – was about to dawn.[3] Condorcet's choice of a round number of stages conferred a notable harmony upon his vision of progressive enlightenment, which influenced many later reformers, despite the fact that the route to benevolent change was far from easy.

Most stage theories, however, tend to stick with more manageable totals than ten. The number three is very popular, as will become apparent. And, in addition, the binary contrast of two has numerous advocates, concentrating especially on a single transformation scene from 'before' to 'after'. All these formats allow for a variety of interpretations within the clarity of a numbered framework, keeping history's progressions within manageable bounds. Clearly, stage theories reject the viewpoint that sees the past as nothing but a jumbled mass of incoherent data. After all, history is more than 'just one damned thing after another'[4] – not least because countless things happen all at once and because, among those countless things, some 'damned' developments are more important than others. Yet the characteristic problem with stage theories is the obverse of excess fragmentation: that is, they tend to excess simplicity with, furthermore, the frequent assumption – usually taken for granted rather than in any way proved – that these stepped pathways are universal for all people.

Stages and the Whole

Both linear and cyclical models of history are readily adaptable to incorporate discrete changes, which fit into many different 'shapes'. Traditional mythologies in a number of cultures make reference to this idea. A golden age gives way to a silver age, which gives way to a bronze age and then perhaps – in some versions – an iron age, and at some point returns (even if with difficulty) to an original golden age.[5]

In all cases, the length of time between one point of stage or 'stadial' transition and the next remains a matter for individual calculation, according to the selected criteria. Analysts who investigate very long-term transformations characteristically think big. For instance, the Russian radio-astronomer Nicolai Kardashev proposed a well-known classification of galactic civilisations that envisages three levels of technical development: in the first (K1), resources are derived from one home planet; in the second (K2), the energies of a local star (in our case, the sun) will be harnessed; and in the third stage (K3), the civilisation has made a technical hyper-leap to utilise resources from an entire galaxy.[6] On that basis, we earthlings have scarcely begun. Armed with this historical model, Kardashev began in 1963 to search for advanced civilisations in outer space and quickly announced, to some excitement, the detection of a possible K3-world in a fluctuating radio source, labelled CTA-102. But, in fact, the signal was that of a pulsing quasar, at the core of a far-distant galaxy.

Clearly, however, the designation of the core stages is affected by the criteria that matter to the person designating them – and to those who are convinced by any given model. Another, quite different prototype was advanced in the mid 1950s by C.S. Lewis, who was a Christian apologist as well as novelist and scholar. For him the real criteria for *Describing the Times* are spiritual.[7] He accordingly dismissed all historical period labels, from classical to medieval to Renaissance, and divided literary history into three new stages. These are 'pre-Christian', 'Christian' and ultimately 'post-Christian', which latter period of degeneration he feared had begun in the nineteenth century. It was a bold claim, not least because, if applied to the study of literature, it would abolish his own professional position as Professor of 'Medieval & Renaissance' English at Cambridge University. But Lewis's colleagues were bemused rather than converted by his schema, which anyway had nothing to say about the non-Christian literary world.

Common to all these stage theories is an interest in identifying significant differences within history. That idea was caught by the German philosopher J.G. Fichte in the early nineteenth century: 'There is not only *Time*,' he wrote resoundingly, 'but there are *times*, and succession of times – epoch after epoch, and age succeeding age.'[8] By differentiating between different eras, the emphasis falls upon the meaning of the past, rather than merely the passing of calendar years. A few dramatic turning points are highlighted, too, making history instantly memorable.

So in 1998 one exercise in global futurology suggests that all humanity may be considered as sharing a common period of 'pre-civilisation' from the start of biological evolution to the advent of organised agriculture in c. 8000 BCE. Then follows a prolonged 'ancient history', which continues until very recent times. Coming soon, however, is the true modernity of 'mondo-culture', of which today's globalisation is but an early intimation. According to this timetable, our collective descendants in five thousand years' time will look back at the year 2000 as the fulcrum of change when 'modern times' finally began.[9] Here is another signally long-focus model, with the added excitement of placing ourselves at the hub of history. Today's immediate contentions are swept into a lengthy procession, based upon the ever-popular threefold classification. However, within such a super-lengthy timescale – with only two real turning points, in 8000 BCE and 2000 CE – all finer distinctions between different eras in the past, and between different cultures at any given moment in time, become entirely lost.

Nonetheless, the recourse to a named and numbered history, with a finite set of stages, has considerable attraction. It appeals to the human capacity to count and to read significance into combinations of digits. And it also reflects a sense of history's capacity for change, in this case projected onto different states of history over time.

Words, after all, are evasive and open to many interpretations. Numbers, by contrast, appear crystalline and definite. Being unchangeable over time, they reflect permanence. They hold out the promise of accuracy and the prospect of further calculations based upon a secure foundation. Hence they seem capable of resolving quandaries with elegant precision.

Many traditions deploy an intricate profusion of number symbolism. So in Hindu cosmology fifty-two represents the fleeting or transitory moment. Or the same tradition sees in the enigmatic number thirteen (unlucky in orthodox Christian numeration) the possibility of transformation and the ability to overcome obstacles.[10] Precise figures keep track of diversity. That can be seen in the grandeur of the Hindu Ages (*Yuga*) of history, which together make great cycles (*Mahayuga*), which are located in turn within even greater aeons (*Kalpa*) lasting thousands of millions of years. The range is dizzying but still tethered in time, which stretches from aeons to the 'twinkling of an eye'. The four *Yuga* – *Krita*, *Treta*, *Dvapara* and *Kali* – with the properties respectively of gold, silver, bronze, and iron, have proportionately varied timespans. The *Kali Yuga* extends for 432,000 human years; the *Dvapara Yuga* for twice as long; the *Treta Yuga* three times as long; and the golden years of the *Krita Yuga* four times as long, for 1,728,000 years.[11] There are also variant calculations which offer different results. Nonetheless, it is conventionally argued that the current *Kali Yuga* began in 3102 BCE, which means that this era of 'hard times' not only prevails today but will also continue for many millennia.

Of course, it is self-evident that not all problems are explicable by pure numbers. The question has to be right before the answer makes sense. Such a warning was teasingly conveyed in the satire, *The Hitch Hiker's Guide to the Galaxy*. In its central spoof scenario, the super-computer, Deep Thought, cogitates for seven and a half million years to determine 'the Ultimate Question of Life, the Universe and Everything'. Eventually, the response is given as: 42.[12] It is a great tribute to the multiple of three key primes: $2 \times 3 \times 7$. Yet it is an answer answerless. The choice of this number, incidentally, suggests a sly tribute to the maestro of time-and-space dislocation, Lewis Carroll, whose King of Hearts in the underground world of *Alice* announces that rule 42 is 'the oldest rule in the book'. This is a comparatively rare example of humour in numbers. (And Alice caps the joke by objecting, logically enough, that if rule 42 is really the oldest then it should come first.)

As it happens, there is an esoteric connection here too. One venerable Jewish Talmudic tradition, as recounted in the twelfth century, holds that the cabbalistic holy name for the divine is spelt with 42 letters, although this has a mysterious meaning vouchsafed only to the wise.[13] It is a good example of recondite number symbolism, which depends not just upon numeracy but upon a cultural tradition ready to see signs in numbers.

Both the Jewish and Christian traditions have been greatly influenced in this way. Among the many exercises in numerology based on hints within specific biblical texts, one fugitive tract of 1675, written by an earnest Protestant divine, may be cited. It recalculated the cryptic 'number of the Beast' – the designation of Satan which is 666. Instead, the tract declared that the real solution is . . . 42.[14] However, this revisionist theology was too Delphic and the argument remained obscure. It is true that the mysterious number also appears in one of Revelation's prophecies, that the Beast/Satan will reign on earth, just before the end of the world, for the span of 'forty *and* two months'. But the kaleidoscope of imagery about the last battle of Armageddon is too complex to render into an easy timetable. The symbolism of numbers thus needs an understood framework to make sense. Otherwise their apparent precision is deceptive and indeed positively distracting.

For that, among other reasons, there are also significant intellectual traditions that reject subdivisions in favour of unity or, if accepting some elements of subdivision, consider that such characteristics are unimportant in comparison with the power of unity. One example was proposed in the spiritualised vision of Pierre Teilhard de Chardin. A highly unorthodox Jesuit priest and palaeontologist, he argued in 1959 that all people globally are beginning to share a convergent consciousness. As units in space, individuals remain individuals but they simultaneously form part of a broader process. 'Space represents a momentary section of the flow which is endowed with depth and coherence by Time,' de Chardin observed. Hence behind global diversity and conflict, he detected a new 'technico-cultural knitting together of human society'. This trend would lead to an ultimate *point Omega*, or true unity. Biology and human history would merge, as humanity – the 'thinking species' – generates one super-consciousness that finally meets with the divine, 'outside Time and Space'.[15] It was a very personal vision, unorthodox even in its millenarianism, foretelling the union of individual psyches into a godly whole. All the earlier stages in history thus count down to one.

Biological 'oneness', uniting all humans whether genetically or behaviourally, has also provided the basis for theories of deep continuity. For example, the world view of Evolutionary Psychology, discussed in chapter 2, does not deny that there may be local differences and changes over time. These are, however, assumed to be purely epiphenomenal – minor variants to a fundamental pattern. The single-minded model of the Stone-Age-derived human biology/psychology declares that the human reproductive imperative is all-powerful. As a result, historical diversity and cultural variety are not interpreted as stages in historical development but as permutations upon an already fixed theme.

'Sexual selection through mate choice can potentially explain anything you can ever notice about evolved human behaviour as something that needs explaining.'[16] Thus remarks evolutionary psychologist Geoffrey Miller, with ultra-sweeping confidence. All forms of cultural production, such as the urge to write books or to paint pictures, are thus interpreted as either direct or indirect forms of courtship display. By reducing everything to one instinct, the model attempts to place history within a secure and unified framework, cutting a swathe through complexity by identifying one core motivation. It leaves unexplained both the extent of cultural variation and the nature of significant changes over time. And in particular the model cannot account for much non-reproductive behaviour, such as (say) why post-menopausal women should bother to write books, when their chances of genetic self-reproduction following this form of courtship display are biologically nil. Nonetheless, the psychological model finds assurance in oneness, which is inscribed in history from the beginning, rather than, de Chardin-like, emerging at the end.

However, there is not an absolute gulf between unified models and stage theories. Underlying the detection of key turning points, which are taken to distinguish between the different eras, there is usually one defining principle, such as Kardashev's intergalactic technological imperative, or Condorcet's faith in the march of liberal education.

Spiritual visions provide an example of oneness that can also, in particular circumstances, accommodate stages within history. A belief in cosmic wholeness or unity is central to many forms of religious thought. The holiness of the 'one' acknowledges the authority of divine creation. Outside and beyond the fret and bustle of everyday affairs, stand the unchanging 'alpha and omega', the first and last things.

Within the holistic consciousness of Islam, for example, there is a strong faith in monotheism (*tawhīd*). Everything therefore unfolds within that absolute framework of divine unity. However, that has not precluded Islamicist studies of historical change, as has already been cited in the case of the celebrated cyclical theories of Ibn Khaldūn. In effect, he saw a series of economic stages, mutating from early simplicity into settled luxury, with an ever-present danger of degeneration.[17] But others focus instead upon the unity behind these variations. There is thus a gamut of responses within Islam. Today the purist doctrines of Wahhabism, for example, stress that the past and the present are spiritually the same. That means, among other things, that the preservation of historical monuments (even of shrines that are venerated by fellow Muslims) is rejected if these visible objects are seen as distracting attention from the divine.

Even within deep 'oneness', however, an implicit two-stageism may develop, particularly if fundamental changes are sought in the present, which is seen as polluted, in order to restore a primitive purity. Hence the true believer's pilgrimage through history may well incorporate calls for radical discontinuity. There is scope for renewal on the way, at significant *Milestones*, in the phraseology of Egypt's Sayyid Qutb, one of the mid twentieth-century inspirers of fundamentalist activism. Hence he declaed that: 'Islamic society is not just an entity of the past, to be studied in history, but it is a demand of the present and a hope of the future.'[18]

Selecting stages, whether one or many, is thus an exercise that is influenced by the perspective of the enquirer. History's divisions do not just 'emerge' from the evidence effortlessly. Ultimately, it is that element of arbitrariness of choice that makes stadial theories both fascinating to analyse and simultaneously open to critique. By combining numbers and history, to make a coherent grand design, these approaches have been remarkably influential. The next section accordingly looks at some of the most popular numbering schemes, which provide convenient stepping stones to travel mentally up and down the centuries.

Numbered Stages

Two is a particularly mighty number for registering binary contrasts and complementary opposites.[19] It therefore launches this section, which focuses upon the number of stages that are commonly identified within long-run histories. In application to human life, two immediately signifies difference. Dichotomous motifs thus recur plentifully in many systems of cultural classification: man/woman; right-hand/left-hand; up/down; front/back; day/night; on/off; yes/no; good/bad; divinity/devil. In a celebrated synthesis, the traditional Chinese polarities of *yang* and *yin* incorporate the complementary forces of the hot, masculine, positive principle (the sun) and the cool, feminine, negative principle (the moon).

When applied to history over time, duality highlights significant change: from 'before' to 'after' or from 'earlier' to 'later'. The dichotomy may be merely a matter of alternative epochs, following one upon another. Yet a contrasting 'two' also contains scope for opposition and conflict.

Binary models are good, therefore, for highlighting moments of dramatic transformation, especially if accompanied by turmoil and conflict, even while binaries are less useful for explaining slow trends or no-change over long periods of time. The pace of technological and industrial development in nineteenth-century Europe, for instance, prompted some well-known dichotomies. One formulation came from the German sociologist Ferdinand Tönnies. He argued in 1887 that, as societies become more industrialised, they move from a simpler stage of *Gemeinschaft*, marked by cohesive, tightly knit communities, to a new complex stage of *Gesellschaft*, characterised by an impersonal, and starkly competitive, individualism. This much-quoted binary carries elegiac implications of social loss.

Yet deciding which features of change are benevolent and which are to be deplored remains a matter of judgement. Others in the same years saw positive outcomes. From Britain, Herbert Spencer gladly announced that technological improvements were lifting humanity from barbarism to a higher 'civilisation'.[20] And from Germany, too, came an alternative account. The sociological analysis of Emile Durkheim depicted a seismic shift from old, automatic work routines, based upon back-breaking labour in the fields, to a new 'organic' solidarity within factory workshops. In this way, he explained, the chronic subdivision of labour was being counteracted by the creative initiative of the workforce, through trade unionism and collective organisation.[21] Hence Durkheim saw industrial development as promoting scope for the very social cohesion that his close contemporary Tönnies saw industrial society as destroying.

Other dualities in economic history posit contrasts between: pre-industrial/ industrial; underdeveloped/developed; backward/advanced; premodern/ modern; or, in older terminologies, between 'savagery' and 'civilisation'; or 'primitivism' and 'culture'. And metaphors are borrowed from the familiar daily alternation between light and dark. So when agonising over the apparent triumph of European fascism in the 1930s, Karl Jaspers mused that history constantly oscillates between a creative 'Law of Daytime' and the destructive 'Passions of Night'. It was a view well known to German philosophy. Kant in 1798 dubbed it 'Abderitism' (contradiction) – or, historically, a regular switching between periods of progress and counter-periods of regression. As a model of alternation, it was also named poetically by J.G. Herder as 'the labour of Penelope', referring to the patient spouse of Homer's *Odyssey*, who wove her web by day and unravelled her work by night.[22]

Generally, verdicts upon binary stages tend to be clear about the attribution of praise or blame. Thus, if seen sadly, history is degenerating from good times to bad; or, if viewed optimistically, it is progressing from old backwardness to 'new, improved' times. Thus, as already discussed in the previous chapter, 'modernity' is seen by its protagonists as distinctly better than the benighted 'olden days', just as 'postmodernity' in turn is considered by its theorists as notably superior to the arrogant hubris of 'modernity'. In each case, being on the 'right' side of history provides a good psychological boost to those who are certain of its momentum.

Unusual among binary models of transformation was the ultra-pessimistic model of Michel Foucault, who enjoyed overturning clichés on all sides of the philosophical spectrum. When interpreting the development of penal policy in mass industrial societies, he saw neither degeneration nor progression but merely a switch from one parlous state to another. Instead of punishment by the old, primitive means of assaulting the body (flogging, pillorying, or hanging) there was a move instead to a would-be rationalist system of control by containment and redeployment (incarceration in prison, hard labour, deportation). But the outcome still confirms for Foucault the oppressive power of all regimes of control.[23] In this way, his anarcho-pessimism functions as a good antidote to liberal reformers who tend to assume that 'progressive' reforms will always have 'progressive' social outcomes. On the other hand, Foucault's binary model is over-schematic. The development of penal policies was not as dualistic as he implies; nor are prison regimes habitually (outside totalitarian systems) as 'total' in their control as he was wont to assume.

Pessimistic binaries in history may even produce a certain element of fatalism. There is no point in seeking change if it brings degeneration, or at least no real improvement. However, even degenerative binaries can provide hope by indicating that history contains alternatives even to an apparently totally entrenched status quo. For that reason, one version of women's history proposed that before the long rule of men, which was widespread in all global cultures, there was a vanished earlier era when women prevailed.[24] So the mythic matriarchy of the 'great Goddess' preceded the historic patriarchy of phallocentric society. Consequently, gender roles are not static but, by implication, are ripe, even overdue, for further transformation. In fact, most feminists do not endorse this particular version of women's history, because evidence for the vanished matriarchy is scanty. Nonetheless, binary models of past changes can subtly encourage hopes of new dialectical developments to come.

Three stages, which are by far the most common within stadial models, show a marked increase in interpretative possibilities. The total is small enough to be conceptually clear, while great enough to incorporate momentum and diversity. Sometimes dubbed the 'perfect number' on a par with the familiar three-dimensionality of space, three adds to the argumentative polarity of two the 'organic' wholeness of one.[25] Moreover, it has a significant temporal dynamism. If duality in human history is represented by a man and a woman, so the addition of a child makes a trio which progresses into the next generation. Three thus avoids the either/or dogmatism of binary alternatives. It offers a 'third way'.

Although particularly common within Indo-European thought systems, triadic formulations are far from confined to them. For instance, the moral framing of Confucianism envisages a treble process of social enlightenment, which steps from primitivism, to simple order, to a higher harmony.[26] Similarly, the separate forces of *yang* and *yin*, when fused together, make a third synthesis, encompassing both. And within Indo-European thought, the spiritual power of 'three' is well known. Hindu manifestations of the divine (*trimurti*) incorporate Brahmā the creator, Visnu the preserver, and Siva the destroyer. In mainstream Christianity, the godhead is envisaged as the Trinity of Father, Son and Holy Spirit, although there have always been alternative Christian views – heresies to the orthodox – that see but the single unity of divinity. Added to these formulations, Pythagorean thought in classical Greece saw a threefold momentum to change, which takes things forward – from beginning – to middle – to end. Or the saga can run onwards into the unknown that is to come: from past – to present – to future.

Encouraged in this way, there are many permutations of triadic history, which are usually defined and explained. But sometimes the magic number on its own is enough. So a children's history primer of 1936 (secularist in tone and unperturbed by the unfolding global turmoil) declared staunchly: *Man Has Climbed: A History of the World ... With a Map showing Three Stages of Civilisation.*[27]

Historical interpretations are generally, however, more ambitious and often provide distinctive names for the different epochs. A very popular three is simply: Ancient/Medieval/Modern, which is alternatively given a different chronology as Premodern/Modern/Postmodern. Or another, from a related but separate intellectual tradition (discussed in the following section), is the Marxist triad of Feudalism/Capitalism/Communism.

Among many triple-stage theories, it is worth highlighting three in particular. One comes from Joachim di Fiore, a twelfth-century biblical scholar and mystic. He was, like Giambattista Vico and Giuseppe di Lampedusa in later generations, a man from the Italian south, at the Mediterranean crossroads where change and resistance to change collide.[28] Joachim was not the first, by any means, to think 'in threes'. But his vision proved notably influential. He drew many complex shapes for history, including a threefold Tree of History (*see* illustration 19) which projected the Trinity into an unfolding epic. Stage one is the Age of the Father; the second, the Age of the Son; and the third (yet to come), the Age of the Holy Spirit. Rather than seeing these as temporal divisions, Joachim envisaged them as successive states of mind – from fear, to

19 Joachim di Fiore's *Tree of History*, from a thirteenth-century manuscript, envisages the distinctive stages of history growing intricately, like a branching tree.

faith, to divine love. But his stages were applicable to history and often translated into millennial hopes for the imminent arrival of the third and best age.
Accordingly, a semi-clandestine Joachimite prophetic tradition outlasted him
by some centuries. It may have influenced Dante, for example, into expecting
an imminent spiritual turning point. And elements of this approach still
survive without specific attribution. For instance, the New Age zodiacal
history that was popular among hippies in the 1970s contains quasi-
Joachimite stages, as the Age of Aries (the Father), is followed by the Age of
Pisces (Christ the Son, the 'fisher of men'); and, impendingly, by the new Age
of Aquarius (the Age of Love).[29]

Much more terrestrial but equally emphatic is a second triadic system, as
propounded by Giambattista Vico in early eighteenth-century Naples.[30] He
borrowed the traditional imagery of historical 'ages' but yoked them into a
dynamic model. Each great era of history, he believed, represented a significant organising principle, which expresses a stage in human development.
Initially, there was an ancient Age of the Gods. Life was simple, if sometimes
violent, and people were ruled over by kings. Then followed the Age of
Heroes, when a feudal aristocracy prevailed by might, while, lastly, there
prevails the Age of Men, in which people develop reason and laws but also risk
becoming slothful and over-civilised.[31] This model was underpinned, for Vico,
by divine providence but was detached from a Christian commentary. It was
intended indeed as a global scenario, applicable to all societies. Furthermore,
Vico warned that the Age of Men will not automatically last for ever, if people
lose too much of their primitive simplicity. In that case, the sequence will
revert to its origins and recommence, making a cyclical or slowly spiralling
history.

A third triadic model is secular in its detail, like that of Vico, but much
more resolutely optimistic. It comes from Auguste Comte, whose dictum that
'everything is relative' has already been noted as declaring his belief in
change, not stasis. He saw three historical stages, on the basis of his belief in
a scientific 'Law of the Three Periods'.[32] 'All thoughtful persons can verify for
themselves its operation . . .' he assured his readers. 'We can test it, as we have
tested other laws, by observation, experiment, and comparison.' In fact,
global history cannot be rerun and re-verified. Nonetheless, Comte built
confidently upon what he defined as a progressive law generating the growth
of human knowledge. A primitive Age of Theology came first, with its ruling
ideas based upon religion, followed by a more settled Age of Metaphysics,
when ideas were drawn from abstract theories. The third stage was his own
era. He named it the Age of Science or (in his preferred terminology)
'Positivism', based upon industrialism and the framing of knowledge into
verifiable general laws.

Comparing their histories, all three of these tripartite models begin with eras of religion: Joachim's Age of the Father, Vico's Age of the Gods, Comte's Age of Theology. But the trajectories are variable. For Joachim, the end is other-worldly, the Age of the Spirit, while for Vico and Comte the destination is terrestrial: the Age of Men, the Age of Science. The implications are variable too. Both Joachim and Comte (who was acquainted with Joachimite prophecies) view the outcome optimistically, but Vico was less certain. Triadic models thus fit into millenarian, cyclical and linear histories, while all invoking a resonant number in their support. Comte, in addition, claimed the authority of science for his 'rule of three'.

Beyond this number, however, things generally become more complicated. Five-stage histories, for example, are relatively uncommon, although they can be found. After all, this number has considerable significance too. There are five senses; and, in traditional Chinese cosmology, there are five elements (water, fire, wood, metal, soil). Pluralist models based upon larger numbers embrace greater diversity. They still, however, sustain a clear narrative, which is based upon an expected sequence of numbered items. Indeed, any readers who felt a slight jolt when the reference at the start of this paragraph jumped from three to five without mentioning four have paid tribute to the weight of expectation that is attached to regular sequencing.

Different examples indicate the narrative clarity plus additional complexity of fivefold models. One mid nineteenth-century study applied this number to European intellectual life, declaring that its history progressed from primitive Credulity, through successive stages of Inquiry, Faith and Reason, before ending, glumly, with Decrepitude.[33] This was intended to parallel the human life cycle: from infancy, childhood, youth and maturity, on to ultimate senescence. But numbering the 'Ages of Man' is a selective exercise. Shakespeare after all found seven, echoing the same rotation but adding birth and death to the five stages that have just been cited. It was a popular motif of a lifetime in identifiable phases, as depicted in the traditional woodcut shown in illustration 20.

Or the model may be not organic stages of growth but epochs of economic transformation. The American historian Walt Rostow detected five stages within such a process. His sequence covers: (1) traditional society; (2) the preconditions of growth; (3) take-off; (4) the 'drive to maturity'; and ends with (5) the contemporary age of mass consumption. Rostow subtitled his study *A Non-Communist Manifesto*[34] to stress his disagreement with the Marxist economic stages, which he thought too rigid. Yet Rostow's model has been criticised in turn. It assumes that the 'take-off' is short and steep, like that of an aeroplane, while trajectories of economic change are much more variegated. Furthermore, Rostow's very long first era of traditionalism compresses

20 A Christian version of *The Wheel of Life* (1460) applies stage-theories to the human life cycle, from the cradle (*lower left*) to the grave (*lower right*).

together many different experiences, unconvincingly, from the Stone Age to the preconditions of growth and the first steam engine in 1769.[35]

Thus even the greater flexibility offered by multi-stage models has not saved them from criticism. Moreover, as the complexities expand, so the memorability of specific schemas declines. Nonetheless, six has had a resounding cosmological affirmation, with *Just Six Numbers: The Deep Forces that Shape the Universe*.[36] This details many of the basic 'constants' that are detected within the physical cosmos.

And seven has some historical advocates too.[37] This latter number has particular potency in biblical numerology. As has been mentioned already, the original creation of the world in seven days was taken as prophetic of a world history of seven thousand years, on the grounds that 'one day is with the Lord as a thousand years'.[38] Much serious effort was accordingly devoted to calculating the correct dates, including by eminent theologians like St Augustine, because the sixth millennium would end by ushering in the final millennial rule of Christ and his saints. However, no sevenfold history managed to ignite the same popular interest that was attached to the Joachimite triadic stages, which were easier to grasp and had greater prophetic urgency.

Only one other low digit has really challenged the power of twofold or threefold models, and that is the number four. Harmony, balance, felicity, plenitude are among its attributes.[39] It evokes the four seasons, the four points of the compass; for Christians, the four gospels and the four arms of the Cross; in Galenic medicine, the four humours; for Buddhists, the 'four noble truths'; and in Hindu teachings, the four *vedas* (sacred books) and the four *yugas* (great ages of the world). Mathematically, this number sums all its lower primes in every combination whether one plus three or two plus two or two times two. With such ballast, it stands robustly 'four square'. It is closed rather than open, finite rather than limitless. Indeed, in some cultural traditions – for example, Japanese – four signifies not merely completion but finality and death. Histories so represented thus tend towards achievement or, alternatively, to closure.

Specific calculations were prompted by prophetic references in the Old Testament to the (unidentified) 'four empires' or four great 'monarchies'. Jewish and Christian scholars did their best to match these with recorded epochs. One *Key of History*, published in 1558, decided that they were the four successive empires of Babylon, Persia, Greece and Rome.[40] For Protestants with a particular reading of the Bible, the question was crucial, as providing a guide to the timing of Christ's second coming. This would inaugurate his kingly rule over the fifth and final monarchy, according to the sect known specifically as the 'fifth monarchists'. But the due date was never agreed and, with time, interest in the fourfold imperial model waned. Even so, Christian histories were slow to shed all references to these details. For example, a Victorian children's history of 1857, which provided charts of world events from Adam and Eve to the recent Crimean War, included precise dates for the four 'universal monarchies', which were quietly and no longer prophetically sited between the fall of Babylon and the birth of Christ.[41]

Equipoise and harmony, meanwhile, predominate within two secular versions of quadriform history.[42] The radical Henri Saint-Simon in the early nineteenth century identified four stages. For him, they were formed of two sets of twinned eras, with 'ancient' history stretching from the origins of humanity to Moses, and then on to Socrates; while 'modern' history ran from Socrates to Muhammad, and then to Saint-Simon's own time. This was bold in its harmonious multiculturalism. It provides a reminder, too, that, in this era, irenic scholars like the British orientalist Sir William Jones were trying hard to reconcile the Biblical chronologies with those of other cultures – in his case, awkwardly cramming the great Hindu *Yuga* into the years since 4004 BCE, following the creation of the world as dated by the authority of the Protestant Archbishop Ussher.[43]

Ignoring such constraints, however, Saint-Simon's fellow radical Charles Fourier took even-numbered prophecy to new heights. His *Theory of the Four Movements* (1808) gave all animal and vegetable life an anticipated timespan of eighty thousand years, entirely bypassing traditional biblical scholarship. In history's first two epochs, humanity will 'ascend' from chaos to the 'apogee of happiness' – for Fourier, this was imminently due – after which two further epochs mark a 'descent' from harmony to death. Furthermore, each of the four main stages has eight sub-periods. So Fourier imagined an intricate world history in concord with thirty-two mini-eras.

Four can, however, acquire a less even-handed momentum, if it is reinterpreted as three past stages plus one in anticipation. So in *The Fourth Great Awakening*, the American economic historian Bob Fogel predicts for the twenty-first century the coming of a new egalitarian society. That will follow, he believes, from three past eras, now completed, of 'techno-physio evolution'. They have set the stage for a spiritual and communal awakening.[44] Another quadriform prediction can be seen in the futurologist Bruce Mazlish's claims for an imminent *Fourth Discontinuity*. This is based initially upon a dictum from Sigmund Freud, to the effect that the human ego has already had three great shocks: the first being when Copernicus 'dethroned' the earth from the centre of the solar system; the second being when Darwin 'dethroned' *Homo sapiens* from being above 'brute' animals; and the third being when Freud 'dethroned' human reason by revealing the role of the unconscious (Freud here paying himself a generous compliment). After these intellectual jolts, Mazlish foretells a fourth great blow to our pride. This will come from superintelligent computerised robots, with which mechanical beings humans will 'co-evolve', so finally 'dethroning' human brainpower.[45] It is a fair warning. On the other hand, it can be argued that our confidence has not so far dwindled with the aid of powerful tools but rather grown – even to overconfidence.

Marked alike by ingenuity and variety, all these compressions of long-term history into compact numbered stages do their best to make sense of complexity. So much effort has not, however, produced consensus, or any sign of one.

Marxist Stages

One central difficulty within many stage theories is the problem of explaining why, when and how an established system, that underpins not just a passing generation but an entire epoch of many generations, should mutate into another. If there are in-built tendencies for change, then why do great transformations not happen more frequently? The most common answer is to make reference to 'organic' growth or decay. Yet that asserts little more than the inevitability of change. It does not explain when and how great transformations in history actually happen – or, alternatively, do not happen, since great upheavals do not occur every day.

Marx and Engels were well aware of this question, since, when they were formulating their ideas of revolutionary transformation, stadial-histories were very much 'in the air'. To explain the linkages between past and present was an urgent task, as Fichte had announced: 'The philosopher, in order to be able rightly to characterise any individual Age, and, if he will, his own, must first have understood *a priori*, and thoroughly penetrated into the signification of Universal Time, and all its possible Epochs.' In Fichte's own view, human history was engaged in a progressive march from crude Instinct towards a divinely sanctified life of Reason. And he envisaged five stages on the epic journey, with his own era at the fulcrum, representing stage three 'precisely in the middle of Universal Time'.[46]

But Fichte's model still did not explain why such changes should happen. Nor did the historical lectures of Hegel, grand in their sweep as they were, provide that clue. Having inserted the dialectic and contradiction into the grand narrative, it was still unclear as to why changes occurred at specific times. Hegel thus added also his own reference to organic growth: a tree produces first buds, then blossom and then fruit. So the march of ideas would grow in dialectical stages, which move around the globe, as summarised in his pithy triad: 'The East knew and to the present day knows only that *One* is Free; the Greek and Roman world, that *Some* are free; the German World [Hegel's term for Christian Europe] knows that *All* are free.'[47] But buds, blossom and fruit are not really dialectical 'opposites'; and, moreover, communities living through history are more like long-enduring forests with compound long-term destinies than they are like single trees which blossom in sequence and then, eventually, die.

Keenly aware of the importance of economic or 'material' factors, Marx and Engels looked instead to economic history. In Scotland, the social philosopher Adam Ferguson had already specified three stages of change, as humanity progresses from a state of 'rudeness' to a higher stage of 'polished and commercial' life. Firstly, economies are based upon hunting and fishing. Then comes either herding, in the case of nomadic societies, or settled agriculture, in farming regions. And, eventually, there is a flowering of trade, with its concomitant social polish. Another variant came from Adam Smith, the analyst of the 'hidden hand' of economic exchange. He turned Ferguson's three epochs into four by counting shepherding as a separate stage between hunting and farming.[48]

Shedding the harmony that underpinned these particular stadial models, Marx and Engels then fused the changing material 'infrastructure' with the dialectical friction of class conflict, to produce a theory of history-as-revolution, as has already been noted. And their model of change became the most influential and controversial of all stage theories.

Ultimately, the problems within Marxism have outweighed its merits. It has been tested by history to virtual destruction. Yet it is worth stressing its initial scope and passion, which won it so much support. As a world view, it is 'omnipotent because it is true', declared Lenin.[49] By comparison with the elaborated Marxist ideas about economic and social history, most of the other stage theories, discussed above, appear relatively thin and perfunctory in their historical detail.

Numbers formed part, but only part, of the Marxist world view. There are repeated but not exclusive references to 'threes'. Marx and Engels did not count the stages rigidly. Each 'mode' or system of economic production would eventually yield to an alternative, they explained. Just as the era of aristocratic 'feudalism' (based upon serf labour) had been revolutionised into bourgeois 'capitalism' (based upon waged labour), so the newly arrived capitalist era, which they were already zealous to overthrow, would also be revolutionised into a new system of proletarian 'communism' (based upon collective labour).

This schema contained an implicit 'three' and it certainly conveyed much of the fervour of secularised Joachimite prophecy. Change was dynamic and unstoppable. Marx and Engels summarised not only the past impact of commercialisation but also the future impact of industrialisation. Hence their triad of feudalism/capitalism/communism had, in the view of all committed Marxists, the authority of history behind it. It was not choice but destiny. Capitalism's fall and communism's triumph were therefore, the *Manifesto* specified, 'equally inevitable'.[50]

Moreover, there was another dynamic triad that was being produced by economic change. When reviewing the social structure of capitalist society specifically, Marx identified a three-tier hierarchy of landowners (aristocracy), capitalists (bourgeoisie) and workers (proletariat). Each group represented one of the economy's key productive forces (land, capital and labour, respectively). That generated three contending social forces within the middle stage of history's threefold expansion, adding more triadic momentum to the revolutionary process.

By dissecting 'capitalist' society in this way, Marx and Engels allowed no overlapping between what were defined as the separate sectoral interests of the rival classes, although in reality many landowners invested in businesses, just as successful businessmen also purchased land, while numerous professional men flourished on the strength of their intellectual capital, without being either bosses or landowners. Nonetheless, the underlying social process was intrinsically conflictual, according to Marx and Engels. Already, they were sure that the bourgeoisie had ruthlessly overthrown the old feudal lords. So one of the three contending classes was on the ropes. That heightened Marx's belief that further changes were near. 'Society as a whole is more and more splitting up into two great hostile camps, into two great classes directly facing each other', the *Manifesto* specified.[51] The decks were clearing for a final crisis, as the three were already counting down to two, on the way to proletarian unity.

Marxist theory became in due course more complex, as it was further developed by Marx and Engels and, later, by a formidable band of Marxist scholars. Nonetheless, as a world view, it always retained the concept of contrasting stages, each one inaugurated by a revolutionary reformulation that occurs once the contradictions of the previous stage have become too great to be contained any longer.

Specifically, however, Marx did allow himself to become more flexible about the number of 'modes of production'. When looking back, with Engels, at the origins of society, he endorsed a stage of 'primitive communism', which was taken to apply to early tribal societies.[52] Then there followed an 'ancient' system of production, based upon slave-ownership, which accommodated the history of classical Greece and Rome. And, on occasion, Marx referred to a separate 'Asiatic' mode of despotic communalism, which was required to incorporate the economies of the East, which to western eyes appeared unaccountably static.

Still, however, the emotional and political thrust of Marxism remained triadic. It saw history as changing from an old, outmoded stage to a new but unstable alternative, and then to a third, much better and qualitatively different solution. Marxists could therefore attack the state of affairs in phase two, without being trapped into calling for a return to phase one. Moreover, the formula was adaptable to many different conditions around the globe, given that economic exploitation was not hard to find, and that the prospect of a better alternative was attractive.

Devoted followers believed that Marx had inaugurated a new era in historical studies. It provides 'the only certain, scientific solution', commented one

Soviet philosopher,[53] who was certain that the materialist 'laws' of Marxism were the equivalent of the Newtonian laws of gravity in physics. The different stages seemed to provide an ordered model of transformation over time. 'History has, in fact, authoritatively certified the truth of scientific communism', as another Marxist author declared, serenely, in 1980.[54] It was especially the materialist base that was taken as the determinant, 'in the last instance', of all political, intellectual and cultural 'superstructures',[55] thus enabling all other aspects of life to be 'located' by reference to their economic context.

Within the Marxist stages, 'revolution' and macro-change are centrally represented; and even micro-changes can be accommodated into the model as generating the 'contradictions' that will eventually explode into revolution. However, the forces of tradition and persistence are completely discounted. In this regard, Marxism is the obverse of theories that see only continuity: rejecting entirely a 'timeless' biology that sees human nature as unchanging and socio-cultural 'nurture' as irrelevant, the Marxist emphasis falls instead upon a 'transformable' environment and a 'malleable' nurture, which is contrasted with a supposedly blank 'nature' that can be changed in response to society's communal will.

Intellectually, this opened a potential pathway to political and intellectual dogma. Organisationally, Lenin made this possible by institutionalising the role of the communist party as *ipso facto* the representative of the proletarian masses. And, in their name, various dictatorial rulers trod this route. The problems were particularly starkly revealed when communist beliefs in transformationism were crudely applied to the sciences, as in the Stalin-approved theories of Pavlovian psychology and of Lysenkoist genetics – initially praised as a new 'Soviet Darwinism'. Yet these supposedly superior and 'proletarian' alternatives to 'bourgeois' teachings were no more than state-supported pseudo-sciences, as their critics within Marxism bravely insisted.[56]

Indeed, philosophically and historically, an absolute dichotomy between a 'real' (material) world and an 'ideal' one of ideas and consciousness has proved a false one. Marx derived this assumption from Hegel. He had indeed argued that the Ideal led the Material. But Marx believed that he had found Hegel's formulation 'standing on its head' and had righted it, 'to discover the rational kernel within the mystical shell'.[57] That remedial action placed the Material over the Ideal, hence justifying the Marxist mantra: 'It is not the consciousness of men that determines their being, but, on the contrary, their social being that determines their consciousness.' Yet once the dichotomy between the Material/ Ideal is abandoned, there is no one single 'determining' force. Consciousness helps to create social being, as much as vice versa. Consequently, as the Marxists discovered, economic factors no longer delineate a few, big, homogeneous stages – and the zigzagging revolutionary dialectic of history, as defined by Marx and potentially organised by Lenin and the communist party leadership, loses its triumphal clarity.

Critiquing Marxist Stages

Going back to earliest times, then, it is highly doubtful whether the first tribal societies were as egalitarian and cooperative as the theory of 'primitive communism' declared them to be. There were many different forms of social organisation, from kingship to group communities. Nor was there one static 'mode of production' throughout the long span of 'prehistory' but many differing adaptations to different circumstances.

Then the 'ancient' economic system, supposedly based upon slave-owning, revealed its own problems. Not only did classical Greece and Rome, which between them constituted the Marxist exemplars for this stage in history, have examples of free labour within their bounds, but so, confusingly, did some allegedly capitalist economies employ many unfree workers. The most notorious example of this in Marx's day was the institution of slavery in the 'capitalist' USA, which prompted Marx to dismiss the obstinate southern plantation-owners as 'historical anomalies'.[58] And they did, of course, obligingly for Marxist theory, lose the American Civil War that followed in the mid nineteenth century. Nonetheless, the continuing persistence of slavery or semi-slavery in supposedly free labour markets both then and today indicates that the institution is hard to eradicate,[59] with complex roots in historically generated ethnic, gender and age-related power imbalances as well as in labour-market conditions.

Another set of problems simultaneously beset the despotic 'Asiatic' mode. It was not satisfactory to group great swathes of 'oriental' history into one static category. Moreover, it was not clear how the Asiatic mode was supposed to fit into the overall sequence of change.[60] Did it precede capitalism, or could a society jump directly from 'oriental despotism' into communism? No one was sure. 'Asiaticism' did at least encourage a search for alternatives to Eurocentric theories of history but the concept raised more problems than it solved. Some tried to 'save the phenomenon' by defining the Asiatic economy in the case of China as one in which landlords flourished by controlling neither labour nor capital, but instead the power of the bureaucratised state, which inserted another, different stage of post-feudal bureaucracy. Yet political activists, like the young Mao Zedong, did not worry about such refinements. For him, the old Chinese empire was certainly not timelessly 'Asiatic' but, in classic Marxist terms, nothing but a dying 'feudal landlord state' – that was thus ripe for overthrow by the forces of history.[61]

Furthermore, if there was a separate trajectory for the Orient, then other world-regions might expect variation too. This sort of revisionist heresy was accordingly excluded from the 1938 Soviet handbook to *Dialectical and Historical Materialism*, published in the name of Joseph Stalin and promulgated with his full authority. According to this summary, there were five stages to be expected universally, running from: tribalism – to slave-ownership ('ancient') – to feudalism – to capitalism – and, finally, to socialism, as the seamless prelude of communism.[62]

Orthodoxy, however, was hard to sustain as historical research continually complicated the picture. There was no agreement as to when Europe's own transition from 'ancient' to 'feudal' mode occurred. After all, the Roman Empire's prolonged decline in the fifth century CE was puzzlingly divided by hundreds of years from the advent of feudal tenures (noble fiefdoms under royal authority) in the tenth or eleventh centuries CE.[63] Moreover, the entire concept of 'feudalism' as an epoch in history is disputed.[64] And other places have different timetables. The Roman Empire did not fall in Byzantium until the mid fifteenth century, thus giving eastern Europe a quite different experience. And what about elsewhere? Was there a stage (say) of Japanese 'feudalism' and, if so, how far did it differ from the European version? Scholars disagree in their answers.[65]

Over time, the concept faltered and hybridised. There are variants, according to recent book titles, such as *Bastard Feudalism, Belated Feudalism, Client Feudalism, Developed Feudalism, New* or *Neo-Feudalism*, and even *Modern Feudalism* – the latter detected in twentieth-century Egypt.[66] The term, however, retains a polemical value in opposition to any form of oppressive landlordism. Hence Gustave Flaubert's only half-joking advice in the later nineteenth century still holds good: 'FEUDALISM. No need to have one single precise notion about it: *thunder against.*'[67]

Problems are typically highlighted when key moments of transformation from one stage to another need to be dated. Thus, just as there is uncertainty about the shift from 'medievalism' to 'modernity' (as discussed in the previous chapter), so there are notable disputes among Marxist historians about any parallel transition from (medieval) 'feudalism' to (modern) 'capitalism'.[68] Estimates range variously from the fifteenth to the nineteenth centuries, including or not including, according to choice, England's 'bourgeois' or not-so-bourgeois mid seventeenth-century revolution en route.

Above all, just as 'modernity' has become overstretched, so too has 'capitalism'. At one point, some Marxists opted for subdividing this stage. Its first form became 'merchant' or 'commercial capitalism' with the expansion of trade in sixteenth-century Europe (matched by 'mercantilist' economic policies – another controversial concept), while its second form was 'industrial capitalism', beginning with the classic steam-powered Industrial Revolution of the later eighteenth century. But subdividing Marx's unitary stages was heresy to the orthodox. Backed by Stalin, official Marxism rejected this approach.[69]

Meanwhile, an alternative precursor stage for economic transformation has been proposed. Before factory-based urban/industrialism in the eighteenth century, there was a seventeenth-century phase of proto-industrialisation based upon domestic industries in the countryside. Or was there? This alternative has also failed to find favour, either within or outside Marxism, because, while true of some industries, ruralisation was far from the experience of all.[70] In effect, economic change does not proceed so neatly across the board; and economic historians are also unable to agree. No doubt for this reason, economists tend to scorn the 'fuzzy messages of history', though actually the historical range of divergencies helps to explain the present-day failures of economic nostrums when one policy is applied willy-nilly in many different socio-cultural contexts.

Returning to Marx, his own core concept of 'capitalism' simply contained too much forced tidiness to work as a definition for one unitary stage stretching over many centuries. For him, there was one core economic process with but one matched set of labour relationships. That was an unfettered and commercialised system, in which privately owned capital employs a property-less workforce. For its economic expression, he referred his readers to industrialising Britain – but for its political expression (here weakening the symmetry of the model) to revolutionary France in 1789. Moreover, Marx was confident that capitalism would not last long, as it was battered by recurrent slumps and was heading for inevitable crisis. The growing poverty of the masses, alongside the flaunted wealth of the rich, would transmute, he believed, into the anger that would launch a revolution. These were not absurd expectations, given the marked turbulence of the nineteenth-century growth economies. However, in the longer run, things developed otherwise.

Not only do industrial economies continue to update their technologies and to enrich the majority (though far from the totality) of their populations – and to an extent learn to tame the extreme cycles of slumps and booms – but the systems of production and distribution have not remained exclusively in the hands of a few capitalists. Instead, many different versions of 'mixed' economies have emerged, with differing combinations of part-private and part-public (state or trust) ownership. Furthermore, with the international transfer of capital, skilled labour and technological know-how, 'backward' societies in the right circumstances can leapfrog some of the problems and processes of industrial development by borrowing from 'advanced' ones.[71] There are therefore plural pathways which lead to different forms of economic transformation.

Accordingly very many variants of 'capitalism' have been identified by different experts during the twentieth century. These range from admiring to hyper-critical. In the latter category, there are accusations of (for example) *Bandit Capitalism, Casino Capitalism, Crony Capitalism, Monopoly Capitalism* or *Racial Capitalism,* as seen in recent book titles. But there are favourable studies too. Hence (taking again only a few examples from many) there are discussions of *Caring Capitalism, Democratic Capitalism, Eco-Capitalism, Hip Capitalism* and/or *Welfare Capitalism.*

Lenin in fact began to multiply the complexities. His *Imperialism: The Highest Stage of Capitalism* (1916) argued that the exploitation of the workers by European capitalism had already extended to become a global process.[72] As a result, the revolutionary struggle had to spread worldwide to match. This particular refinement allowed the Marxist message to spread beyond the commercially and industrially transforming economies to which Marx had at first applied it. As a significant amendment to the canon, it was popularised by Stalin, who enshrined it within the orthodoxy.[73] Yet not all industrialising economies do have an 'imperialist' phase, in terms of formal rule over subject peoples. And even in terms of 'indirect' rule, the relationships of industrially successful powers with poorer economies are far from identical and far from equally or simply exploitative.

Moreover, the twists and turns of international politics also sprang their own paradoxical results. When Stalin later found himself at war with 'totalitarian capitalism' in the form of Nazi Germany, he allied Soviet communism with 'imperialist' Britain and the 'capitalist' USA in order to save Russia's proletarian revolution. In that, he succeeded, at least for a time. But, while one result of the Second World War was to encourage the European powers to decolonise, another was to confer upon Soviet Russia a de facto unofficial 'empire' in eastern Europe that lasted for almost fifty years. Unexpected in theory, it made sense politically, albeit not for its victims. However, Stalin did not present this regional hegemony as a 'higher stage' of communism.

Further surprises were also to follow. In 1989–91, at the end of the Cold War between Soviet Russia and the USA, the 'wrong' stage of history, in terms of Marxist predictions, collapsed. Communism was rejected in eastern Europe by the very people in whose name the proletarian revolution was being run. And the system then imploded in the Soviet Union, its official heartland, too. The red flag was defeated, not primarily from outside, but following unstoppable discontent within and ultimate economic failure, based upon attempted mass transformationism without reference to well-regulated markets (the adjective is important) as a flexible and responsive mechanism for calibrating opportunities against costs.

Insofar as communism is surviving elsewhere, it is doing so by translation into distinctly mixed forms, which include elements of commercialism officially denounced as 'capitalist' and cultural referents traditionally rejected as 'bourgeois'. Thus, when discussing contemporary China, for example, analysts variously identify a 'market communism' or a 'neo-Confucian-communism'.[74] 'True' Marxists may also argue that so far nothing has been tried but a rigid 'state socialism' or, worse, a hybrid denounced in one inventive phrase as 'Stalino-feudalism'. If that analysis is accepted, then an egalitarian communism still remains a possible future destiny of history. But not now via the old 'inevitable' Marxist stages.

Analysts in the post mode are already dissecting *Post-Communism*. And there are problems with 'capitalism' too. Officially victorious, it is no longer presented as one single stage of economic history with one set of labour relationships within it.

Instead, 'capitalism' as a significant terminology chiefly survives in rhetorical usages. Academically, it is more generally used as a headline than a detailed category, meaning something like international commerce and/or factory industrialism and/or workers' oppression (but rarely, now as a stage in history). For right-wing polemicists, 'capitalism' indicates the merits of globalisation and unfettered labour markets (sometimes plus political support for the USA), even though the economies and social politics of the 'capitalist' world are now very variegated.

On the left, the concept undeniably retains its hostile reference to 'fat cat' industrial bosses. There has also been a serious attempt at redefining its economic evolution. Over time, it has mutated into *Late Capitalism* – or so it was suggested by the Trotskyist/Marxist economist Ernest Mandel in 1972, designating it as 'late' specifically because he believed that the final meltdown was nigh.[75] And in that conclusion, his analysis, though insightful about tensions within global commercialisation, was proved wrong. Nonetheless, Mandel's endgame-phraseology suggested an intriguing alignment with the parallel 'end-of-modernity' debates, prompting the American cultural theorist Fredric Jameson in 1984 to identify *The Cultural Logic of Late Capitalism* as *Postmodernism*.[76] However, this yoking of two unstable concepts has not really saved either. So, just as some now analyse 'post-postmodernism', others write of *Post-Capitalism*, while many others simply ignore both terms.

Gradually, over time, historical concepts become overstretched and, as that happens, lose meaning. And 'capitalism'/'communism' as stages in history, along with 'modernity', and all their hybrid variants, have now lost their clarity as ways of shaping history. To reiterate, therefore: the processes that these words attempt to capture certainly need examination – but the analysis cannot be done well if the historical labels acquire afterlives of their own which bear decreasingly adequate reference to the phenomena under discussion.

Problematic Stages

Attractive elements of stadial theories are their claims to explain the sweep of change across the centuries, and the leading quality of key periods within that. 'Systems elaborate things; they interpret the world,' commented Theodor Adorno, 'while the others really keep protesting only that it can't be done.'[77] This was a wry tribute, especially coming from a highly unorthodox Marxist-influenced philosopher whose own *Negative Dialectics* simultaneously argued that 'the whole is the false'. His approach thus tried to turn Hegel inside out, rather than upside down, and to leave everything in doubt. For that reason, Adorno's critical method offered no alternative historical pattern, other than a stern warning against the risks of 'totalising' visions from others – which did ultimately imply an unsatisfactory conclusion of essential randomness.

Broad-based stadial theories, meanwhile, do also have the potential for being adapted and shared between different intellectual traditions. An arresting example can be seen in an attempt, in the 1960s, to find a convergence between Marxism and Islamicism. Thus the influential Iranian religious thinker Alī Sharī'atī saw history as a process of faith and fight. The Marxist stages were, for him, too much focused upon systems of economic production. Instead, religious struggle takes the dynamic role of class struggle. And the outcome will be a new spiritualised communalism, which will end the age-old private ownership of the means of production – but not in the way that Marx foresaw.[78] This cross-cultural synthesis again attracted considerable attention for a while, but latterly has been eclipsed by alternative Islamic models of change.

All these stage histories meanwhile remain very revealing about the pre-occupations of those who frame them. The factors that are assumed to drive their transformations, however, often remain too culture-bound to apply globally. That criticism was noted by Saint-Simon, who sniffed that: 'Hitherto, *history* has been badly divided.'[79] His own culturally pluralist response was to include Moses, Socrates and Muhammad, as has already been noted. But others could as plausibly seek the inclusion of (say) Zoroaster, Confucius and Buddha, making the outcome yet more diverse but much less easy to synthesise, especially when all the other spiritual teachers of Eurasia, the Americas, Africa and Australasia are included too.

Collectively, the general problem is that of fitting sometimes different and sometimes similar experiences across all world cultures within one set of stages in linear sequence. Too many aspects of history refuse such corralling. Indeed, while stage theories do well at highlighting fundamental transformations, they consistently underplay both deep continuities and the micro-changes that bridge turning points.

Interestingly, many of these criticisms were made by the controversial historians' critic Oswald Spengler when writing his own panoramic *Decline of the West* in 1922. He denounced the Eurocentrism of his colleagues, advocating plural trackways instead (as discussed in the next chapter). Spengler also dismissed the westernised triad of ancient/medieval/modern. He did not doubt that these stages were already 'meaningless'. And he added: 'It is a quite indefensible method . . . to begin by giving rein to one's own religious, political or social convictions and endowing the sacrosanct three-phase system with tendencies that will bring it exactly to one's own standpoint.'[80] It was a justifiably sharp critique. Spengler, however, was tempted to offer his own prediction instead. He foresaw a struggle between 'money' (capitalism) and 'blood' (a racialised nationalism), with the defeat of 'money' leading to a new Caesarism or populist dictatorship. This was prescient about the rise of Hitler's Third Reich (another three) in Germany and, for a while, in fascist Europe, but was entirely wrong about its ultimate victory. As Spengler had himself pointed out, a few numbered historical stages are just too restrictive to encapsulate the whole of global history, let alone to predict its future as well.

Shaping History – Time Pieces

All societies have ways of locating themselves in time and history. That is far from saying that the popular recall of the past is perfect. On the contrary, many are the complaints that people today – led especially, it seems, by the young – are constituting a heedless 'Now Generation' that knows nothing of olden times. 'Speak so much of memory because there is so little of it left,' the French historian Pierre Nora exclaimed dramatically in 1989. And he is not alone in expressing such anxieties.

Upon closer examination, however, it can be seen that such fears are not only wrong but profoundly wrong. People may not remember the things that historians might believe that everyone ought to remember. But functioning individuals readily recall events and episodes relating to their own lives, and those of their close associates and of all those wider groups whose fortunes matter to them. Any association that attracts strong emotion, whether organised around a live religion (say) or a dedicated football club (to take a different example) is likely to generate strong memories. In addition, people generally have some sense of the inter-connectedness of the present to a much longer past, whether influenced by cultural traditions that see time as a line or time as a cycle or some other pattern. Things that came 'before', though hazy in detail, are accessible in myths and organised histories. So the present is tethered into a much longer span of time – and is framed within space/geography too. Furthermore, people know that they do not need to recollect everything individually, as information and beliefs are habitually shared and exchanged with others to create complex maps of 'social' memory.[1]

The capacity of healthy humans to habituate themselves within time stems intimately from our biological being. All mammals, including ourselves, have an 'internal clock' which is coordinated by a small sensory organ attached to the brain, known as the pineal gland or, more poetically, as the inner 'third eye'. It enables us to process environmental stimuli so that our biorhythms are coordinated in response to daily and seasonal changes in light and darkness. The 'interiority' of this instinctive experience makes the temporal process seem at once familiar and yet hard to express in words. Added to that, the (relatively) large human brain makes us unusual among mammals in our biologically adapted capacity not only to store consciously large quantities of information from beyond the immediate moment but also to analyse such information regularly and systematically. Armed with such resources, we respond both instinctively and actively to time, not only synchronically but also diachronically.

How different the normal consciousness of a healthy human is from amnesia is revealed by a statement from a medical patient who did lose chunks of his memory for some months, after a bruising accident. The anonymous man recorded in 1931 the disorientation that resulted:

> I had a feeling of puzzlement upon my mind, not unlike that which one may experience on waking from a deep sleep in a strange place. . . . The immediate past seemed to be a 'perfect and absolute blank', and . . . I found little comfort in the thought that I was so far normal as to be able to recognise such a blank as being extraordinary.

In this case, the memory loss was relatively mild, as the patient still recollected his learned skills of language and numeracy; and he was alert enough to realise that something was 'missing'. In the most severe cases, however, people who have no mental 'reach' beyond the very immediate moment cannot function unaided and indeed are found to have 'shed' elements of their former time-framed personality.

Because of the importance of both individual and 'social' memory, communities typically have many techniques for recording the past and for recalling information for discussion or action. And, living within the time–space continuum, people manage to log historical points of reference both by devising communicable accounts of the past that are time-ordered and/or by using the trigger of 'fixing' information by spatial orientation.

Historically, much the oldest means of shaping and recollecting significant past events is by visiting places that are 'memory-laden', so using the specificity of geography and the power of visual memory. This technique applied for millennia before the invention of calendars and clocks.

An example that is now well known is the 'Dream-Time' of the indigenous people of Australia. They traditionally see the land not as a separate and apparently empty space but as a living spiritual and physical environment, which binds everything together. Within this, their historic legends of the world's origins merge the past and present together. And these communal memories are tapped by regular journeys ('walkabouts') to visit the places that act as memory markers. It was a historical tragedy when this custom was entirely misunderstood as feckless 'wandering' by the European settlers who arrived in the nineteenth century to contend for the land. The outcome saw the displacement of the indigenous people not only from their accustomed territories but also from their history markers, generating among them and their descendants a cultural disorientation that has been hard to overcome.

In fact, it was once strongly believed by those living within clock- and calendar-based communities that those who live without these aids to time measurement are somehow 'timeless'. For example, the Nuer people of southern Sudan were famously so depicted in 1940 by the English anthropologist E. E. Evans-Pritchard. He based his assessment not only on their way of life but especially upon the gulf in terminologies. '[They] have no expression equivalent to "time" in our language, and they cannot, therefore, as we can, speak of time as though it were something actual, which passes, can be wasted, can be saved, and so forth.' Instead, the Nuer operated by reference to only relatively few and non-standardised units of temporality, entirely without a sense of precision.

Yet their 'loose' style of reckoning made sense within the context of a nomadic lifestyle. Hence later anthropological studies have come to stress how intricately people's attitudes are mediated by their own cultural traditions and their immediate socio-economic requirements.[2] The Nuer's sense of time was different from that of Evans-Pritchard, but it was not missing. The seasonal rhythms of the pastoral year – when to take the herds to the camps or when to plant crops – were well understood. Significant occurrences were also remembered at special holy places; and the Nuer had a complex repertoire of myths and legends to tell them about the past, as well as a lively prophetic tradition to forecast the future. By these means, people were orientated in both time and space. Moreover, many of these traditional accounts are still told and retold today, providing a cultural link between older and newer styles of recounting history, even amidst the brutal turmoil of regional civil wars within Sudan and the maelstrom of forced population displacements.

Using specific locations as memory-prompts certainly remains widespread across all cultures, both oral and literate. This is one notable sign of continuity through time. Either places on their own have symbolic significance; or their meanings are enhanced by the construction of monuments, shrines, memorials, obelisks, carvings, plaques, and other markers. Battlefields and disaster zones, where large numbers of people died, are particularly likely to be commemorated, but homage is paid to peaceful history too. So it is possible to find (rare) statues to comedians as well as (abundant) statues of warriors.

Not only places but simply the names of places, in extreme circumstances, evoke an entire history too. The first military use of nuclear weapons is recalled by 'Hiroshima', which was uranium-bombed on 6 August 1945. This word is known to many who have only a vague idea about the city's actual location on Japan's Honshu Island. (But Nagasaki, devastated by plutonium-bomb three days later, does not have the same name-symbolism.) Or in southern Poland, 'Auschwitz', the Germanic rendering of the town of Oświęcim, recalls the Nazi Holocaust against the European Jews and all others deemed to be 'blood' enemies of the Third Reich. Again, this place was not the only site of a concentration camp for state-organised mass murder. Its name has, however, become the grim shorthand for a global memory and warning alike.

Locating history in time, however, does not invariably require precise framing by dates and places. Traditionally, the sense of temporality, in pre-calendar communities, was loosely structured, and so were mythic accounts of the past. 'Once upon a time', 'many moons ago', 'time out of mind', 'when the world was young', 'in days of yore' are phrases that evoke distance and simultaneously enhance recognition by their formulaic quality. They introduce the array of myths, legends, sagas and traditional verses that convey allegorical information about the past and, often, moral messages about the present too. 'Where are the sultans, the kings? Now they are corpses! / Palaces with many queens' quarters, now ruins!' exclaimed an anonymous fragment of Swahili epic verse in eighteenth-century east Africa. These mournful lines, while unspecific about time and incident, impart due wariness about the fleetingness of worldly glory – with a reminder that all heroic quests contain hazards.

Myth-histories were in circulation long before the advent of literacy and they continued thereafter too. Indeed, many classic myths, now written down for popular consumption, are widely enjoyed to this day, for their poetry and imaginative power, in yet another mark of continuities in human modes of communication.

Nonetheless, a different style of history-writing also gradually emerged within literate and calendar-based societies. When the temporal process is measured precisely, an orderly framework is provided and events can be recorded and 'set' in time. The origin of the world can be given a precise date – as can predictions of its end. Divided into pieces, time appears more manageable; the shape of history more easily clarified; and human activities, both religious and secular, more readily coordinated. And, within measured calendrical systems, diachronic thought is undertaken more consciously and systematically, and so too is planning for the future.

Creating a calendar is in itself a form of mental ordering, as undertaken on the strength of the astronomical observations of countless unknown 'sky-watchers'. Their efforts translated the human capacity to 'read' time into a regular notation which was then shared across the generations, being revised and updated in the process. In some pre-literate societies, astronomical sightings were associated with special sites where crowds of people gathered. Thus places like Stonehenge – and the other 360-plus stone circles in Britain and northern France, dating back some four or five thousand years – probably began as grand ceremonial theatres for the observation of time. In this way, communal histories located in place were then heightened by verification along astronomical sight lines.

From the time of ancient Babylon in the first millennium BCE, the advent of formal calendars was associated with the parallel development of settled agriculture, established government and sufficient levels of elite literacy and numeracy. Once adopted, the impact of these devices quickly spread. They were used by rulers to organise regular systems of taxation and administration, as well as to specify ritual dates, and to coordinate economic life. Following the calendar thus meant following a system of power, as seen, for example, in traditional China where the Han emperor marked his inauguration in 221 BCE by banning all rivals to the imperial calendar, which was annually adjusted to keep pace with the seasons by imperial astronomers, working in the imperial observatory, under his supreme authority.

But giving order to time was never something that was just imposed from above. Entire community lifestyles became and remain organised around accepted calendars.[3] These become framers of consciousness, memories and daily routines. As a result, there is great resistance to radical revision to calendrical systems which, unless exceptionally disrupted by external events, characteristically retain great continuity over time and so enhance inter-generational cultural compatibilities. On the other hand, minor adaptations are tolerated, if with some grumbling. For example, the notorious riots that supposedly greeted a modest reform of the calendar in mid eighteenth-century England, did not actually happen. It was a later myth that angry crowds assembled crying 'Give us back our eleven days', when the dates in September 1752 were adjusted to match the more astronomically accurate Gregorian calendar of mainland Europe. However, it is interesting that the possibility of popular riots in such circumstances seemed entirely plausible, so that accounts of the riots written by later generations became accepted as historically genuine, until only recently when their mythic nature was revealed.

Without widespread preparation for change, it is much easier to announce calendrical innovations than it is to entrench them in daily life. That was duly discovered by the leaders of the French Revolution. In 1792 they introduced an ambitious new decimal calendar, with each day divided into ten hours (each with a hundred minutes) and each week extended to ten days. The renamed months (still pegged at twelve) were standardised at thirty days apiece, and the five left-over days were dedicated as public holidays. So, with a flourish, 22 September 1792 became Day 1 of Revolutionary Year 1. However, both the Catholic Church for theological reasons, and the French workforce for practical ones as well, resisted the abolition of the seventh day of rest and/or worship. Hence the new decimal system was already floundering when it was jettisoned by Napoleon Bonaparte as Emperor in 1805. The old duodecimal notation – derived ultimately from the time-measurement system of ancient Babylon – triumphed, as it triumphs still today. Interestingly, however, while the new system of time measurement was not a success, France's new system of spatial measurements did eventually gain acceptance, with decimal metres and kilometres being introduced gradually in 1790 and made compulsory in 1840.

There is thus a trade-off, in such intimate matters of time measurement, between what can potentially be done and what is accepted socially. Each innovation may face potential opposition or local grumbling, as for example when people complained at the 'cold' artificiality of mechanical clock-time, when it was first introduced. Throughout all this, great ingenuity has been expended on finding ways of tracking the passing hours and minutes, whether by use of running water, or shifting sands, or burning candles, or smouldering incense, or ringing bells, or by watching the shadows cast by sunbeams on sundials. And the uses of time, thus measured, have also been variegated and flexible. So some communities, who live in latitudes away from the equator, have traditionally allowed seasonal variations in the working 'hour', which was extended in the summer daylight but abbreviated in midwinter.

Clocks, as the products of calendrically aware societies, enhance the awareness of time measurement; and, with the greater precision of clock-construction, there have come ever greater possibilities for precise time management, with enhanced social synchronisation and coordination. Moreover, far from discouraging a sense of history, the sense of an unfolding temporality, which can be calibrated both in the long-run and in the instant, encourages the stabilising of history into this framework. Human memory systems normally remain pre-clock-and-calendar-referenced in that we do not usually remember things by reference to their dates, unless the dates are exceptional in some way. Nonetheless, people who live in societies with precisely structured and measured time know that there is an accepted and tested chronology into which events can be fitted, thus situating history within both a short- and long-term framework.

Many early mechanical clocks specifically demonstrated the sharedness of temporality by being put on public display. One sixteenth-century example can be viewed today within Strasbourg Cathedral. This magnificent clock not only shows the hours and minutes but sets them within a cosmic and spiritual frame by displaying also updated astronomical information and the procession of Catholic feast days. The temporal ordering of the world, made visible to all, is a sign of the value attached to such knowledge. And an array of public clocks around the world, sited wherever people gather together in numbers, continue today to chime the message of shared temporality.[4] One elegantly minimalist example (see illustration 21) can be found in the heart of contemporary Berlin. The clock's flickering panels invite the viewers to calculate the hours and minutes for them-selves, as the patterned lights constantly change in response to the steady electronic pulse of atomic time.

Technical difficulties in getting instruments to work with the required precision have historically meant that the early mechanical clocks, pioneered in Europe from the thirteenth century onwards, were clumsy and not very reliable. Eventually, however, technological improvements, made with much trial and error and tugged by buoyant consumer demand, led to the invention of miniaturised and accurate timepieces for personal use. So the spread of privately owned clocks began from the sixteenth century onwards, followed by privately owned watches from the eighteenth century onwards. All time-imbued humans can understand their message, so their ultimate market is universal. And the quest for ever-improved accuracy of timekeeping continues, down to today's ultra-precise atomic clocks and ubiquitous digital displays. 'No one knows what time is,' comments David Landes, the historian of chronometry: '. . . But we sure know how to measure it.'[5]

As timekeeping devices have become widely available a number of cultural and organisational adaptations have followed. Not only has the length of an hour become standardised, but so have duodecimal timekeeping systems the world over, completed with international agreements on designated global time zones in 1884. Lifestyles and work-styles in urban and commercial societies are accordingly organised around shared timetables. Punctuality becomes a social virtue; and 'wasting' the fleeting moments is deplored. Mentalities are not just time-imbued, but become much more intently 'time-conscious'.[6] And because the human consciousness still does not track temporal change precisely, there are ubiquitous reminders, both visually and in broadcast messages.

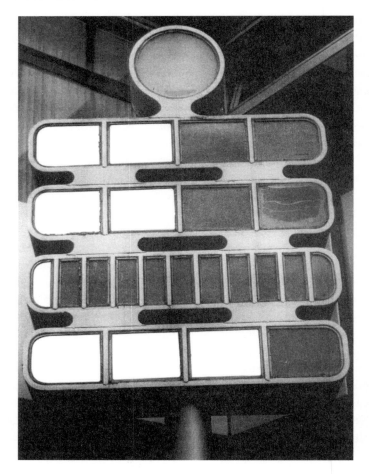

21 The twenty-four-hour clock 'Mengenlehre Uhr' next to Berlin's Europa Centre invites onlookers to calculate the time from an ever-changing pattern of coloured lights – in this case at the precise moment of 12.08.*

* The timer light at the top switches off/on every sixty seconds, with a new lighted panel being illuminated minute by minute. In the top row, each panel marks five hours; in the second row one hour; in the third row five minutes; and in the fourth row one minute.

Within societies that are so saturated with precise timekeeping, there is no lack of historical information set within this ordered framework. There are anniversaries and commemorations, both pleasant and melancholic. And there are huge industries of historical writing, archiving, museum-displaying, broadcasting, interpreting and debating. Indeed, the more precisely time is defined, the more accurately the past can be structured within the vast temporal panorama.

Nonetheless, as already mentioned, anxieties are still expressed about the dangers of a failure in social or collective memory. The insistent nowness of the here-and-now, influenced particularly by the battering pressures of instant communication, can seem overwhelming. Indeed, just as people living in non-clock-and-calendar societies were once thought of as 'timeless' and insufficiently aware of the passing moments, so now there are reverse worries that people in time-saturated societies may become too minute-by-minute time-harried and insufficiently aware of the long term.

Ultimately, however, the complex human responses to temporality will always find ways of adjusting timetables to human requirements, as well as vice versa. And temporal living will always remain based upon an intricate trade-off between an immediate sense of the present, that is infused and tempered by recollections of the past, and anticipations of the future. How all these attitudes are cultivated will remain matters of individual and communal negotiation, whether memories be 'stored' in time or by place. To flourish best, people need a good set of personal and communal 'markers', based on an understood history and geography (both of the global region where they live *and* of other contrasting regions), albeit with a continuing flexibility in the interpretative schema to allow for updating in the light of experience and study. This intrinsic timefulness of human living also explains why 'broken' historical memories are harmful to individuals and communities. By the same token, interactive projects to relocate and to recover what can be recovered are beneficial. Provided that the study of history is not perma-frozen into predetermined dogma, the process is one that always entails weighing, assessing, debating and concluding, to find the range of possibilities, probabilities and certainties. These procedures constitute the basic template for all the mechanisms that allow humans to piece history together in time.

CHAPTER 7

Multiple Dimensions

It is often said, rather sweepingly, that people do not learn from the 'dead' past, which anyway never repeats itself. But all the components of that remark are misleading. The past is not simply 'dead'. Significant elements survive into the present. The past may thus provide instructive parallels between one period of time and another, even if no events are literally rerun. And we learn too from happenings that are rare and strange as well as from those that are habitual and routine. All this renders knowledge of both past and present into an invaluable resource. After all, we cannot learn directly from the future, because that is unknown. But the past forms and informs us, as we are in time and time is in our very bones.

Intermittently, it is true that we may gain instruction and sometimes inspiration from the more or less speculative dreams, prophecies, plans, forecasts and warnings about things that have yet to unfold. Yet all these future projections are launched, however imaginatively, from the ever-changing present, which incorporates so much from the past. The history of futurology, then, is part of history – and thus part of the historic resources available for understanding the art of living in time.

Given that importance, it is not surprising that all people have their own ways of imparting knowledge about the past, whether conveyed by oral or written means, and whether focusing upon secular or spiritual traditions or both. For that reason, the history of how humans study history is itself a subject of significance in its own right.[1] This chapter accordingly reverts to the question of how we can best frame the multi-dimensionality of the past without, on the one hand, forcing things into preset stages or patterns that suit some cultural traditions and not others but, on the other hand, without fragmenting knowledge into meaningless details that are unattached in time.

One foundational motive for the study of history globally is to provide an explanatory framework that welds the distant past, however hazily surmised, into lived experience. In pre-literate societies, this role was commonly undertaken by myth-histories. These narratives combine allegorical meanings with historical sweep, in accounts that continue to be enjoyed today for their sheer story-telling powers.[2] 'Once upon a time' is distant but not so distant that its mythic deeds cannot be savoured. 'This is how the story . . . / Was handed down to me / By my father and my ancestors. / This is also how I learned the traditions . . ? ends an account by a memory man (*griot*) in northern Senegal.[3] Such histories, often chanted or sung, and repeated with special emphasis at festivals and commemorations, mesh communities into time.

A semi-fabulous sense of 'deep history' also reappears as the starting point in very many early written histories. For instance, the classic Japanese *Ko-Ji-Ki*, or *Records of Ancient Matters*, dating from the early eighth century CE, begins the global saga with the first coupling of the gods that brought forth a new world: 'So in the dimness of the great commencement, we, by relying on the original teaching, learn the time of the conception of the earth and of the birth of islands; . . . [and] the establishment of men . . ?.[4] Such stories are generally presented matter of factly. So the fourteenth-century Icelandic *Saga of Thorstein*, which was a written version of a venerable oral tradition, was brisk: 'The Beginning of this Saga is, that a king named Loge ruled that country which is north of Norway.' Yet this hero had a past that stretched into the mists of time. Loge 'was the fairest of men, . . . like . . . his kinsmen, the giants, from whom he [was] descended'.[5]

The blending of a prior 'age of gods' into a later age of mortals was a common device – and it was echoed by Giambattista Vico, who has already been noted as invoking a heroic 'Age of the Gods' to begin his three-stage global history. By such means, the distant past is rendered familiar, almost domesticated, within the contours of a communicable story. Indeed, 'narrative is a guardian of time', comments one theorist of historical philosophy.[6] Accounts of the past, however, do not have to be given in the strictest of chronological sequences, any more than stories have to be recounted so simply. The point, rather, is that the present gains a firm footing in a communicable history. And that remains the case today, although now the study of the past is shared between many disciplines, from astrophysicists who study the past of the cosmos to futurologists who study past and present forecasts to see if we can also 'write' the future.

Another strong motive for recording and assessing historical data is triggered especially by the wish to preserve dramatic and unusual information within communal memory. So as well as the desire to 'begin at the beginning' there is also the need to retell great events, so that epic deeds are not forgotten. For example, the 'foundational parent' of European history-writing, Heredotus, began his famous study of the Graeco-Persian wars in *c.* 425 BCE with a specific explanation: 'Herodotus of Halicarnassus writes this History, that the Memory of things past may not be extinguish'd by Length of Time. . . .'[7] And, in a different continent and a different era, the same desire to explain extraordinary events to posterity was recorded in very similar words. In 1605 Garcilaso de la Vega, a man of half-Spanish half-Peruvian–Inca origins, was inspired to write about the first arrival of the Spanish in Florida, as a way of understanding, *inter alia*, the chain of events that led to his own cultural origins. 'As time passed, my desire to preserve this story increased . . .' he explained, because 'it was unworthy and regrettable that [such epic events] should remain in perpetual oblivion.'[8]

Providing explanations from which all might learn constitutes a third and powerful reason for studying the past. China's influential historian Sima Qian accordingly ended each section of his narrative with a commentary, headed 'The Grand Historian remarks'.[9] In this way, he drew points of special significance to the attention of readers, launching a historiographical style that has been much emulated by later Chinese historians.

An impulsion to convey stored information about the past is widespread in all cultures. This propensity can be viewed as integrally linked to the communicative capacity of human speech based upon memory; and the propensity gained additional momentum once histories were written down, as recorded information could outstrip the capacity of individual storage and could also reach extended audiences beyond those within immediate hearing range. One atavar who did his best to inculcate a sense of the past was Rashìd al-Dìn, the polymathic physician who became Grand Vizier of the Persian Empire in the fourteenth century. His *Compendium of Chronicles* sought to elucidate both 'philosophical truths and natural laws' based upon the history of the known world, including sources from China. Copies of his handwritten text were widely circulated as well as deposited in mosque libraries. And he further ordered that two complete transcripts were to be made annually, in Arabic and Persian, to transmit his works to posterity, although this precaution did not prove sufficient to protect all his texts against the hazards of time.[10]

Taking the 'long view' by putting immediate events into historical context gives people a chance to gain critical distance. The subject's potential for calm meditation led Francis Bacon to another crisp dictum: that 'histories make men [humanity] wise'.[11] Furthermore, by recollecting past options, including past errors, the possibilities of future change are enhanced. One very celebrated remark to that effect came from George Santayana, the Castilian-born American social philosopher: 'Those who cannot remember the past are condemned to repeat it.'[12] As a literal claim, this can be disputed, since events, whether forgotten or not, are not replicated exactly. Santayana, however, sought to highlight the role of collective memory. Communities with good knowledge resources have greater opportunities for innovation and renovation than those with only limited awareness. Santayana was not advising specifically about the need to learn from history's disasters; but his maxim can be interpreted in that way, which is why it is prominently inscribed at Poland's Holocaust Memorial Museum at Auschwitz (Oświęcim). Here the crucial need for historical understanding is explicit – at a deeply sombre site that all humans should visit at some point in their lives.

How far people on a day-to-day basis need to access collective memory, and particularly the written resources in which it is recorded and interpreted, varies from person to person according to circumstances. Many get by without too much precise information. They manage with a general sense of the recent past and a hazier notion of 'long ago', although many have significantly detailed knowledge about matters of personal concern. But the point is not that all can and will remember equally. It is rather that people, individually and collectively, have available the massive resources of applied study to record and to test/contest memories. Debating the past is a global concern, as much as debating the present: the two are inextricably mixed, as the global repertoire of 'shapings' indicates.

Time Frames Revisited

As the study of human history continues to expand, propelled particularly by the growth of an internationalising historical profession, so the task of framing the ever-multiplying stock of information and analysis is becoming ever more complex. Interpretations generally seek some intermediate point between the rival extremes of seeing only change or seeing only continuity. And they do so within the global repertoire of strategies for shaping history that have been discussed throughout this study. These possibilities are then applied to interpretations both of significant moments and of long-term trends in history – as discussed in the rest of this section.

Bedrock for all organised study of the past on an international basis is the acceptance of a common calendar with an agreed and accurate chronological sequencing, which allows for the translation of dates into and out of the many variant calendars in use around the world. Of course, the human capacity for memory considerably pre-existed the invention of all time-measuring devices. Nonetheless, logging historical information in abundant detail and with a quest for accuracy needs a reliable chronological framework. This was slowly established, by dint of centuries of accumulating global effort by astronomers; and the calendrical measurement of time is now scientifically underpinned by ultra-precise measurements by atomic clocks, which attune the earth-count to the cosmological framework, in the form of Universal Time (UT).[13]

International celebration of a globally shared temporal awareness came agreeably at the very start of the year 2000 CE. Although this date had little significance in itself for people outside the Christian tradition, it was nonetheless widely, though not universally, celebrated around the world. In effect, it was taken as a milestone in an immensely lengthy collective effort at year-counting. The effect also consolidated a universal style of international celebration, with fireworks showering brilliant lights into the midnight sky. Among the participant displays, that from officially communist China was particularly apt – not that the date 2000 has any particular significance in Chinese history, whether from a Marxist or a Confucian perspective, but because China was the country which pioneered the peaceful art of pyrotechnic display, so generating a symbolic language of celebration that has global appeal.

Writing histories within the agreed framework of a long-counting global calendar gives historians immediate freedom to vary their chosen timespans, while remaining within a structured whole. Historical studies are therefore short focus or long term, narrow beam or wide angle, or anywhere in between, just as physicists now measure and study time in both small units and great ones, over an exceptionally wide range: from the Planck microsecond or $10^{(-43)}$, the shortest physically meaningful instant of time, to the cosmologists' billions of projected future years.[14]

Throughout, the challenge is to weigh the relative force of continuity and different degrees of change. For example, when looking at the history of specific days of crisis, the effect highlights the possibilities of revolutionary upheaval. One notable exemplar became an instant classic. American journalist John Reed's *Ten Days that Shook the World* caught the whirlwind excitement of the apparently impossible as the communists came to power in Tsarist Russia in October 1917. The obvious risk of a close-focus study is that the significance of the short term is exaggerated, as against the long term. But diachronic time provides its own corrective. While the Russian Revolution is still historically of great significance, its meaning post-1991 differs from its promise in November 1917. Then the revolutionary activist Maria Spiridonova announced proudly to the new Congress that 'There is no force in the world which can put out the fire of the Revolution'.[15] Yet the Soviet regime has been extinguished. And, in a harsh irony, Spiridonova spent virtually all her adult life incarcerated in Russian prisons, before 1917 as an enemy of the Tsars and then, after 1918, in detention as one of the many comrades who were purged by the Bolshevik leadership.

Other studies of history's 'shaking days' reveal that far from every example chosen by historians remains as memorable today as the initial turbulence once seemed likely to be.[16] Not only does the effect of passing time have a flattening effect, as already noted; but the forces of historical persistence or continuity have had time to operate as a brake upon turmoil, eventually softening and absorbing the effects of crisis.

Single days of notoriety are subject to the same potential change in perspectives. For example, still unknown is the ultimate significance of the deadly assault upon Manhattan's World Trade Center by an elusive group of Al-Qaeda militants on 11 September 2001 (known as 9/11 in the American style of signalling the month before the day). One study quickly offered a permutation of the 'shaking' motif with *Two Hours that Shook the World*.[17] And in terms of international news coverage, that assessment was undoubtedly correct. Yet those who declared that 'everything has changed' were only writing history's first draft. Elements of continuity began to reassert themselves, absorbing some of the shock. Six months later, the counter-claims were equally inflated: 'Nothing has changed after all.' The long-term verdict, however, has not yet emerged, because the wider ramifications of the assault are still unfolding worldwide, not least since the attack galvanised the USA's foreign policy into a highly interventionist phase. These developments are challenging public opinion everywhere to clarify its responses both to American military activism (upon which Americans themselves are divided) and to Wahhabist-Islamic direct-action militancy (upon which Islamic opinion also differs). The dynamic outcome, however, both in terms of events and perceptions, remains yet to be seen.

Characteristically, the heightened emotions that emerge in response to immediate crisis tend to encourage exaggerated extrapolations from the present. Then, when things calm down somewhat, the opinion often switches with equal exaggeration the other way. Something of this dualism between 'all' or 'nothing' can be seen in the cyclical hopes and fears that fuel speculative financial booms, when investors initially believe that 'the sky's the limit' and rush to invest, even ahead of economic plausibility, and then, once doubts set in, rush to disinvest in an excessive panic that leads to outright slump or a sharp corrective downturn.[18]

If taking a short focus tends to exaggerate the extent of change, and the potential for continuing change, the converse applies to studies of the very long run. The further back that knowledge reaches, the thinner becomes the evidence and the less precise the reconstructed chronology of human history. In that case, significant developments long ago are assessed in large blocks of time, just as geologists group the evolution of the earth's surface into immensely prolonged geological eras. Things tend to seem frozen into a common 'prehistory' as it is sometimes discouragingly entitled – discouraging, since it is certainly part of human history. The result is that intermediate demographic, migrational, climatic, epidemiological and familial fluctuations in fortune, which were of great moment to the generations living through them, tend to be suppressed.

On the other hand, very big turning points stand out clearly, at least in retrospective study. These include biological macro-changes, such as the era when, some 4.2 million years ago, the upright hominids became separated from the great apes to form the 'archaic' humans. (All dates are subject to revision.) Or another key period, some two hundred thousand years ago, was of great significance for us: it saw the first anatomically 'modern' big-brained humans (genus: *Homo sapiens*) become successfully established in Africa. Their descendants then began to migrate extensively, adapting to diverse environments and becoming globally ubiquitous.[19] Or another change of great historical moment occurred some thirty to forty thousand years ago, when the humans of what is known as the Cro-Magnon era outlasted the Neanderthals to become the sole inheritors of the many hominid lineages.

This sort of long-span account tends to highlight a few transformations in an otherwise lengthy 'old' Stone Age, which began some 2.6 million years ago, with the advent of *Homo habilis*, the first makers of stone tools.[20] On the other hand, the pace of change always remains a matter of debate, since every one of these major transformations took a long time to become established, so that analysis blends into evolutionary micro-change as well.

Climatic factors are also best studied with a diachronic perspective, because that allows long-term trends and turning points to be distinguished from short-term fluctuations. Only after the retreat of the most recent Ice Age, in *c.* 10,000 BCE, has the relatively much more humanity-favourable global environment encouraged a historically new and more settled way of life. Hence the entire saga of relatively 'recent' human history is taking place within a historically brief window of opportunity, so far sustained between the perils of renewed deep freeze on the one hand and those of excess global warming on the other. Given that there is no guarantee that things will not again change fundamentally, it highlights the framing importance of climatic history.[21]

Geologically, the post-Ice Age era is known as the Holocene (meaning 'entirely recent') in which we now live. This changed environment provided suitable conditions for the application of human ingenuity to establish organised crop cultivation in perhaps *c.* 8000 or even 9000 BCE. The extent of change, from wandering to settled communities, was far from rapid and definitely not universal. But by *c.* 6000 BCE there is convincing evidence for animal husbandry combined with wheat- and barley-farming in a number of places around the eastern Mediterranean and also in the Indus Valley; as well as rice- and millet-growing in China and south-east Asia; maize and bean cultivation in central America; and drained clearances for yams and taro in Papua New Guinea.[22] These initiatives are often taken as marking a 'new' Stone Age, or

'Neolithic' era but historical opinion now tends to avoid pinning overly precise labels on long-span changes.

However, one element that stabilised the earth's geographical configuration is insufficiently emphasised by historians. As a result of continuing climatic change the sea-level by *c.* 4000–5000 BCE had risen to approximately its present height (with continuing global-regional fluctuations), being augmented by melting ice from the receding Ice Age.[23] This change sealed the continents into their current boundaries, closing some historic land routes between them. It means that the sea and its tides, often considered to be 'timeless' factors, also have their own intricate history.

Interestingly, one early exemplar of the thematic approach to the global past was written on just that subject. In 1861 the inventive French historian Jules Michelet published his rhapsodic meditations on *La mer*, mingling alarm and admiration as he discussed everything from whales to great storms to mermaids to the benefits of sea-bathing.[24] It was a style of presentation that was far removed from strict chronology or from traditional 'kings and battles'. But it fitted Michelet's own interpretation, which was influenced by his intellectual debt to Vico – both of them envisaging a history that is shaped into spirals rather than straight lines. A framework chronology therefore provides scope for non-linear as well as linear accounts. The references to specific dates provide temporal anchors, without expecting the exposition to be presented to readers in strict chronological order.

Long-span overviews, as much as close-impact studies, raise the same sort of questions about the interweaving of changes and continuity, but projected onto different scales. In practice, historians choose the time frames and approaches that suit their particular sources and the particular issues that they seek to elucidate. The common chronology does not in itself dictate any specific temporal choices, although centuries, or combinations of centuries, are often taken as building blocks for historical periodisation.

Between the first emergence of cuneiform writing in the fourth millennium BCE[25] and the early twenty-first century, there are some six thousand years in which literacy has been known at least somewhere in the world (needless to say, it was initially the preserve of a tiny minority) and from which written records survive, albeit very patchily from the early days. For that reason, this era is sometimes taken as dating the start of human 'history' (once also dubbed the start of 'civilisation') as opposed to its 'prehistory'. And, even without these specific labels, the turning point is highly significant. Between then and now there have been only 240 generations of people, assuming stereotypically one demographic generation to renew itself every twenty-five years: a large number in relation to any individual lifespan but a tiny number, in terms of cosmic history. It is in relation to the relatively 'recent' experiences of humanity in the last six thousand years – between the long perspective of many millennia and the short focus of a few days – that the conventional period divisions are broadly applied, and increasingly debated.

Coincidentally, it may be noted that the fourth millennium BCE has often been retrospectively nominated as a standard 'start' date in a number of cultural traditions, though in all cases there were a variety of alternative calculations. Thus in the Christian calendar, in the Protestant Archbishop Ussher's revised estimate, the creation of the world occurs in 4004 BCE; in the Jewish spiritual year-count, everything commences in *anno mundi* 3761 BCE; and in Hindu cosmology, which goes back long before the fourth millennium, the current great cycle, the *Kali Yuga*, begins in 3102 BCE.[26]

Dividing up this lengthy timespan, about which now great quantities of information are available, is not subject to rule; and should not be. Nonetheless, there are numerous subdivisions that are conventionally accepted, for ease of teaching and communication. As has already been argued in earlier chapters, the chronologies and conceptual designations of these periods are now tending to become hazy, as the established categories have become overstretched by too many variant applications. Furthermore, the definitional problems are multiplied when any temporal subdivisions are borrowed from one historical tradition and applied incautiously to the experiences of all other people.

'Freezing' time into conventional periods tends to encourage a belief that each period has a special character, which is then evoked to explain things within that period, so risking a purely circular argument. An accompanying problem is that the preceding epoch, before any era that is being studied, is often viewed as being diametrically 'opposite', thus obscuring links and continuities across time. The outcome of studying the past in terms of separate eras may generate a perceptual fragmentation, when people 'see the past as a plurality of unconnected periods', as sociologist Norbert Elias warns from an adjacent discipline.[27]

Nevertheless, the answer to debates on periodisation is not to produce arbitrarily yet another dispensation, because that only generates a new set of problems. The perennial intertwining of historical continuity with variants of change means that there are always grounds to challenge one set of definitions or to propose another set. As it is, there are often many quiet adjustments to the customarily accepted period dates, in the light of fresh research. However, the various 'names' allotted to the different epochs tend to remain unchanged – no doubt partly in tribute to the force of continuity and partly because conceptual alternatives are not easily agreed.

Consequently, there is always scope to reconsider the conventional ways of dividing up the past. It is strange that historians, who are generally so careful to define and to justify their sources and methods, have not done more to explain and to justify their chosen time frames. These, and the period designations that are attached to them, urgently need a conscious airing and reconsideration, as matters of communal interest – and not just within each period 'enclave'. A greater clarity of time frames and terminologies, plus a greater awareness of the overlappings between and within significant cultures and eras, will also improve the possibilities for genuine cross-cultural comparisons. And, as all epochs and all regions are longitudinally subject to a changing balance between continuity, micro-change and macro-change, history students should productively study not only short-focus periods but long-span historical themes as well.

For all this, chronological references remain crucial as the key means to locate things in time-space. Chronologies, however, need good, not outmoded, interpretative packaging to make the chosen time frames really significant, while overlapping as well as successive trends may also be accepted.

Playfully, the Belgian artist René Magritte once imagined *Time Transfixed* (1938), in a frozen, rootless moment of mystery (*see* illustration 22). Yet the clocks in life don't stop, so the challenge is to link both the moments *and* the aeons.

Considering Pluralities

There have been numerous calls for a 'pluri-dimensional' study of history, to step outside the old conventional narratives and, among other things, to avoid ethno-centrism. So the human past has been compared to a huge 'polyphonic' symphony of many voices from many people.[28] As this section explores, however, it has not been easy to find an agreed format.

Such pluralistic declarations have certainly helped to promote a greater egalitarianism in the expression of social attitudes by historians. People who live in non-literate societies, for example, are no longer condescended to as 'primitive' and somehow not 'really' part of history. And, from a global perspective, all cultures and the many alternative and sometimes competing traditions within cultures are understood to constitute, axiomatically, part of the historical whole. Some heroes (of both sexes) are still retained. But it is realised that these admired figures may come from many places around the world; and that one nation's champions do not automatically command reverence elsewhere. Indeed, there is something of an unofficial search for a wider social, cultural and gender range of past individuals or groups who can be studied with admiration and yet also with historical verisimilitude. Meanwhile, the universal villains tend to be leaders whose regimes have

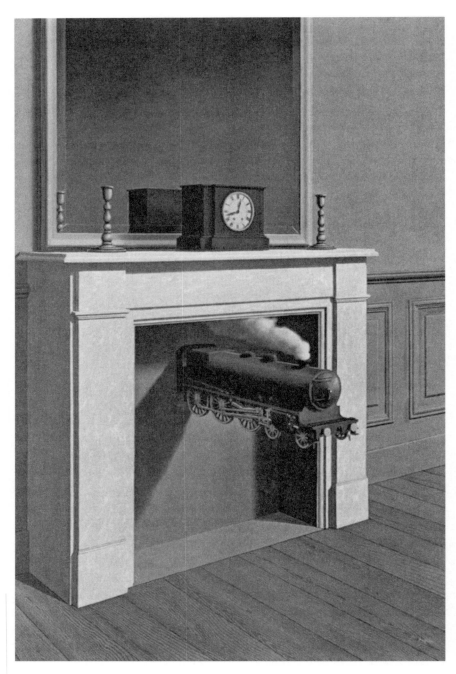

22 Magritte's *Time Transfixed* (1938) offers a frozen moment of mystery in illustration of an atomised world, with no links between cause and effect.

knowingly perpetrated mass murder, but it frequently requires the sifting effect of time, and the fading of immediate loyalties, to establish precisely who do or do not fall into this category.

Not only is there a move towards 'fair play' for all peoples, so there is too a new interest in multiple themes, both expected and unexpected. Objects that might seem merely mundane, such as the humble potato, have been the subject of their own dedicated studies.[29] Indeed, a plethora of past things are now studied longitudinally, often bypassing all conventional period distinctions. Such themes are potentially able to liberate historians, as 'from a restrictive and artificial scaffolding', in the words from Massimo Montanari that have already been quoted.[30] But the new pluralism brings fresh challenges in its turn. A liberated diversity makes it even more difficult to put these studies together within a common historical frame and makes comparison across cultures even more complex.

Arnold Toynbee famously faced the problem of global synthesis which, after a lifetime of endeavour, he likened to the juggler's task of keeping many balls in the air without losing coherence.[31] His massive twelve-volume world history (1934–61) was intent upon avoiding Eurocentrism by taking every world 'civilisation' seriously on its own terms and within its own timetable. By that means, Toynbee hoped to discover the scientific 'laws' of historical fluctuations that caused empires to rise and to fall. It was an impressive enterprise of encyclopedic range.

Yet Toynbee's intellectual edifice ran into more and more problems as it proceeded. His own attention turned, as the volumes progressed, from finding scientific laws to discovering the spiritual 'meaning' of history in the unity of humankind. And his critics were generally stern about the unresolved problems of classification and explanation within the Toynbee schema. His work was 'intellectually dangerous and totally false', charged one adversary; 'a terrible perversion of history', agreed another, who was equally uninhibited in voicing outright rejection.[32] Toynbee therefore triggered debate rather than consensus.

Especially notable among the difficulties in the 'comparative civilisations' approach is the compartmentalisation of global 'cultures' to identify their distinctive historical cycles. It may wrongly be assumed that each tradition is a separate entity and, moreover, that each is internally homogeneous. That is a possibly accurate view of closed communities who live or have lived in isolation in remote or inaccessible parts of the globe. Historically, however, the model of separate and homogeneous cultures underestimates the extent of pluralism within great 'civilisations' and it also ignores the regular movements of people, ideas and technologies between them.

Humans come from a travelling species: historically, 'out of Africa', as geneticists report. And Eurasia in particular, as the globe's biggest land mass, has repeatedly seen great migrations, often over long distances, whether from east to west, west to east, from northern latitudes to the lusher terrains of the south, or back again. In relatively recent times, from the sixteenth century onwards, there has been a massive European global diaspora. And in the nineteenth and especially the twentieth centuries, there have been global contraflows from mid-Eurasia, known as the Middle East, and from east and south-east Asia – for example, with outflows of people from the Indian subcontinent to Africa and western Europe, and from China to establish 'Chinatowns' in many of the world's great cities. These movements also meet and mingle with a multi-generational African diaspora, which has taken people to the Americas and their descendants on to Europe, and in some cases back to Africa. Such repeated mixings and overlappings complicate comparisons between 'big blocs' of apparently separate global cultural traditions, making the range of permutations ever greater.

Thus two recent contributions to a Toynbee-like modelling of historical cycles demonstrate, once more, the appeal of tracing patterns, as well as the intractabilities of the task. Peter Turchin focuses upon the internal dynamics of resources within agrarian states in order to test the prospects of their territorial rise or fall. The temporal parameters for long-lasting empires can thus be contrasted with those of brief-lived ones. There are always, however, problems in defining the 'lifespan' of power systems, which do not invariably have clear start and end dates, but mutate and evolve as well as rise and fall. And it is also difficult to build into the models the irruption of forces from outside whatever phenomenon is being explored.[33] For L.D. Snyder, the units for assessment are human 'culture-systems'. Assuming these to be clearly separable one from another, he calculates a classic 'cultural cycle' of rise and fall to last some three to four hundred years. However, there are many historical variations. Cultures mutate within as well as overlap and borrow from others. As a result, the periodicity is less than certain, whether past or present. 'Our Macro-Macro Chart does suggest that something significant should be happening in 2000,' Snyder notes with reference to a 'Western cycle' that is deemed to start in 1750. Yet he adds cautiously: 'but that analysis is based on a ±100 years, and has no real theoretical foundation.'[34]

Bloc regional contrasts do, however, lend themselves well to comparative presentations over time. That style was used by Oswald Spengler in conjunction with his stern critique of all Eurocentric models of history – a decade before Toynbee's enterprise began. Special charts were constituted to cue the achievements in religion, culture and politics of different 'civilisations' at similar points in time. So Spengler displayed Indian, Chinese, Egyptian, Hellenic (classical), Arabian and western history (post 900 CE) within parallel lines. Again, his range was impressive, albeit with some idiosyncratic touches.

By his own era, he complained, there was a 'Degradation of abstract thinking into professional lecture-room philosophy'[35] – though presumably he exempted his own ideas from this stricture. Even Spengler's boldness, however, had limits: his global coverage was incomplete, omitting Africa, Australia and Central/South America.

Comparative visual displays of regional variations, nonetheless, remain good at showing the simultaneity of differences around the globe. Hence an illustrated (non-Spenglerian) volume, entitled *Timelines of the Ancient World*, provides encyclopedic information in a grid format, from the beginnings to *c.* 1500 when 'ancient' times come to a halt. Anyone wishing to know (say) what other great buildings were constructed in the third century BCE when Stonehenge reached its peak (*c.* 2100 BCE) can compare it with the Great Pyramid at Giza (2550 BCE) and the Ur-Nammu Ziggurat in Mesopotamia (2100 BCE), or the Indus Valley's vanished cities of Harappa and Mohenjo-daro (*c.* 2500 BCE), or La Galgada temple in Peru (2300 BCE).[36] This layout is effectively pluralist. However, there are always dangers of cramping global diversity when history is interpreted under the headings of no more than five world-regional blocs, as well as missing the cross-linkages (both peaceful and bellicose) between these blocs – linkages which themselves vary considerably over time.

Giving due weight to both separation and unity remains one of the most difficult tasks for historians who write world histories. Many excellent ones continue to be produced;[37] but, no doubt warned by the critical battering that both Spengler and Toynbee experienced, today's experts generally refrain from detecting any grand 'laws' or inevitable cycles within human affairs. A bold few, like the North American political analyst Francis Fukuyama, are prepared to predict the 'end of history', in his case meaning by the 'end' not the imminent demise of history but its long-term evolutionary target (as the 'end' of an acorn is an oak tree). Here the study of the past was consciously invoked as the basis of future prediction. To some excitement within the USA, history's outcome was revealed to be a US-style pluralist democracy.[38] Viewed from elsewhere, however, the case seems unproven.

Instead, the tenor today tends to stress complexity and the collapse of simple 'grand narratives'. The stories are now pluralistic. In adjacent subject disciplines, significantly, there is something of a 'turn to history' too. As anthropology and sociology increasingly rediscover change over time, however, so the permutations of explanatory frameworks grow ever more diverse. Another keen North American commentator, in this case a philosopher turning to history, has recently suggested that there are three strands of geology, biology and human culture that unfold in parallel. Exploring these over the past millennium from 1000 to 2000 CE suggests a picture of flux and non-linearity. Hence variability becomes the key theme, rather than either continuity or sustained long-term developments. This conclusion should encourage 'a more *experimental* attitude toward reality', the author decides, though 'reality' is not expected to disappear.[39]

Plurality of themes, people, periods, places, trends and non-trends are thus fully debated. Historians respond too with very variegated styles of exposition, mingling analysis and interpretation with narrative. As already noted, there is a deep-seated myth that argues that history-writing is always presented in chronological sequence. However, that is very far from the case. Themed studies of old, like Michelet's historical rhapsody on the sea which has already been mentioned, or panoramic studies in recent times, like Theodore Zeldin on the intimate history of human sexuality, consciously avoid the banalities of mere date-ordering.[40]

Nor is there now, if there ever was, a rigid distinction between the 'West' that is taken to assume a linear outcome to history and the 'East' that allegedly favours cyclicality. Instead, the analytical cross-currents run vigorously in all directions. As the Indian poet K.N. Daruwalla writes, teasingly: 'In a curved universe, a straight metric line / is floundering in a rut / you must give it multiple meanings . . .'.[41] This is being amply and emphatically done on all sides.

Within this cornucopia of approaches, however, there have been relatively few probes into how the big picture is held together. There is a ceaseless deluge of data and analysis rather than a dissection of how a pluri-dimensional past actually operates in multiple dimensions. However, one serious conceptualisation has come from Fernand Braudel, the French historian whose emphasis upon 'deep continuities' has already been noted. His answer was not to divide whole-history into segments by period of time but instead to consider three distinct levels, or strata, of temporality.[42] These run longitudinally throughout history in all epochs and locations.

While never adopted as a working model by his fellow historians, this sent into circulation a Braudelian notion of time as multi-tiered – a view that continues to resurface in speculations about the nature of time.[43] In turn, Braudel himself acknowledged being inspired by the Russian-born sociologist Georges Gurvitch. His analysis had depicted variable sorts of social temporality, as people live by different rhythms and timetables.[44] It was an approach that also recalled that of Berdyaev. His threefold model has already been cited, proposing an immediate psychological time nested within an unfolding historical time, which is nested in turn within an all-embracing cosmic time.

By contrast with the theoretical models of Gurvitch and Berydaev, the interpretation developed by Braudel was very consciously anchored in the specificities of placement. Its very historical 'locatedness' makes it the pioneering model for all multi-stranded histories. For Braudel, underpinning everything is the persistence of the long term, *la longue durée*, which is expressed in global geography and ecology. 'All the stages, all the thousands of stages, all the thousand explosions of historical time can be understood on the basis of these depths, this semi-stillness. Everything gravitates around it.'[45] Above this solid base, there comes a middle or intermediate realm of historical trends or 'conjunctures', which are generated by human societies. This tier embraces many significant fluctuations, whether economic, demographic, political or military. And, thirdly, there is the surface level, *'l'histoire événementielle'*, the micro-history of events, which are generated by individuals. At first sight, this tier seems exciting and action packed. Yet events, for Braudel, are but ephemeral and ultimately delusive. They are, he specified: 'surface disturbances, crests of foam that the tides of history carry on their strong backs'.

Braudel's maritime allusion was apt in coming from a historian of the sea. It is as old as the planet. Hence the apparent maritime permanence, beneath the foam cresting the waves, may encourage a sense of underlying continuity. Braudel's survey of *The Mediterranean* thus began with an intensive exploration of the framework of regional geography before surveying the lesser vagaries of climatic change, economic transactions, contending empires and wars. However, the persistence of mountains, plains, coastlines, islands and the great sea is not so helpful for (say) framing the historical interpretation of trans-regional intangibles, such as the history of ideas or international law or religion or scientific practice or mathematical logic or myriad other themes. Not all factors, in other words, are equally affected by regional/local geography: some are global and trans-regional, or partial but inter-regional.

Furthermore, there are numerous conceptual difficulties within Braudel's model. His division between separate tiers or layers (*paliers*) is too schematic and rigid. In practice, the aspects of history that Braudel attributes arbitarily to the short term (events/individuals/politics), to the medium term (trends/ societies/economies) and to the long term (structures/cultures/geography) all overlap, since any or all of these processes operate within the short, medium and/or long term, and all can have effects in the short, medium and/or long term, with feedback effects from all upon any or all the others – as well as countervailing pressures.

Individuals and events, at the 'surface' level, are particularly more complex and deep-rooted in their impact than Braudel implied – and he certainly underestimated their potential role in diachronic terms. For instance, history has been deeply affected by the role of charismatic religious teachers (and their successors) who establish religions that survive for millennia. And there are many other examples of significant interventions both by individuals and by groups of people. At Braudel's intermediate level, moreover, the shifts in economies and societies are left unexplained, and their connections with politics and events unexplored. And at the fundamental level, the global environment, including its climate, its physical geography and the human contribution – variously cultivating, destroying, building and rebuilding – is not as static and unchanging as Braudel claimed. Mountain ranges, for example, emerge at differing speeds in contrasting circumstances, the Alps being, in geomorphological terms, a relatively 'sudden' creation.[46] In his own personal terms, Braudel's vision of a timeless geography may have sprung from an idealised memory of the 'unchanging' rural France of his childhood, as has already been mentioned. Moreover, his personal distaste for mere 'events' was certainly heightened during his 'gloomy' years of captivity by the German army during the Second World War, when he explained that he did his best to take the 'long view' – and wrote from memory a first draft of his massive study of the Mediterranean.[47]

Either way, Braudel's three tiers of time, like a layer-cake, are too rigidly separated and, at their base, not only too immobile but also too monolithic. A stress upon geohistory as the overwhelmingly important source of continuity at the deep base of things in fact precludes consideration of other forms of continuity. The rates of change at all levels are also much more variegated and interactively meshed than Braudel allowed. Thus, ultimately, a tiered system of stratified layers does not provide a successful basis for explaining macro-change in history. While Braudel had led the way in applying a pluralist model, his detailed configuration simply allots different rates to different phenomena without explaining how they are linked. In his case, moreover, the model designedly discounts the likelihood of major transformations, other than occasional geographical upheavals.

So attempts at stratifying history into different levels that work to different rates of temporal change run up against the problem of inter-connectedness. Neither the selected layers nor the separately posited rates of change work in isolation. Braudel's model has the attraction of elegant simplicity in its specification; but it assumes stability without explaining change, and it does not indicate how the various short-, medium- and long-term factors may either interact or counteract one another. All later multivariate models, however, may be viewed as, if not Braudelian, then at least post-Braudelian.

Distinguishing between different time-spans with differently appointed characteristics thus quickly runs into problems of rigidity when applied to historical complexity. The same debates have attended another tripartite division of time which was proposed in 1965 precisely for studying variations within the geohistory that was, for Braudel, the deep core of stability. This geomorphological model from geologists Schumm and Lichty envisaged a geologic span of very slow adaptation (long ago), which embraces a 'modern' epoch of graduated developments (the last millennium), which in turn embraces the present-day moment of micro-change (one year or less). The outcome drew attention, stimulatingly, to differential rates of change, and encouraged similar debates about whether these short-, medium- and long-term variables were co-dependent or independent. But this model, too, has been critiqued as too arbitrary in its core specifications and too schematic in its core chronological divisions.[48]

When the variables and timescales are multiplied too far, however, all these tiered pictures become far too inchoate. A variant attempt by the social historian Peter Laslett posited a grid system showing four separate rates of transformation in human history, crossmatched with nine different types of social, political, cultural or economic alteration. However, he concluded that even this degree of complexity was probably insufficient.[49] And his multivariate classification of characteristic 'paces' for different sorts of change over different time frames was in effect halted upon the drawing board.

Rather than separate tiers or sorts of temporality, then, each with their separate characteristics, it is more helpful to envisage *within* one complex temporality a range of different dimensions that continuously interact, intersect and counteract longitudinally. Such an alternative allows for flexibility, overlapping and fuzzy boundaries. At one point, the British-American historian Lawrence Stone threw out the suggestion, which he did not develop further, that the developing past constitutes 'a non-linear, multiple-loop feedback system, with many semi-independent variables, each responsively reacting to the influence of some, or all, of the others'.[50] That stimulating proposition goes beyond the idea of separate layers or divided strata of history. The only proviso is that there is no need to exclude all forms of linearity from the picture, as Stone appears to do. It is certainly misleading to assume that the entirety of history must run along straight lines. On the other hand, it is equally dogmatic to exclude the possibility of some long-term linear development, which takes place gradually, the whole being contained within a multi-dimensional process that includes both continuity and the different rates and forms of transformation. Indeed, most of Stone's own applied historical studies were precisely concerned with elucidating trends, and also establishing deviations and variations within trends.

Dimensions within History

Here the analysis of *The Shape of History* has argued throughout the book for an interlocking or loosely 'braided' three-dimensional history, in which the three strands combine and intertwine continuously, though not necessarily evenly, within time – or, more properly, within time-space. An invented term for this process is 'trialectical' – with the light friction not of bipolar opposites but of tripartite meshing.

Moreover, the component elements apply to everything: to geology, and to societies, and to cultures, and to individuals alike, holding the whole together in dynamic tension. Hence the considered picture may be taken not as anti-Braudelian but definitely as post-Braudelian.

Establishing the three dimensions within history has been undertaken in the previous chapters, by reference to the repeated themes that recur again and again throughout the immensely varied world repertoire of historical writings. Although there is an endless array of possible meanings of the past, its shape emerges from their collective intersections. These repeated features are defined as continuity (or persistence), micro-change (or momentum) and macro-change (or turbulence). These features are all diachronic, occurring throughout history, as well as synchronic, and they interact as do the three dimensions of space. It should be stressed once more that the pattern is never a neat one. If the trialectical linkages are imagined like a plait or braid,[51] then it is a very tangled one, with many loops, overlaps, bypasses, loose strands, knots, breaks and feedbacks, yet still operating within a general power of equilibriation.

Because the mesh is ever-interlocking, all aspects are equally affected by continuity and by the varieties of change. It would be simpler if things were otherwise. But it cannot be simply said that (for example) geology and geography represent the element of continuity, while (say) society or culture represent slow change, and (say) politics and war represent dramatic upheaval. Alas for simplicity, but the strands of history cannot be parcelled out onto separate time dimensions, each moving at their own separate pace. 'Big' organising factors, like demographics, climate, biology, technology, economics, culture, ideas, literacy, religion, politics, science, all can persist, can develop slowly, and can mutate rapidly.

Remarkable reminders of the element of continuity in human affairs do have the power to arrest attention. So when the five-thousand-year-old body of Ötzi, the Tyrolean Ice-Man, was discovered in 1991, it was at first thought to be the relatively recent corpse of a hapless mountaineer who had frozen 'some decades ago'. But in fact his cadaver had been preserved in the snow since his lonely death on a high Alpine ridge sometime between 3300 and 3200 BCE (at the time when literacy was first emerging, though he himself was a pastoralist, not a scribe).[52] Thus his immediate species recognisability was a sign of the biological closeness of his epoch with ours.

Meanwhile, the slow processes of evolution are affecting all humans, as well as all other living creatures, over a much longer timespan that stretches well back before the birth and death of Ötzi. At the same time, however, biology is also subject to macro-change. For example, interventionist medicine is now 'meddling' with gradual evolution by providing people with artificial body aids, comprising anything from spectacles to hearing aids, false teeth, prosthetic limbs, heart pacemakers, hip replacements and an astonishing range of organ transplants. Survival is no longer for the physically 'fittest' alone (to cite a famous phrase coined not by Darwin but by Herbert Spencer) – or rather, developing technologies are offering the chance to redefine the means of biological 'fitness'. Indeed, all efforts at mutual aid and succour between humans have long tried to provide communal buffers against the random hazards of life in a turbulent world. So our survival has 'naturally' been a social-cum-biological process, repeatedly raising ethical and practical issues that are ones of collective concern. The debates about cloning constitute an urgent case in point.

Whenever a direct question is posed – does the study of human history reveal a basic template of continuity tempered by change? or, alternatively, a process of change tempered by continuity? – most people, though never all of them, tend to select the second of the two options. However, a better reply would be to reject both alternatives. Not only do 'continuity' and 'change' constantly intermix but 'change' is too slack and overused a term to convey the fullness of the patterning.

Three rather than two variables remain constantly in operation throughout. Continuity and micro-change are the more 'normal' features in the sense of being immediately familiar on a day-to-day basis. Yet it does not take much study of either history or current affairs to realise that turbulence, radical discontinuities and macro-changes always reappear, even after lengthy periods when calm appears to hold sway. True, it is the nature of 'shock' upheavals that they seem to generate surprise or consternation when they actually occur, no matter how repeatedly such possibilities are predicted. Such reactions indicate the strength of our habitual attachment to routine and the disturbance felt when it is rudely interrupted. The power of turbulence, however, is always latent, even when not apparent.

These triadic dimensions recur in many contexts. For example, policy options may represent the polar alternatives of conservatism, gradualism and revolutionary transformationism. In monolithic regimes, such choices generally remain canvassed within the ruling group. But, in more open political systems, the three alternatives may also form the basis of rival political parties: favouring conservatism, gradualism or revolution. However, given the characteristic tanglements of history, the alignments are never perfectly neat. Thus there are characteristic debates within conservatism, as to how far things should be conserved and how far changes should be tolerated (and even, on occasions, how far drastic changes are needed to return things to their 'proper' state). And, at the other end of the spectrum, revolutionary political parties find it hard to be revolutionary on every issue. Plans for radical economic restructuring may coexist with much more traditional attitudes on (say) gender relationships or sex. In the early Russian revolution, for example, Lenin's moment of curbing the transformative momentum came in June 1920 when he denounced 'left-wing' communism, dubbing it an 'infantile disorder' within the movement. For him, the purists who opposed all tactical compromises represented not the true interests of the people but mere 'petty bourgeois anarchism'.[53]

History's variant dimensions, in other words, keep returning, as upheavals disturb even the most committed conservative or the forces of restraint and tradition curb even the most dedicated revolutionary. Gradualists who favour micro-change are at least prepared for the possibility of innovation. They can claim to 'go with the flow'. On the other hand, they too risk either being tugged by tradition and inertia to be more cautious than they intend or being ambushed by upheaval to find that they have unleashed forces that they cannot control.

Appeals to deep continuity, nonetheless, remain available in all circumstances as effective psychological ballast for any cause that is under threat or facing crisis and upheaval. Thus in 1941 Joseph Stalin, officially the revolutionary leader of international communism, quickly called upon traditional Russian patriotism in order to repel Hitler's invading German forces, and as quickly rehabilitated the previously despised aristocratic generals who had defeated Napoleon's invading army in 1812. Impressively, too, after the 1991 fall of the Soviet regime, the compliment to national solidarity was repeated. While most monuments to former communist leaders have been removed and many formerly destroyed buildings are being reconstructed, the bronze equestrian statue of Marshal Zhukov, the military architect of the Red Army's defeat of Hitler, still stands resplendently in the centre of Moscow.

Prospective changes, meanwhile, may be advocated with reference to either of the other two dimensions. Thus the rival merits of slow, incremental, emollient gradualism or, alternatively, of drastic discontinuity in the form of a 'short, sharp shock' are canvassed, in many different policy contexts. Such debates are found not only at public policy level but in personal and spiritual matters too. So in classical Buddhism, for example, the best pathway to spiritual enlightenment is disputed between the protagonists of the Gradual Way and those who support the Sudden Way.[54]

Today therapies for people seeking to change their routine behaviour tend to stress the gradualist benefits of small actions repeated on a day-by-day basis, as in the 'twelve steps' of one well known detoxification programme. However, there are also advocates of rapid transformational change, as may happen in the case of religious conversion. Indeed, in medical history, there was, at one stage, a highly literal application of 'shock therapy' to change people's mental configuration, in the form of the now controversial application of electroconvulsive shocks to the human brain.

Radical measures can nonetheless either be or seem to be the best option in extreme circumstances. Thus, recently, one of the most notorious examples of 'shock therapy' as public policy has come with the decision, in the case of Russia's post-Soviet restructuring after 1991, to adopt – with the encouragement of many international economists – an economic policy of sudden market liberalisation.[55] It meant that this country underwent a drastic ideological experiment twice in the twentieth century, once into communism and once out of it. These rapid transformation policies recall what Berdyaev termed an 'either-all-or-nothing' strain within Russian thinking, although the relevant ideologies have international as well as national roots. And great changes have followed, including undesired as well as desired ones. 'What we thought would be easy turned out to be painfully difficult', as Russia's free-marketising President Boris Yeltsin admitted in a confessional speech at his surprise resignation on 31 December 1999. It is a comment that many political leaders could echo today.

Understanding the historical context in time and space is therefore required – whether seeking to support or to oppose any given action – in order to improve the chances of success, whether acting slowly, rapidly or not at all, within a multidimensional cosmos that incorporates persistent continuities as well as transformative possibilities.

Acknowledging the potential for change – in processes, people and ideas – entails accepting that some 'truths' are local and contingent. These may be adapted or updated over time, in the light of better information or different circumstances or both.

Having said that, however, understanding the power of continuity also entails recognition that other 'truths' are time-invariant and therefore, for all intents and purposes, are timeless. These are absolutes, within this cosmos. Human knowledge of those truths changes over time; and we may be mistaken in our formulation of them. In principle, however, there are time-invariant truths that we can strive to identify. One such proposition is that 'we don't know everything'. Yet that is a positive truth, not a denial of its possibility. The all-too-obvious fact that we do not know everything does not mean that we know nothing. Diachronic time thus incorporates elements of persistence that remain true through-time as well as elements that change, whether rapidly or slowly.[56]

People when they change their minds often feel the tug of these different dimensions. Sometimes there is the famous *coup de foudre* – the sudden moment of revelation. In those circumstances, the radical transformation is palpable, whether exciting or upsetting. Yet, on other occasions, ideas may change imperceptibly, updating as circumstances alter. One effective way therefore to champion a desired innovation is to assert that it is coming anyway, encouraging people to shed their resistance in order to conform with 'the times'. The radical Saint-Simon noted that 'herd' effect, with the sardonic comment: 'It is so sweet to swim with the tide.'[57] Only after a while do people then realise, perhaps with a start, that they have changed their minds on some issue without remembering exactly when.

Anecdotally, a classic tripartite account (which recurs in a number of variant forms) portrays a common sequence of responses to startling new ideas. At first a strange theory is greeted with laughter and derision as merely outlandish. Then, if the new view is repeated with more emphasis, people become angry, asserting that it is contrary to orthodoxy. But, finally, after more repetition, ideas are changed. People then remark that they knew the new view all along – and ask why they are being bothered with something so obvious.[58] This sequence does not work in all cases, as there are always some accepters who quickly welcome new ideas and some resisters who never agree. Yet the anecdote shows how the mind can initially feel distaste for novelty but then cushion the surprise by making a covert jump to assimilate the new into apparently long-accepted truisms. Hence the sometimes almost startling speed with which radical concepts are not only circulated but accepted and 'domesticated', even though the very different process of implementing novel ideas can be surprisingly sluggish when pitted against the forces of institutional and personal inertia.

Perhaps it should be reiterated, at this point, that the three dimensions of continuity/micro-change/macro-change are not causal agencies in their own right. Instead, they constitute the defining framework and provide the 'hooks' within the cat's cradle of history within which causation works. Logically, the end result is the sum of everything that happens, including the tiniest micro-change, which also contributes to the whole. Within that totality, however, analysts rightly highlight and weigh the relative significance of specific factors and combinations of factors – whether major or minor – as appropriate for the given outcome that is being explained or interpreted.[59] Very long-term results tend to be more readily explained in terms of very long-term trends and causation; but short term outcomes, if sufficiently momentous, often depend upon a combination of short-, medium- and long-term causes in interactive combination. So the patterns shift and recombine, but not inexplicably.

History within Time

Identifying the dimensions within history, which unfolds within time, means that it is not necessary – indeed, it is entirely misleading – to allot different characteristics to different 'sorts' or 'types' of time.

Fashions for subdividing temporality into separate categories have certainly been found in sociology, notably in the work of Georges Gurvitch which has already been mentioned. He found a dazzling array of up to eleven different times, from *la longue durée* (which impressed Braudel) to a short, sharp 'explosive time', not excluding 'time the deceiver' and 'time the surpriser'. Many of these sociological categories, however, refer to the time-tables that are generated by different communities. So 'town time' can be contrasted with 'country time', 'monastic time' with 'secular time', and so on. The subject is a fascinating one, as humans are exceptional in being a species with highly variable lifestyles;[60] and these variations are also readily internalised into people's mindsets. Nonetheless, these permutations of 'social time' as lived and understood occur within one historical time-space: they are sub-times, not separate times.

Philosophically, the habit of subdividing temporality has also had some famous advocates, though far from all philosophers subscribe to this approach. One originator of the style was the British theorist of anti-realism J. M. E. McTaggart. He divided temporality, in a famous 1908 essay, into three series, prosaically named A, B and C, as the basis for his attempted logical demolition of time-as-longitudinal-process.[61] For him, there was just a continuous present that uses calendrical markers whose sequences are purely a matter of convention, like the order of letters in an alphabet. McTaggart's viewpoint tallied with his (non-Christian) faith in reincarnation, since he believed that people live many successive lives during one long never-ending Now. Some supporters were indeed convinced. And they tried, albeit unsuccessfully, to contact McTaggart in a seance, four years after his physical death.[62] That did not in itself either prove or disprove his logic. But McTaggart's analysis did not manage to banish all references to 'before' and 'after', so temporality crept back into his picture after all. Moreover, the conventional markers that he invoked, such as calendars and alphabets, depend completely upon time when used in consecutive communication.

Other philosophers, meanwhile, did not subdivide temporality in order to deny it but rather to allot different characteristics to allegedly different *sorts* of time, within the human consciousness of temporality. Berdyaev's threefold model has been the most influential among such approaches. Yet the arbitrary nature of his categorisation is apparent when his version is contrasted with rivals. For example, Berdyaev's compatriot, the Russian philosopher Sergei

Alexeyev had earlier proposed a different triad. This comprised physical time (where Einsteinian relativity applied); ontological or philosophical time (as understood by human thought and capable of being absolute); and psychological time.[63] Yet another variant followed from Pitirim Sorokin, the Russian-born sociologist who made his career in the USA. He preferred five categories: physico-mathematical time; biological time; psychological time; metaphysical time; and socio-cultural time. His philosophical notations here began to merge into Gurvitch-style social timetables reflecting diversities in human lived experience.

None of these arbitrary classifications, however, showed that the temporal process, as opposed to human perspectives upon the same, is itself subdivided into different categories, each with its own characteristics. Instead, time is a holistic phenomenon and process – or, more accurately, it is the time-space continuum that operates as a whole. It is within such a framework that history unfolds in multiple dimensions.

Human responses to all this are undoubtedly very rich and culturally significant. Again, however, there is not one special category known as 'psychological time' that has one special set of characteristics. Personal responses to temporality are variegated, from individual to individual, and from culture to culture, with their very different temporal conventions.

That the human consciousness is time-immersed may be taken as axiomatic. Such a case was certainly argued by one of the twentieth century's most troubled philosophers of time. From a Catholic artisan family in Germany's Black Forest, Martin Heidegger shared in Europe's intellectual turmoil of the 1920s and 1930s, when many of these models of disjointed temporality were propounded. In *Being and Time* (1927), he located human consciousness within the matrix of a 'triunic' time that combines past, present and future. Heidegger therefore rejected the 'thin' view that sees each 'Now' as a tiny instant in isolation. With a methodology of philosophical introspection, he further postulated that humans have a threefold temporal awareness, incorporating an immediate sense of within-timeness (*Innerzeitkeit*); plus an encompassing 'everydayness' (*Zeitlichkeit*), by which individuals interpret the era in which they live; and, linking both, a 'longitudinal' notion of shared historicality with others (*Geschichtlichkeit*).[64]

Notable among all these interpretations are the conceptual recurrence of 'threes' and the desire also to differentiate between diachronic and synchronic sensibilities. However, none of these classifications has been tested against external evidence that others think/respond in the same way. Individuals have many contrasting views on time (some are reviewed in the next chapterlink) and cultural traditions differ considerably too. Heidegger in his own later works switched to a four- rather than threefold vision.[65] Yet his analysis was highly self-referential and difficult to test. As a result, the Heidegger-style 'inwards' approach to time studies via the identification of different times from different forms of consciousness has faltered, quite apart from the fact that he himself has become controversial for sharing too much personal 'everydayness' with German fascism in the mid 1930s.

Among the responses to these arguments one of the most important and historically minded has come from the French theorist Paul Ricoeur. He proposes that people link their differently sensed temporalities by using narrative (whether historical or fictional) to 'map' their lived time onto cosmic or universal time.[66] This may be termed a post-Heideggerian position. It is helpful and perceptive upon the central role of story-telling to convey through-time experiences.

Against that, however, not all histories, whether personal or global, are conveyed by simple narratives. Other styles, either alternatively or in tandem, include episodic accounts, broken story-lines, in-depth analysis and synchronic immersion (as opposed to diachronic fables). And, above all, it still remains far from proven that all people everywhere do see time as sectionalised and thus needing to be re-welded, in the way that Ricoeur, post-Heidegger, assumes. It is just as plausible that narratives come from integrated senses of temporal process as from fragmented ones.

Exploring multiple dimensions within history thus does not mean that time itself is subdivided into different 'times' with different characteristics. Nor does it imply that the human consciousness of time is similarly frag-mented too. On the contrary, these dimensions of persistence/momentum/turbulence operate *within* a holistic time-space whose synchronic and diachronic properties we can grasp and study both simultaneously – and longitudinally.

Frameworks and Contingency

Multidimensionality means that historians' interpretations are not then preset into any specific form. They can analyse lines of development *and* cycles, in appropriate circumstances, without having to choose permanently between one or the other. In economic history, for example, long-term trends of indus-trial growth may take an ultimately linear form, while trade cycles of invest-ment and output display a marked, if irregular, cyclicality within such long-term trends.

Contingencies and hazards are specifically accommodated within such multidimensional frameworks too. Both macro- and micro-change can generate the unexpected, and macro-change positively entails an element of surprise, though the degree of surprise will vary. One English historian made an oft-quoted assertion about the shape of history: 'I can see only one emergency following upon another as wave follows upon wave . . . [marking], in the development of human destinies, the play of the contingent and the unforeseen.'[67] The author was H.A.L.Fisher, writing in 1935 at a time of particular turmoil – thus adapting his own long-term convictions in the light of an immediate sense of crisis. However, his sensitivity to the brooding menace of mid-1930s politics did not prevent him from analysing the twists and turns of recent European history, as surprises are in principle just as explicable, after the event, as are normalities.

Indeed, as has already been noted, the unexpected category throws light upon the expected, and vice versa, in a way that would be impossible were everything in flux or everything preset. H.A.L. Fisher for one was not afraid of detecting a framework that underlay the fluctuations and contingencies of international politics. Thus in his very next sentence he expressed a long-term Whiggish confidence in the diachronic outcome: 'The fact of progress is written plain and large on the page of history.'

Nowadays, historians are generally less effusive in their terminology. And historical 'inevitability' is rarely invoked with such confidence. Yet the deeply historic challenge of studying both the different-past and the similar-past remains as essential as it always has been to understanding the cosmos in time, and ourselves within it.

Underlying all historical explanations is the assumption that history is not so fragmented as to be beyond explanation; and that history unfolds within a consecutive time-space that is ultimately coherent. These features are potentially knowable by time-based humans. Historical causation can therefore be studied and communicated to others, even if the answers are subject to debate and revision. By contrast, the relatively small number of philosophers and theorists who deny the possibility of cause and effect, logically reject not only historical sequentiality but also consecutive time – a viewpoint antithetical to sustained knowledge.

Expressing visually or diagrammatically the cat's cradle or disorderly 'braid' of history, within which causation works, is a hard task. The untidy elements of turbulence/friction/dynamics have to mesh into the interlocking elements of patterning/structures/persistence, in a way that is simultaneously coherent and disorderly. Suggestive examples can be found in three-dimensional kinetic art with inbuilt movements of unexpected shapes and materials in strange designs. Or the intricate double helix that holds the sequencing of the human genome can be viewed as a prototype of ordered diversity.[68] Diagrams of scrambling complexity are found too in charts displaying the mathematics of movement, or in scientific reconstructions of the bio-physical origins of the universe.[69]

The illustration below displays a cheerful figure of 'braiding' in a Nepalese popular print of twining serpents, which are life-spirits in Buddhist iconography. Together, they provide a gauge against the danger of exogenous challenge (like a lightning strike). The representation is not intended to show 'history' as such, but its interwoven tangle can be viewed as an imaginary web of life, surging from the earth and watched over benignly (in the popular

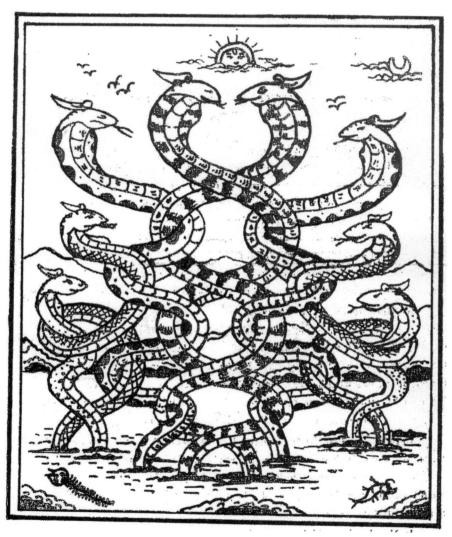

23 'Braided' life forces are shown in the entwined forms of eight serpents, or life-spirits, as adapted from a Nepalese Buddhist good-luck print.

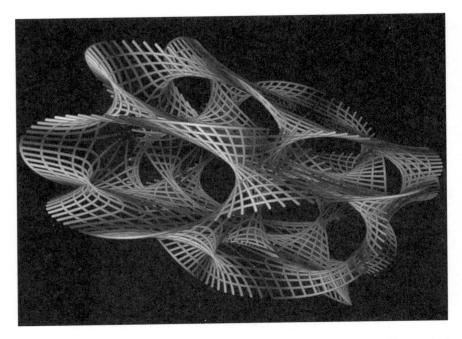

24 This computer-graphic representation imagines the micro-microscopic 'Superstring' particles which hypothetically mesh to originate matter.

print) by the sun and moon. There is an interesting design comparison with the adjacent illustration which conveys a scientist's concept of the super-strings or tiny, tiny micro-filaments of proto-matter that mesh dynamically to form matter at the start of time.

Ultimately, however, the multidimensional historical process looks not like a print or a diagram but singularly like the cosmos as a whole.

Questing to comprehend the frictive interplay between frameworks and contingencies is accordingly a universal theme, across many disciplines. Research in non-equilibrium physics, for instance, now directs attention upon the longitudinal qualities of time. Not only do temporal dynamics unite both order and disorder into a braided history, but they do so unidirection-ally. Time's asymmetries, as much as its symmetries, were present at the origins of everything, and continue to apply to every speck of dust throughout time-space.

So is shaped an entire cosmic history. The tensile force of non-equilibriation – between the component dimensions of continuity and transformation, of certainty and uncertainty – is emphasised by Ilya Prigogine, the Russian-born Belgian physicist of temporal dynamics, as integrally part of the whole:

We have achieved a non-contradictory description of nature rooted in dynamical instability. [This view steers a 'narrow' path between complete determinism and complete chaos.] Why is the arrow of time always pointed in the same direction? This can only mean that our universe forms a whole. It has a common origin that already implied time-symmetry breaking . . . [And in a later chapter] Time and reality are irreducibly linked. . . .[70]

Shaping History – Time Power

Understanding the forces of temporality provides one of the great themes of human enquiry.[1] Much lore is enshrined, not only in learned study, but communally, in myths, literature and proverbs.[2] Clues are thus provided to the paradoxical properties of time as daily encountered. It not only 'moves' and takes specific forms – but it also, simply but inexorably, *is*. Human perceptions and responses are explored here, panoramically, to enjoy as well as to acknowledge time-power.

Definitions and advice are often contradictory, as befits the mysterious nature as well as the apparent consequences of temporality. This all-embracing force can, after all, achieve opposite results simultaneously. So time heals/time destroys; time remembers/time forgets; time is wise/time is foolish; time is magisterial/time is 'sluttish' (a Shakespearean phrase); time is an ally/time is an enemy; time is fleeting/time is dragging; time is very old/but time is also newly minted moment by moment.

Perceptions

One response to this quixotism is to joke. An old riddle enquires, 'What is it that, the more one has of it, the less one has of it?' And the answer is: 'Time'. But, in general, the theme is too abstract to be a subject for immediate humour. At most, a dry wit captures the paradox. Thus Jonathan Swift was sardonic in his observation that 'Every man desires to live long; but no man would be old.' Indeed, even in cultures that especially value maturity as an esteemed stage in the human life cycle, it is venerability, rather than decrepitude, which is the quality to be admired. Hence a traditional Russian proverb offers an alternative approach: 'Better to live well than long.'

Decay and death are known as prime agents of time. It is a destroyer and a thief, with an especial love of stealing youth and beauty. 'But we breathe, we change! We lose our hair, our teeth! Our bloom! Our ideals!' mourns Hamm in Samuel Beckett's brooding drama of world death and ultimate *Endgame*. Cultures that esteem the appearance of being young are especially aware of the passing of time. 'We never get back our youth,' as Dorian Gray mourns at the denouement of Oscar Wilde's fictional resistance to growing old. The forces of temporality assert their power quite impersonally, even though for humans the effects are highly personal. The illustration overleaf provides an artistic rendering of Age attacking Youthful Beauty, at the behest of Father Time, with his hourglass signalling that none can escape — and Beauty is defenceless against the coming onslaught.

So relentless is the temporal process that it provides a source of gloomy relish for pessimist philosophers, like Arthur Schopenhauer. 'Every evening we are poorer by a day,' he noted. Indeed, every twenty-four hours we are that much closer to eventual death. After all, 'Dry trees fall and green ones as well,' as a Meru saying from Tanzania confirms stoically.

Yet history can produce positive outcomes too. 'Time the destroyer is time the preserver', concluded T.S. Eliot, drawing upon spiritual teachings of rebirth from conflagration. Time has the capacity to soothe grief and heal wounds. Therefore it is the 'great physician'. As the years pass, furthermore, time allows a long-term perspective that corrects old errors. Thus it has distinguished offspring, according to an old saying, condensed into a maxim by Francis Bacon. 'Truth is the daughter of Time.' (One waspish commentator countered in reply that 'errors, heresies, falsehoods' are among its offspring too.) Miguel de Cervantes meanwhile nominated an alternative parent for truth, 'whose mother is History', still locating its emergence in the unfolding diachronic. So 'Time will tell', adds an old saying. 'Truth will out,' agrees another. And, in his role as a scientific experimenter, Francis Bacon adds a further stroke of optimism. For him, time is 'the greatest innovator'; or, popularly, 'Time works wonders'.

Those who believe that they are working with this mighty force have an especial confidence. Consequently, the statesman William Gladstone was magisterial when speaking in the British House of Commons in 1866 about the coming of democracy: 'Time is on our side.' And he was eventually proved to be correct, not only for Britain but for many countries around the world. A rather different trend was hymned in the 1960s, a century after Gladstone. This time participants in the internationalised youth culture of the 1960s could join vocalist Mick Jagger of the Rolling Stones in singing his claim-song: 'Time, time, time is on my side; yes it is . . .'. Whether true liberation — in sexual or political lives — has arrived or is yet to arrive, the refrain nonetheless speaks exuberantly of transformative possibilities, whilst

25 *Time Orders Old Age to Destroy Beauty* (1746), by Batoni: the young woman cannot resist the marks of time but, beyond the dark cavern, there is a distant vista of spring and renewal.

implying that those who resist are signally failing to understand the inner momentum of history.

Conversely, therefore, those who wish to defer change signal an alternative mantra: 'The time is not ripe.' But who decides the question of ripeness? It is a matter of judgement and hence, frequently, of disagreement. Whether any given innovation is a temporary blip or a harbinger of long-term transformation becomes fully transparent only when the outcome has itself become history.

Options

Negotiating between the dimensions of continuity, micro-change and macro-change at any given moment always allows scope for alternatives, even if these are only very minor ones. Such options are the cardinal components of temporal experience: indicators that we live within the extraordinary temporal fusion of flexibility and fixity. If the entire cosmos were in total flux, then choice would be meaningless because there would be no settled points against which to measure choice. But, equally, if all were fixed and static, then options, even at the margins, would be impossible.

Instead, we navigate between, freighted with experience but aware that each moment is different from the one that came before. Hence Life 'must be lived forwards', urged the Danish philosopher, Søren Kierkegaard, in his most famous dictum, but 'understood backwards'.[3] He added too that, because things are never in perfect repose, perfect understanding is impossible. Just to complicate things, of course, it is not necessary to envisage the past as being located behind the present: it may be projected in any direction – upwards, downwards, forwards, backwards – provided that it is contiguous also with here-now, with which it is diachromeshed. The Kierkegaardian point, however, remains: we study to understand the past retrospectively, while adventuring onwards into the future.

Proverbial advice for coping with daily events certainly faces in all directions. Care for the future – looking onwards – forms a big part of the task. Think of things to come. 'A stitch in time saves nine.' Undertake a small repair now to save a great effort later. 'No time like the present.' Be ready. 'Redeem the time!' Use the moments well. 'There is a tide in the affairs of men,' advised Shakespeare; 'and of women', parodied Lord Byron, mingling jest with romantic gallantry. Seize time by the proverbial forelock. 'Strike while the iron is hot.' Opportunities don't come twice in the same guise. 'Go and dare before you die,' urged Goethe. 'Time and tide wait for no man'. Delay will only make problems worse. 'Procrastination is the thief of time.' The early bird will find food. And, as a Ghanaian proverb neatly states, always remember that 'The late-comer's fish is in the sea.' Act while you can. Every moment is valuable: indeed, 'Time is money!', though definitely not the sort that can be banked. 'Never put off until tomorrow what you can do today.' And, even if some people's own years on earth are limited, they should try at least to plant a seedling that will bear fruit for others in years to come, as a generous Islamic *hadith* or religious precept recommends.

On the other hand, *past* experience – looking at history – prompts plentiful good advice too. 'Look before you leap.' Consider carefully. 'Haste makes waste', as a proverb from ancient Sumeria warned, with ever-relevant wisdom. Think twice before taking an important step. 'Marry in haste, and repent at leisure.' Baby, take your time. 'Measure seven times and cut once,' as a Russian homily sagely advises. Above all, learn from experience. 'A burnt child dreads the fire.' Remember that things not only can but do go wrong. 'Once bitten, twice shy.' So think things through. Take a deep breath before starting to run. More haste, less speed. Some things, once done, cannot be undone. 'Only fools rush in . . .'. Don't panic. 'Tomorrow is another day.' Play the game long.

With all this, however, don't become so preoccupied with the future or with the past that enjoyment of the *present* – the immediate and irreplaceable here-and-now – is lost. 'Seize the moment.' *Carpe diem*: live for the day. So the thirteenth-century Chinese poet Liu Yin advised, when contemplating the transience of love and magnolia flowers: 'This year make not plans for next year:/Tomorrow's affairs will not be those of today.' While thoughts can travel to past and future, existence happens in the present moment: 'Quick now, here, now, always – ' in T.S. Eliot's orgasmic wording. Enjoy things as they unfold. Learn even from disasters. And, if there have been delays, then don't hesitate to make up for lost time: 'better late than never.' Meanwhile, 'Eat, drink and be merry, for tomorrow we die.' On that theme, D. H. Lawrence provided some purple prose of emotion, written shortly before his own premature death from tuberculosis, to remind all his fellow creatures: 'We ought to dance with rapture that we should be alive and in the flesh, and part of the living, incarnate cosmos.'

Or an escape from the urgency of temporal awareness is always possible, up to a point. Asleep, we are not conscious of its progression. And, in idle reverie, the untethered mind can temporarily 'lose track of time'. Even people in the most intensely clock-bound cultures do not watch the clock incessantly. Attention is readily distracted, especially by strong sensations, such as those generated by unfettered movement at high speed, or by sexual ecstasy or by great exhilaration, overwhelming fear, agonising pain, deep preoccupation, creative absorption, or by any altered state of consciousness, with or without drugs or drink to assist the process.

But gentler measures also serve. 'Let us abolish the ticking of time's clock with one blow,' suggests one of Virginia Woolf's time-wrapped characters in her 1931 novel, *The Waves*. Her recommended tactic to shut out the passing of the years is to sit, quiet and warm, tenderly secluded with a lover, in the flickering firelight: 'Come closer.' The art of deep relaxation has not gone. Even in frenzied lifestyles, there is scope for slowing things down and taking things 'easy', as revealed in current debates about the inevitability or otherwise of 'fast' and 'slow' time.[4] While some cultural traditions are sympathetic to 'speedy' action in everything, including food, others take a quite different view. There is always the allure of deferring until '*mañana*'. And, even amidst hyper-busy scenes in hyper-busy communities, the age-old continuity of leisurely gossiping and chatting is still encountered everywhere.

Spiritual meditation and philosophical exploration provide yet more ways of bypassing time's relentlessness. In Buddhist teachings, for example, the 'highest repose' is reached by musing on things beyond this world. The technique of rapt contemplation, sometimes including the monotonous repetition of a mystic word or phrase, allows thoughts to fly free. All forms of spiritual meditation seek to lighten the burden of time, including the guilt of the present and the inevitability of death. It is the quest well defined by William Blake's pithy phrase in his *Auguries of Innocence*, '[to] Hold infinity in the palm of your hand/And eternity in an hour'. Or echoed in the words of Bangladeshi poet Furrukh Ahmed in praise of spiritual renewal: 'For all skies and all oceans/See the outline of a new promise gleaming bright:/*And in every particle of sand a mountain's surmise*'.

Time Frames

Apart from such dreamlike moments of time abstraction, the mind normally meshes anticipation and retrospection seamlessly together as part of the concerns of the present. Looking to things yet to come means thinking 'through time', whether hoping, fearing, desiring, dreading, guessing, predicting, dreaming, planning, rehearsing, calculating, debating or debunking. Emotions as well as rational calculations entwine. Indeed, so great can be the anticipation of some desired event that its actual arrival may be relatively disappointing, because so much of the pleasure has been discounted in advance. And the reverse happens too. Dreaded outcomes are sometimes greeted almost with relief if they turn out better than anticipated.

Admittedly, much of this future thinking, whether by individuals or communities, tends to focus upon anticipated events that are relatively close at hand. It is much harder to arouse serious interest in very long-term eventualities, even when warnings of potential problems are couched in the most urgent terms. The 'nowness' of 'here-now' tugs our thoughts to hover around 'now'.

Retrospection – the 'remembrance of things past' – is, however, an integral part of present-moment consciousness, not only as things are recalled from personal experience but also because thoughts, aided by evidence, can encompass much earlier times. Mental processes run in parallel with temporality, which is the condition for their operation. Thus past sorrows and past pleasures alike cast long shadows onto people's subsequent attitudes, ideas and emotions. Laments for the vanished 'snows of yesteryear' are particularly poignant. And, bleakest of all, there is fierce regret at things that have gone wrong but cannot subsequently be righted. That anguish is vented, but unavailingly, in the cry from Shakespeare's Richard II: 'Oh call back yesterday, bid time return . . .'.

Thinking beyond the present to past and future certainly acts as a warning against excess pride and overconfidence in the immediate moment. There have been and will be other lives, other times. 'Who has stood among the ruins of Carthage, Palmyra, Persepolis [the ancient Persian capital, burnt by Alexander the Great] or Rome without being moved to reflect on the transience of empires and men, to mourn the loss of the rich and vigorous life of bygone ages?' Hegel once demanded, with sympathetic rhetoric. But people's responses to traces of the distant past, needless to say, are far from uniform. Some are indifferent. Or others stress not so much today's empathy with earlier experience but rather the oddness of 'strange ways and strange peoples'.

'The past is a foreign country: they do things differently there,' wrote novelist L. P. Hartley, plangently, dreaming from the 1950s of a stylised pre-1914 England. And his phrase is borrowed approvingly by historians who are anxious to highlight the 'otherness' of earlier times. '*Tempora mutantur, nos et mutamur in illis*': 'times change and we change within them', as the well-known Latin tag had long ago confirmed. This makes for a style of history-writing that stresses the undeniable elements of discontinuity over time, even at the cost of downplaying continuities. 'Let the dead past bury its dead.'

Other historians, by contrast, prefer to stress the force of tradition and living continuities, despite sundry other changes. 'The past is never dead. It is not even past.' So ran the verdict of a lawyer in William Faulkner's novel *Requiem*. This rival dictum has been much repeated too. People who live in the long aftermaths of bitter conflicts, like Faulkner in the American Deep South, are all too well aware of the continuing legacy of old anguish. 'So we beat on, boats against the current, borne back ceaselessly into the past,' agreed F. Scott Fitzgerald, another American author who was perennially tugged between the vivid present and the lost brightness of old illusions. But it is not only past sadness that endures. There are positive legacies too. Ideas and information, especially when written down, can outlast the moment of their gestation. And there are many imperceptible inheritances that persist amongst us unawares. 'The fundamental things apply/As time goes by . . .'. Between them, these opposing perspectives – the 'dead past' and the 'living past' – indicate the rival weightings of continuity and transformation, which are left for posterity to negotiate.

Witnessing

Moreover, we all simultaneously make and witness history. Time-bound, we see daily a complex planet that has survived from long before our emergence. Its shape and form and living beings are products of the trialectical mix of continuity, micro-change and macro-change. 'Look back on Time, with kindly eyes . . .' suggests Emily Dickinson, embracing an acceptance even of regret. Above our heads, the stars in the night sky are collectively signalling the long history of the cosmos. Their light has reached the earth after travelling across vast distances in deep space, which also means from deep time. Indeed, our own planetary system is contributing to the radiance. If therefore some adventurous humans could jump instantly (say) to the Pole Star, keeping all senses and brainpower intact, they would be able to see the gleaming light from the earlier history of our own sun. Engagingly, it was once speculated that this light-beam would constitute the equivalent of a moving film projection into space of past events on earth. That might theoretically allow us to travel to another star to review any details of history that we wished to check. However, the scenario is too fanciful. Viewed from another star, the visible radiance of our solar system would come from the sun, entirely subsuming any additional reflections from the earth and other orbiting planets.

Nonetheless, the human presence in time-space is now being signalled not by a notional light-beam of filmic history but instead by the daily 'chatter' or 'leakage' of transmitted electronic 'noise'. This disturbance is potentially detectable by far-distant listeners with suitably sensitive radio receivers. Admittedly, to date there has been absolutely no indication that there is an audience 'out there'. Scientific opinion remains divided about the possibility, with considerable scepticism being expressed.[5] As the eminent physicist Enrico Fermi once demanded, aptly enough, in response to a fervent assertion that there must be lots of intelligent life scattered across the universe: 'Okay, but where is everybody?'

While answers are potentially awaited, scientific projects have been launched to investigate the active possibilities. In the search for extra-terrestrial intelligence (SETI),[6] signals have been systematically transmitted to indicate that sentient beings are living here, on planet earth. Will any potential listeners understand the message? (*Perhaps.*) Will they respond? (*Uncertain.*) And will we be able to decode any reply? (*Also uncertain.*) The difficulties of communication will be truly galactic. And any sallies of interplanetary humour will almost certainly fall flat.

However, we will have one thing in common with all new companions encountered anywhere within this cosmos. We will all be part of the same all-shaping, paradoxical temporality that waits for no one.

That elemental fusion is noted by Argentina's doyen of world literature Jorge Luis Borges, who, having speculated that time is but an illusion, concludes superbly:

> And yet, and yet . . . Time is a river which sweeps me along – but I am the river; it is a tiger which destroys me – but I am the tiger; it is a fire which consumes me – but I am the fire.

CHAPTER 8

History Past and Future

Time's outwardness and inwardness mean that we not only observe but simultaneously live the process. And, as a result, we share it too, since we all belong within this universal framework.

A free verse by Aleksander Wat, translated into English from the Polish, expresses just such a visceral, wrenching sense of communal destiny, from a poet whose own life-history was ground between the rival forces of twentieth-century Europe's competing ideologies:

> With my skin I measured uncountable dimensions of time-space, with it I fathomed the flights of youth and the downfalls of the age of defeats. / To be in the skin, in everyone, in every skin of every one . . .'[1]

How humans experience individually and collectively, within and without, the intertwined components of continuity and transformationism, as these forces frame recollections of the past and anticipations of the future, forms the final theme for consideration.

Recollecting the Persistent Past

Continuities provide *through-time stability*, as well as vested interests and inertia. For individuals, bodily continuity throughout each lifetime frames all experience, while memories simultaneously carry building blocks of stored information that integrate the present with the past and help to prepare for the immediately expected future.[2] The capacity for remembering, however automatically, is an essential mechanism of personal being and for all forms of mental cognition including speech.

At times there are moments of half recognition, when a new scene seems oddly familiar or a new acquaintance seems immediately like an old friend. In such cases, the novelty has very instantly meshed into a deeply persistent template within our memories. On other occasions, however, the extent of strangeness or disruption is overwhelming. Then 'the times' seem jangled and 'out of joint', in Shakespeare's sharp phrasing.[3] The jolting effect reveals how normally we expect a seamless continuity to prevail.

While there are many cultural variations in the temporal rhythms of community lifestyles, all people, whether living in calendrical societies or not, are normally able to make distinctions between the present, the recent past and a remoter past. The role of memory as a means of providing a temporal as well as spatial 'location' is not only conscious and cerebral but also subconscious and instinctive.

Hence recollections are readily triggered by sensory perceptions. This was the basis for Marcel Proust's famous account of his sudden recall of his vanished youth, '*le temps perdu*', which was not, after all, entirely lost to his conscious mind but flooded back, when he tasted again a small sweet cake dipped in tea as he had often done in his childhood.[4]

Sensory awareness of cross-time similarities is considerably refined, in the human species, by conscious thought; but at a very basic level it is a capacity shared with other sentient creatures that have instinctual forms of temporal orientation.[5] In the human case, the pre-calendrical antiquity of memory is shown in the fact that past events, even comparatively recent ones, are commonly remembered without precise dates attached to them, unless special efforts have been made to 'store' that information.

Flaws and fallibilities in remembering are often bewailed. At the same time, however, the human mind has a formidable power to absorb and to retain. For example, most people keep almost effortlessly throughout a lifetime their knowledge of the structures and working vocabularies of the language (or languages) that they learn in childhood. Such information can, of course, be supplemented by reference to 'stored' assistance, in the guise of dictionaries and grammars. But the basic linguistic usages have 'grown' into the very framework of people's minds, in the form of knowledge that is hardly recognised as remembered knowledge until perhaps memory may start to fail in illness or old age.

Aids to recollection also use the persistence of structured signs as triggers. Memories can thus be jolted, classically, by marks or drawings on trees, walls, rocks or ceremonial posts. Or symbolic markings may convey cues for an entire repertoire of historical and cultural information. For instance, the indigenous Americans traditionally used wood carvings and woven wampum belts for this purpose. The illustration opposite shows a nineteenth-century maple 'memory-stick' or ceremonial cane. Its markings of pegs and incisions allow the initiate to recite the roll-call and history of the Iroquois chiefs. The mnemonic aid is elegant in its economy – and forms a non-technological precursor of the

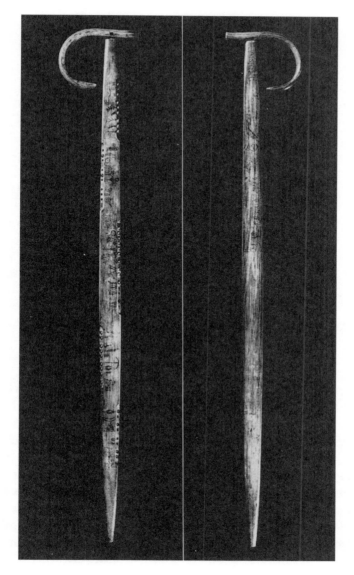

26 The ceremonial memory-stick of the North American Iroquois (c. 1860) was a visual prompt, with special markings for recalling the history and rituals of the chiefs.

dazzling powers of the computerised memory-sticks invented in the early twenty-first century. (*See* illustration overleaf.)

With today's preservation and circulation of written, printed and electronic data, our communicable memory-stocks dramatically expand and magnify

27 A computer memory-stick in the early twenty-first century holds within its 6.5 cm ×
2 cm frame as much as 256 megabytes of electronically stored information.

the role of individual memories. In that way we collectively have access to far
more than any one person alone could ever assimilate and recall. For instance,
the world community of mathematicians in the early twenty-first century
proves some three hundred thousand theorems each year in aggregate, to the
required standards of the research community.[6] Yet even the most diligent
practitioners could not hope to keep mental track of this 'exploding galaxy' of
knowledge. Instead, they learn where and how to 'look things up' from stored
resources, which constitute a form of human-created persistence (or would-
be persistence, since all stored resources are potentially vulnerable to loss,
attrition and decay).

In this way, continuity can also become *additive*, so that when micro- and
even macro-changes do occur they may coexist with, rather than automatically
replace, older ways.

One daily example comes from the biological history of human communication systems. Much older even than speech is the art of conveying messages
by using noise, gestures and 'body language'.[7] Eventually, it happened that

significant sounds became codified into fluent and expressive spoken words, perhaps some two hundred thousand years ago (estimates of the date vary very considerably).[8] Yet the ancient techniques of gesturing and 'face-work' continue unabated alongside vocalisation: not mirroring the talk precisely but providing a free-form adjunct, which is adroit enough not only to underline a message but also, if needs be, to negate it. These 'extra languages' exist world-wide, even while different communities (and groups within communities) have many differing social conventions that crucially frame their meanings.

Another example of persistence-plus in modes of communication can be seen in the widespread human enjoyment of music. This is a feature across all cultures and all eras of history, with the major variations being at individual level in the differing degrees of personal response. Again, the human capacity to use repetitive noise, as in hooting or whistling, or to make rhythmic sounds, with percussive objects, considerably predates speech.[9] Yet those techniques of communication were far from halted by the shift to talking. Instead, they have been transmuted by social endeavour into the torrent of music in its myriad forms, with or without words, which is broadcast daily throughout the world – its format adroitly combining persistence with alteration to convey moods as well as messages that are 'beyond words'.

Adjusting to the Adaptive Past

Transformation, meanwhile, is simultaneously part of everyday experience. In its form of little-by-little incrementalism, or micro-change, it is *adaptive*, allowing for continuous adjustments to differing circumstances.

Applied to human memory, the power of gradual adaptation can be seen in the constant processes of mental updating, undertaken partly consciously but chiefly subconsciously. By this means, information and impressions are variously retained or shed. So much happens, moment by moment, and so much is learned as well as experienced directly over a lifetime, that it is impossible to recollect everything. For that reason, it is normal for the human memory, unaided, to be patchy, to fade, to 'play tricks', as well as to retain and to store. In effect, by being tolerably selective, with banked 'reserves' of information, people are functioning normally, although when minds begin to shed too much this trait becomes a warning sign of ill health.[10]

Such gradual adaptationism in response to changing circumstances is a classic example of micro-change, and in the same way, little by little, people can also train or 'will' their memories to remember more effectively and more systematically. The various mnemonic devices that have been invented for the purpose often use the technique of 'placing' information mentally, which adds spatial cues to locate intellectual ones.

Augmenting persistence by micro-change then leads to *accumulation*. In terms of social and cultural history, that can be seen in the pooling of ideas to generate collective memories and communal know-how. As a result, people acquire information about many things not experienced personally. Myths and shared interpretations of history provide historical depth.[11] And oral tradition has its own power and conventions: dealing not so much in hard data but in diachronic messages. It is also true that these legacies from the past are imperceptibly updated and re-rendered from generation to generation. The effect, however, is to confirm an accumulating legacy: 'Far far away, I hear the voice / That time will not take away', as a Brazilian funeral song declares, borrowing traditional music to create a twentieth-century popular classic, the *Sentinela*.[12]

When to the communicative power of speech is added the creative art of writing, and then the efficacious craft of printing ('this most beautiful invention'), the ability to preserve and extend the human corpus of knowledge is immensely multiplied. In the right circumstances, words may thus outlast their authors, so greatly strengthening the mental traffic between the generations over very long periods of time.

Of course, far from every text, once printed, gains public attention, either in its own day or later. 'The greater portion are forgotten', noted Arthur de Gobineau deflatingly.[13] And it is certainly the case that the 'conversation' between past authors and their later readers is one-sided, because past authors cannot correct or contradict subsequent interpretations of their work.

Nonetheless, subject to these special asynchronous conditions, messages can be sent through time. 'I have achieved a monument more lasting than bronze, / and loftier than the pyramids of kings, / . . . I shall not wholly die . . .' wrote Horace exuberantly in 23 BCE, circulating handwritten copies of his *Odes* in Rome under the Emperor Augustus.[14] And his self-faith proved to be justified. Two thousand years later, his texts have been transmuted into print, while the Roman Empire, to whose power he was subject, has long disappeared. Furthermore, not only his words survive, but so do numerous commentaries upon his work by intervening generations. Hence collections of printed works act as multilayered reservoirs of accumulating knowledge, to be drawn upon when required.

Significant losses are part of the story, for example when oral cultures are overrun by literate ones, before people realise the interest and value of taking stock of the old ways. (But curious later generations often labour, painstakingly – and not always successfully – to recover such lost information retrospectively.)

If micro-changes then accumulate sufficiently in a specific direction, they produce, alongside loss, *trends*. In other words, historical fluctuations are not always purely random in their impact. Again such processes do not last for ever but they do persist, sometimes for very long spans, as in the case of biological evolution, which occurs alongside biological persistence. 'Order is something which unfolds in time,' comments Simone Weil, in philosophic meditation upon the human condition.[15]

For human affairs, the cumulative effect is enhanced by our species' capacity for developed communication, which means that ideas and examples can be explicitly as well as implicitly shared between many, whether strangers or close associates. The role of education (and not just schooling) is significant here, as it generally takes place in micro-stages and is a conscious means of trans-generational transmission. With the advent of literacy among at least a technical elite (if not all political rulers), the capacity to consult stored cultural capital in the form of written or enumerated information, without needing the presence of the author, first greatly multiplied the communicative possibilities[16] – alongside (and not in lieu of) the continuing power of face-to-face communication.

Upon this basis, complex societies and enduring power systems, stretching far beyond the immediately local, are structured. Historically, literate societies have been, from time to time, defeated by illiterate ones. Yet formalised literacy and numeracy skills since their first crystallisation have never disappeared from somewhere on the globe; and these skills have also emerged spontaneously in more than one time and place in history. That very fact indicates something of the impulsion for codifying human knowledge and extending human communicative powers. With such skills, once they are multiplied, there develops too the basis not only for spatially extended political and cultural systems, but also for more popularly intensive participation within them.

Within the last two centuries – and particularly since the 1950s – the spread of mass literacy on a global (though not yet completely universal) basis,[17] is expanding the effect exponentially. Contacts and knowledge are multiplying together. Already in the 1960s, the lively information exchange was dubbed by techno-analyst Marshall McLuhan as aiding the formation of a 'global village'.[18] It was a good phrase. Today, however, the trend could more plausibly be located within an ever-growing global community of townees.[19] And, with access to organised knowledge, there is following too the spread of popular participation in 'politics' and political culture, broadly defined. Named 'democracy' long before it was interpreted in terms of the right to vote, this trend was greeted presciently in the mid nineteenth century by the French social theorist, Alexis de Tocqueville. It was already defeating absolute kings and hereditary aristocrats, he remarked, and its greatest impact was yet to come.[20] In this way, micro-changes in human knowledge resources, and popular access to them, are tilting, as they extend, into macro-change.

Coping with the Turbulent Past

Radical discontinuities, whether welcomed or otherwise, are sources of *turbulence*. These upheavals occur within the natural order and, by extension, similarly within human affairs.

Shock disasters, because of their exceptional nature, are particularly hard for individuals to absorb. A really heavy battering, both emotional and physical, tends to overload all sensory and mental faculties. When accompanied by over-whelming noise, flashing lights, disrupted and fearsome surroundings and agonising danger, exceptional shocks are capable of producing the well-known cases of disorientation described as battle trauma, such as shell shock in the trenches of the First World War.

Terrifying violations of normal order are hard to absorb into routine memories. One tactic in response is to isolate disturbing recollections by thinking about them as little as possible, whilst communicative therapies offer alternative methods for talking problems 'out'. In both cases, the aim is to limit the damage. Some therapists make the further claim that memories can be entirely repressed, only then for a forgotten trauma to be identified, unex-pectedly, while the victim is in therapy. Experts, however, seriously question whether people, once past the 'unremembering' stages of early infancy, ever obliterate all disastrous memories.[21] Instead, the mind has the capacity to compartmentalise, using the power of persistence to 'lock' away unpleasant thoughts in the hopes that they may fade. This 'willed forgetting' is the reverse of the mental capacity for 'willed remembering', which is used in memory exercises. 'Locking' away unpleasant memories is, however, far from easy, with the result that traumas, injuries and injustices are often all too vividly remembered or return in flashbacks.

Not only individuals but entire communities are seared by historical disas-ters too. The long legacy of collective memories, as transmitted between the generations, ensures that particularly bitter historical conflicts are not just confined to one era but extend, with successive aftershocks, for long periods of time, generating *macro-friction* and hostility. Civil wars ('brother against brother') as well as religious and/or ideological contests (believer against believer) and exceptionally brutal treatments of one community by another (the powerful against the weak) are particularly prone to leave diachronic resentments that are hard to resolve.

Coping with problematic historical legacies such as these needs the tribute of historical accuracy, historical empathy and generosity from history's victors, although it may be added that those who appear to have immediately 'won' a historical contest do not always turn out to be the winners over the long term. The tasks of reconciliation are hard but not impossible. At times, it requires a new macro-change to cope effectively with the fallout from past macro-destruction, as evinced in the resolution: 'this must never happen again'. Easier said than achieved; but a new phoenix may rise from the fire. As Hannah Arendt, philosopher and refugee from Hitler's Germany, recorded warily: 'There remains also the truth that every end in history necessarily contains a new beginning; this beginning is the promise, the only "message" which the end can ever produce.'[22]

That history contains major *transformational* possibilities is demonstrated within human communications. Here change had a positive effect. The advent of speech, when significant sounds were first combined to convey words and sentences with significant meaning, was a turning point for our species. These new skills, using the 140-plus sounds made by the human larynx, may have been learned very rapidly, within a generation, or they may have evolved more slowly from proto-languages;[23] but, historically, the outcome was a macro-transformation.

Furthermore, speech in every language contained within it the possibility that words and numbers could be written and conveyed impersonally. So literacy emerged spontaneously in different parts of the globe at different times: in Sumeria from *c.* 3500 BCE; in Egypt shortly afterwards from *c.* 3000 BCE; in China from *c.* 1500 BCE or perhaps earlier; and in Mayan Central America from *c.* 300 CE. Since then, numerous writing systems have come and gone; but the plurality of the experience is visible today in the 'diverse oneness' of the world's array of scripts and alphabets.[24]

Communications remain at the heart of later transformations too. There was no automatic transition from handwriting to print technology. But eventually it was done. Early wood-block texts were in circulation in eighth-century CE China and extensively by the tenth century.[25] And the technology subsequently became known in Europe where, in the German commercial city of Mainz, Johan Gutenberg pioneered the first mechanical press, using moveable metal type.[26] These were the macro-technological transformations that made possible the slower but cumulative micro-spread of literacy. Especially by the nineteenth century, when the printing press was mechanically powered, books became available in bulk and variety, with a new durability, textual accuracy and economy.

But the spoken word had its own later Gutenberg equivalent. What is known as 'secondary orality', or speech at a distance, now supplements the written word in an audio-visual culture that is accessible to the illiterate, as well as the literate, worldwide. Beginning with the invention of the telephone in the 1870s, radio boosted the fluent spoken word, while film and television ('the universal eye') boosted the flowing visual image, plus words.[27] However, the new electronic technology, upon which this is based, embraced equally the world – and skills – of literacy.

Now dextrous human hands, that historically chipped the first tools from flintstones, are being used to tap words, numbers and commands onto keyboards. Electronic computing (developed in the 1940s, after much prior experimentation) has generated a new systematic accession to human memory and human brainpower; and computing facilities are fast spreading from old mainframes to new personalised machines at home and work. So there is a new and fast-expanding electronic 'noosphere' – the global knowledge-sphere that Teilhard de Chardin detected alongside the 'biosphere', the earth-zone that sustains life, and the 'geosphere' or wider planetary context.[28]

Those who have access to the technology have access to stupendous computational power; as well as to nearly instant electronic mail (complete with viruses), via the internet; and to the information grid, beautifully named as the 'web' (inaugurated in 1992). This interactive network system was being used, at the millennial moment of 1 January 2000, by some 275 million people worldwide[29] – still a minority amongst the globe's 6 billion-plus, but a distinctly sizeable one. Here is an unfolding macro-transformation, through which more and more humans are living. In one sense it is taking its time, from the first experiments with electricity in the mid eighteenth century, but it is also accelerating in the later twentieth/early twenty-first centuries, with a classic macro-signal of radical discontinuity: immense power at the flick of an on/off switch.

Already there is great hype and sceptical counter-hype. Is the internet *the* 'latest thing' since the Industrial Revolution, muses one commentator, or merely the 'latest thing' since the latest 'latest thing'?[30]

All these media of communication are potent tools for the communication and discussion of history. They may be used to reiterate old wounds or to spread new disinformation. But they simultaneously have the capacity to extend the forum for sharing historical understanding and debate, as the cultural foundation stones for global community.

Anticipating the Three-Dimensional Future

The past, as it merges with the present, provides ample evidence of human experiences of the familiar mixture of persistence, with its components of stability–location–addition, micro-change, with its elements of adaptation–accumulation–trend, and radical discontinuity, with its contribution of turbulence–friction–and macro-transformation.

On the strength of that long history, it is also likely that the same features will be manifested within different circumstances in the future.

Accordingly, we can be certain about uncertainty, which means that we know something definite about things to come. There are likely to be great transformations that cannot now be anticipated. Yet we can simultaneously make informed estimates and assess the probabilities of continuities and unfolding micro-trends, albeit without the security of full and final knowledge.

Persistence in human affairs will, for example, remain apparent in the characteristic pre-calendrical framings of memory: thus we will not suddenly start to recollect past events and impressions with precise dates and times inevitably attached to them. Similarly, our very ancient and pre-speech predilection for musical sounds is highly unlikely to disappear but instead will continue to flourish – always busily adapting and adopting the latest technologies. Moreover, it is not hard to predict too that direct and personal face-to-face communications will remain essential – at home, at work, at school. For example, behavioural scientists like B. T. Skinner who argued in the 1950s that the availability of mass television would turn it into the chief medium for teaching, with a tireless TV monitor available to instruct students round the clock, have been proved wrong. Fifty years on, education still depends chiefly upon face-to-face interaction, though it is now the computer not the television whose role is being debated.[31]

Expectations of persistence apply unhesitatingly in the basic structures of the physical universe too, making it possible to calculate both regularities and irregularities. Inspired by that hope, the Marquis de Laplace in early nineteenth-century France dreamed of a precise science of prediction. To a true historical understanding, he dramatically exclaimed in 1812, 'nothing would be uncertain, and the future, as the past, would be present to its eyes'.[32] As knowledge of the cosmos was developing, old puzzles were being solved. In 1758/9, for example, the return to visibility of Halley's Comet triumphantly confirmed a prediction first made by the English astronomer Edmond Halley over fifty years earlier.[33] What had seemed random was scientifically explicable.

However, a silent caveat, 'other things being equal', remains in operation. Thus Halley's Comet will be seen again from earth in 2063 but only provided that something unforeseen (such as collision with space debris) does not derail it. The exceptional, however truly exceptional, is never impossible, as the 'singularity' of the primal Big Bang indicates.

Even the most apparently firm predictions thus have some margin of error, however tiny. These variations inform the possibilities/probabilities that underpin exercises in risk assessment. For instance, scientists reliably calculate that the waste currently generated by nuclear programmes will have a radioactive half-life of tens of thousands of years. We are thus bequeathing a hazardous storage problem to our descendants over many generations. That risky legacy is therefore one thing that we do know about the future. On the other hand, if an effective system of waste deactivation is one day invented, then that particular burden will be lifted; and future scenarios will be other than we can now envisage.

Alongside a future of persistence, moreover, there will also be a future of gradual adaptation. Biological evolution is not expected to halt; nor will rocks cease to crumble, and rivers to silt, and ice to melt or to freeze – even if the grand geo-climatic context of all these micro-changes may do so.

Similarly, in human affairs, there are long-standing gradual trends that are likely to remain in operation, though not necessarily for ever. It is highly probable that the spread in literacy will continue; and, now too, the spread of computer literacy. Such micro-changes will also entail, as part cause and part effect, further public participation in matters of global concern. It is therefore not hard to predict that the uneven distribution of the world's resources and the state of the global environment will be issues of ever-increasing importance. Contentions over such questions are, paradoxically, easier to resolve in times of prosperity than in times of hardship but too often it takes a crisis to force decisions onto the agenda.

Gradual adaptations cannot be assumed to continue unbrokenly, as trends are either slowed by the 'tug' of continuity and/or redirected by greater discontinuities. As a result, expectations based on indefinite extrapolations from immediate data often 'overshoot' because contradictory possibilities are underestimated. Political predictions of even the near future often turn out to be wrong.[34] And today, for instance, forecasts of an intensified 'westernisation' conflict with rival claims that the next hundred years will become the 'Asian Pacific' century. A feminist meanwhile might counter that the future will be female. Or we may recall the historically justified dictum: 'Always something new out of Africa'.

Technological predictions are particularly prone to extrapolate from the potentially possible to the probable without allowing for intervening factors and alternative developments. Futurologists in the 1970s, who were enthused by the first space flights, were quick to forecast that travel and settlements in space would soon become routine. One envisaged mining on the moon by 1995, and an entire satellite city in regular earth orbit by 2001. But neither outcome has (yet) materialised. The astronauts remain few in numbers. Instead, unmanned probes are becoming instead our proxy voyagers in deep space. Moreover, it is possible that the entire costly rocket-fuelled technology of the pioneering era may yield to an alternative energy regime. Lightweight 'solar-sailing' crafts, far from the earth's gravitational pull and powered by the energy of sunshine, are already being canvassed.[35] Thus it is relevant to recall that technological developments are always framed within practical viability, as well as being tempered by their social acceptability or otherwise.

Today's prophetic fears about future problems are not absolute templates for trends that cannot be avoided but instead should be taken as urgent invitations to devise intelligent evasive action. The reverse applies in the case of prophetic hopes. It cannot be assumed that any desired changes will continue into the future ad infinitum. They will need assistance to continue and supportive action to prevent derailing.

Future macro-changes, meanwhile, remain by definition the most difficult of all future developments to predict. Much transformational talk in the early twenty-first century relates to the human relationship with the electronic media. Some warnings are simply exaggerated. Once, for example, it was predicted that the spread of television ownership would kill live theatre, cinema going and public entertainments. But not so. And now there are fears that 'new technology' in the form of computers and the worldwide web will kill 'old-style' portable books.[36] However, this is too melodramatic. It is much more likely that a new digitised book production will be sought to make the old and new complementary, in the 'additive' way of humans with their best inventions.

The same proviso applies to the use of computers in teaching. Because students habitually learn not only from tutors but also from one another, within regularised frameworks, it is unlikely that all education will be individualised and technologised. Instead, real-time live interactions will remain at the familiar core of human exchanges, while learning at a distance will keep a special role for self-motivated people and for those without live access to face-to-face communications.

Most crucially, too, there is no inevitability in the predicted coming of a techno-evolutionary crisis in our relationship with computing power. The robots that we currently design and use are not infallibly bound to develop into a never-sleeping rival species ('*robo sapiens*') to supersede the dozy humans, who have not yet outgrown the biological requirement for regular slumber. Nor is the coming of a hybrid 'cyborg', half-human and half-machine, at all inevitable.[37]

Techno-warnings such as these invite the incorporation of suitable controls to prevent unwanted outcomes. In the mid eighteenth century, Denis Diderot jokingly predicted that humans might one day evolve into nothing but heads. That would follow because: 'we walk so little, work so little, but think so much'.[38] Yet we have not grown big heads (except psychologically) but instead we have devised and built extra-bodily computational assistance instead. How we use these new technologies will continue to depend upon our choices – and prophetic science fiction writers are already ahead of the game in envisioning worlds with a robot power that is designed to assist rather than to harm humans.[39]

Combining persistence with adaptation and transformation makes the future opaque but not unimaginable. It therefore follows that some predictions will eventually be upheld but not necessarily in the expected manner or with the expected results. Enthusiasts, it has been well noted, tend to foreshorten the forecast timespan – their eagerness adding allure to their prophetic vision while clouding the intervening problems that have to be resolved before the new outcome can be accomplished.[40]

Simultaneously, however, many prophecies err entirely. The onwards route, in the eloquent phrasing of Jorge Luis Borges, always remains open: 'Time forks perpetually towards innumerable futures.'[41] And poised between the retrospective and the prospective there remains the familiar here-now. So too the narrator of Borges' infolded story of forking pathways realises, 'Centuries of centuries, and only in the present do things happen'.

Fortunately, for the most part, the routines of daily living blur the historic weight of individual actions and decisions moment by moment – each one as quickly come as gone beyond recall. Multidimensionality takes the edge off inexorability. The illustration opposite is by Salvador Dalí who became, with his celebrated motif of the melted clock, the foremost twentieth-century artist of disordered time. In this variant, he pays surreal tribute to Lewis Carroll, the surreal fabulist of alternative worlds: the clock melts and halts, but the human-made time-marker is also pierced by the onwards force of a fiery tree of life to symbolise renewal. So emerges a complex future from a complex past.

The Shape of History

Studying history is therefore always work in progress, not because historians cannot agree but, more fundamentally, because all our evidence and experience are situated within an asymmetrical time and are therefore always expanding and changing the perspectives. Yet this developmental component is an essential part of the subject's strength. If human understandings of history become ossified, then the result is like a 'stuck' collective memory, which is ultimately as damaging to a community as it is for individuals who cannot adjust to changing times.

Between them, the efforts and debates between and across the generations do contribute to build a richer, deeper and more accurate understanding of the past, including an ability to refute false accounts that are not congruent with the evidence. And it is not hard to predict that humans will continue to undertake, review, assess, debate and critique the study of history as the vital basis of human knowledge.

28 Salvador Dalí's illustration of the Mad Hatter's Tea-Party from *Alice in Wonderland* allows a fiery tree of life to pierce his iconic image of a subversively melting clock, while an enigmatic key rests nearby.

Collectively, the global repertoire combines to suggest that the shape of the past is multidimensional. And the same will apply to the shape of the future. Specifically, the case has been made for three dimensions of persistence/micro-change/radical discontinuity: a trialectical braid or mesh of history. The components wax and wane in relative importance over time but the creative tension between them always holds.

Numbering the elements within the mix precisely is, however, much less important than acknowledging the force of pluralities within a coherent whole, as it is sustained between fragmentation and inertia.

'Three-dimensionality' is therefore a convenient way of referring to the many-sided elements within persistence/adaptation/fiery turbulence. It is surely for that reason that this prime number recurs within so many philosophical systems and has recurred so frequently within the classifications cited throughout this study. Its emphasis within Christian theology and within Hindu thought form two significant examples. But there are also traditions of 'oneness' that recall the emphasis upon an ultimate holism. And these perceptions recur because they relate to something fundamental.

Combining many-and-one with respect to temporality is acknowledged in a dictum which declares as much: 'Time has three dimensions and one positive pitch or direction.'[42] This comment was made in the later nineteenth century. Cryptically expressed by England's most unorthodox Catholic priest-poet Gerard Manley Hopkins, it referred to past/present/future as the three dimensions. Furthermore, in terms of understanding time, it clearly preceded the Einsteinian rethinking as the time-space continuum. Yet the dictum neatly encapsulates an observable state of affairs that is worth reiterating.

This study has accordingly argued that three-dimensionality is found within history and operates longitudinally throughout past and present and, prospectively, the future. The cosmic framework for all this is not time on its own but time as part of the dynamic and temporally asymmetric time-space continuum. It is the absolute that contains both absolutes and relativities. And it is within this time-space framework that *the shape of history has three dimensions and one direction.*

Time Frames and History

Evidence for history's dynamic combination of persistence, adaptation and transformation can be seen everywhere. The mixture is apparent within ourselves: both physically, as living amalgams of carbon, hydrogen, oxygen, nitrogen and other trace elements, that precede and survive us in other forms; and psychologically, within our personalities and consciousness, which throughout a lifetime cope or strive to cope with existing in time and surviving/changing within it.

The same combination is seen within the physical environment all around. Some elements appear to survive granite-like and unchanged from the past, while others are changing slowly from past to present, and yet other things are dramatically new. Human actions and, in some cases, non-actions, contribute to these processes. As an interventionist not to say meddling species, we have had and continue to have a notable impact upon our local environment. That means that much of what passes for untrammelled 'nature' is not in fact entirely untouched and 'raw'. We ourselves form part of the earth's dynamic ecosphere, both influenced by and influencing its development.

Nevertheless, there are limits to our scope. The global trialectic comes from forces that are not only within ourselves but are also outside ourselves and our control. Whatever happens, the arrow of temporality flies onwards. Good moments pass, and disastrous inheritances too. 'And when stampeding Space confines me / Time returns and delivers me / Time Time . . .'.[1] (This voice from Martinique is that of Aimé Césaire, who suggests both the pain of the African forced diaspora and the ultimate possibility of a rerooting in company with timeful humanity.)

Far beyond the reach of this world, the greater cosmos displays similar but quite impersonal traits of persistence, adaptation and radical discontinuities. Continuance, for example, seems to apply to the imperceptible 'dark matter' (whether cold or warm) that is thought to pervade the universe and may constitute as much as 90 per cent of its mass. If confirmed, this phenomenon may be considered as providing ballast to the system, with an array of clustered particles, their nature so far undetected, acting as the equivalent of a cosmological constant.[2]

By contrast, the dramas of destruction and renewal are more readily detected. Star-births are signalled by a pearly glow – as seen, for example, in the 'vast stellar nursery' known as the Orion Nebula – and star-deaths by the sudden flaring of a supernova on the verge of burnout. And past extinctions can also be traced. In the Crab Nebula (in the Taurus constellation), there is a 'ghostly patch of grey light' which marks the location of a fast-spinning neutron star or pulsar. This radioactive remnant is all that is left from a supernova explosion some six thousand light years away, that was reported (though not in those terms) by eyewitnesses from earth in 1054.

Yet it is not necessary to wait for exceptional dramas in order to view in the night skies the evidence for multiple processes at work. Look up and in general there is reassuring continuity. The stars are not jumbled randomly between one night and the next. Instead, they remain majestically 'fixed' in their places. They do apparently rotate, as in fact the earth rotates, but they are undeviating within their established constellations. The 'shooting' stars that flare through the skies in comet storms provide the mutable contrast that demonstrates the stability of the general rule. If all were similarly on the move, then we would be deeply perplexed and without stable 'bearings'.

On the other hand, there are gradual celestial changes whose movement is visible too. Consider the shapes of the star galaxies. These characteristically take the form of spider-armed spirals or great elliptical clusters. Not only are the contours of these astral groupings gradually changing but their locations are imperceptibly moving too. These incremental processes are far too slow to be witnessed from night to night. But their past trackways can be seen. View the photographic evidence of a spiral galaxy, such as our own galaxy, the Milky Way (see illustration 29). The elegantly trailing 'arms' mark the course of its slow Catherine-wheel rotation over time. The stars are clustered along the concentrated shock waves which emanate from the heart of the galaxy and are then swept off line, giving each galaxy its own signature pattern of past micro-change.

And look once more. At the radiant heart, the dense core of stars indicates the dramatic transformation that first launched the galaxy. At some point, an unstable cloud of turbulent cosmic dust and gas coalesced and collapsed into the burning energy that shines in a mass of stars. That explosive 'punch' has not yet been dissipated, even while the shock waves are slowly dispersing outwards. Thus the

29 The distinctive shape of a spiral galaxy, here shown in an artist's depiction of the Milky Way, recurs in many variant forms as its formative shock waves slowly disperse in trailing arms of stars, welding turbulence with slow change and day-to-day continuity.

mixture not just of continuity and change, but of continuity with different rates and sorts of change, is detectable everywhere: both close at home and stretching far beyond our immediate horizons. ''Tis Compound Vision –' mused Emily Dickinson, America's distinctive poet of pellucid perceptions: 'Light – enabling Light – / The Finite – furnished / With the Infinite . . .'.[3]

All these overlappings reaffirm the point made at the start of this study, that the long term is always detectable in the immediate moment, just as the synchronic moment is always meshed into a diachronic frame. Because of that intimate linkage between past and present, studies of time need to take account of both perspectives. It is not enough just to peer intensely into a micro-micro-second – the analysis must also be longitudinal. A new 'temporal turn' has already been detected within philosophical studies.[4] And Time is a 'coming' theme in other fields as well,[5] looking at the world not only 'in the round' but also 'in the long'.

Of course, all these references should really be to time-space or, as the physicists prefer, space-time. One hundred years after Minkowski and Einstein, their integral conjunction should be taken as commonplace. One way of envisaging the continuum is to consider time as providing the energistic dynamo and space its locational expression. Thus the history it contains in turn throws light on the nature of time-space itself.

Be that speculation as it may, it is undoubtedly within the framework of temporality and spatiality that history unfolds. Its outcome, when viewed longitudinally, is shaped by the three interlocking dimensions that have been explored throughout this study. As a result, it is also argued here that one-dimensional labels for periods of the past are generally unhelpful, and become increasingly so when the original usages become outworn over time or when they are applied inappropriately to other historical traditions. The challenge instead is to find multidimensional ways of interpreting the combination of persistence, accumulation and transformation that between them shape the past and present and, prospectively, the future too.

Multiplying many historical dimensions makes one historical process, whose contours match those of the cosmos. And this complex saga unfolds within the one time-space that we inhabit, whose qualities are at once deeply strange and deeply familiar. So we live and make history: '. . . *Once out of time and your chance is gone.*'[6]

Notes

Chapter 1

1. From T. S. Eliot (1888–1965), 'Burnt Norton', *The Four Quartets* (Faber 1st edn, 1944), pp. 9, 13.
2. For interpretations, *see* A.F. Aveni, *Skywatchers of Ancient Mexico* (Austin, 1980), pp. 156–8; K.A. Read, *Time and Sacrifice in the Aztec Cosmos* (Bloomington, 1998), pp. 212–16; and R. Hassig, *Time, History and Belief in Aztec and Colonial Mexico* (Austin, 2001).
3. D. Hume (1711–76), *A Treatise on Human Nature* (1739), Vol. 1, pp. 123, 119–20.
4. St Augustine (354–430), *Confessions*, trans. and ed. H. Chadwick (Oxford, 1991), 11:xiv, p. 230.
5. Stellar data provide prime evidence for dating the age of the universe: *see* J. Gribbin, *The Birth of Time: How We Measured the Age of the Universe* (1999), pp. 45–60, 123–9, 140–7, 167–71, 178–80, 192–208.
6. C.A. Ronan, *The Universe: From the Big Bang to the End of Time* (1991), pp. 36–7, 178–9, 194; and J. Silk, *On the Shores of the Unknown: A Short History of the Universe* (Cambridge, 2005). Further discussions are also available in R.B. Partridge, *3K: The Cosmic Microwave Background Radiation* (Cambridge, 1995); and M. Bartusiak, *Einstein's Unfinished Symphony: Listening to the Sounds of Space-Time* (Washington DC, 2000).
7. J. Maynard Keynes (1883–1946), *A Tract on Monetary Reform* (1923), p. 80.
8. J. Barbour, *The End of Time: The Next Revolution in Our Understanding of the Universe* (1999), esp. pp. 324–5. For contrasting discussions, *see also* R. Healey, 'Can Physics Coherently Deny the Reality of Time?' [answering no] and J. Ismael, 'Remembrances, Mementos, and Time-Capsules', both in C. Callender (ed.), *Time, Reality and Experience* (Cambridge, 2002), pp. 293–316, 317–28.
9. C.K. Raju, *The Eleven Pictures of Time: The Physics, Philosophy and Politics of Time Beliefs* (New Delhi, 2003), pp. 385–8.
10. G. Böwering, 'The Concept of Time in Islam', *Proceedings of the American Philosophical Society*, 141 (1997), esp. pp. 57–62.
11. *See* R. Penrose, 'On Gravity's Role in Quantum State Reduction', in C. Callender and N. Huggett (eds), *Physics Meets Philosophy at the Planck Scale: Contemporary Theories in Quantum Gravity* (Cambridge, 2001), pp. 290–304. In the same vein in the same volume, see too J. Christian, 'Why the Quantum must Yield to Gravity', pp. 305–38. Experiments using the Ligo system (US) and the Geo 600 detector (Europe) are currently seeking to measure fundamental gravitational waves: *The Guardian*, 5 Nov. 2005, p. 8; and other physicists are exploring causal set theories that may unite quantum theory and relativity: see 'The Riddle of Time', *New Scientist*, 15 Oct. 2005,

pp. 30–3. Further significant comments on these themes are found too in G. Ghirardi, *Sneaking a Look at God's Cards: Unravelling the Mysteries of Quantum Mechanics*, trans. G. Malsbary (Princeton, 2005), pp. 448–54.

12. On this question, see A. J. Ayer, 'Statements about the Past', in his *Philosophical Essays* (1963), pp. 167–90.

13. L. Smolin, *The Life of the Cosmos* (1997), pp. 286–9.

14. St Augustine, *Confessions*, 11:xi, pp. 228–9.

15. B. Davies, *About Time: Einstein's Unfinished Revolution* (1995), pp. 15, 31–2, 44–77. The extent to which Einstein borrowed/adapted/absorbed ideas already current, especially those of Henri Poincaré (1854–1912), remains debated: *see* Raju, *Eleven Pictures of Time*, esp. pp. 146–69, 461–3. And for the social/cultural/scientific context, *see* S. Kern, *The Culture of Time and Space, 1880–1918* (1983).

16. Cited in H. Hobhouse, *The Crystal Palace and the Great Exhibition: Art, Science and Productive Industry* (2002), p. 27. See also J. Stein, 'Reflections on Time, Time-space Compression and Technology in the Nineteenth Century', in J. May and N. Thrift (eds), *Timespace: Geographies of Temporality* (2001), pp. 106–11, 119; and W. Schivelbusch, *The Railway Journey: The Industrialization of Time and Space in the Nineteenth Century* (Berkeley, 1986).

17. I. Newton (1642–1727), *Principia Mathematica*, trans. by A. Motte as *The Mathematical Principles of Natural Philosophy* (1729), Vol. 1, p. 9.

18. H. Minkowski (1864–1909), 'Space and Time' (1908), repr. in J. J. C. Smart (ed.), *Problems of Space and Time: Readings* (New York, 1964), p. 297.

19. *See* variously J. Bernstein, *Einstein* (1991), pp. 39–42, 53–61, 90–1; Davies, *About Time*, pp. 44–77; H. Fritzsch, *The Curvature of Spacetime: Newton, Einstein and Gravitation* (New York, 2002); and illustration in Ronan, *The Universe*, pp. 18–19. See also M. Lockwood, *The Labyrinth of Time: Introducing the Universe* (Oxford, 2005), for discussion of the mutual interplay between physics and philosophy.

20. For W. K. Heisenberg (1901–76), see D. C. Cassidy, *Uncertainty: The Life and Science of Werner Heisenberg* (New York, 1991).

21. *Time* magazine, 24 September 1979, facing p. 64. Einstein himself had no intention of parenting either scepticism or subjectivism. And he rejected as completely unscientific a colleague's suggestion that individual electrons chose how to react when exposed to radiation: *see* letter from Einstein, 29 April 1924, in M. Born (ed.), *The Born–Einstein Letters: Correspondence between Albert Einstein and Max and Hedwig Born* (1971), p. 82.

22. *Time* magazine, 31 December 1999.

23. A. Comte (1798–1857), *The Positive Philosophy* (1830–42) trans. H. Martineau (1875 edn), Vol. 2, pp. 58, 457. For Comte's ideas of relativity and his precursors, *see* too M. Pickering, *Auguste Comte: An Intellectual Biography*, Vol. 1 (Cambridge, 1993), pp. 48, 113, 120, 127, 153, 206, 282–3, 516–17, 578, 634, 683–4. And for acceptance of 'the relativity of all knowledge', *see* Herbert Spencer, *First Principles* (1862; 1899), pp. 50–72.

24. K. R. Burich, 'The Moral and Philosophical Origins and Implications of Relativity', in D. P. Ryan (ed.), *Einstein and the Humanities* (New York, 1987), p. 22.

25. S. L. Jaki, 'The Absolute beneath the Relative: Reflections on Einstein's Theories', ibid., p. 14, neatly criticising 'the absolutisation of the relative by those who are busy relativising the absolute'. *See* also R. P. Feynman (1918–88), 'Relativity and the Philosophers', in his *Six Not-So-Easy Pieces* (1998), pp. 73–7; and discussions in I. Hinckfuss, *The Existence of Space and Time* (Oxford, 1975); G. J. Whitrow, *The Nature of Time* (1975), pp. 133–9, 142–4; E. E. Harris, *The Reality of Time* (New York, 1988), esp. pp. 34–7, 41–8, 151–9; D. Cockburn, *Other Times: Philosophical Perspectives on Past, Present and Future* (Cambridge, 1997), pp. 3–13; and R. D. Ingthorsson, *Time, Persistence, and Causality: Towards a Dynamic View of Temporal Reality* (Umeå, Sweden, 2002).

26. For a critique of relativity run to excess, *see* R. Boudon, *The Poverty of Relativism*, trans. P. Hamilton (Oxford, 2004).

27. W. Friedman, *About Time: Inventing the Fourth Dimension* (Cambridge, MA, 1990), pp. 67–84; A. Polakow, *Tense and Performance: An Essay on the Uses of Tensed and Tenseless Language* (Amsterdam, 1981), pp. 62–93, 94–117, 129, 146–7; A.G.B. ter Meulen, *Representing Time in Natural Language: The Dynamic Interpretation of Tense and Aspect* (Cambridge, MA, 1997); and A. Hübler, *The Expressivity of Grammar: Grammatical Devices Expressing Emotion across Time* (Berlin, 1998). But for a philosophical defence of tenselessness, see R. Le Poidevin, *Change, Cause and Contradiction: A Defence of the Tenseless Theory of Time* (Basingstoke, 1991); and critique by W.L. Craig, *The Tenseless Theory of Time: A Critical Examination* (Dordrecht, 2000).

28. H. Vaughan (1625–95), 'The World' (1655), in L.C. Martin (ed.), *The Works of Henry Vaughan* (Oxford, 1914), p. 466.

29. On this theme, *see* J. MacDonald, *The Arctic Sky: Inuit Astronomy, Star Lore, and Legend* (Toronto, 1998), pp. 192–202.

30. F. Braudel (1902–85), 'Histoire et sciences sociales: la longue durée', *Annales: E.S.C.*, 4 (1958), pp. 725–53; repr. in his *Écrits sur l'histoire* (Paris, 1969), pp. 41–83; and trans. in his *On History* (1980), pp. 25–54. *See also* below, pp. 29, 31–2, 208–10.

31. M.M. Bakhtin (1895–1975), 'Toward a Methodology for the Human Sciences', in his *Speech Genres and Other Late Essays*, trans. V.W. McGee (Austin, 1986), p. 170.

32. Variegated strands within Buddhist thought are explored in H.S. Prasad (ed.), *Essays on Time in Buddhism* (Delhi, 1991).

33. U.K. Heise, *Chronoschisms: Time, Narrative and Postmodernism* (Cambridge, 1997), pp. 14–46.

34. For this term, *see* E. Grosz, *Space, Time and Perversion: Essays on the Politics of Bodies* (New York, 1995), p. 112; and also J. Derrida (1930–2004), 'Ousia and Gramme', as quoted in D. Wood, *The Deconstruction of Time* (Evanston, IL, 2001), pp. 260–1, 269, 270.

35. *See* T. Siegfried, *Strange Matters: Undiscovered Ideas at the Frontiers of Space and Time* (Washington, DC, 2002), pp. 78–9, 187, 195–213, 235–54; M. Kaku, *Parallel Worlds: A Journey through Creation, Higher Dimensions, and the Future of the Cosmos* (New York, 2005), pp. 183–226, 237–40, 256–83; and L. Randall, *Warped Passages: Unravelling the Universe's Hidden Dimensions* (2005). But for a critique, *see* P. Woit, *Not Even Wrong: The Failure of String Theory and the Continuing Challenge to Unify the Laws of Physics* (2006).

36. Wells's imaginary time traveller, who shared his creator's intellectual zest, urges that 'There are really four dimensions, three which we call the three planes of Space, and a fourth, Time,' adding also that 'Scientific people . . . know very well that Time is only a kind of Space': H.G. Wells (1866–1946), *The Time Machine* (1st edn, 1895), pp. 3, 5.

37. For 'other' spiritual dimensions, see an early example of four in A.T. Schofield, *Another World: Or, the Fourth Dimension* (1888); and a more recent example of five, as in J. Hick, *The Fifth Dimension: An Exploration of the Spiritual Realm* (Oxford, 1999). A comprehensive fusion of theology and physics was also proposed as two dimensions by the German theologian Karl Heim (1874–1958), on which *see* A.A. Eerikäinen, *Two Dimensions of Time: The Dimensional Theory of Karl Heim* (Frankfurt am Main, 2003).

38. Having decided to use this formulation, I was then encouraged to find that others have done so too, suggesting that the alternative phrase is 'in the air'. For examples, *see* the British geographers J. May and N. Thrift (eds), *Timespace: Geographies of Temporality* (2001); the Danish musicologist E. Christiensen, *The Musical Timespace: A Theory of Music Listening* (Aalborg, 1996); the Chinese moral teacher L. Cheng-Ming, *Behind Civilisation and History: Towards Understanding Man in Time-Space* (2001); and, a real

pioneer, the Czech philosopher of science M. Čapek, 'Time-space rather than Space-time', in his *New Aspects of Time: Its Continuity and Novelties* (Dordrecht, 1991), pp. 324–42. The phrasing is also deployed in a special analytical sense, which differs from the above examples, by the German philosopher of identity, Martin Heidegger (1889–1976), whose *Zeit-Raum* invokes a primordial multi-dimensional state that he held to have preceded ordinary space and time: *see* D. Wood, *The Deconstruction of Time* (Evanston, IL, 2001), pp. xxi–xxii, 263.

39. Thought-provoking and beautifully illustrated essays explore these themes in K. Lippincott and others, *The Story of Time* (1999).

40. *See* N. Berdyaev (1874–1948), *The Meaning of History*, trans. G. Reavey (1936), p. 15; also *Slavery and Freedom*, trans. R. M. French (1940; 1943), pp. 257–64; and *The Beginning and the End*, trans. R. M. French (1952), p. 206. For context, see too D. B. Richardson, *Berdyaev's Philosophy of History: An Existentialist Theory of Social Creativity and Eschatology* (The Hague, 1968), pp. 37–43. And *see* below pp. 217–18.

41. *See* Edmund Husserl (1859–1938), *On the Phenomenology of the Consciousness of Internal Time*, trans. J. B. Brough (Dordrecht, 1990); J. Derrida, *Speech and Phenomena: And Other Essays on Husserl's Theory of Signs*, trans. D. B. Allison (Evanston, IL, 1973), p. 64; and D. Moran, *Introduction to Phenomenology* (2000), esp. pp. 4–22.

42. W. S. Rendra, 'The World's First Face', from his *Ballads and Blues: Poems* (Kuala Lumpur, 1977), pp. 68, 70.

Chapterlink 1–2

1. Time travel in fiction is generally presented with great seriousness, to assist the suspension of disbelief, although there are comic and parodic variants. For overviews, *see* B. Aldiss and D. Wingrove, *Trillion Year Spree: The History of Science Fiction* (Thirsk, 1986; 2001); B. Foote, *The Connecticut Yankee in the Twentieth Century: Travel to the Past in Science Fiction* (New York, 1991); A. Roberts, *Science Fiction* (2000); and G. Slusser, P. Parrinder and D. Chatelain (eds), *H. G. Wells's Perennial Time Machine* (Athens, GA, 2001).

2. The scientific possibilities and/or impossibilities are debated in B. Parker, *Cosmic Time Travel: A Scientific Odyssey* (New York, 1991); C. B. Pickover, *Time: A Traveller's Guide* (New York, 1998); P. Davies, *How to Build a Time Machine* (2001); J. R. Gott, *Time Travel in Einstein's Universe: The Physical Possibilities of Travel through Time* (2001); J. Al-Khalili, *Black Holes, Wormholes and Time Machines* (Bristol, 1999); and Kaku, *Parallel Worlds*, pp. 111–45, 172–8, 304–7.

3. See J. P. Telotte, *Science Fiction Film* (Cambridge, 2001).

4. S. Hawking, 'The Future of the Universe', in L. Howe and A. Wain (eds), *Predicting the Future* (Cambridge, 1993), p. 22.

5. For an affectionate introduction to the genre, *see* W. H. Armytage, *Yesterday's Tomorrows: A Historical Survey of Future Societies* (1968). More recent studies include M. Keulen, *Radical Imagination: Feminist Conceptions of the Future . . .* (Frankfurt am Main, 1991); D. Klaić, *The Plot of the Future: Utopia and Dystopia in Modern Drama* (Ann Arbor, 1991); G. Claeys and L. T. Sargent (eds), *The Utopia Reader* (New York, 1999); and D. D. Kilgore, *Astrofuturism: Science, Race and Visions of Utopia in Space* (Philadelphia, 2003).

6. P. Davies, *About Time: Einstein's Unfinished Revolution* (1995), pp. 57–8: equivalent results were later produced by experiments in accelerating subatomic particles at the European Commission for Nuclear Research (CERN) particle accelerator near Geneva.

Chapter 2

1. *See* H.L. Bergson (1859–1941), *Creative Evolution,* trans. A. Mitchell (1911), p. 320; and discussion in R. McLure, *The Philosophy of Time: Time before Times* (2005), pp. 9–38.

2. This is a convention, not a revealed truth, and it is always possible to speculate that one plus one might be defined as something other than two. Yet in such an eventuality, that would imply an alternative internally consistent counting system applicable to another scale of properties, rather than no mathematical rules at all.

3. *See* synopsis by M. Ascher and R. Ascher, 'Ethnomathematics', in I. Grattan-Guinness (ed.), *Companion Encyclopedia of the History and Philosophy of the Mathematical Sciences* (1994), Vol. 2, pp. 1545–54; and details in M. Ascher, *Ethnomathematics: A Multicultural View of Mathematical Ideas* (Pacific Grove, CA, 1991), pp. 140–9, 188; and T. Gladwin, *East is a Big Bird: Navigation and Logic on Puluwat Atoll* (Cambridge, MA, 1970).

4. On this, consult R. Cooke, *The History of Mathematics* (New York, 1997), p. 15; and G. Ifrah, *The Universal History of Numbers: From Prehistory to the Invention of the Computer* (1998), pp. 23–46.

5. Ibid., pp. 340–6, 355, 409, 416, 419–20, 587–90: specifying estimated date on p. 420.

6. Cooke, *History of Mathematics,* pp. 325–51; and D.V. Schrader, 'The Newton–Leibniz Controversy', in F.J. Swetz (ed.), *From Five Fingers to Infinity: A Journey through the History of Mathematics* (Chicago, 1994), pp. 509–20.

7. Indeed, the Sumerian time travellers would also recognise a number of other conventions, derived from their mathematical system based upon multiples of sixty, such as the division of an hour into sixty minutes; a minute into sixty seconds; and a circle into 360 degrees: Ifrah, *Universal History,* pp. xxi, 91–5; H. Crawford, *Sumer and the Sumerians* (Cambridge, 1991), p. 56.

8. Ifrah, *Universal History,* p. xxiv; R. Penrose, *The Road to Reality: A Complete Guide to the Laws of the Universe* (2006).

9. G.W. Patrick (ed.), *The Fragments of . . . Heraclitus of Ephesus on Nature* (Baltimore, 1889), pp. 88–9, 103.

10. R. Herrick (1591–1674), *Poems,* ed. L.C. Martin (1965), p. 139.

11. Ecclesiastes 1: 2, 4–5, 9.

12. Wheeled transport was used from the fourth millennium BCE, while the oldest surviving examples date from the third millennium: *see* S. Piggott, *The Earliest Wheeled Transport from the Atlantic to the Caspian Sea* (1983), pp. 14, 16, 49, 61–3, 239–40.

13. *See* F. Braudel (1902–85), *On History,* trans. S. Mathews (1980), p. 33; and further discussion on pp. 208–10.

14. I. Lissner, *The Living Past: The Great Civilisations of Mankind,* trans. J.M. Brownjohn (1957), p. 141.

15. 'Invented' capitals such as Madrid in Spain (chosen 1651), St Petersburg in Russia (founded 1703; capital 1712–1918), Washington in the USA (planned 1791), Ottawa in Canada (1855), New Delhi in India (1912), Ankara in Turkey (1923), Canberra in Australia (1927) and, most recently, Brazil's new city of Brazília (planned 1957) then in turn need time to acquire their own history and traditions.

16. V.F.S. Sit, *Beijing: The Nature and Planning of a Chinese Capital City* (Chichester, 1995), esp. pp. 29–35, 42–9; and R. Terrill, *Flowers on an Iron Tree: Five Cities of China* (1976).

17. A. Waldron, *The Great Wall of China: From History to Myth* (Cambridge, 1990), pp. 5–6, 13–29, 56–9, 140–64, 194–226; and map, pp. xiv–xv.

18. A. Ravaglioli, *Piazza Navona: Centro di Roma* (Rome, 1973). *See also* on urban links between past and present, A. Woodward, *Rome, Time and Eternity* (Upton upon Severn, 1995); and D. Montagnon, *Rome* (Cologne, 2001).

19. *See* e.g. Charles de Secondat, Baron de Montesquieu (1689–1755), *Spirit of Laws*, ed. D. W. Carrithers (Berkeley, 1977), p. 289 (Book 19): 'Nature and the climate rule almost alone over the savages; customs govern the Chinese; the laws tyrannise in Japan; morals had formerly all their influence at Sparta; [and] maxims of government, and the ancient simplicity of manners, once prevailed at Rome'.

20. H. T. Buckle (1821–62), *History of Civilization in England* (1857), Vol. 1, pp. 807, 852.

21. Braudel, *On History*, p. 28.

22. F. Braudel, *The Identity of France, Vol. I: History and Environment*, trans. S. Reynolds (1988), pp. 18, 263–4; and *Vol. II: People and Production* (1990), p. 677.

23. *See* for example S. Schama, *Landscape and Memory* (1995).

24. For a fascinating survey, *see* esp. F. A. Yates (1899–1981), *The Art of Memory* (1966).

25. Compare J. Verne (1828–1905), *From Earth to Moon and a Trip round It* (1865; 1995), p. 108; and S. Berthon and A. Robinson, *The Shape of the World* (1991), p. 9 and facing illustration.

26. D. Crystal (ed.), *The Cambridge Encyclopedia of Language* (Cambridge, 1987), p. 5.

27. From 'The Nun's Priest's Tale', in F. N. Robinson (ed.), *The Works of Geoffrey Chaucer* (1957), p. 203.

28. D. Crystal, *An Encyclopedic Dictionary of Language and Languages* (Oxford, 1992), pp. 185–6, 342.

29. Ibid., p. 405. *See also* pp. 67–9, 108–9.

30. D. Hume (1711–76), 'An Inquiry Concerning Human Understanding' (1749), in T. H. Green and T. H. Grose (eds), *Hume's Essays: Moral, Political, and Literary* (1882), Vol. 2, p. 39.

31. Charles Davenant (1656–1714), *Circe: A Tragedy* (1st edn, 1677), p. 17.

32. Pierre Bourdieu (1930–2002), *Sociology in Question*, trans. R. Nice (1993), pp. 46, 86–8.

33. I. Opie and P. Opie, *The Lore and Language of Schoolchildren* (Oxford, 1967), pp. v–x, 1–10.

34. Braudel, *Identity of France*, Vol. 2, p. 230.

35. Salman Rushdie, *Midnight's Children* (1981), p. 341.

36. M. D. Leakey, 'Footprints in the Ashes of Time', *National Geographic*, 155 (April 1979), pp. 446–57: of the two or probably three barefoot walkers, one had a longer stride, indicating a hominid with a height of 1.4 metres (4 feet 7 inches); a second, shorter companion walked nearby at the same time, while a third may have followed moments later, treading in the steps of the first and blurring the prints slightly. All were hominids of a genus now classified as *Australopithecus afarensis*, who are named after the Āfar Triangle in Ethiopia, where archaeologists first found and identified them.

37. J. Shreeve, *The Neandertal* [sic] *Enigma: Solving the Mystery of Modern Human Origins* (1996), pp. 93–4, 97, 122–3, 126–7, 188–206, 270–6, 296–8, 311–12, 335–42; and S. Oppenheimer, *Out of Eden: The Peopling of the World* (2004), pp. 47–9, 103–5, 347–8.

38. G. Vico (1668–1744), *Principles of the New Science*, ed. T. C. Bergin and M. H. Fisch (Ithaca, NY, 1968), p. 96: para 331.

39. Terence, *The Self-Tormentor*, I, I: '*Humani nil a me alienum puto*'.

40. One influential example was K. Lorenz's *On Aggression* (1967).

41. R. Dawkins, *The Selfish Gene* (Oxford, 1989), pp. 3, 11, 33–5, 45–7. Hence he argues that, while humans can rise above their selfish natures, altruism is always learned and never natural: pp. 200–1.

42. J. Beddoe, *The Anthropological History of Europe* (Paisley, 1912), p. 188.

43. L. L. Cavalli-Sforza, P. Menozzi and A. Piazza, *The History and Geography of Human Genes* (Princeton, 1996), pp. 16–20, esp. p. 19. And *see also* S. Olson, *Mapping Human History: Discovering the Past through our Genes* (2002). But for a counterview, *see* V. Sarich and F. Miele, *Race: The Reality of Human Differences* (Boulder, CO, 2004).

44. For an attempted scientific methodology, *see* R. B. Dixon, *The Racial History of Man* (New York, 1923), pp. 8–45, 475–523. And for context, *see* G. M. Fredrickson, *Racism: A Short History* (Princeton, 2002); and E. Barkan, *The Retreat of Scientific Racism: Changing Concepts of Race in Britain and the United States between the World Wars* (Cambridge, 1992).

45. A. de Gobineau (1816–82), *The Inequality of Human Races* (1853/5), ed. O. Levy (1915), pp. 146–7, 150–2, 179–81, 205–7.

46. D. Mason, *Race and Ethnicity in Modern Britain* (Oxford, 1995), pp. 6–9, 12–14.

47. *See* variously S. J. Gould, *The Mismeasure of Man*, revised edn (1997); S Rose, L. J. Kamin and R. S. Lewontin, *Not in Our Genes: Biology, Ideology and Human Nature* (1984); and S. Rose, 'Escaping Evolutionary Psychology', in H. Rose and S. Rose (eds), *Alas, Poor Darwin: Arguments against Evolutionary Psychology* (2000), pp. 247–65.

48. This point is further discussed on p. 65.

49. S. Goldberg, *Male Dominance: The Inevitability of Patriarchy* (1979), p. 194.

50. J. Levy (now Eales), 'Women in Chess: Mid-Nineteenth–Early Twentieth Century', *British Chess Magazine* (1981), pp. 402–4; and her 'Women and Chess' (in preparation). Compare with S. Baron-Cohen, *The Essential Difference: Men, Women, and the Extreme Male Brain* (2003), pp. 2–9, 183–5.

51. Relevant debates/disagreements are found in C. N. Degler, *In Search of Human Nature: The Decline and Revival of Darwinism in American Social Thought* (New York, 1991), pp. 293–309; L. Rogers, *Sexing the Brain* (2000), esp. pp. 10, 18–22, 33–4, 93–6, 100–2, 115–16, 123–4, 128–32; M. Hines, *Brain Gender* (Oxford, 2004), esp. pp. 183, 188, 213, 218, 228; S. Jones, *Y: The Descent of Men* (Boston, 2005); and J. Roughgarden, *Evolution's Rainbow: Diversity, Gender and Sexuality in Nature and People* (Berkeley, 2004), esp. pp. 159–81.

52. D. M. Buss, *Evolutionary Psychology: The New Science of the Mind* (Boston, 1999), p. 20. For a measured reassessment of biological/cultural interaction, consult also C. Badcock, *Evolutionary Psychology: A Critical Introduction* (Cambridge, 2000).

53. R. Thornhill and C. T. Palmer, *A Natural History of Rape: Biological Bases of Sexual Coercion* (Cambridge, MA, 2000).

54. D. M. Buss, 'Sex Differences in Human Mate Preferences: Revolutionary Hypotheses Tested in 37 Cultures' (1989), repr. in L. Betzig (ed.), *Human Nature: A Critical Reader* (New York, 1997), pp. 175–90.

55. Among many critiques of the static assumptions within Evolutionary Psychology, *see* the measured discussion in D. J. Buller, *Adapting Minds: Evolutionary Psychology and the Persistent Quest for Human Nature* (Cambridge, MA, 2005), esp. pp. 476–81, for a summary of the case for a continuously adaptive rather than 'fixed' human nature.

56. C. P. Cavafy (Kavafis) (1863–1933), 'He Swears' (1915), in his *Collected Poems*, ed. G. Savidis (1998), p. 41.

57. K. Marx (1818–83), 'The Eighteenth Brumaire of Louis Bonaparte', in D. McLellan (ed.), *Karl Marx: Selected Writings* (Oxford, 2000 edn), p. 329.

58. E. Burke (1729–97), *Reflections on the Revolution in France*, ed. C. C. O'Brien (1979), p. 106.

59. G. di Lampedusa (1896–1957), *The Leopard* (Milan, 1958), trans. A. Colquhoun (1963), p. 29.

60. E. J. Hobsbawm, 'Inventing Traditions', in E. J. Hobsbawm and T. Ranger (eds), *The Invention of Tradition* (Cambridge, 1973), pp. 1–14.

61. C. H. Ward-Jackson and D. E. Harvey, *The English Gypsy Caravan* (Newton Abbott, 1972), pp. 11, 15, 28–34, 39–40, 43.

62. I. M. Pei, with E. J. Biasini, *Les grands desseins du Louvre* (Paris, 1989), p. 11.

63. H. Cronin, *The Ant and the Peacock: Altruism and Sexual Selection from Darwin to Today* (Cambridge, 1991), p. 3.

64. Lorenz, *On Aggression*, p. 232.

65. A. Cowley (1618–67), 'The Mistress, VI: Inconstancy' (1647), in T.O. Calhoun et al. (eds), *The Collected Works of Abraham Cowley* (Newark, 1993), Vol. 2, p. 30.
66. J-B. Alphonse Karr (1808–90), *Les Guêpes* (Jan. 1849; repr. 1859), 4 ser., p. 305.
67. M. Livio, *The Accelerating Universe: Infinite Expansion, the Cosmological Constant, and the Beauty of the Cosmos* (New York, 2000), p. 237.
68. T. Hey and P. Walters, *The New Quantum Universe* (Cambridge, 2003), p. 315.
69. A. Pais, *'Subtle is the Lord . . .': The Science and the Life of Albert Einstein* (Oxford, 1982), pp. 284–8.
70. On this, *see* D. Goldsmith, *Einstein's Greatest Blunder? The Cosmological Constant and Other Fudge Factors in the Physics of the Universe* (Cambridge, MA, 1995), pp. 106–10, 130–1, 140–1; Livio, *Accelerating Universe*, pp. 122–30, 171–2, 258; S.W. Hawking, 'The Cosmological Constant', in W.H. McCrea and M.J. Rees (eds), *The Constants of Physics* (1983); Siegfried, *Strange Matters*, pp. 140–59; and J. Barrow, *The Constants of Nature: From Alpha to Omega* (2002).

Chapterlink 2–3

1. Issues of cyclicality are explored in M. Eliade, *The Myth of the Eternal Return: Cosmos and History* (1954; 1989); G.W. Trompf, *The Idea of Historical Recurrence in Western Thought: From Antiquity to the Reformation* (Berkeley, 1979).
2. J.B. Priestley (1894–1984) explored moveable time in three plays: *Dangerous Corner* (1932), *Time and the Conways* (1937) and *I Have Been Here Before* (1937), while J.W. Dunne (1875–1949) explained his belief in time-transcendence in *Experiment with Time* (1927), *Serial Universe* (1934), *The New Immortality* (1938) and *Nothing Dies* (1940).
3. J. Potocki (1761–1815), *The Saragossa Manuscript: A Collection of Weird Tales*, ed. R. Caillois (1962), p. 153. The original French text appeared in St Petersburg (1804/5), updated in Paris (1813); and in Polish (1847). Critical interest revived in the 1950s, with new editions and the cult film adaptation, *The Manuscript Found in Saragossa*, starring Zbigniew Cybulski (dir. Wojciech Jerzy Has, 1965; in fresh print, 2000).
4. *See* variously A. van Schendel, 'The White Woman', in R. Huijing (ed.), *The Daedalus Book of Dutch Fantasy* (Sawtry, Cambs., 1993), p. 284; and lyrics/music by A. and M. Bergman, with M. Legrand, *The Windmills of Your Mind* (EMI: Metro-Goldwyn-Mayer Music Inc., 1968), performed with many minor variations to the wording.
5. For belief in reincarnation, transmigration of souls, and metempsychosis (rebirth into non-human as well as human forms), *see* S.J. Kaplan (ed.), *Concepts of Transmigration: Perspectives on Reincarnation* (Lewiston, NY, 1996); D.R. Eylon, *Reincarnation in Jewish Mysticism and Gnosticism* (Lewiston, NY, 2003); and studies listed in L. Kear (ed.), *Reincarnation: A Selected Annotated Bibliography* (Westport, CT, 1996). For debates on past-life memories, *see also* H. Tendam, *Exploring Reincarnation: The Classic Guide to the Evidence for Past-life Experiences* (1987; 2003) and M. Harris, *Sorry – You've Been Duped!* (1986). In addition, the internet hosts numerous websites reporting reincarnation beliefs/testimonies, as well as debunking websites, and websites debunking the debunkers.
6. See D.H. Fischer, *The Great Wave: Price Revolutions and the Rhythm of History* (New York, 1996), esp. pp. 273–7, 415–19; P. Hall, 'The Intellectual History of Long Waves', in M. Young and T. Schuller (eds), *The Rhythms of Society* (1988), pp. 37–62; E. Mandel, *Long Waves of Capitalist Development: The Marxist Interpretation* (Cambridge, 1980). For a proffered exemplar, *see also* J.S. Goldstein, *Long Cycles: Prosperity and War in the Modern Age* (New Haven, 1988); and a reassessment of the 'strange attractions of tides and waves', in C. Freeman and F. Louçã, *As Time Goes By: From the Industrial Revolutions to the Information Revolution* (Oxford, 2001), pp. 93–122.

Chapter 3

1. *See* the pertinent comment in A. Gerschenkron (1904–78), *Continuity in History and Other Essays* (Cambridge, MA, 1968), p. 11.
2. M. Saad, *Thermodynamics: Principles and Practice* (Upper Saddle River, NJ, 1997), pp. 1–2, 20, 95–7, 209–10, 824–7: the first law of thermodynamics states the principle of conservation, that energy can be converted from one form to another; and the third law explains that changes due to heat loss vary with circumstances, diminishing as temperatures fall to an (unattainable) absolute zero. Meanwhile, a fourth protocol, or zeroth law, defines the principles of temperature and thermal equilibrium.
3. Patrick (ed.), *Heraclitus*, p. 94.
4. H. A. Simon, *Models of Man, Social and Rational: Mathematical Essays on Rational Human Behaviour in a Social Setting* (New York, 1951), p. 97.
5. *See* variously D. North, *Understanding the Process of Economic Change* (2005); G. D. Snooks, *Economics without Time: A Science Blind to the Forces of Historical Change* (Basingstoke, 1993), pp. 15–20, 41–2, 62–72, 115–16; W. Macmillan, 'Mathematical Programming Models and the Introduction of Time into Spatial Economic Theory', in T. Carlstein, D. Parkes and N. Thrift (eds), *Timing Space and Spacing Time, Vol. 3: Time and Regional Dynamics* (1978), pp. 51–65; and discussion in Freeman and Louçã, *As Time Goes By*, esp. pp. 120–2, 123–35, 371–2.
6. A. Lewington and E. Parker, *Ancient Trees* (1999), pp. 8–12, 179–85.
7. N. G. Jablonski and G. Chaplin, 'The Evolution of Human Skin Coloration', *Journal of Human Evolution*, 39 (2000), pp. 57–106.
8. This possibility was suggested by C. Darwin (1809–82), *On the Descent of Man, and Selection in Relation to Sex* (1871), Vol. 1, pp. 26–7. *See* too D. R. Brothwell, V. M. Carbonell and D. H. Goose, 'Congenital Absence of Teeth in Human Populations', in D. R. Brothwell (ed.), *Dental Anthropology* (Oxford, 1963), pp. 179–90; G. J. Armelagos et al., 'Post-Pleistocene Facial Reduction, Biomechanics and Selection against Morphologically Complex Teeth', *Human Evolution*, 4 (1989), pp. 1–7; C. Loring Brace, 'Krapina, "Classic Neanderthals", and the Evolution of the European Face', *Journal of Human Evolution*, 8 (1979), pp. 527–50; and F. H. Balkwill, *The Testimony of the Teeth to Man's Place in Nature* (1893), p. 175.
9. C. Darwin, *On the Origin of Species by Means of Natural Selection: Or, the Preservation of Favoured Races in the Struggle for Life* (1859), pp. 450–6, 479–80.
10. Charles Lyell (1797–1875), *Principles of Geology* (1830), Vol. 1, p. 73. For context, *see* too R. Porter, *The Making of Geology: Earth Science in Britain, 1660–1815* (Cambridge, 1977); S. J. Gould, *Time's Arrow, Time's Cycle: Myth and Metaphor in the Discovery of Geological Time* (1991); and M. Rudwick, *Bursting the Limits of Time* (Chicago, 2005).
11. *See* R. Redfern, *Corridors of Time: . . . Earth's History as Exposed in the Grand Canyon* (1980).
12. Quoted favourably by Darwin in his *Origin*, pp. 194, 460, 471. Darwin was influenced by the Swedish botanist Carl von Linné [Linnaeus] (1707–78), who had earlier invoked the tag in his magisterial 1751 classification of plants: see C. Linnaeus, *Philosophia Botanica* . . . (Vienna, 1763 edn), p. 31, sect. 77.
13. Henry, Lord Brougham (1778–1868), 'Address Delivered on the Opening of the Newton Monument at Grantham, 1858', in his *Tracts, Mathematical and Physical* (1860), p. 282.
14. Aristotle (384–322 BCE), *Physics*, ed. D. Bostock (Oxford, 1996), Bk 3/1, p. 56; and his *De Generatione et Corruptione*, in W. D. Ross (ed.), *The Works of Aristotle*, Vol. 2 (Oxford, 1930), Bk 2/6, 333b5.
15. M. T. Cicero (106–43 BCE), *The Nature of the Gods*, trans. P. G. Walsh (Oxford, 1997), pp. 66–7, Bk 2, sect. 56.
16. M. F. Quintilian (35? – *c.* 100 CE), *Institutiones Oratoriae*, X, 3/i.

17. See G.W. Leibniz (1646–1716), *Nouveaux essais sur l'entendement humain* (1765), ed. E. Boutroux (Paris, 1885), pp. 29–30, 135.
18. T. Robinson (c. 1640–1719), *An Essay towards a Natural History of Westmorland and Cumberland . . . to which is Annexed, A Vindication of the . . . Mosaick System of the Creation* (1709), Annexe p. 114.
19. For this maxim in astronomy, see M. Maimonides (1135–1204), *The Guide of the Perplexed*, trans. M. Friedlander (1881–5), Vol. 2, p. 54. The best-known advocate of analytical parsimony is William of Ockham (c. 1287–1347), after whom the technique of excising the extraneous is known as 'Ockham's razor'.
20. Newton, *Mathematical Principles*, Vol. 2, p. 202.
21. Darwin, *Origin*, p. 489; and *Descent of Man*, Vol. 1, pp. 177, 184. While Darwin wrote cautiously of descent (ancestry), a poetic evocation of the message became instead: Mathilde Blind, *The Ascent of Man* (1899).
22. M. Kimura (1924–94), *The Neutral Theory of Molecular Evolution* (Cambridge, 1983). See also J. Monod, *Chance and Necessity: An Essay in the National Philosophy of Modern Biology* (Paris, 1970), trans. A. Wainhouse (1974), p. 117, on the 'vast reservoir of fortuitous variability' within biology; and S.B. Carroll, *Endless Forms Most Beautiful: The New Science of Evo Devo and the Making of the Animal Kingdom* (2006).
23. For optimality or otherwise, see summaries in M.R. Rose and G.V. Lauder, 'Post-Spandrel Adaptationism', and R. Amundson, 'Historical Development of the Concept of Adaptation', in M.R. Rose and G.V. Lauder (eds), *Adaptation* (San Diego, 1996), pp. 1–8, 11–53. And for pattern-forming, see P. Ball, *The Self-Made Tapestry: Pattern Formation in Nature* (Oxford, 1999), esp. pp. 1–15, 77–109, 252–67.
24. See variously E.C. Scott, *Evolution vs. Creationism: An Introduction* (Berkeley, 2005); M. Pigliucci, *Denying Evolution: Creationism, Scientism, and the Nature of Science* (New York, 2002); N. Eldredge, *The Triumph of Evolution and the Failure of Creationism* (New York, 2000); and C.W. Mitchell, *The Case for Creationism* (Grantham, 1994).
25. T.R. Malthus (1766–1834), *An Essay on the Principle of Population* (1798); and Darwin, *Origin*, p. 63.
26. W.H. McNeill, *Plagues and Peoples* (Oxford, 1977), pp. 5–14, and *passim*.
27. D.J. Weatherall, 'The Genetics of Common Diseases: The Implications of Population Variability', in D. Chadwick and G. Cardew (eds), *Variation in the Human Genome* (Chichester, 1996), pp. 300–8.
28. 'The twenty-first century will bring a savage test,' warns A. Karlen, *Man and Microbes: Disease and Plagues in History and Modern Times* (New York, 1995), p. 230. See also in P.R. and A.H. Ehrlich, *The Population Explosion* (1990), pp. 12–13: 'Why isn't Everyone as Scared as We Are?'
29. Quotations from M. Mwangi, *The Last Plague* (Nairobi, 2000), pp. 335–6, 449.
30. R. Jakobson (1896–1982), *Main Trends in the Science of Language* (1973), p. 23.
31. L.L. Cavalli-Sforza and M.W. Feldman, *Cultural Transmission and Evolution: A Quantitative Approach* (Princeton, 1981), p. 54.
32. Tae Hung Ha, *Maxims and Proverbs of Old Korea* (Seoul, 1970), p. 106.
33. For the 2000-plus new words and phrases which have entered into current English usage since 1980 alone, see E. Knowles and J. Elliott (eds), *The Oxford Dictionary of New Words* (Oxford, 1997).
34. H.B. Adams (1838–1918), *The Education of Henry Adams: An Autobiography* (Boston, 1918), p. 451.
35. J. Aitchison, *Language Change: Progress or Decay?* (1981), pp. 190–221. See also M. Tallerman (ed.), *Language Origins: Perspectives on Evolution* (Oxford, 2005); and G. Deutscher, *The Unfolding of Language* (2005).
36. C.F. Voegelin and F.M. Voegelin, *Classification and Index of the World's Languages* (New York, 1977); and Crystal (ed.), *Encyclopaedia of Language*, pp. 283–5.

37. A. Parkes, *An Introduction to Computable Languages and Abstract Machines* (1996), pp. 12–24.
38. Darwin, *Descent of Man*, Vol. 1, p. 60.
39. E. L. Eisenstein, *The Printing Press as an Agent of Change: Communications and Cultural Transformation in Early–Modern Europe* (Cambridge, 1979), Vol. 1, pp. 80–3; and case study by K. S. Rajyashree, 'Consequences of Printing on the Written Marathi', in S. I. Hasnain (ed.), *Standardization and Modernization: Dynamics of Language Planning* (New Delhi, 1995), pp. 108–25.
40. *See* R. Keller, *Language Change: The Invisible Hand in Language* (1994), pp. 78–80, 95–107, 114–23, 152–4; R. Lass, *Historical Linguistics and Language Change* (Cambridge, 1997), pp. 292, 295–324; and D. Lightfoot, *The Development of Language: Acquisition, Change and Evolution* (Oxford, 1999), esp. pp. 77–110, 148–50, 207–26.
41. J. Wilkins (1614–72), *An Essay towards a Real Character, and a Philosophical Language* (1668), p. 8.
42. E. Haugen, *Blessings of Babel: Bilingualism and Language Planning* (Berlin, 1987), pp. 13–18; J. Edwards, *Multilingualism* (1995), pp. 33–9, 55–60, 83–8; and Crystal (ed.), *Encyclopaedia of Language*, pp. 360–3.
43. *See* Dawkins, *Selfish Gene*, pp. 192–201, 322–32; and at greater length, S. Blackmore, *The Meme Machine* (Oxford, 1999).
44. E. P. Thompson (1924–93), *The Making of the English Working Class* (1963), Preface, p. 13.
45. R. Jacobsen (1907–94), 'Now', in his *Night Open: Selected Poems* (Freedonia, NY, 1993), p. 184.
46. Anon., *The Laughing Philosopher* (Dublin, 1777), p. 91.
47. On this theme, *see* Folke Dovring, 'Peasantry, Land Use, and Change', *Comparative Studies in Society and History*, 4 (1961/2), pp. 364–74.
48. S. Piggott, *The Earliest Wheeled Transport: From the Atlantic Coast to the Caspian Sea* (1983), pp. 14–16, 31–3, 59–63, 239–40; M. A. Littauer and J. H. Crouwel, *Wheeled Vehicles and Ridden Animals in the Ancient Near East* (Leiden, 1979); and L. Tarr, *The History of the Carriage* (1969), pp. 9, 26–30, 87–109.
49. R. W. Bulliet, *The Camel and the Wheel* (Cambridge, MA, 1975), pp. 7–21, 27, 110, 140, 175, 216–17.
50. For examples, *see* J. Needham, *The Shorter Science and Civilisation in China*, Vol. 4 (Cambridge, 1994), pp. 43–58, 111–30, 155–85, 220–66; and T. S. Reynolds, *Stronger than a Thousand Men: A History of the Vertical Water Wheel* (Baltimore, 1983).
51. G. Basalla, *The Evolution of Technology* (Cambridge, 1988), p. 2 and illus. pp. 6–7.
52. *See* G. Kubler, *The Shape of Time: Remarks on the History of Things* (New Haven, 1962), pp. 48–9, 77–82; and also A. Hart-Davis, *Eurekaaargh! Inventions that Failed* (1999).
53. T. G. Dobzhansky (1900–75), 'Man and Natural Selection', *American Scientist*, 49 (1961), p. 285.
54. E. L. Jones, *Growth Recurring: Economic Change in World History* (Oxford, 1988), pp. 73–84.
55. A. Smith (1723–90), *An Inquiry into the Nature and Causes of the Wealth of Nations* (1776), ed. R. H. Campbell, A. S. Skinner and W. B. Todd (Oxford, 1976), Vol. 1, p. 456.
56. R. R. Nelson and S. G. Winter, *An Evolutionary Theory of Economic Change* (Cambridge, MA, 1982), pp. 9, 17–20; and R. R. Nelson, *Understanding Technical Change as an Evolutionary Process* (Amsterdam, 1987). *See also* P. Steadman, *The Evolution of Designs: Biological Analogy in Architecture and the Applied Arts* (Cambridge, 1979), pp. 83–6, 225–6, 229–36; Basalla, *Evolution of Technology*, pp. 21–5, 26–49, 121, 124–9; and, for the perennial borrowing, anticipating and sharing of ideas, the anecdotes in T. Rothman, *Everything's Relative: And Other Fables from Science and Technology* (New York, 2003).

57. S. Butler (1835–1902), 'Darwin among the Machines', in *Christchurch N.Z. Press* (13 June 1863), repr. in H.F. Jones (ed.), *The Note-Books of Samuel Butler* (1912), pp. 42–6, esp. p. 46.

58. B. Mazlish, *The Fourth Discontinuity: The Co-Evolution of Man and Machines* (New Haven, 1993), pp. 216–33; and *see* below, pp. 245–6.

59. A.R. Wallace (1823–1913), 'The Development of Human Races under the Law of Natural Selection', *Anthropological Review* (May 1864); repr. in his *Contributions to the Theory of Natural Selection* (1870), p. 315.

60. F. Bacon (1561–1626), *Novum Organum: Or, True Suggestions for the Interpretation of Nature* (1844), p. 59, Bk 1, sect. lxxxiv.

61. D. Diderot (1713–84), in S.J. Gendzier (ed.), *Denis Diderot's The Encylopedia: Selections* (New York, 1967), p. 97.

62. *See* case study in J. Smith, *The Speckled Monster: Smallpox in England, 1670–1970, with Particular Reference to Essex* (Chelmsford, 1987).

63. J. Haygarth (1740–1827), *An Inquiry How to Prevent the Small-Pox . . .* (Chester, 1784), p. 223; and his *Sketch of a Plan to Exterminate the Casual Small-Pox from Great Britain . . .* (1793). And *see* p. 94.

64. M. Livi-Bacci, *A Concise History of World Population* (Oxford, 1992), pp. 106–13.

65. R.S. Westfall, *Never at Rest: A Biography of Isaac Newton* (Cambridge, 1980), p. 274. For an engaging history of the giant-metaphor, see R.K. Merton, *Standing on the Shoulders of Giants: A Shandean Postscript* (New York, 1965).

66. K.R. Popper (1902–94), *Objective Knowledge: An Evolutionary Approach* (Oxford, 1972), pp. 261–5.

67. R. McKie, *Ape-Man: The Story of Human Evolution* (2000), p. 179.

68. H. Spencer (1820–1903), *Social Statics: Or, the Conditions Essential to Human Happiness Specified* (1851), p. 65, pt 1, ch. 2, sect. 4.

69. Leibniz, *Nouveaux essais*, pp. 29–30, 135.

70. Basalla, *Evolution of Technology*, p. 57.

Chapterlink 3–4

1. *See* L. Gardner, *Bloodline of the Holy Grail: The Hidden Lineage of Jesus Revealed* (Shaftesbury, 1996), pp. 335–45; with Stuartist website at *http://www.royalhouseofstuart. org.uk* and a debunking alternative at *http://www.chivalricorders.org/royalty/fantasy/ stuart.htm*. For another speculative interpretation of the putative descendants of Christ and Mary Magdalene, nominating via the Merovingians 'at least a dozen families in Britain and Europe today, with numerous collateral branches', *see* M. Baigent, R. Leigh and H. Lincoln, *The Holy Blood and the Holy Grail* (1982), esp. pp. 368–9; and for other speculations about Christ and Mary Magdalene, *see* W.E. Phipps, *Was Jesus Married?* (New York, 1970); and idem, *The Sexuality of Jesus: Theological and Literary Perspectives* (New York, 1973), pp. 61–71.

2. D. Brown, *The Da Vinci Code* (2003): the heroine decodes the mysteries of the Holy Grail by using cipher-breaking skills learned at Royal Holloway, University of London – in an agreeable tribute to the talented students of this internationalist college. This brief touch of realism within Brown's fictional romp has prompted more than one new applicant to come to Royal Holloway to study cryptography, as my colleagues in the Computer Science Department have confirmed.

3. *See* J. Bunyan (1628–88), *The Pilgrim's Progress* (1678); and the stress upon the widespread appeal of this text, which has been translated into over two hundred languages, in C. Hill, *A Turbulent, Seditious, and Factious People: John Bunyan and his Church* (Oxford, 1988), pp. 373–80.

4. *See* J. B. Bury's classic *The Idea of Progress: An Inquiry into its Origin and Growth* (1920); as well as discussions in F. E. Manuel, *Shapes of Philosophical History* (1965); R. Nisbet, *History of the Idea of Progress* (1980); and C. Lasch, *The True and Only Heaven: Progress and its Critics* (New York, 1991).

5. G. Stedman Jones, *An End to Poverty? A Historical Debate* (2004).

6. Narrative techniques are reviewed in H. P. Abbot (ed.), *The Cambridge Introduction to Narrative* (Cambridge, 2002); S. Chatman, *Story and Discourse: Narrative Structures in Fiction and Film* (Ithaca, 1978); and D. Bordwell, *Narration in the Fiction Film* (1993).

Chapter 4

1. M. T. V. T. Lago and A. Blanchard (eds), *The Non-Sleeping Universe* (Dordrecht, 1999).

2. Discussed in T. D. Kendrick, *The Lisbon Earthquake* (1956); J. Z. de Boer and D. T. Sanders, *Earthquakes in Human History: The Far-Reaching Effects of Seismic Disruptions* (Princeton, 2005), pp. 88–105; and, for the 1755 post-quake tidal waves, P. A. Pirazzoli, *Sea Level Changes: The Last 20,000 Years* (Chichester, 1996), p. 131.

3. F. M. A. de Voltaire (1694–1778), *Candide: ou l'optimisme* (Paris, 1759), trans. as *Candid: Or, All for the Best* (1759), p. 132. His specific target was G. W. Leibniz, *Théodicée* (1710), trans. as *Theodicy: Essays on the Goodness of God, the Freedom of Man and the Origin of Evil* (1952), esp. p. 98.

4. An early twentieth-century text, for example, stressed the new approach in its title: see O. Lodge, *Modern Scientific Ideas, Especially the Idea of Discontinuity* (1927), p. 13.

5. C. R. Hartington (ed.), *The Year without a Summer? World Climate in 1816* (Ottawa, 1992). For an overview of natural cataclysms and their geographical incidence, *see* variously L. Newson, *Atlas of the World's Worst Natural Disasters* (1998); and L. Davis, *Encyclopedia of Natural Disasters* (1993).

6. Plato (428–347), *Timaeus*, ed. A. E. Taylor (1929), pp. 19, 23. *See also* commentary in ibid., pp. 131–3; and in W. L. Friedrich, *Fire in the Sea: The Santorini Volcano – Natural History and the Legend of Atlantis* (Cambridge, 2000), esp. pp. 82–93, 99–103, 138–57. However, Plato's account, which was not presented as a first-hand report, located his imagined Atlantis outside the Mediterranean, just beyond the pillars of Hercules at Gibraltar/Ceuta, rather than within the Mediterranean itself.

7. C. Yong et al. (eds), *The Great Tangshan Earthquake of 1976: An Anatomy of Disaster* (Oxford, 1988), pp. 1, 57–8. Even this heavy mortality was outdone by a mega-quake in China in 1556, which is said to have killed well over 750,000 people (but figures from this era are hard to verify).

8. See J. L. Doob, *Stochastic Processes* (New York, 1953).

9. Hear, for example, *Electronic Music* (EMF, Canada, 1997) by the French-Greek maestro of electronic music, Iannis Xenakis (1922–2001).

10. G. Cuvier (1769–1832), *Recherches sur les ossemens fossiles* . . . (1812); later reissued as *Discours sur les révolutions de la surface du globe* . . . (Paris, 1825/6). *See also* D. Outram, *Georges Cuvier: Vocation, Science and Authority in Post-revolutionary France* (Manchester, 1984), pp. 141–60.

11. L. Huxley, *Life and Letters of Thomas Henry Huxley* (1900), Vol. 1, p. 176.

12. S. J. Gould (1941–2002) introduced this term in a joint article by himself and N. Eldredge, 'Punctuated Equilibria: An Alternative to Phyletic Gradualism', in T. J. M. Schopf (ed.), *Models in Paleobiology* (San Francisco, 1972), pp. 82–115; also repr. in N. Eldredge, *Time Frames: The Rethinking of Darwinian Evolution and the Theory of Punctuated Equilibrium* (1986), pp. 193–223. *See also* T. Palmer, *Controversy: Catastrophism and Evolution – the Ongoing Debate* (New York, 1999), pp. 127–37, 143; R. Corfield, *Architects of Eternity: The New Science of Fossils* (2001), pp. 129–30, 142–5,

296–7; and restatement in S.J. Gould, *The Structure of Evolutionary Theory* (Cambridge, MA, 2001).

13. Eldredge, *Time Frames*, pp. 39–40, 106, 121; S.M. Stanley, *Extinction* (New York, 1987), pp. 7, 91–107, 128, 132–71; Palmer, *Controversy*, pp. 171–2, 187–9, 190–7, 340–2.

14. For this view, *see* F.J. Teggart (1870–1946), *Theory of History* (New Haven, 1925), repr. as *Theory and Processes of History* (Berkeley, 1977).

15. Stanley, *Extinction*, pp. 208–18.

16. T. Dobzhansky et al., *Evolution* (San Francisco, 1977), p. 466.

17. *See* I. Glynn and J. Glynn, *The Life and Death of Smallpox* (2004); and D.R. Hopkins, *Princes and Peasants: Smallpox in History* (Chicago, 1983), pp. 310, 317.

18. M. Davis, *Late Victorian Holocausts: El Niño Famines and the Making of the Third World* (2001).

19. *See* variously R. Conquest, *The Harvest of Sorrow: Soviet Collectivisation and the Terror-Famine* (1986; 2002), pp. 299–307, calculating the Soviet death toll at 12 million, including the famine and accompanying terror; D.L. Yang, *Calamity and Reform in China: State, Rural Society and Institutional Change since the Great Leap Famine* (Stanford, 1996), pp. 21–41, 37–8, calculating famine-induced premature mortality at anything from 16.5 to 30 million (a wide range); and C.H. Twining, 'The Economy', in K.D. Jackson (ed.), *Cambodia, 1975–8: Rendezvous with Death* (Princeton, 1989), pp. 109–50.

20. *See* J. Gleick's *Chaos: Making a New Science* (New York, 1987); as well as C. Brown, *Chaos and Catastrophe Theories* (Thousand Oaks, CA, 1995), pp. v–vi, 1, 48; J.L. Casti, *Complexification: Explaining a Paradoxical World through the Science of Surprise* (1994); and M. Buchanan, *Ubiquity: The Science of History . . . Or Why the World is Simpler than We Think* (2000).

21. J. Barkley Rosser, *From Catastrophe to Chaos: A General Theory of Economic Discontinuities* (Dordrecht, 1991), pp. 12, 18–30, esp. p. 23.

22. A. Marshall (1842–1924), *Principles of Economics* (1890), Vol. 1, p. vi.

23. O. Cromwell (1598–1658), from I. Roots (ed.), *Speeches of Oliver Cromwell* (1989), pp. 73, 76. *See* too C. Hill, 'The Word "Revolution"', in his *A Nation of Change and Novelty: Radical Politics, Religion and Literature in Seventeenth-Century England* (1993), pp. 100–20.

24. Examples include E. Petre, *The Fate of France: . . . [compared with] . . . the Happy Revolution in England . . .* (1690); R.B. [N. Crouch], *The History of the House of Orange: . . . till the Late Wonderful Revolution* (1693); and Anon., *A Collection of* [Voting] *Lists: . . . ever since the Glorious Revolution . . .* (1715).

25. An early example is M. D'Odoucet, *Révolution française . . .* (Paris, 1790); or L. Romilly, *Thoughts on the Probable Influence of the French Revolution upon Great Britain* (1790). Compare earlier with R. Price (1723–91), *Observations on the Importance of the American Revolution: And the Means of Making it a Benefit to the World* (1785).

26. *See* C. Fourier (1772–1837), *Theory of the Four Movements* (1808), ed. G. Stedman Jones and I. Patterson (Cambridge, 1996), pp. 99, 104. *See also* D. Bell, 'Charles Fourier: Prophet of Eupsychia', in M. Blaug (ed.), *Dissenters: Charles Fourier; Henri de St Simon; Pierre-Joseph Proudhon; John A. Hobson* (Aldershot, 1992), pp. 197–214; and P.M. Pilbeam, *French Socialists before Marx: Workers, Women and the Social Question in France* (Teddington, 2000), pp. 14–16, 40–3, 76–7, 108–10.

27. C.J. Guarneri, *The Utopian Alternative: Fourierism in Nineteenth-Century America* (Ithaca, 1991).

28. For Saint-Simon (1760–1825), *see* A.J. Booth, *Saint-Simon and Saint-Simonism: A Chapter in the History of Socialism in France* (1871), p. 38.

29. P-J. Proudhon (1809–65), *General Idea of Revolution in the Nineteenth Century* (Paris, 1851; trans. 1923), pp. 13–14, 239, paraphrasing Deuteronomy, 32:39: 'I kill and I make

alive; I wound and I heal.' For variant interpretations of Proudhon's radical populism, consult: C. Gaillard, *Proudhon: Heraut et philosophe du peuple* (Paris, 2004); E. Hyams, *Pierre-Joseph Proudhon: His Revolutionary Life, Mind and Works* (1979), esp. p. 276; and J. S. Schapiro, 'Pierre Joseph Proudhon, Harbinger of Fascism', in Blaug (ed.), *Dissenters*, pp. 94–117.

30. W. Blake (1757–1827), 'The Marriage of Heaven and Hell' (*c.* 1793), in G. Keynes (ed.), *Poetry and Prose of William Blake* (1961), p. 181.

31. I. Kant (1724–1804), *Idea for a Universal History with a Cosmopolitan Purpose* (1784), in H. Reiss (ed.), *Kant's Political Writings* (Cambridge, 1970), pp. 43, 44. See also M. Despland, *Kant on History and Religion* (Montreal, 1973), p. 33.

32. G. W. F. Hegel (1770–1831), *Lectures on the Philosophy of World History*, in Hoffmeister edn, ed. D. Forbes (Cambridge, 1975), pp. 124–5, 127, 130–1, 170. See also C. Taylor, *Hegel* (Cambridge, 1975), pp. 389–427; J. McCarney, *Hegel on History* (2000); and T. P. Pinkard, *Hegel: A Biography* (Cambridge, 2000). Hegel's very complex writings were initially circulated in bowdlerised versions, edited by the 'deservedly obscure' H. M. Chalybaus: *see* ibid., p. xi.

33. Mazlish, *Riddle of History*, pp. 146–51; and K. R. Popper, 'What is Dialectic', *Mind: A Quarterly Review of Psychology and Philosophy*, 49 (1940), pp. 403–26.

34. K. Marx and F. Engels (1820–95), *Communist Manifesto* (1848), in McLellan (ed.), *Marx: Selected Writings* (2000 edn), p. 246. *See too* G. Lichtheim, *Marxism: An Historical and Critical Study* (1961), pp. 6–9, 12, 22–8, 39–62.

35. F. Engels, *Socialism: Utopian and Scientific* (1892), in K. Marx and F. Engels, *Selected Works in Two Volumes* (Moscow, 1962), Vol. 2, p. 153.

36. G. A. Wetter, *Dialectical Materialism: A Historical and Systematic Survey of Philosophy in the Soviet Union* (1958); Z. A. Jordan, *The Evolution of Dialectical Materialism: A Philosophical and Sociological Analysis* (1967).

37. Engels, 'Speech at the Graveside of Karl Marx' (Highgate Cemetery, 1883), in Marx and Engels, *Selected Works*, Vol. 2, p. 167. In 1871 Marx presented the first volume of *Das Kapital*, to Darwin, who mildly hoped that their researches would 'in the long run' add to 'the Happiness of Mankind': *see* K. Padover, *Karl Marx: An Intimate Biography* (New York, 1978), p. 364; and context in D. A. Stack, 'The First Darwinian Left: Radical and Socialist Responses to Darwin, 1859–1914', *History of Political Thought*, 21 (2000), pp. 682–710.

38. M. Kaufmann, *Utopias: Or, Schemes of Social Improvement from Sir Thomas More to Karl Marx* (1879), p. 248. For Marx's contemporary reputation, *see also* E. J. Hobsbawm, 'Dr. Marx and the Victorian Critics', in his *Labouring Men* (1964), pp. 239–49.

39. For Li Ta-chao [Li Dazhao] (1888–1927), *see* M. Meisner, *Li Ta-chao and the Origins of Chinese Marxism* (Cambridge, MA, 1967), p. 63.

40. V. I. Lenin (1870–1924), *What is to be Done?* trans. S. V. Utechin and P. Utechin (Oxford, 1963), esp. pp. 144–7, 150, 152–4, 186–7, 192.

41. While acknowledging insights from Marx, Julius Nyerere (1922–99) distinguished his village communalism from state-directed communism: *see* variously J. K. Nyerere, *Freedom and Unity/Uhuru na Umoja: A Selection from Writings and Speeches, 1952–65* (1967), pp. 121–2, 206–7, 208; C. Legum and G. Mmari (eds), *Mwalimu: The Influence of Nyerere* (1995), pp. 32–45; and A. V. Y. Mbelle, G. D. Mjema and A. A. L. Kilindo (eds), *The Nyerere Legacy and Economic Policy Making in Tanzania* (Dar es Salaam, 2002).

42. C. McClintock, *Revolutionary Movements in Latin America: El Salvador's FMLN and Peru's Shining Path* (Washington DC, 1998), pp. 63–73.

43. For such discussions, *see* M. Desai, *Marx's Revenge: The Resurgence of Capitalism and the Death of Statist Socialism* (2002); and works cited there.

44. On policies in 1970s China, *see* S. Chakrabarti, *Mao, China's Intellectuals and the Cultural Revolution* (New Delhi, 1998), esp. pp. 76–99, 116–27; and R. J. R. Kirkby,

Urbanisation in China: Town and Country in a Developing Economy, 1949–2000 AD (1985), pp. xii, 76, 86.

45. *See* for a study of Romanian settlement planning or 'systematisation' (*sistematizare*) in application to Feldioara (Braşov country), S.L. Sampson, *National Integration through Socialist Planning: An Anthropological Study of a Romanian New Town* (New York, 1984), pp. 17–18, 30–40, 285–305.

46. *See, inter alia,* C. Brinton, *The Anatomy of Revolution* (1939); L. Stone, 'Theories of Revolution', *World Politics,* 18 (1965/6), pp. 159–76; P. Calvert, *Revolution* (1970); I. Kramnick, 'Reflections on Revolution: Definition and Explanation in Recent Scholarship', *History & Theory,* 11 (1972), pp. 26–63; J. Krejči, *Great Revolutions Compared: The Search for a Theory* (Brighton, 1973), p. 212; and E. Kamenka, 'Revolutionary Ideology and "The Great French Revolution of 1789 – ?"', in G. Best (ed.), *The Permanent Revolution: The French Revolution and its Legacy, 1789–1989* (1988), esp. pp. 85–99.

47. G. Farmer and D.J. Hamblin, *First on the Moon: A Voyage with Neil Armstrong, Michael Collins, Edwin E. Aldrin jnr* (1970), p. 268.

48. R.D. Launius, *Frontiers of Space Exploration* (Westport, CT, 1998), p. 24; and for global witnessing, *see* T. Green, *The Universal Eye: World Television in the Seventies* (1972), pp. 1–2.

49. N. Perrin, *Giving up the Gun: Japan's Reversion to the Sword, 1543–1879* (Boston, 1979), pp. 7–18; and context in Numata Jirō, *Yōgaku/Western Learning: A Short History of the Study of Western Science in Early Modern Japan* (Tokyo, 1992), pp. 26–9, 162–3, 168–9.

50. *See* N.D. Cooks, *Born to Die: Disease and New World Conquest, 1492–1650* (Cambridge, 1998).

51. A. Recinos and D. Goetz (trans), *The Annals of the Cakchiquels; and Title of the Lords of Totonicapán* (Norman, OK, 1953), pp. 115–16.

52. L.L. Cavalli-Sforza and F. Cavalli-Sforza, *The Great Human Diasporas: The History of Diversity and Evolution* (New York, 1995), pp. 121–3, and map, p. 122.

53. H.S. Klein, *The Atlantic Slave Trade* (Cambridge, 1999), esp. pp. 210–11; R. Law, *The Slave Coast of West Africa, 1550–1750: The Impact of the Atlantic Slave Trade on African Society* (Oxford, 1991), esp. pp. 1–4, 350; and P.E. Lovejoy, *Transformations in Slavery: A History of Slavery in Africa* (Cambridge, 1983). For a recent retelling, *see also* S. Schama, *Rough Crossings: Britain, the Slaves, and the American Revolution* (2005).

54. P. Rivière, *Christopher Columbus* (Stroud, 1998), pp. 9–23, 26–32, 38–9, 43; and M.H. Davidson, *Columbus Then and Now: A Life Reexamined* (Oklahoma, 1997), pp. 62–96, 273–9, 282.

55. B. Tedlock, *Time and the Highland Maya* (Albuquerque, NM, 1992), pp. xiii–xv, 209–13.

56. Among a huge literature, *see* J. Walvin, *Slavery and the Slave Trade: An Illustrated History* (1983), pp. 82–98; S. Stuckey, 'Slavery and the Circle of Culture', in J.W. Harris (ed.), *Society and Culture in the Slave South* (1992), pp. 100–27; and W.E. Cross, 'Black Psychological Functioning and the Legacy of Slavery: Myths and Realities', in Y. Danieli (ed.), *International Handbook of Multi-Generational Legacies of Trauma* (New York, 1998), pp. 387–400.

57. *See* comments in W.A. Clark (ed.), *From Tejano to Tango: Latin American Popular Music* (New York, 2002); P. Fryer, *Rhythms of Resistance: African Musical Heritage in Brazil* (2000), pp. 8–12; A. Kebede, *Roots of Black Music: The Vocal, Instrumental and Dance Heritage of Africa and Black America* (Englewood Cliffs, NJ, 1982); and J. Collins, *African Pop Roots: The Inside Rhythms of Africa* (1985), esp. pp. 8–11.

58. R. Rorty (ed.), *The Linguistic Turn: Recent Essays in Philosophical Method* (Chicago, 1967).

59. Compare T.S. Kuhn, *The Structure of Scientific Revolutions* (Chicago, 1962), esp. pp. 47–9, 52–76, 79–80, 86–90, 100–5, 150–7; and M. Foucault (1926–84), interviewed in F. Elders (ed.), *Reflexive Water* (1974), pp. 150, 156.

60. *See* commentaries in J. Krige, *Science, Revolution and Discontinuity* (Brighton, 1980), pp. 9–10, 15–19, 214–15, 218; and I.B. Cohen, *Revolution in Science* (Cambridge, MA, 1985), pp. 22–5.
61. K.R. Popper, *The Logic of Scientific Discovery* (1959), esp. pp. 276–81.
62. E.W. Constant, *The Origins of the Turbojet Revolution* (Baltimore, 1980), pp. 3–5, 178–94, 241–6, esp. p. 4, showing grid of technologies upon which the new turbojet depended. For approaches to technological change, *see also* M.K. Matossian, *Shaping World History: Breakthroughs in Ecology, Technology, Science and Politics* (Armonk, NY, 1997); and J.E. McClellan and H. Dorn, *Science and Technology in World History: An Introduction* (Baltimore, 1999).
63. E.J. Hobsbawm, *Industry and Empire: An Economic History of Britain since 1750* (1968), p. 1.
64. Luce Irigaray, *Thinking the Difference: For a Peaceful Revolution*, trans. K. Montin (1994).
65. See J. Blau, *The Renaissance of Modern Hebrew and Modern Standard Arabic: Parallels and Differences in the Revival of Two Semitic Languages* (Berkeley, 1981), p. 157, and esp. P. Wexler, *The Schizoid Nature of Modern Hebrew: A Slavic Language in Search of a Semitic Past* (Wiesbaden, 1990).
66. For the extent of the current challenge, *see* D. Nettle and S. Romaine, *Vanishing Voices: The Extinction of the World's Languages* (Oxford, 2002).
67. Marx and Engels, *Communist Manifesto* (1848), in McLellan (ed.), *Marx: Selected Writings* (2000 edn), p. 248.
68. W. Shakespeare, *The Tempest* (1611), Act 5, Scene 1.
69. W.B. Yeats (1865–1939), 'Easter, 1916', in R.J. Finneran (ed.), *W.B. Yeats: The Poems* (1983), p. 180: 'All changed, changed utterly: / A terrible beauty is born.'
70. See N. Yushij [A. Esfadiyâri] (1896–1959), 'Cold Ashes', in M. Kianush (ed.), *Modern Persian Poetry* (Ware, 1996), p. 64; and D. Randall (1914–2000), *Cities Burning* (Detroit, 1968), p. 3.

Chapterlink 4–5

1. For apocalypticism and narrative closure, *see* F. Kermode, *The Sense of an Ending: Studies in the Theory of Fiction* (New York, 1967; 2000), while, in a different vein, M. Peckham, *Man's Rage for Chaos: Biology, Behavior and the Arts* (New York, 1965) looks at chaotic intrusions into orderly arts.
2. Consult variously Ronan, *The Universe*, pp. 168–71, 178–9; F. Close, *End: Cosmic Catastrophe and the Fate of the Universe* (1988), pp. 180–1, 197–200, 215; Kaku, *Parallel Worlds*, pp. 42–4; and F. Hoyle, G. Burbidge and J.V. Narlikar, *A Different Approach to Cosmology: From a Static Universe through the Big Bang towards Reality* (Cambridge, 2000).
3. Fascinating accounts and full references to a rich literature are provided in N. Campion, *The Great Year: Astrology, Millenarianism and History in the Western Tradition* (1994); C. Keller, *Apocalypse Now and Then: A Feminist Guide to the End of the World* (Boston, MA, 1996); R. Bray, *Awaiting the Millennium: A History of End-Time Thinking* (Leicester, 1998); E. Weber, *Apocalypses: Prophecies, Cults and Millennial Beliefs through the Ages* (1999); and A. Amanat and M. Bernhardsson (eds), *Imagining the End: Visions of Apocalypse from the Ancient Middle East to Modern America* (2000). For a sceptical fusillade against apocalyptic believers, *see also* R. Abanes, *End-Time Visions: The Road to Armageddon?* (New York, 1998).
4. Examples are plentiful in F. Carey (ed.), *The Apocalypse and the Shape of Things to Come* (1999); F. Van der Meer, *Apocalypse: Visions from the Book of Revelation in Western Art* (Antwerp, 1978); and N. Rosenthal et al., *Apocalypse: Beauty and Horror in Contemporary Art* (2000).

5. Relevant here is the material in J. R. Stone, *Expecting Armageddon: Essential Readings in Failed Prophecy* (2000).
6. D. Adams (1952–2001), *The Restaurant at the End of the Universe* (1980), p. 124; also in *The Hitch-Hiker's Guide to the Galaxy: A Trilogy in Five Parts* (1979–84; collected edn, 1995), p. 250.

Chapter 5

1. G. Waldman, *Introduction to Light: The Physics of Light, Vision, and Color* (Mineola, NY, 2002), pp. 28–31, p. 30: [Light] 'has both wave and particle properties, and the more any experiment reveals one aspect, the less it reveals the other'.
2. Quotations come from three Christian thinkers who, in their different ways, rejected the materialism and secularism of later twentieth-century society: *see* R. Guardini, *The End of the Modern World* (1956; repr. 1998), p. 200; C. S. Lewis (1898–1963), *Miracles: A Preliminary Study* (1947), p. 199; and H. Lindsey, *The 1980s: Countdown to Armageddon* (New York, 1980; Basingstoke, 1983), p. 8.
3. On this, consult J. P. Bloch, *New Spirituality, Self and Belonging: How New Agers and Neo-Pagans Talk about Themselves* (Westport, CT, 1998), pp. 2–4, 7–11, 121–3; P. Heelas, *The New Age Movement: The Celebration of Self and the Sacralisation of Modernity* (Oxford, 1996); and esp. for the Theosophical Society, J. G. Melton, 'A History of the New Age Movement', in R. Basil (ed.), *Not Necessarily the New Age: Critical Essays* (Buffalo, NY, 1988), pp. 35–53.
4. Swami Wassermann, *Now You See It; Now You Don't – Catching the Creator by the Tail: Mystic Procedure in the Age of Aquarius* (Wicklow, 1988).
5. For the Hindu cycle of changing *Yuga* (sometimes *Juga*) or ages of the world as taking 4,320,000 years to revolve, *see* T. R. Trautmann, 'Indian Time, European Time', in D. O. Hughes and T. R. Trautmann (eds), *Time: Histories and Ethnologies* (Ann Arbor, 1995), p. 169.
6. R. M. Pirsig, *Zen and the Art of Motorcycle Maintenance: An Inquiry into Values* (1974; 1979) was advertised as a text 'that will change the way you think and feel about your life'.
7. For problems of definition, *see* B. S. Turner (ed.), *Theories of Modernity and Postmodernity* (1990); M. R. Rose, *The Post-Modern and the Post-Industrial: A Critical Analysis* (Cambridge, 1991); S. Best and D. Kellner, *Postmodern Theory: Critical Interrogations* (Basingstoke, 1991); C. Jencks (ed.), *The Post-Modern Reader* (1992); H. Bertens, *The Idea of the Postmodern: A History* (1995); and J. Frow, 'What was Postmodernism?', in his *Time and Commodity Culture: Essays in Cultural Theory and Postmodernity* (Oxford, 1997), pp. 13–63.
8. J. F. Lyotard (1924–98), *The Postmodern Condition: A Report on Knowledge* (1979), trans. G. Bennington and B. Massumi (Manchester, 1984), pp. 15, 37. For an *ur*-critique of historical writing that inspired many postmodernist thinkers, *see also* H. V. White, *Metahistory: The Historical Imagination in Nineteenth-Century Europe* (Baltimore, 1974); and, among many responses, E. Breisach, *On the Future of History: The Postmodernist Challenge and its Aftermath* (Chicago, 2003), pp. 193–208.
9. As illustrated in C. Jencks, *The Architecture of the Jumping Universe: A Polemic – How Complexity Science is Changing Architecture and Culture* (1995).
10. *See* e.g. A. Kroker and M. Kroker (eds), *Body Invaders: Sexuality and the Postmodern Condition* (Basingstoke, 1988); and, for a literary application of the thematic contrast, read D. Lodge, *Nice Work: A Novel* (1988).
11. A. Codrescu, 'Comrade Past and Mister Present' (1986), cited in M. Cornis-Pope, *The Unfinished Battles: Romanian Postmodernism Before and After 1989* (Iasi, 1996), pp. 7, 178.

12. K. Jenkins, 'Introduction', in K. Jenkins (ed.), *The Postmodern History Reader* (1997), pp. 3, 206 – the later phrase quoting Jacques Derrida.
13. P. Osborne, *The Politics of Time: Modernity and Avant-Garde* (1995), p. 3. *See too* W. Welsch, *Unsere postmoderne Moderne: Zweite, durchgesehene Auflage* (Weinheim, 1988): 'our postmodern modernity'.
14. For critiques, *see* T. Eagleton, *The Illusions of Postmodernism* (Oxford, 1997); B. Smith, 'The Last Days of the Post Mode', *Thesis Eleven*, 54 (1998), pp. 1–23; G. Browning, *Lyotard and the End of Grand Narratives* (Cardiff, 2000), p. 171; and R. Rorty, 'The Continuity between the Enlightenment and Postmodernism', in K.M. Baker and P.H. Reill (eds), *What's Left of Enlightenment: A Postmodern Question* (Stanford, CA, 2001), pp. 19–36.
15. S. Brodribb, *Nothing Matters: A Feminist Critique of Postmodernism* (Melbourne, 1992); and D. Lyon, *Postmodernity* (Buckingham, 1994), p. 80.
16. Federico de Onis (1888–1966) in his 1934 study of Spanish and Spanish-American poetry, dated the era of modernism as 1896–1905, postmodernism as 1905–1914, and *ultramodernismo* as 1914–32.
17. D. Hebdige, *Hiding in the Light: On Images and Things* (1988), p. 181.
18. G. Myerson, *Ecology and the End of Postmodernity* (Cambridge, 2001), p. 74. But for a more positive view of postmodern thought in relation to environmentalism, *see* T. Jagtenberg, *Eco-Impacts and the Greening of Postmodernity* (Thousand Oaks, CA, 1998).
19. E.J. Hobsbawm, *Age of Extremes: The Short Twentieth Century, 1914–91* (1994). For a critical overview of contrasting interpretations of the twentieth century, *see also* M. Salvati, *Il Novecento: interpretazioni e bilanci* (Rome-Bari, 2001; 2004).
20. A.J. Toynbee (1889–1975), *A Study of History, Vol. 5: The Disintegrations of Civilisations, Part One* (1939), p. 43.
21. Marx and Engels, *Communist Manifesto* (1848), in McLellan (ed.), *Marx: Selected Writings* (2000 edn), p. 248; and *see* above, p. 110. The phrase recurs in the title of M. Berman, *All That is Solid Melts into Air: The Experience of Modernity* (New York, 1982); yet is often favoured by postmodernists too.
22. Cited in M. Banniard, 'Rhabanus Maurus and the Vernacular Languages', in R. Wright (ed.), *Latin and the Romance Languages in the Early Middle Ages* (1991), p. 168.
23. A. Szakolczai, *The Genesis of Modernity* (2003), esp. p. 240.
24. P. Oppenheimer, *The Birth of the Modern Mind: Self, Consciousness, and the Invention of the Sonnet* (New York, 1989), esp. pp. 3–4, 12, 23–4, 39–40, 173, 185–6, with the Emperor Frederick II (1194–1250), at whose cultivated court the first sonnets were written, proposed as the first truly 'modern' ruler: ibid., pp. 12, 185–6.
25. L. Hunt (ed.), *The Invention of Pornography: Obscenity and the Origins of Modernity, 1500–1800* (New York, 1993).
26. For René Descartes (1596–1650), *see* J. Cottingham, *Descartes: Descartes' Philosophy of Mind* (1997), p. 3; and D. Judovitz, *Subjectivity and Representation in Descartes: The Origins of Modernity* (Cambridge, 1988).
27. *See* J.I. Israel, *Radical Enlightenment: Philosophy and the Making of Modernity, 1650–1750* (Oxford, 2001); and Jan de Vries and Ad Van der Woude, *The First Modern Economy: Success, Failure and Perseverance of the Dutch Economy, 1500–1815* (Cambridge, 1997).
28. Compare R. Porter, *Enlightenment: Britain and the Making of the Modern World* (2000); A.L. Beier, D. Cannadine and J.M. Rosenheim, *The First Modern Society: Essays in English History* (Cambridge, 1989); and A. Herman, *The Scottish Enlightenment: The Scots' Invention of the Modern World* (2002; 2003).
29. For Kant, *see* J.F. Rundell, *Origins of Modernity: The Origins of Modern Social Theory from Kant to Hegel to Marx* (Oxford, 1987).

30. G. Himmelfarb, *The Roads to Modernity: The British, French and American Enlightenments* (New York, 2004).

31. *See* p. 108. For earlier technological innovations, *see also* J. Gimpel, *The Medieval Machine: The Industrial Revolution of the Middle Ages* (1977), including (p. xi) the erroneous verdict that by the later 1970s the wellsprings of human technological invention had finally become exhausted.

32. J. Shakerley, *The Anatomy of Urania Practica: Or, A Short Mathematical Discourse . . .* (1649), p. iii.

33. R. Koselleck, *Critique and Crisis: Enlightenment and the Pathogenesis of Modern Society* (1959; trans. 1988).

34. For S. Freud (1856–1939), *see* H. Ferguson, *The Lure of Dreams: Sigmund Freud and the Construction of Modernity* (1996); and one of many critiques of Freud and Freudianism in F. Crews, *Follies of the Wise* (Emeryville, CA, 2006).

35. P. Mandler, 'The Consciousness of Modernity? Liberalism and the English National Character, 1870–1914', in M. Daunton and B. Rieger (eds), *Meanings of Modernity: Britain from the Late-Victorian Era to World War II* (2001), pp. 119–44.

36. For Charles Baudelaire (1821–67), *see* M. Hamburger, *The Truth of Poetry: Tensions in Modern Poetry from Baudelaire to the 1960s* (1969), p. 1: 'The importance of Baudelaire, then, can be taken for granted here . . . as the father of modern poetry . . .'.

37. Contrast chronologies in N. Cheetham, *New Spain: The Birth of Modern Mexico* (1974), p. 314; with W. Canak and L. Swanson, *Modern Mexico* (Boston, MA, 1998), p. 17; and R. Gallo, *Mexican Modernity: The Avant-Garde and the Technological Revolution* (2005).

38. Compare for Egypt, M. W. Daly (ed.), *Modern Egypt: From 1517 to the End of the Twentieth Century* (Cambridge, 1998); G. Annersley, *The Rise of Modern Egypt: A Century and a Half of Egyptian History, 1798–1957* (Edinburgh, 1994); and R. Meijer, *The Quest for Modernity: Secular Liberal and Left-Wing Political Thought in Egypt, 1945–58* (2002); and, for Libya, A. A. Ahmida, *The Making of Modern Libya: State Formation, Colonization and Resistance, 1830–1932* (Albany, NY, 1994); M. Khadduri, *Modern Libya: A Study in Political Development* (Baltimore, 1963) on Libyan independence in 1949; and J. Wright, *Libya: A Modern History* (1982), pp. 127–30, 132–6, for the advent of Gaddafi.

39. *See* T. Megarry (ed.), *The Making of Modern Japan: A Reader* (Dartford, 1995), pp. ix–xix; as well as T. C. Smith, 'Japan's Aristocratic Revolution', in ibid., pp. 57–66; and M. B. Jansen, 'The Meiji State, 1868–1912', in ibid., pp. 67–88.

40. Another historian finds a 'baroque' era in sixteenth- and seventeenth-century Europe, leaving the eighteenth century to start the 'modern': *see* R. Blackburn, *The Making of New World Slavery: From the Baroque to the Modern, 1492–1800* (1997), esp. pp. 20–3.

41. *See* pertinent comments in G. Rozman, *Urban Networks in Russia, 1750–1800, and Pre-Modern Periodisation* (Princeton, 1976), esp. pp. 5–12, 16–40; and, for parallel issues as debated by literary scholars, *see* too L. Besserman (ed.), *The Challenge of Periodisation: Old Paradigms and New Perspectives* (New York, 1996).

42. C. Okigbo (1932–67), 'Path of Thunder' (posthumously pub., 1968), in his *Labyrinths: With Path of Thunder* (1971), p. 72. For the Nigerian civil war, in which Okigbo died fighting for an independent Biafra, *see* T. Falola, *The History of Nigeria* (Westport, CT, 1999), pp. 119–26; and for turmoil in 1967–8 more generally, *see* A. Marwick, *The Sixties: Cultural Revolution in Britain, France, Italy and the United States, c. 1958–c. 1974* (Oxford, 1998), pp. 584–675; M. Kun, *Prague Spring, Prague Fall: Blank Spots of 1968*, trans. H. Csatorday (Budapest, 1999); and L. Barcata, *China in the Throes of Cultural Revolution: An Eye-Witness Report* (New York, 1968).

43. A. Compagnon, *The Five Paradoxes of Modernity*, trans. F. Philip (New York, 1994).

44. 'There is debate about when it really got started, whether it can be thought of as a homogeneous phenomenon, and what its key characteristics might be': P. Cooke, *Back to the Future* (1990), pp. 9–10. *See* too, on problems of definition: M. Bradbury and J. McFarlane, 'The Name and Nature of Modernism', in their *Modernism, 1890–1930* (1976), p. 11; M. Levenson, *A Genealogy of Modernism: A Study of English Literary Doctrine, 1908–22* (New York, 1984), p. vii; A. Eysteinsson, *The Concept of Modernism* (Ithaca, 1990), p. 1; and H. Heynen, *Architecture and Modernity: A Critique* (Cambridge, MA, 1999), p. 3.

45. C. Jencks, 'Preface: Post-Modernism – The Third Force', in Jencks (ed.), *Post-Modern Reader*, p. 10.

46. D. Ayers, *Modernism: A Short Introduction* (Oxford, 2004), p. ix.

47. T. J. Clark, *Farewell to an Idea: Episodes from a History of Modernism* (1999), p. 15. This is based upon a 'free and easy' approach that does not seek precise definitions, 'in hopes that most readers know it [modernity] when they see it': ibid., p. 7.

48. Consider U. Becks-Malorny, *Paul Cézanne, 1839–1906: Pioneer of Modernism* (Cologne, 1995); and A. Callen, *The Art of Impressionism: Painting Technique and the Making of Modernity* (New Haven, 2000).

49. *See* T. Parsons and I. Gale, *Post-Impressionism: The Rise of Modern Art* (1992); B. Thomson, *The Post-Impressionists* (Oxford, 1983), pp. 9–10; and for P. Picasso (1881–1973), *see also* J. Weiss, *The Popular Culture of Modern Art: Picasso, Duchamp and Avant-Gardism* (New Haven, 1994); and M. C. Fitzgerald, *Making Modernism: Picasso and the Creation of the Market for Twentieth-Century Art* (New York, 1995).

50. For W. Gropius (1883–1969) and Modernism, see E. S. Hochman, *Bauhaus: Crucible of Modernism* (New York, 1997), p. 1.

51. R. E. Krauss, *The Originality of the Avant-Garde and Other Modernist Myths* (Cambridge, MA, 1985), pp. 5–6, 9.

52. Postmodernism has been similarly hailed as another rebellious variant within modernity: *see* comment in K. Tester, *The Life and Times of Postmodernity* (1993), p. 28.

53. S. H. Spender (1909–95), *The Struggle of the Modern* (1963).

54. S. Lublinski, *Der Ausgang der Moderne: Ein Buch der Opposition* (Dresden, 1909).

55. For J. A. A. Joyce (1882–1941), *see* J. S. Atherton, *The Books at the Wake: A Study of Literary Allusions in James Joyce's Finnegans Wake* (1959), p. 54; M. Levitt, *James Joyce and Modernism: Beyond Dublin* (Lewiston, NY, 2000); and A. Charles, *James Joyce: Modernism and Postmodernism* (Oxford, 1995).

56. For S. Beckett (1906–89), *see* R. Begam, *Samuel Beckett and the End of Modernity* (Stanford, 1996).

57. For J. Cage (1912–92), *see* M. Roth, *Difference/Indifference: Musings on Postmodernism, Marcel Duchamp and John Cage* (Amsterdam, 1998).

58. The ambiguities of S. Dalí (1904–89) are analysed in D. Ades, *Dalí* (1995); R. Radford, *Dalí* (1997), esp. pp. 321–32; and M. J. LaFontain, *Dalí and Postmodernism: This is not an Essence* (Albany, NY, 1997).

59. L. Tickner, *Modern Life and Modern Subjects: British Art in the Early Twentieth Century* (New Haven, 2000), p. 184. An ultimate stress upon diversity *within* a long twentieth-century modernity, rather than after it, is conveyed by essays in M. Nava and A. O'Shea (eds), *Modern Times: Reflections on a Century of English Modernity* (1996); and by an encyclopedic survey by H. Foster and others, *Art since 1900: Modernism, Antimodernism and Postmodernism* (2004).

60. For example, it is hard to classify a long-lived architectural chameleon like American architect Philip Johnson (1906–2005), on whose career *see* F. Schulze, *Philip Johnson: Life and Work* (New York, 1994).

61. C. Jencks, *Late Modern Architecture and Other Essays* (1980), p. 30.

62. J. Mordaunt Crook, *The Dilemma of Style: Architectural Ideas from the Picturesque to the Post-Modern* (1987).

63. *See* C.S.B., *Modernism: What it is and Why it was Condemned* (Edinburgh, 1908); R. Elliott, *Modernism: Is it from Heaven or of Men?* (1929); and comments in B. Bergonzi, *The Myth of Modernism and Twentieth-Century Literature* (Brighton, 1986), p. xiii.

64. Contrast W-B. Zhang, *Confucianism and Modernisation: Industrialisation and Democratisation of the Confucian Regions* (Basingstoke, 1999); R. Combes, *The Tao of Modern Living* (2000), updating traditional Chinese maxims in intended humour; J. James and A. James, *Modern Buddhism* (Bradford on Avon, 1987); D. Smith, *Hinduism and Modernity* (Oxford, 2003); N. Hanif, *Islam and Modernity* (New Delhi, 1997); J. Gray, *Al-Qaeda and What it Means to be Modern* (2004); and R. Hutton, *The Triumph of the Moon: A History of Modern Pagan Witchcraft* (Oxford, 1999).

65. D. McDonagh, *The Rise and Fall and Rise of Modern Dance* (1990).

66. *See* variously A. Appel, *Jazz Modernism: From Ellington and Armstrong to Matisse and Joyce* (New York, 2002); and B. Ulanov, *A History of Jazz in America* (1958), pp. 235–7, 308–9, 313–15.

67. For the attack upon C. Monteverdi (1567–1643), *see* G. M. Artusi, *L'Artusi: Overo delle imperfettioni della moderna musica* ... (Venice, 1600); and for A. Schönberg (1874–1951), *see* M. Hansen, *Arnold Schönberg: Ein Konzept der Moderne* (Kassel, 1993). Dramatic musical change in the early twentieth century was greeted by E. Duncan in 1915 as *Ultra-Modernism in Music: A Treatise on the Latter-Day Revolution in Musical Art* (1915).

68. M. Weiner (ed.), *Modernization: The Dynamics of Growth* (New York, 1966), p. 1.

69. This phrase was coined by the poet Paul Valéry (1871–1945): *see* Compagnon, *Five Paradoxes of Modernity*, p. xv.

70. L. L. Martz, *Many Gods and Many Voices: The Role of the Prophet in English and American Modernism* (Columbia, MO, 1998). Compare also S. N. Eisenstadt, *Japan and the Multiplicity of Cultural Programmes of Modernity* (Hong Kong, 1994); S. N. Eisenstadt (ed.), *Patterns of Modernity, Vol. 2: Beyond the West* (1987); Z. Bauman, *Modernity and Ambivalence* (Cambridge, 1991); and S. Gunn, *History and Cultural Theory* (Harlow, 2006), pp. 107–30.

71. Contrast P. Brooker, *Modernity and Metropolis: Writing, Film and Urban Formations* (Basingstoke, 2002); J. Donald, *Imagining the Modern City* (1999); and S. Inwood, *City of Cities: The Birth of Modern London* (2005); with M. Ogborn, *Spaces of Modernity: London's Geographies, 1680–1780* (1998); and E. McKellar, *The Birth of Modern London: The Development and Design of the City, 1660–1720* (Manchester, 1999).

72. J. Habermas, 'Modernity: An Unfinished Project' (1981), trans. N. Walker, in M. Passerin d'Entrèves and S. Benhabib (eds), *Habermas and the Unfinished Project of Modernity: Critical Essays* (Cambridge, 1996), pp. 38–55.

73. W. S. W. Lim, *Alternative Post(Modernity): An Asian Perspective* (Singapore, 2003), p. v. *See* too for a postcolonial critique of Eurocentricity in historical visions, R. J. C. Young, *White Mythologies: Writing History in the West* (2004).

74. B. Latour, *We Have Never Been Modern*, trans. C. Porter (New York, 1993), pp. 10–12, 46–8, 75, 145.

75. C. Hill (1912–2003), 'A One-Class Society?' in his *Change and Continuity in Seventeenth-Century England* (1974), pp. 216–17, reviewing P. Laslett (1915–2001), *The World We Have Lost* (1965), pp. 226–7.

76. *See*, for long post-medieval continuities, H. M. Cam (1885–1968), *What of the Middle Ages is Alive in England Today?* (1961).

77. Anon. publishing as 'A Lady', *A Sketch of Universal History, from the Earliest Times, to the Year 1763; Distinctly Divided into Ages and Periods, for the Assistance of the Memory* (1786), p. 1: 'History may be divided, with respect to time, into Ancient History, that of the Middle Age [starting in Year 1], and Modern.'

78. A. Hauser (1892–1978), *The Social History of Art: Vol. 1, From Prehistoric Times to the Middle Ages*, ed. J. Harris (1999), pp. xxxi, 109, 175, 230–43.

79. See J. Guitton, *The Modernity of St Augustine*, trans. A.V. Littledale (1959); and K.J. Mullany, *Augustine of Hippo: The First Modern Man* (New York, 1930).

80. J.J. Cohen, *The Postcolonial Middle Ages* (Basingstoke, 2000).

81. J. Baudrillard, *The Illusion of the End* (Paris, 1992), trans. C. Turner (Cambridge, 1994), p. 10.

82. N. Berdyaev (1874–1948), *The End of Our Time* (1933), pp. 11, 69–120. A similar Christian appeal to a spiritualised medievalism comes too in Guardini, *End of the Modern World*, pp. 1, 7–26, 51, 186–7, 214–18.

83. G. Barraclough (1908–84), '*Medium Aevum*: Some Reflections on Medieval History and on the Term "The Middle Ages"', in his *History in a Changing World* (Oxford, 1955), pp. 54–63. *See also* L. Patterson, 'The Place of the Modern in the Late Middle Ages', in Besserman (ed.), *Challenge of Periodisation*, esp. pp. 51–4.

84. M. Montanari, *The Culture of Food*, trans. C. Ipsen (Oxford, 1994), p. xii.

85. R.M. Rosen (ed.), *Time and Temporality in the Ancient World* (Philadelphia, 2004). All the essays in this collection, which cover a range of eras and places, repay close attention.

86. G. Seferis (formerly G. Seferiadis) (1900–71), 'Sixteen Haiku', in E. Keeley and P. Sherrard (eds), *George Seferis: Collected Poems* (Princeton, NJ, 1995), p. 46.

87. J. White, *The Eighteen Christian Centuries* (Edinburgh, 1860), p. 3.

88. R. Sorabji, *Time, Creation and the Continuum: Theories in Antiquity and the Early Middle Ages* (1983), esp. pp. 193–252; and E.G. Richards, *Mapping Time: The Calendar and its History* (Oxford, 1998), pp. 107, 224–6, 326.

89. Compare J. Ussher (1581–1656), *The Annals of the Old and New Testament* (1650–4; repr. 1658), pp. [v], 1; and J. Lightfoot (1602–75), *A Few and New Observations upon the Book of Genesis* (1642), p. 4.

90. K. Jaspers (1883–1969), *The Origin and Goal of History*, trans. M. Bullock (1953), p. 260. For context, *see* too S. Kirkbright, *Karl Jaspers – a Biography: Navigations in Truth* (New Haven, 2005).

Chapterlink 5–6

1. See I. Kant, 'An Answer to the Question "What is Enlightenment?"' (1784), in Hans Reiss (ed.), *Kant's Political Writings*, trans. H.B. Nisbet (Cambridge, 1970), p. 58; and J.S. Mill (1806–73), *The Spirit of the Age*, first pub. in *The Examiner* (1831), ed. F.A. Von Hayek (Chicago, 1942), p. 2, 6.

2. M. Arnold (1822–88), *Stanzas from the Grande Charteuse* (1855), in K. Allott (ed.), *The Poems of Matthew Arnold* (1965), p. 288.

3. J. Gleick, *Faster: The Acceleration of Just about Everything* (1999; repr. 2000), p. 6.

4. Compare E. Burke (1729–97), *Reflections on the Revolution in France* (1790), ed. C.C. O'Brien (Harmondsworth, 1969), p. 170; and P.B. Shelley (1792–1822), *Hellas: A Lyrical Drama* (1st edn, 1822), p. 51: final chorus, to which Shelley appended a note (p. 57) acknowledging that 'to anticipate however darkly a period of regeneration and happiness is a more hazardous exercise' than to prophesy war.

5. V. Woolf (1882–1941), 'Mr. Bennett and Mrs. Brown' (1924), repr. in her *Collected Essays* (1966), Vol. 1, pp. 320–1. For context, *see also* Woolf on the Post-Impressionist Exhibition in letter to V. Dickinson, 27 Nov. 1910, in N. Nicolson with J. Trautmann (eds), *The Flight of the Mind: The Letters of Virginia Woolf (Stephen), Vol. 1, 1888–1912* (1975), p. 440; and V. Woolf, 'Old Bloomsbury' (written early 1920s), in her *Moments of Being: Unpublished Autobiographical Writings*, ed. J. Schulkind (1976), pp. 173–4. The first evening of frank talking occurred at some point during the years 1904–7 when Woolf lived at 46 Gordon Square, in London's Bloomsbury: for cultural

context, *see* H. Lee, *Virginia Woolf* (1996), pp. 287–81; and J. Briggs, *Virginia Woolf: An Inner Life* (2005).

6. Naming the epoch is a very personal response. Readers are invited to record their own verdict on today's times as 'an age of . . .' or a 'century of . . .'. Summarising an entire era *convincingly* in a short phrase is not as easy as it might seem, but it's a creative way of encapsulating key aspects of history. Try it and see.

Chapter 6

1. F.S. Fitzgerald (1896–1940) not only named the boom years but also assessed their ending after the 1929 stock-market crash: see his *Tales of the Jazz Age* (New York, 1922) and 'Echoes of the Jazz Age' (1931), repr. in his *The Crack-Up, with Other Pieces* (Harmondsworth, 1968), pp. 9–19.

2. J.W. Bashford (1843–1919), *Problems of the Twentieth Century* (Chicago, 1895), p. 10. Prohibition was added as the 18th Amendment to the US Constitution in 1919 and repealed by the 33rd in 1933.

3. M. de Condorcet (Jean-Antoine-Nicolas Caritat) (1743–94), *Esquisse d'un tableau historique des progrès de l'esprit humain* (Paris, 1795), trans. as *Outline of an Historical View of the Progress of the Human Mind* (Philadelphia, 1796), pp. 23, 250–93. *See also* K.M. Baker, *Condorcet: From Natural Philosophy to Social Mathematics* (Chicago, 1975), pp. 349–50; and p. 85, above.

4. This oft-repeated dictum, which was initially applied to 'Life' (not to history), was propounded by the American journalist and publisher, Elbert Hubbard (1859–1915).

5. Campion, *The Great Year*, pp. 59–64.

6. S.J. Dick, *Life on Other Worlds: The Twentieth-Century Extraterrestrial Life Debate* (Cambridge, 1998), pp. 214, 222–3.

7. C.S. Lewis, *De Descriptione Temporum/Describing the Times: An Inaugural Lecture* (Cambridge, 1955), p. 3. This rejection of the 'medieval' coincided with a similar attack by the historian Geoffrey Barraclough, for which *see* p. 147.

8. J.G. Fichte (1762–1814), 'The Vocation of the Scholar' (1794), in W. Smith (ed.), *The Popular Works of Johann Gottlieb Fichte* (1889), Vol. 1, p. 226.

9. B. Buzan and G. Segal, *Anticipating the Future* (1998), pp. 220–1, 268–9.

10. F.W. Bunce, *Numbers: Their Iconographic Consideration in Buddhist and Hindu Practices* (New Delhi, 2002), pp. 63, 123.

11. *See* variously Trautmann, 'Indian Time', pp. 168–71; M. Stutley, *Hinduism: The Eternal Law* (Wellingborough, 1985), pp. 44–5; L.W. Fagg, *Two Faces of Time* (Wheaton, IL, 1985), pp. 75, 80–1; Ifrah, *Universal History of Numbers*, pp. 421–6; and R. Thapar, *Time as a Metaphor of History: Early India* (Delhi, 1996), pp. 7–9, 44.

12. Adams, *Hitch-Hiker's Guide*, pp. 130, 135. And for 42 in *Alice*, see L. Carroll (C.L. Dodgson) (1832–98), *Alice's Adventures in Wonderland* (1865) in M. Gardner (ed.), *The Annotated Alice* (2000), p. 125. Various websites also discuss the significance of number jokes in Adams and Carroll, ingeniously but generally inconclusively.

13. Maimonides, *Guide of the Perplexed*, Vol. 1, p. 234.

14. R. Franklin (1630–1703), *A Discourse on Antichrist . . . Shewing that the Number of the Beast Ought not to be Translated 666 but 42 Only . . .* (1675). The relevant texts are found in Revelation, 13:5, 18.

15. P. Teilhard de Chardin (1881–1955), *The Future of Man* (Paris, 1959), trans. N. Denny (1964), pp. 32, 84, 122, 124, 273–4, 302.

16. G.F. Miller, 'Sexual Selection for Cultural Displays', in R. Dunbar, C. Knight and C. Power (eds), *Evolution of Culture: An Evolutionary View* (Edinburgh, 1999), pp. 71–91, esp. p. 80.

17. *See* C.F. Robinson, *Islamic Historiography* (Cambridge, 2003), esp. pp. 3–17, 172–86. For Ibn Khaldūn, *see* p. 54.
18. S. Qutb (1903–66), *Milestones* (New Delhi, 1981), *passim*, incl. p. 194. On Islam and attitudes to history, consult N.J. Delong-Bas, *Wahhabi Islam: From Revival and Reform to Global Jihad* (2004), pp. 8–9, 24–6, 56–61, 199–201, 256–65, 272–4, 288–9; R. Firestone, *Jihad: The Origin of Holy War in Islam* (New York, 1999); G. Kepel, *Jihad: The Trail of Political Islam*, trans. A.F. Roberts (2002); and, for a critique of Wahhabism and a defence of preserving venerated shrines, H. Algar, *Wahhabism: A Critical Essay* (Oneonta, NY, 2002), pp. 43–4, 54–6.
19. For a global review, *see* R. Needham (ed.), *Right and Left: Essays on Dual Symbolic Classification* (Chicago, 1973).
20. H. Spencer, *Progress: Its Law and Cause* (1857), in *Spencer's Essays: A Selection* (1907), pp. 7–8, 12–13, 20–1.
21. E. Durkheim (1858–1917), *The Division of Labour in Society*, trans. W.D. Halls (Basingstoke, 1984), pp. 84–5.
22. *See* J. Wahl, *Philosophies of Existence: An Introduction to the Basic Thought of Kierkegaard, Heidegger, Jaspers, Marcel, Sartre*, trans. F.M. Lory (1969), pp. 58–9; and for Kant and J.G. Herder (1744–1803), *see* Manuel, *Shapes of Philosophical History*, pp. 73–4.
23. M. Foucault, *Surveiller et Punir* (Paris, 1975), trans. as *Discipline and Punish: The Birth of the Prison* (1977), pp. 7–23; and *see* p. 107.
24. R. Miles, *The Women's History of the World* (1989), pp. 19–78.
25. *See* J. Barit, 'The Lore of Number', in Swetz (ed.), *From Five Fingers*, p. 98; and Bunce, *Numbers*, pp. 19–21.
26. Wei-Bin Zhang, *Confucianism and Modernisation*, pp. 42–5.
27. F.J. Gould (1855–1938), *Man Has Climbed: A History of the World for Young and Old in 29 Pages: With a Map Showing Three Stages of Civilisation* (1936).
28. For J. di Fiore (*c.* 1135–1202), *see* M. Reeves, *Joachim of Fiore and the Prophetic Future* (1976), pp. 2, 27–8, 41–58, 166–75; idem, *The Prophetic Sense of History in Medieval and Renaissance Europe* (Aldershot, 1999); and M. Reeves and W. Gould, *Joachim of Fiore and the Myth of the Eternal Evangel in the Nineteenth Century* (Oxford, 1987), p. 3, and *passim*. For Vico and G. di Lampedusa, *see also* pp. 39, 46, 55.
29. For the Age of Aquarius, *see* p. 125.
30. For Vico, *see* pp. 39, 55; and for context, P. Rossi, *The Dark Abyss of Time: The History of the Earth and the History of Nations from Hooke to Vico*, trans. D. Cochrane (Chicago, 1984).
31. *See* variously Mazlish, *Riddle of History*, pp. 34–41; Manuel, *Shapes of Philosophical History*, pp. 55, 58; and C. Miller, *Giambattista Vico: Imagination and Historical Knowledge* (New York, 1993), pp. 32–4.
32. Comte, *Positive Philosophy*, Vol. 2, p. 158.
33. J.W. Draper (1811–82), *History of the Intellectual Development of Europe* (1864), Vol. 1, p. 19.
34. *See* W.W. Rostow (1916–2003), *The Stages of Economic Growth: A Non-Communist Manifesto* (Cambridge, 1960), p. 4.
35. For differing interpretations of the steam engine, *see* pp. 72, 108, 136.
36. M. Rees, *Just Six Numbers: The Deep Forces that Shape the Universe* (1999).
37. For an example, *see* F. Eveleigh, *Seven Ages of History and Progress: A History of the World and its People from Remote Ages to Modern Times* (1971). For a recent literary 'seven', *see* C. Booker, *The Seven Basic Plots: Why We Tell Stories* (2004), incl. pp. 229–34; and from a physics–biology overview perspective, *see* too E. Chaisson, *Epic of Evolution: Seven Ages of the Cosmos* (New York, 2006).
38. Richards, *Mapping Time*, p. 84; Campion, *Great Year*, pp. 99–103, 506–11.
39. Ibid., pp. 151–60; Bunce, *Numbers*, pp. 22–4.

40. J. Philippson of Sleidan (1506–56), *The Key of History: Or, a Most Methodicall Abridgement of the Four Chiefe Monarchies, . . .* (1627), first publ. in Latin in 1558. *See also* Manuel, *Shapes of Philosophical History*, pp. 14–19; and B.S. Capp, *The Fifth Monarchy Men: A Study in Seventeenth-Century English Millenarianism* (1972), pp. 20–4, 59, 69, 167.

41. Anon. (A. Smyth), *The Panorama of History: Presenting in Bold Relief the Leading Facts of Universal History . . .* (1857), Charts 1 and 2.

42. Compare H. Saint-Simon, 'On the Division of History' (1807/8), in K. Taylor (ed.), *Henri Saint-Simon, 1760–1825: Selected Writings on Science, Industry and Social Organisation* (1975), p. 95; and Fourier, *Theory of the Four Movements*, table facing p. 48.

43. W. Jones (1746–94), 'On the Chronology of the Hindus', *Asiatick Researches*, Vol. 2 (1788), as quoted in Trautmann, 'Indian Time', pp. 183–4: thus the *Krita Yuga* was deemed to begin with Adam and Eve, the *Treta Yuga* with Nimrod the biblical hunter, the *Dvapara Yuga* with the biblical Raamah/or Indian King Rama, and the *Kali Yuga* with Buddha. For general context, *see also* E.W. Said (1935–2003), *Orientalism* (1978; in 1985 edn), pp. 77–9, 122.

44. R.W. Fogel, *The Fourth Great Awakening and the Future of Egalitarianism* (Chicago, 2000).

45. B. Mazlish, *The Fourth Discontinuity: The Co-Evolution of Humans and Machines* (New Haven, 1993), pp. 3–7, 195–8, 231–3.

46. J.G. Fichte, *The Characteristics of the Present Age* (1806), trans. W. Smith (1847), pp. 3–4, 6–10, 16, 64, 258–9.

47. Neatly put in the first English translation of Hegel: see G.W.F. Hegel, *Lectures on the Philosophy of History*, trans. J. Sibree (1857), p. 110. And *see* p. 100.

48. Compare A. Ferguson (1723–1816), *An Essay on the History of Civil Society* (Edinburgh, 1767), pp. 123, 148, 277; and A. Smith (1723–90), *Lectures on Jurisprudence*, ed. R.L. Meek et al. (Oxford, 1978), p. 14.

49. V.I. Lenin, 'Three Sources and Three Constituent Parts of Marxism', as cited in G. Catephores, *An Introduction to Marxist Economics* (Basingstoke, 1989), p. xi. For the intellectual context, *see* esp. L. Kolakowski, *Main Currents of Marxism: Its Rise, Growth and Dissolution*, trans. P.S. Falla (Oxford, 1978; New York, 2005), 3 vols.

50. Marx and Engels, *Communist Manifesto*, in McClellan (ed.), *Marx: Selected Writings*, p. 255. *See also* discussion on pp. 100–2.

51. Ibid., p. 246.

52. *See* F. Engels, *The Origin of the Family, Private Property and the State* (Zurich, 1884), reflecting the significant impact upon Marx and Engels of a pioneering study of the Iroquois people by American anthropologist, L.H. Morgan (1818–81), *Ancient Society* (1877).

53. For F.V. Konstantinov's analysis in 1951, *see* A.J. Gregor, *A Survey of Marxism: Problems in Philosophy and the Theory of History* (New York, 1965), p. 272. And for Engels's 1883 speech comparing Marxism to the laws of Darwinism in biology, *see* p. 101.

54. G. Shakhnazarov, *Futurology Fiasco: A Critical Study of Non-Marxist Concepts of How Society Develops*, trans. V. Schneierson (Moscow, 1982), p. 8.

55. Summarised in F. Engels, *Anti-Dühring* (Leipzig, 1878), ed. C. Palme Dutt (1936), p. 32; expanding the declaration by Marx that 'The mode of production of material life conditions the social, political, and intellectual life process in general': *see* K. Marx, 'Preface to A Critique of Political Economy' (1859), in McClellan (ed.), *Marx: Selected Writings*, p. 425.

56. For the work of Ivan P. Pavlov (1849–1929) in psychology, and T.D. Lysenko (1898–1976) in biology, *see* critique in Z.A. Medvedev, *The Rise and Fall of T.D. Lysenko*, trans. I.M. Lerner (New York, 1969), esp. pp. 244–53. Relevant discussions appear also in Gregor, *Survey of Marxism*, pp. 258–81; and E. van Ree, *The Political*

Thought of Joseph Stalin: A Study in Twentieth-Century Revolutionary Patriotism (2002), pp. 185–7.

57. Two quotations come from K. Marx, 'Afterword' to second German edn of *Das Kapital*, Vol. I (1873), in Marx and Engels, *Selected Works*, Vol. 1, p. 456; and K. Marx, 'Preface to *A Critique of Political Economy*' (1859), in McClellan (ed.), *Marx: Selected Writings*, p. 425. *See* too discussion in D. Campbell, *The Failure of Marxism: The Concept of Inversion in Marx's Critique of Capitalism* (Aldershot, 1996).

58. K. Marx, *Grundrisse der Kritik der politischen Ökonomie* (c. 1857/8), trans. as *Pre-Capitalist Economic Formations*, ed. E. J. Hobsbawm (1964), p. 119.

59. Although slavery was outlawed internationally by declaration of the United Nations General Assembly in 1948, the UN and other organisations are still campaigning against many contemporary forms of slave or un-free labour, including child servitude, around the world. Full information is available from UN websites, including those sponsored by the Commissioner for Human Rights and the International Labour Organisation, and from the website of Anti-Slavery International.

60. *See* the summary in S. P. Dunn, *The Fall and Rise of the Asiatic Mode of Production* (1982); and further details in L. Krader, *The Asiatic Mode of Production: Sources, Development and Critique in the Writings of Karl Marx* (Assen, Netherlands, 1975); M. Sawer, *Marxism and the Question of the Asiatic Mode of Production* (The Hague, 1977); M. Godelier, 'The Concept of the Asiatic Mode of Production and Marxist Models of Social Evolution', in D. Seddon (ed.), *Relations of Production: Marxist Approaches to Economic Anthropology* (1978), pp. 209–57; B. O'Leary, *The Asiatic Mode of Production: Oriental Despotism, Historical Materialism and Indian History* (Oxford, 1989); B. Brugger and D. Kelly, *Chinese Marxism in the Post-Mao Era* (Stanford, 1990), pp. 19–35; and Said, *Orientalism*, pp. 153–6.

61. The 'feudal landlord state', running from 1000 BCE to 1840, was the third in Marxist China's officially promulgated five-stage history: *see* G. Minhai, *Feudalism in Chinese Marxist Historiography* (Copenhagen, 1992), p. 12.

62. J. V. Stalin (1878–1953), *Dialectical and Historical Materialism* (1938), in Engl. trans. (Moscow, 1939), p. 32. On its authorship, *see also* van Ree, *Political Thought of Stalin*, pp. 255–72, 278–83.

63. *See* discussions in R. A. Brown, *Origins of English Feudalism* (1973), pp. 21–32, 83–94; P. Anderson, *Passages from Antiquity to Feudalism* (1978), pp. 112–27, 182, 270–5, 284–5; and S. Reynolds, *Fiefs and Vassals: The Medieval Evidence Reinterpreted* (Oxford, 1994).

64. 'It must be admitted that the word feudalism, which was to have so great a future, was very ill-chosen,' notes Marc Bloch (1886–1944), in his *Feudal Society*, trans. L. A. Manyon (1962), p. xviii. And *see* Reynolds, *Fiefs and Vassals*, pp. 1–14, esp. pp. 3–7.

65. *See* P. Duus, *Feudalism in Japan* (New York, 1993), pp. 3–12; and, for problems in making valid international comparisons, Rozman, *Urban Networks in Russia*, pp. 8–33.

66. A. El Azhary Sonbol, *The New Mamluks: Egyptian Society and Modern Feudalism* (Syracuse, NY, 2000).

67. For G. Flaubert (1821–80), *see* J. Barzun (ed.), *Flaubert's Dictionary of Accepted Ideas* (1954), p. 38.

68. The debates are rehearsed in P. Sweezy et al., *The Transition from Feudalism to Capitalism* (1976); R. J. Holton, *The Transition from Feudalism to Capitalism* (Basingstoke, 1985); and R. S. Duplessis, *Transitions to Capitalism in Early Modern Europe* (Cambridge, 1997), pp. 4–5, 303–8.

69. For M. N. Pokrovsky (1868–1932), author of *History of Russia from the Earliest Times to the Rise of Commercial Capitalism* (1910–12; revised 1924–5) and his rejection by Stalin, *see* Barber, *Soviet Historians*, pp. 19–23, 57–66, 142–3; and G. M. Enteen, *The Soviet Scholar-Bureaucrat: M. N. Pokrovsky and the Society of Marxist Historians* (Philadelphia, PA, 1978), pp. 37–42, 48–9, 161–4, 179–84, 195–6.

70. *See* F. F. Mendels, 'Proto-Industrialisation: The First Phase of Industrialisation Process', *Journal of Economic History*, 32 (1972), pp. 241–61; and critique in L. A. Clarkson, *Proto-Industrialisation: The First Phase of Industrialisation?* (Basingstoke, 1983), esp. pp. 51–7.
71. As pointed out by A. Gerschenkron, 'Reflections on the Concept of "Pre-Requisites" of Modern Industrialisation', in his *Economic Backwardness in Historical Perspective* (New York, 1965), pp. 31–51.
72. For this study, written in 1916, Lenin drew upon the British liberal economist J. A. Hobson (1858–1940), *Imperialism: A Study* (1902).
73. J. V. Stalin, *Foundations of Leninism* (1922; New York, 1932), p. 8.
74. On this, *see* variously Wei-Bin Zhang, *Confucianism and Modernisation*, esp. pp. 204–8, 211–15; W. T. de Bary, *Asian Values and Human Rights: A Confucian Communitarian Perspective* (Cambridge, MA, 1998), pp. 119, 134–9; and A. J. Gregor, *Marxism, China and Development: Reflections on Theory and Reality* (New Brunswick, NJ, 1995).
75. E. Mandel (1923–95), *Late Capitalism* (Frankfurt am Main, 1973), trans. J. de Bres (1975), esp. pp. 10, 589. Mandel's agile theoretical repositionings are satirised in the figure of Ezra Einstein in T. Ali's novel *Redemption* (1990).
76. F. Jameson, 'Postmodernism, or the Cultural Logic of Late Capitalism', *New Left Review*, 146 (July–Aug. 1984), pp. 53–92; later expanded into a book with the same title: *Postmodernism: Or, the Cultural Logic of Late Capitalism* (1991). *See also* J. Goody, *Capitalism and Modernity: The Great Debate* (Oxford, 2004); and comment in previous chapter, p. 130.
77. T. W. Adorno (1903–69), *Negative Dialectics* (1966), trans. E. B. Ashton (1990), p. 20.
78. For Alī Sharī'atī (1933–77), *see* H. Enayat, *Modern Islamic Political Thought: The Response of the Shi'i and Sunni Muslims to the Twentieth Century* (1982), pp. 152–9.
79. Taylor (ed.), *Henri Saint-Simon*, pp. 94–5.
80. *See* O. Spengler (1880–1936), *The Decline of the West, Vol. 1: Form and Actuality* (1922), trans. C. F. Atkinson (1926–9), p. 16; and his *The Decline of the West, Vol. 2: Perspectives of World-History*, pp. 506–7. And *see* too K. P. Fischer, *History and Prophecy: Oswald Spengler and the Decline of the West* (New York, 1989); and J. Farrenkopf, *Prophet of Decline: Spengler on World History and Politics* (Baton Rouge, 2001).

Chapterlink 6–7

1. *See* esp. E. Zerubavel, *Time Maps: Collective Memory and the Social Shape of the Past* (Chicago, 2003), *passim*; F. Hertog, *Régimes d'Historicité: Présentisme et Expériences du Temps* (Paris, 2003); A. Gell, *The Anthropology of Time: Cultural Constructions of Temporal Maps and Images* (Oxford, 1992); and K. C. Pinto, 'Capturing Imagination: The Buja and the Medieval Islamic *Mappa Mundi*', in N. Yavari et al. (eds), *Views from the Edge* (New York, 2004), pp. 154–83.
2. On this, consult J. Fabian, *Time and the Other: How Anthropology Makes its Object* (New York, 1983); and case studies in S. E. Huchinson, *Nuer Dilemmas: Coping with Money, War and the State* (1997); P. Nabokov, *A Forest of Time: American Indian Ways of History* (Cambridge, 2002); R. J. Thornton, *Space, Time and Culture among the Iraqw of Tanzania* (New York, 1980); W. Friedman, *About Time: Inventing the Fourth Dimension* (Cambridge, MA, 1990), pp. 104–11; and J. S. Amelang, 'Mourning becomes Eclectic: Ritual Lament and the Problem of Continuity', *Past & Present*, 187 (2005), pp. 3–31.
3. *See* esp. Richards, *Mapping Time*; L. Halford-Strevens, *The History of Time: A Very Short Introduction* (Oxford, 2005); G. Declercq, *Anno Domini: The Origins of the Christian Era* (Turnhout, 2000); A. Waugh, *Time: From Micro-Seconds to Millennia – A*

Search for the Right Time (1999); and the insightful case study in R. Poole, *Time's Alteration: Calendar Reform in Early Modern England* (1998).
4. There are many famous clocks on public display around the world but there is, as yet, no illustrated guide to assist clock admirers to find them.
5. D.S. Landes, *Revolution in Time: Clocks and the Making of the Modern World* (2000), p. 202. *See* too E. Bruton, *The History of Clocks and Watches* (2000); S.A. Bedini, *The Trail of Time: Time Measurement with Incense in South Asia/Shih-chien ti tsu-chi* (Cambridge, 1994); and R.R.J. Rohr, *Sundials: History, Theory, and Practice* (New York, 1996).
6. On these themes, *see* G.J. Whitrow, *Time in History: Views of Time from Prehistory to the Present Day* (Oxford, 1989); A. Borst, *The Ordering of Time: From the Ancient Computus to the Modern Computer*, trans. A. Winnard (Cambridge, 1993); B. Adam, *Timewatch: The Social Analysis of Time* (Cambridge, 1995); and a breathless discussion by J. Griffiths, *Pip Pip: A Sideways Look at Time* (1999).

Chapter 7

1. There is scope for a new history of history-writing across and between global cultural traditions, for which themes *see* variously J. Cannon (ed.), *The Blackwell Dictionary of Historians* (1988); and E. Fuchs and B. Stuchtey (eds), *Across Cultural Borders: Historiography in Global Perspective* (Lanham, MD, 2002).
2. *See* J. Mali, *Mythistory: The Making of a Modern Historiography* (Chicago, 2003); and K. Armstrong, *A Short History of Myth* (2005).
3. S. Diop, *The Oral History and Literature of the Wolof People of Waalo, Northern Senegal: The Master of the Word (Griot) in the Wolof Tradition* (Lewiston, NY, 1995), pp. 119–20. For memory-men and -women, *see also* P. Stoller, *The Cinematic Griot: The Ethnography of Jean Rouch* (Chicago, 1992).
4. B.H. Chamberlain, 'A Translation of the *Ko-Ji-Ki*, or *Records of Ancient Matters*' [*c.* 712 CE], *Transactions of the Asiatic Society of Japan*, 10 (1881), suppl., p. 4.
5. 'The Saga of Thorstein', in R.A. Anderson, J. Bjarnason and G. Stephens (trans.), *Viking Tales of the North: The Sagas of Thorstein, Viking's Son, and Fridthjof the Bold* (Chicago, 1877), p. 1.
6. P. Ricoeur (1913–2005), *Time and Narrative*, Vol. 3 (Paris, 1985), trans. K. Blarney and D. Pellauer (Chicago, 1988), p. 241.
7. For Herodotus (*c.* 484–*c.* 420? BCE), *see* I. Littlebury, *The History of Herodotus, Translated from the Greek* (1709), p. 1; and J.L. Myres, *Herodotus: Father of History* (Oxford, 1953), pp. 3, 9–10, 15–16, 19.
8. For Garcilaso de la Vega, el Inca (1539–1616), *see* J.G. Varner and J.J. Varner (eds), *The Florida of the Inca: A History . . . Written by the Inca, Garcilaso de la Vega . . .* (Austin, 1951), pp. xxxvii, 594.
9. For Sima Qian (*c.* 145?–86? BCE), *see* B. Watson (ed.), *Records of the Grand Historian of China, Translated from the Shih chi of Ssu-ma Ch'ien* (New York, 1961), Vol. 2, pp. 104–5; and S.W. Durrant, *The Cloudy Mirror: Tension and Conflict in the Writings of Sima Qian* (Albany, NY, 1995).
10. For Rashìd al-Dìn or Rashìdu'd-Dìn (*c.* 1247–1318), *see* E.G. Browne, *A History of Persian Literature, Vol. 3: Under Tartar Dominion, AD 1265–1502* (Cambridge, 1920), pp. 77–80.
11. F. Bacon, *Essays or Counsels, Civil and Moral* (1625), ed. B Vickers (2002), p. 179.
12. G. Santayana (1863–1952), *The Life of Reason: Or, the Phases of Human Progress, Vol. 1: Introduction and Reason in Common Sense* (1905), p. 284.
13. C. Audoin and B. Guinot, *The Measurement of Time: Time, Frequency and the Atomic Clock*, trans. S. Lyle (Cambridge, 2001), pp. 63–4, 236–7, 241, 263.

14. M. Rowan-Robinson, *The Cosmological Distance Ladder: Distance and Time in the Universe* (New York, 1985), pp. 280–95; B. Greene, *The Fabric of the Cosmos: Space, Time and the Texture of Reality* (2004), pp. 477–81, 492–3.

15. For Maria Spiridonova (1884–1941) in 1917, *see* J.S. Reed (1887–1920), *Ten Days that Shook the World* (New York, 1919), p. 311; and for her role as political assassin, revolutionary symbol, and one of the leaders of the pro-peasant Social Revolutionary Party, renamed the Left Social Revolutionaries, *see* C.I. Steinberg, *Maria Spiridonova: Revolutionary Terrorist*, ed. G. David and E. Mosbacher (1935).

16. Studies listed in ascending day order include: H. MacShane, *Three Days that Shook Edinburgh: Story of the Historic Scottish Hunger March* (Glasgow, 1933; Edinburgh, 1994); A. Cockburn and J. St. Clair, *Five Days that Shook the World: Seattle and Beyond* (2000); H. Fagan, *Nine Days that Shook England: An Account of the English People's Uprising in 1381* (1938); Reed, *Ten Days that Shook the World*; T. Méray, *Thirteen Days that Shook the Kremlin: Imre Nagy and the Hungarian Revolution*, trans. H.L. Katzander (1959); J. Benoist Mechin, *Sixty Days that Shook the West: The Fall of France, 1940*, trans. C. Falls (1963); and, on the 1940 Battle of Britain, R.W. Clarke et al., *The Hundred Days that Shook the World* (Hemel Hempstead, 1969).

17. F. Halliday, *Two Hours that Shook the World: September 11 2002 – Causes and Consequences* (2002) was one graphically entitled study, amidst a torrent of interpretation and analysis.

18. The internet boom/slump in the late 1990s offers a recent example: *see* R. Cellan-Jones, *Dot.Bomb: The Rise and Fall of Dot.Com Britain* (2001), pp. 189–204; Sean Carton, *The Dot.Bomb Survival Guide* (New York, 2000), pp. 247–56; and a revealing business confessional by E. Malmsten et al., *Boo Hoo: A Dot-Com Story from Concept to Catastrophe* (2002).

19. *See* C. Gamble, *Timewalkers: The Prehistory of Global Colonisation* (Stroud, 1993); and Cavalli-Sforza and Cavalli-Sforza, *Great Human Diasporas*.

20. McKie, *Ape-Man*, pp. 57–67, 130–1, 207; and W.B. Wright, *Tools and the Man* (1939), pp. 187–93.

21. *See* B. Fagan, *The Long Summer: How Climate Changed Civilisation* (2004); and D. Macdougall, *Frozen Earth: The Once and Future Story of Ice Ages* (Berkeley, 2004).

22. G. Blainey, *A Short History of the World* (2000), pp. 45–55; N. Roberts, *The Holocene: An Environmental History* (Oxford, 1998 edn), pp. 129–58.

23. H.H. Lamb, *Climate, History and the Modern World* (1982), pp. 106–7, and graph p. 107. For oceanographic variations, *see also* Pirazzoli, *Sea Level Changes*; and B.C. Douglas et al., *Sea Level Rises: History and Consequences* (San Diego, CA, 2001).

24. J. Michelet (1798–1874), *La mer* (Paris, 1861), in Eng. trans. *The Sea* (1875). And consult for context C. Crossley, *French Historians and Romanticism: Thierry, Guizot, the Saint-Simonians, Quinet, Michelet* (1993), pp. 183–250, esp. pp. 183, 193–5, 217, 248.

25. For cuneiform writing in Mesopotamia by *c.* 3500 BCE, *see* M.W. Green, 'Early Cuneiform', in W.M. Senner (ed.), *The Origins of Writing* (Lincoln, NB, 1989), pp. 43–57; M. Van de Mieroop, *Cuneiform Texts and the Writing of History* (1999), p. 9.

26. *See above*, pp. 149, 161.

27. N. Elias (1897–1990), *Time: An Essay*, trans. E. Jephcott (Oxford, 1992), p. 192.

28. *See* e.g. K.N. Chaudhuri, *From the Atlantic to the Arabian Sea: A Polyphonic Essay on History* (Florence, 1995).

29. The classic study is R.N. Salaman (1874–1955), *The History and Social Influence of the Potato* (Cambridge, 1949; 1985). Many other consumables have also found historians, as in J. Goodman, *Tobacco in History: The Cultures of Dependence* (1993) or A. Wild, *Coffee: A Dark History* (2004).

30. *See* p. 147.

31. A. Toynbee (1899–1975), *Mankind and Mother Earth: A Narrative History of the World* (1976), p. xi. For his classifications, *see* his *Study of History* (1934–61), summarised in A. Toynbee, *A Study of History: Abridgement of Vol. 1–6*, by D.C. Somervell (1951), pp. 8, 35, 36.

32. G.J Renier, 'Toynbee's *A Study of History*', in M.F.A. Montagu (ed.), *Toynbee and History: Critical Essays and Reviews* (Boston, MA, 1956), pp. 73–4; and H. Trevor-Roper, 'Testing the Toynbee System', in ibid., pp. 122–4. Compare also verdicts in G. Snooks, *The Laws of History* (1998), pp. 73–89; and R.N. Stromberg, *Arnold J. Toynbee: Historian for an Age in Crisis* (Carbondale, IL, 1972), pp. 39–76, 111–13.

33. P. Turchin, *Historical Dynamics: Why States Rise and Fall* (Princeton, NJ, 2003), pp. 200–4. His approach to spatial ecology is expounded in idem, *Quantitative Analysis of Movement: Measuring and Modelling Population Redistribution in Animals and Plants* (Sunderland, MA, 1998) and its application to human ecology is further extended in idem, *War and Peace and War: The Life Cycles of Imperial Nations* (New York, 2005).

34. For cultural cycle-building, see L.D. Snyder, *Macro History: A Theoretical Approach to Comparative World History* (Lewiston, NY, 1999), *passim*, incl. p. 676. His study is dedicated to Ibn Khaldūn and Arnold Toynbee.

35. Spengler, *Decline of the West*, Vol. 1, end-charts: Table 1, showing the world's spiritual 'epochs' in stages of spring/summer/autumn/winter.

36. From C. Scarre (ed.), *Timelines of the Ancient World: A Visual Chronology from the Origins of Life to 1500* (1993), pp. 94–7, 104–5.

37. Examples include (alphabetically by author): G. Blainey, *A Short History of the World* (2000); C. Cipolla, *The Economic History of World Population* (1978); I.N. Diakonoff, *The Paths of History* (Cambridge, 1999); F. Fernández-Armesto, *Civilizations* (2001); E. Gellner, *Plough, Sword and Book: The Structure of Human History* (1988); E.L. Jones, *Growth Recurring: Economic Change in World History* (Oxford, 1988); M. Livi-Bacci, *A Concise History of World Population* (Oxford, 1992); J.R. McNeill and W.H. McNeill, *The Human Web: A Bird's-Eye View of World History* (2003); L. Mumford, *The City in History: Its Origins, Its Transformations and its Prospects* (1961); C. Ponting, *World History: A New Perspective* (2000); Roberts, *The Holocene*; P.N. Stearns, *Gender in World History* (2000); and H. Thomas, *An Unfinished History of the World* (1989).

38. F. Fukuyama, *The End of History and the Last Man* (1992), esp. pp. 39–51, and pp. 49–50 for table showing the spread of liberal democracies, 1790–1990. *See also* debates within H. Williams, D. Sullivan and G. Matthews, *Francis Fukuyama and the End of History* (Cardiff, 1997).

39. M. de Landa, *A Thousand Years of Non-Linear History* (New York, 1997), p. 273.

40. T. Zeldin, *An Intimate History of Humanity* (1994).

41. K.N. Daruwalla, 'Dialogues with a Third Voice', in B. King, *Modern Indian Poetry in English* (Delhi, 1992), p. 125.

42. For a summary of Braudel's model, *see* his essays on 'History and the Social Sciences' and 'History and Sociology', in his *On History*, pp. 27–33, 74–8.

43. E.g. S.J. Gould mentions the possibility of a three-tiered model of time in distinctly Braudelian terms but without mentioning Braudel: *see* Gould, *Structure of Evolutionary Theory*, pp. 1328, 1330.

44. *See* G. Gurvitch (1894–1965), *La multiplicité des temps sociaux* (Paris, 1958); and comment by Braudel, 'History and the Social Sciences', in his *On History*, pp. 49–50. For Gurvitch's love of classification, *see* too R. Swedberg, *Sociology as Disenchantment: The Evolution of the Work of Georges Gurvitch* (Atlantic Highlands, NJ, 1982), pp. 124–6.

45. For this and the following quotation, *see* Braudel, *On History*, p. 33; and idem, *The Mediterranean and the Mediterranean World in the Age of Philip II*, trans. S. Reynolds (Paris, 1949; 1972), Vol. 1, p. 21.

46. J-P. Burg and M. Ford, 'Orogeny through Time: An Overview', in J-P. Burg and M. Ford (eds), *Orogeny through Time* (Bath, 1997), pp. 1–17, esp. p. 13.

47. Braudel, *On History*, p. 77; and J.H. Hexter (1910–96), 'Fernand Braudel and the *Monde Braudellien*' (1972), in J.H. Hexter, *On Historians: Reappraisals of Some of the Makers of Modern History* (1979), pp. 10, 104–5 – an analysis that Braudel commended.

48. *See* S.A. Schumm and R.E. Lichty, 'Time, Space and Causality in Geomorphology', *American Journal of Science*, 263 (1965), pp. 110–19; and B.A. Kennedy, 'Classics in Physical Geography Revisited', *Progress in Physical Geography*, 21 (1997), pp. 419–23.

49. P. Laslett, 'Social Structural Time: An Attempt at Classifying Types of Social Change by their Characteristic Paces', in M. Young and T. Schuller (eds), *The Rhythms of Society* (1988), pp. 17–36, esp. pp. 20–1, 32.

50. L. Stone (1919–99), 'History and the Social Sciences in the Twentieth Century', in his *The Past and the Present Revisited* (Boston, MA, 1981), p. 41.

51. For this analogy, *see* too D.H. Fischer, 'The Braided Narrative: Substance and Form in Social History', in A. Fletcher (ed.), *The Literature of Fact* (New York, 1976), pp. 109–33.

52. K. Spindler, *The Man in the Ice: The Preserved Body of a Neolithic Man Reveals the Secrets of the Stone Age* (1994), p. 1; and A.T. Chamberlain and M.P. Pearson, *Earthly Remains: The History and Science of Preserved Human Bodies* (2001), pp. 127, 129–31. Ötzi is now preserved at the Museo Archaeologico dell' Alto Adige at Bolzano, Italy.

53. V.I. Lenin, *'Left-Wing' Communism: An Infantile Disorder* (1920), in his *Collected Works*, Vol. 31 (1966), pp. 17–104. *See* too C. Hill, *Lenin and the Russian Revolution* (1947; 1993), pp. 115–16; and E.H. Carr, *The Bolshevik Revolution, 1917–23* (1977 edn), Vol. 3, pp. 181–8.

54. D.S. Ruegg, *Buddha-Nature, Mind and the Problem of Gradualism in a Comparative Perspective: On the Transmission and Reception of Buddhism in India and Tibet* (1989), p. 150.

55. *See* among a large literature G.W. Kolodko, *From Shock to Therapy: The Political Economy of Postsocialist Transformation* (Oxford, 2000); and also N.A. Berdyaev, *The Russian Idea*, trans. R.M. French (1947), pp. 193–8.

56. For a discussion of 'eternalist' (through-time) and 'temporalist' (temporally contingent) interpretations, *see* W. Künne, *Conceptions of Truth* (Oxford, 2003), pp. 249–316. A further discussion is provided in D.M. Armstrong, *Truth and Truthmakers* (Cambridge, 2005).

57. C.H. de Saint-Simon, *Catéchisme des Industriels*, in *Oeuvres de Saint-Simon et D'Enfantin* (Paris, 1875), p. 57.

58. One triadic variant, quoted at a scientists' international conference in 1985, cited the progression from 'This man is nuts' to 'We will have to look at this problem in order to dismiss it' to the eventual 'Of course, I've always known that this was the case': *see* T. Palmer, *Controversy: Catastrophism and Evolution* (New York, 1999), pp. vii–viii.

59. For debates, *see* J.R. Lucas, *Space, Time, and Causality: An Essay in Natural Philosophy* (Oxford, 1984), esp. pp. 69–83, 148–53, 184–9; P. Dowe and P. Noordhof (eds), *Cause and Chance: Causation in an Indeterministic World* (2004); and, on causal modelling, J. Pearl, *Causality: Models, Reasoning and Inference* (Cambridge, 2000).

60. *See*, for example, sociological probes in A. Nakatani, *Contested Time: Women's Work and Marriage in Bali* (Oxford, 1995).

61. Consult J.M.E. McTaggart (1866–1925), 'The Unreality of Time', in his *Philosophical Studies*, ed. S.V. Keeling (1934), pp. 110–31; and his *The Nature of Existence*, ed. C.D. Broad (Cambridge, 1927), Vol. 2, pp. 9–31. *See also* G. Rochelle, *Behind Time: The Incoherence of Time and McTaggart's Atemporal Replacement* (Aldershot, 1998); and R. McLure, *The Philosophy of Time: Time before Times* (2005), pp. 139–64.

62. J.M.E. McTaggart, *Human Immortality and Pre-Existence* (1915); and his *Nature of Existence*, Vol. 2, pp. 176–89. For the unsuccessful seance, *see* G. Rochelle, *The Life and Philosophy of J.McT.E. McTaggart, 1866–1925* (Lewiston, NY, 1991), pp. 201–3.

63. For S.A. Alexeyev (Askoldov) (1870–1945), *see* N.O. Lossky, *History of Russian Philosophy* (1952), pp. 382–3; and for P.A. Sorokin (1889–1968), *see* his *Sociocultural Causality, Space, Time: A Study of the Referential Principles of Sociology and Social Science* (Durham, NC, 1943), pp. 158–225.

64. M. Heidegger (1889–1976), *Being and Time* (1927), trans. J. Macquarrie and E. Robinson (1962), p. 382. *See also* M. King, *A Guide to Heidegger's Being and Time*, ed. J. Llewellyn (Albany, NY, 2001), pp. 134–6, 302–15; R. Polt, *Heidegger: An Introduction* (1999), pp. 157–64; and C.M. Sherover, *Heidegger, Kant and Time* (Bloomington, IN, 1971), pp. 182–212.

65. P. Edwards, *Heidegger's Confusions* (Amherst, NY, 2004), pp. 33–4; and critiques also in A. Feenberg, *Heidegger and Marcuse: The Catastrophe and Redemption of History* (2005); H. Ott, *Martin Heidegger: A Political Life*, trans. A. Blunden (1993); and Wood, *Deconstruction of Time*, pp. xx–xxii, 137–249.

66. P. Ricoeur, *Time and Narrative*, Vol. 3, trans. K. Blarney and D. Pellauer (Chicago, 1988), pp. 104–41; and also K. Simms, *Paul Ricoeur* (2003), pp. 87–98.

67. H.A.L. Fisher (1865–1940), *A History of Europe* (1935), Vol. 1, p. vii. For a survey of historical surprises, mainly relating to the outcome of battles, *see* E. Durschmeid, *The Hinge Factor: How Chance and Stupidity Have Changed History* (1999); and for theoretical discussions, J. Alexander et al. (eds), *The Micro-Macro Link* (Berkeley, 1987); and G. Itzkowitz, *Contingency Theory: Rethinking the Boundaries of Social Thought* (Lanham, MD, 1996).

68. J.D. Watson, *The Double Helix*, retold by D. Maule (2001), pp. 85–95; and P. Goujon, *From Biotechnology to Genomes: The Meaning of the Double Helix* (Singapore, 2001).

69. *See* e.g. S. Kauffman, *At Home in the Universe: The Search for Laws of Self-Organization and Complexity* (New York, 1995), pp. 226–9, 232–3. Other models of complex order are found in surveys of space-time, such as D-E. Liebscher, *The Geometry of Time* (Weinheim, 2005), pp. 5–18; and in diagrams of the mathematics of movement, as in E.J. Kostelich and D. Armbruster, *Introductory Differential Equations: From Linearity to Chaos* (Reading, MA, 1996), pp. 189, 255. A 33-metre-high steel-rod sculpture by Antony Gormley, entitled *Quantum Cloud*, which captures the irregular pattern-making of probabilities, can also be viewed at Greenwich (London), by the River Thames at the Millennium Dome: *see* T. Hey and Patrick Walters, *The New Quantum Universe* (Cambridge, 2003), Plate, p. 314.

70. Quotations assembled from separate passages in I.R. Prigogine (1917–2003), with I. Stengers, *The End of Certainty: Time, Chaos and the New Laws of Nature* (New York, 1997), pp. 162, 187, 188–9. On these debates, consult also D.R. Griffin (ed.), *Physics and the Ultimate Significance of Time: Bohm, Prigogine and Process Philosophy* (Albany, NY, 1986); and P. Coveney and R. Highfield, *The Arrow of Time: The Quest to Find Science's Greatest Mystery* (1991).

Chapterlink 7–8

1. *See* the historical compendium in J.T. Fraser (ed.), *The Voices of Time: A Cooperative Survey of Man's Views of Time as Expressed by the Sciences and by the Humanities* (New York, 1966); and comparative analyses in Lippincott et al., *Story of Time*.

2. Dicta about daily living with time and its effects, including death, appear in all collections of quotations, sayings, proverbs and song, as well as extensively in literature and philosophy. No culture is without such forms of advice and commentary, however variously expressed.

3. Summary of S. Kierkegaard, journal entry, n.d., *c*. 1843, in A. Dru (ed.), *The Journals of Søren Kierkegaard: A Selection* (1938), p. 127.

4. On claims for the contemporary speeding of time-consciousness, *see* J. Gleick, *Faster: The Acceleration of Just About Everything* (2000); and L. Kreitzman, *The 24-Hour Society* (1999); with counter-blasts in favour of 'slow' time from T. H. Eriksen, *Tyranny of the Moment: Fast and Slow Time in the Information Age* (2001) and Griffiths, *Pip Pip: Sideways Look at Time.*

5. *See* e.g. P. D. Ward and D. Brownlee, *Rare Earth: Why Complex Life is Uncommon in the Universe* (2004), esp. pp. 222–9, 235–9, 243–56, 282–5.

6. Consult E. Ashpole, *The Search for Extra-Terrestrial Intelligence* (1990); Dick, *Life on Other Worlds*; D. Lamb, *The Search for Extra-Terrestrial Intelligence: A Philosophical Inquiry* (2001); M. Benson, *Beyond: Visions of the Interplanetary Probes* (New York, 2003); and a sceptical salvo from G. Basalla, *Civilised Life in the Universe: Scientists on Intelligent Extraterrestrials* (Oxford, 2006).

Chapter 8

1. A. Wat (1900–67), 'Ode III', in C. Milosz and L. Nathan (eds), *Aleksander Wat: Selected Poems* (1969), p. 81. *See also* A. Wat, *My Century: The Odyssey of a Polish Intellectual*, ed. R. Lourie (New York, 1990).

2. *See* M. W. Eysenck, *Human Memory: Theory, Research and Individual Differences* (1977), pp. 135–58; and J. T. E. Richardson et al., *Working Memory and Human Cognition* (New York, 1996). On the simultaneous value/fragility of memory, *see* V. Schwarcz, *Bridge across Broken Time: Chinese and Jewish Cultural Memory* (New Haven, 1998); J. Rappaport, *The Politics of Memory: Native Historical Interpretation in the Columbian Andes* (Cambridge, 1990); and theoretical discussion in A. Loizou, *Time, Embodiment and the Self* (Aldershot, 2000), pp. 94–108.

3. W. Shakespeare (1564–1616), *Hamlet*, Act 1, Scene 5.

4. M. Proust (1871–1922), *Remembrance of Things Past, Vol. 1: Swann's Way*, trans. C. K. Scott Moncrieff and T. Kilmartin (1981), p. 51.

5. *See* variously J. M. Pearce, *Animal Learning and Cognition: An Introduction* (Hove, Sussex, 1997), pp. 137–66, 167–94; and C. D. L. Wynne, *Animal Cognition: The Mental Lives of Animals* (Basingstoke, 2001), esp. pp. 189–90.

6. C. A. Pickover, *The Loom of God: Mathematical Tapestries at the Edge of Time* (New York, 1997), p. 21.

7. A classic introduction is provided in E. T. Hall, *The Silent Language* (New York, 1959), pp. 57–81, 188–209. *See also* subsequent studies esp. by A. Leroi-Gourhan, *Le geste et la parole* (Paris, 1964), trans. A. B. Berger as *Gesture and Speech* (Cambridge, MA, 1993); and S. Goldin-Meadow, *Hearing Gesture: How our Hands Help Us Think* (Cambridge, MA, 2004).

8. J. Aitchison, *The Seeds of Speech: Language Origin and Evolution* (Cambridge, 1996), pp. 50–3, 77–92; P. Lieberman, *The Biology and Evolution of Language* (Cambridge, MA, 1984), pp. 327–8; and diagrammatic models of possible sequences of human evolution, from leaving the trees to 'civilisation', in M. Landau, *Narratives of Human Evolution* (New Haven, 1991), pp. 6, 8–9.

9. *See* essays in N. L. Wallin, B. Merker and S. Brown (eds), *The Origins of Music* (Cambridge, MA, 2000); and C. Sachs, *A Short History of World Music* (London, 1949), p. 3.

10. *See* esp. D. L. Schacter, *The Seven Sins of Memory: How the Mind Forgets and Remembers* (Boston, MA, 2001); and, on the history of memory systems, Yates, *Art of Memory.*

11. *See* esp. J. Le Goff, *History and Memory*, trans. S. Rendall and E. Claman (New York, 1992), pp. xi–xii, 51–99; and debates in C. Hoerl and T. McCormack (eds), *Time and Memory: Issues in Philosophy and Psychology* (Oxford, 2001); and D. Draaisma, *Metaphors of Memory: A History of Ideas about the Mind*, trans. P. Vincent (Cambridge, 2000).

12. *Sentinela* by Fernando Brant, as cited in C.A. Perrone, *Masters of Contemporary Brazilian Song: MBP* [música popular brasileira], *1965–85* (Austin, TX, 1989), p. 141.

13. A. de Gobineau, *The Moral and Intellectual Diversity of Races*, ed. H. Hotz and J.C. Nott (Philadelphia, 1856; repr. New York, 1984), p. 407.

14. Quintus Horatius Flaccus (65–8 BCE), *Odes*, Bk 3, no. 30, in B. Radice (ed.), *Horace: The Complete Odes and Epodes* (1983), p. 164.

15. S. Weil (1909–43), *Lectures on Philosophy*, ed. P. Winch, trans. H. Price (Cambridge, 1978), pp. 68–9; and comment in P. Winch, *Simone Weil: 'The Just Balance'* (Cambridge, 1989), p. 51.

16. *See* T. P. Waldron, *Principles of Language and Mind* (1985), pp. 105–18; J. Goody, *The Logic of Writing and the Organisation of Society* (Cambridge, 1986); and his *The Power of the Written Tradition* (Washington, DC, 2000). But for overlappings between literacy and orality, *see* too B.V. Street, *Social Literacies: Critical Approaches to Literacy in Development, Ethnography and Education* (1995), pp. 2–5, 53–5, 75–7, 149–51, 153–9; M. Bloch, 'Literacy and Enlightenment', in K. Schousboe and M.T. Larsen (eds), *Literacy and Society* (Copenhagen, 1989), pp. 15–37; and case study in R. Thomas, *Oral Tradition and Written Record in Classical Athens* (Cambridge, 1989).

17. In 1850 fewer than one in ten of the world's adult population could read and write; in 1995, by contrast, it is estimated that more than three-quarters (77.4 per cent) have basic literacy: compare N. Rassool, *Literacy for Sustainable Development in the Age of Information* (Clevedon, Somerset, 1999), p. 55; and D. Vincent, *The Rise of Mass Literacy: Reading and Writing in Modern Europe* (Cambridge, 2000), pp. 17–18.

18. M. McLuhan (1911–80), *The Gutenberg Galaxy* (1962), p. 31.

19. Data in K. Davis, 'The Origins and Growth of Urbanisation in the World', *American Journal of Sociology*, 60 (1955), pp. 429–37; R. Jones (ed.), *Essays on World Urbanisation* (1975); and G.W. Jones and P. Visaria (eds), *Urbanisation in Large Developing Countries: China, Indonesia, Brazil and India* (Oxford, 1997), p. 1.

20. A. de Tocqueville (1805–59), *Democracy in America*, ed. J.P. Mayer, trans. G. Lawrence (1848; repr. New York, 1969), p. xi.

21. *See* discussions in J. Sandler and P. Fonagy (eds), *Recovered Memories of Abuse: True or False?* (1997); and R.J. McNally, *Remembering Trauma* (Cambridge, MA, 2003), esp. p. 275.

22. H. Arendt (1906–75), *The Origins of Totalitarianism* (1951; in 1986 edn), pp. 478–9. For context, *see* S.J. Whitfield, *Into the Dark: Hannah Arendt and Totalitarianism* (Philadelphia, 1980); and M.B. Hull, *The Hidden Philosophy of Hannah Arendt* (2002), pp. 99–101.

23. *See* J.R. Hurford, 'The Evolution of Language and Languages', in R. Dunbar, C. Knight and C. Power (eds), *The Evolution of Culture: An Interdisciplinary View* (Edinburgh, 1999), p. 188; as well as the essays in Senner (ed.), *Origins of Writing*; and those in S. Houston (ed.), *The First Writing: Script Invention as History and Process* (Cambridge, 2005).

24. J. DeFrancis, *Visible Speech: The Diverse Oneness of Writing Systems* (Honolulu, 1989), pp. 267–9. *See also* A. Nakanishi, *Writing Systems of the World: Alphabets, Syllabaries, Pictograms* (Kyoto, 1975; Rutland, VT, 1980); F. Coulmas, *The Writing Systems of the World* (Oxford, 1989); W.G. Boltz, *The Origin and Early Development of the Chinese Writing System* (New Haven, 1994); and J.M. Unger, *Ideogram: Chinese Characters and the Myth of Disembodied Meaning* (Honolulu, 2004).

25. T. Tsuen-Hsuin, *Paper and Printing*, in J. Needham (ed.), *Science and Civilisation in China, Vol. 5: Chemistry and Chemical Technology – Part 1: Paper and Printing* (Cambridge, 1985), pp. 23–132, 146–8; T.F. Carter, *The Invention of Printing in China and its Spread Westward* (New York, 1925); and M. Edwardes, *East-West Passage: The Travel of Ideas, Arts and Inventions between Asia and the Western World* (1971), pp. 81–2, 90–3.

26. For J. Gutenberg (1394?–1468), *see* V. Scholderer, *Johann Gutenberg: The Inventor of Printing* (1970), p. 8; and S. Füssel (ed.), *Gutenberg-Jahrbuch 2001* (Mainz, 2001). The wider implications are canvassed in L. Febvre and H-J. Martin, *The Coming of the Book: The Impact of Printing, 1450–1800*, trans. D. Gerard (1976); Eisenstein, *The Printing Press as an Agent of Change*; and G. Cavallo and R. Chartier (eds), *A History of Reading in the West*, trans. L. Cochrane (Cambridge, 1999).

27. *See* G. Burton, *Talking Television: An Introduction to the Study of Television* (2000), pp. 34–5, 211–29; and S. McQuire, *Visions of Modernity: Representation, Memory, Time and Space in the Age of the Camera* (1998), pp. 253–7.

28. Teilhard de Chardin, *Future of Man*, pp. 132, 157–9.

29. M. Dodge and R. Kitchin, *Mapping Cyberspace* (2001), p. 4, Table 11; and context in J. Naughton, *A Brief History of the Future: The Origins of the Internet* (1999).

30. R. Lord, *The Net Effect* (2000), p. 228. For rival views, *see* too A. Toffler, *The Third Wave* (1980), p. 18; A. Toffler and H. Toffler, *Creating a New Civilization: The Politics of the Third Wave* (Atlanta, 1995), p. 19; V. Mosco, *Digital Sublime: Myth, Power and Cyberspace* (Cambridge, MA, 2004); and R.L. Glass, *ComputingFailure.com: War Stories from the Electronic Revolution* (Upper Saddle River, 2001).

31. B.F. Skinner (1904–90), 'Teaching Machines' (1958), repr. in his *Cumulative Record* (1961), p. 173. These debates are continued in Mosco, *Digital Sublime*; and R. Land and S. Bayne (eds), *Education in Cyberspace* (2005).

32. P. Simon, Marquis de Laplace (1749–1827), *A Philosophical Essay on Probabilities* (Paris, 1812), trans. F.W. Truscott and F.L. Emory (New York, 1902), p. 4.

33. For E. Halley (1656–1742), *see* J. Muirden, *Observer's Guide to Halley's Comet* (1985), pp. 13–20; and S. Schaffer, 'Comets and the World's End', in L. Howe and A. Wain (eds), *Predicting the Future* (Cambridge, 1993), pp. 52–76.

34. In 1979, a commentator looking at forecasts for 2000 did not foresee the collapse of the USSR or the ending of South African apartheid, while being wrongly sure that the Israeli-Palestinian question would have been resolved: *see* P. Peeters, *Can We Avoid a Third World War around 2010? The Political, Social and Economic Past and Future of Humanity* (1979), pp. 247–50. For the history of forecasting, *see* J. Margolis, *A Brief History of Tomorrow: The Future, Past and Present* (2000); and for the historians' input, consult also D.J. Staley, 'A History of the Future', *History and Theory*, 41 (2002), pp. 72–89.

35. C.R. McInnes, *Solar Sailing: Technology, Dynamics and Mission Applications* (Chichester, 1999), p. 1.

36. Contrast D. Reinking, 'Introduction', in D. Reinking et al., *Handbook of Literacy and Technology: Transformations in a Post-Typographic World* (Mahwah, NJ, 1998), p. xi; and F. Mayor and J. Binde, *The World Ahead: Our Future in the Making* (2001), pp. 313–32.

37. *See* e.g. D.M. Rorvik, *As Man Becomes Machine: The Evolution of the Cyborg* (1970; 1973); Mazlish, *Fourth Discontinuity*, pp. 216–33; and P. Menzel and F. D'Aluisio, *Robo Sapiens: Evolution of a New Species* (Cambridge, MA, 2000).

38. D. Diderot, 'D'Alembert's Dream', in *Rameau's Nephew and D'Alembert's Dream* (1769), trans. L. Tancock (1976), p. 180.

39. For a far-sighted vision of three basic 'laws of robotics', *see* I. Asimov (1920–92), *I, Robot* (1952), p. 21.

40. Comment from G.E. Lessing (1729–81), *The Education of the Human Race*, trans. F.W. Robertson (1872), p. 73.

41. Quotations from J.L. Borges (1889–1986), 'The Garden of Forking Paths', in his *Labyrinths: Selected Stories and Other Writings*, ed. D.A. Yates and J.E. Irby (New York, 1962), pp. 20, 28.

42. G. Manley Hopkins (1844–89), 'Creation and Redemption: The Great Sacrifice' (1881), in C. Devlin (ed.), *The Sermons and Devotional Writings of Gerard Manley Hopkins* (1959), p. 196.

Coda

1. 'Et quand l'Espace galope qui me livre / le Temps revient qui me delivre / le Temps le Temps': from Aimé Césaire, 'Summation', in his *Cadastre: Poems*, ed. E. Snyder (New York, 1973), p. 128.

2. R. Morris, *Cosmic Questions: Galactic Halos, Cold Dark Matter, and the End of Time* (New York, 1993), p. 104.

3. From E. Dickinson (1830–86), 'The Admirations – and Contempts – of time –' in *The Complete Poems*, ed. T.H. Johnson (1975), p. 428.

4. Wood, *Deconstruction of Time*, p. xiv.

5. *See* variously Siegfried, *Strange Matters*, p. 245: 'I think time still holds some surprises'; J. Baggott, *Beyond Measure: Modern Physics, Philosophy and the Meaning of Quantum Theory* (Oxford, 2004), p. 288: 'My recommendation is to watch *time* closely.'

6. The closing dictum comes from Johannes Eckhart (*c.* 1260–1327), the German-born Christian mystic and unorthodox pantheist: F. Pfeiffer, *Meister Eckhart*, trans. C. de B. Evans (1924), Vol. 1, p. 352.

Further Reading

This booklist suggests some starting points for further reading about time and history, citing works in English and English translation to introduce themes that can be discussed in any language. For convenience, the list is divided by broad themes but there is much overlap between the separate sections. The place of publication is London unless otherwise indicated.

Long-Run World Histories

Blainey, G., *A Short History of the World* (2000)
Bryson, B., *A Short History of Nearly Everything* (2003)
Diakonoff, I. N., *The Paths of History* (Cambridge, 1999)
Fagan, B., *The Long Summer: How Climate Changed Civilisation* (2004)
Fernández-Armesto, F., *Civilisations* (2001)
Fukuyama, F., *The End of History and the Last Man* (1992)
Gellner, E., *Plough, Sword and Book: The Structure of Human History* (1988)
de Landa, M., *A Thousand Years of Non-Linear History* (New York, 1997)
Ponting, C., *World History: A New Perspective* (2000)
Roberts, J. M., *The Penguin History of the World* (1995)
Roberts, N., *The Holocene: An Environmental History* (Oxford, 1998)
Scarre, C. (ed.), *Timelines of the Ancient World: A Visual Chronology from the Origins of Life to 1500* (1993)

History of Human Communications

Allan, R. A., *A History of the Personal Computer: The People and the Technology* (2001)
Briggs, A. and Burke, P., *A Social History of the Media: From Gutenberg to the Internet* (Cambridge, 2002)
Coulmas, F., *The Writing Systems of the World* (Oxford, 1989)
Donald, M., *Origins of the Modern Mind: Three Stages in the Evolution of Culture and Cognition* (Cambridge, MA, 1991)
Febvre, L. and Martin, H-J., *The Coming of the Book: The Impact of Printing, 1450–1800*, trans. D. Gerard (1976)
Goldin-Meadow, S., *Hearing Gesture: How our Hands Help Us Think* (Cambridge, MA, 2004)

Goody, J., *The Logic of Writing and the Organisation of Society* (Cambridge, 1986)

Ifrah, G., *The Universal History of Numbers: From Prehistory to the Invention of the Computer* (1998)

Mosco, V., *The Digital Sublime: Myth, Power and Cyberspace* (Cambridge, MA, 2004)

Nettle, D. and Romaine, S., *Vanishing Voices: The Extinction of the World's Languages* (Oxford, 2002)

Ong, W.J., *Orality and Literacy: The Technologising of the Word* (1982)

Vincent, D., *The Rise of Mass Literacy: Reading and Writing in Modern Europe* (Cambridge, 2000)

Population and Economic Histories

Cameron, R., and Neal, L., *A Concise Economic History of the World: From Paleolithic Times to the Present* (Oxford, 2002 edn)

Cavalli-Sforza, L.L. and Cavalli-Sforza, F., *The Great Human Diasporas: The History of Diversity and Evolution* (New York, 1995)

Fischer, D.H., *The Great Wave: Price Revolutions and the Rhythm of History* (New York, 1996)

Jones, E.L., *Growth Recurring: Economic Change in World History* (Oxford, 1988)

Kubler, G., *The Shape of Time: Remarks on the History of Things* (New Haven, 1962)

Landers, J., *The Field and the Forge: Population, Production and Power in the Pre-Industrial West* (Oxford, 2003)

Landes, D.S., *The Unbound Prometheus: Technical Change and Industrial Development in Western Europe from 1750 to the Present* (Cambridge, 1969; 2003)

Livi-Bacci, M., *A Concise History of World Population* (Oxford, 1992)

McClellan, J.E. and Dorn, H., *Science and Technology in World History: An Introduction* (Baltimore, 1999)

McNeill, J.R. and McNeill, W.H., *The Human Web: A Bird's-Eye View of World History* (2003)

Rosser, J.B., *From Catastrophe to Chaos: A General Theory of Economic Discontinuities* (Dordrecht, 1991)

Watts, S.J., *Disease and Medicine in World History* (2003)

Human Socio/Cultural/Biology

Badcock, C., *Evolutionary Psychology: A Critical Introduction* (Cambridge, 2000)

Barkan, E., *The Retreat of Scientific Racism: Changing Concepts of Race in Britain and the United States between the World Wars* (Cambridge, 1992)

Cavalli-Sforza, L.L., Menozzi, P. and Piazza, A., *The History and Geography of Human Genes* (Princeton, 1996)

Fredrickson, G.M., *Racism: A Short History* (Princeton, 2002)

Gribbin, M. and Gribbin, J., *Being Human: Putting People in an Evolutionary Perspective* (1995)

Hines, M., *Brain Gender* (Oxford, 2004)

Hrdy, S.B., *Mother Nature: Natural Selection and the Female of the Species* (1999)

Oppenheimer, S., *Out of Eden: The Peopling of the World* (2003)

Roughgarden, J., *Evolution's Rainbow: Diversity, Gender and Sexuality in Nature and People* (Berkeley, 2004)

Sarich, V. and Miele, F., *Race: The Reality of Human Differences* (Boulder, CO, 2004)

Stearns, P.N., *Gender in World History* (2000)

Zeldin, T., *An Intimate History of Humanity* (1994)

Shaping History

de Boer, J.Z. and Sanders, D.T., *Earthquakes in Human History: The Far-Reaching Effects of Seismic Disruptions* (Princeton, 2005)

Calvert, P., *Revolution* (1970)

Eliade, M., *The Myth of the Eternal Return: Cosmos and History* (1954; 1989)

Gershenkron, A., *Continuity in History and Other Essays* (Cambridge, MA, 1968)

Gould, S.J., *Time's Arrow, Time's Cycle: Myth and Metaphor in the Discovery of Geological Time* (1991)

Hobsbawm, E.J., 'Inventing Traditions', in Hobsbawm, E.J. and Ranger, T. (eds), *The Invention of Tradition* (Cambridge, 1973), pp. 1–14

Lasch, C., *The True and Only Heaven: Progress and its Critics* (New York, 1991)

Lucas, G., *The Archaeology of Time* (2005)

Manuel, F.E., *Shapes of Philosophical History* (1965)

Tassone, G., *A Study on the Idea of Progress in Nietzsche, Heidegger and Critical Theory* (Lewiston, NY, 2002)

Trompf, G.W., *The Idea of Historical Recurrence in Western Thought: From Antiquity to the Reformation* (Berkeley, 1979)

White, H.V., *Metahistory: The Historical Imagination in Nineteenth-Century Europe* (Baltimore, 1974)

Periodisation and History

Arendt, H., 'The Concept of History: Ancient and Modern', in her *Between Past and Future: Eight Exercises in Political Thought*, enlarged edn (1977), pp. 41–90

Barraclough, G., '*Medium Aevum*: Some Reflections on Medieval History and on the Term "The Middle Ages"', in his *History in a Changing World* (Oxford, 1955), pp. 54–63

Besserman, L.L. (ed.), *The Challenge of Periodization: Old Paradigms and New Perspectives* (New York, 1996)

Compagnon, A., *The Five Paradoxes of Modernity*, trans. F. Philip (New York, 1994)

Ermarth, E.D., *Sequel to History: Postmodernism and the Crises of Representational Time* (Princeton, 1992)

Habermas, J., 'Modernity: An Unfinished Project' (1981), trans. N. Walker, in Passerin d'Entrèves, M. and Benhabib, S. (eds), *Habermas and the Unfinished Project of Modernity: Critical Essays* (Cambridge, 1996), pp. 38–55

Jameson, F., *Postmodernism: Or the Cultural Logic of Late Capitalism* (1991)

Jencks, C. (ed.), *The Post-Modern Reader* (1992)

Latour, B., *We Have Never Been Modern*, trans. C. Porter (New York, 1993)

Lyotard, J-F., *The Postmodern Condition: A Report on Knowledge*, trans. G. Bennington and B. Massumi (Manchester, 1984)

Osborne, P., *The Politics of Time: Modernity and Avant-Garde* (1995)

Rose, M.R., *The Post-Modern and the Post-Industrial: A Critical Analysis* (Cambridge, 1991)

The End of History

Amanat, A. and Bernhardsson, M. (eds), *Imagining the End: Visions of Apocalypse from the Ancient Middle East to Modern America* (2002)

Baudrillard, J., *The Illusion of the End* (Paris, 1992), trans. C. Turner (Cambridge, 1994)

Bray, R., *Awaiting the Millennium: A History of End-Time Thinking* (Leicester, 1998)

Campion, N., *The Great Year: Astrology, Millenarianism and History in the Western Tradition* (1994)

Cohn, N., *The Pursuit of the Millennium* (1957)

Duncan, P. J. S., *Russian Messianism: Third Rome, Revolution, Communism and After* (2000)

Friedländer, S. (ed.), *Visions of Apocalypse: End or Rebirth?* (New York, 1985)

Gould, W. and Reeves, M., *Joachim of Fiore and the Myth of the Eternal Evangel in the Nineteenth Century* (Oxford, 2001)

Hill, C., *Antichrist in Seventeenth-Century England* (1971)

Reeves, M., *The Prophetic Sense of History in Medieval and Renaissance Europe* (Aldershot, 1999)

Stone, J. R., *Expecting Armageddon: Essential Readings in Failed Prophecy* (2000)

Weber, E., *Apocalypses: Prophecies, Cults and Millennial Beliefs through the Ages* (1999)

Theories of History/Time

Braudel, F., 'Histoire et sciences sociales: la longue durée', *Annales: E.S.C.*, 4 (1958), pp. 725–53; repr. in his *Écrits sur l'histoire* (Paris, 1969), pp. 41–83; and trans. as 'History and the Social Sciences: The *Longue Durée*', in his *On History*, trans. S. Matthews (1980), pp. 25–63

Breisach, E., *On the Future of History: The Postmodernist Challenge and its Aftermath* (Chicago, 2003)

Elias, N., *Time: An Essay*, trans. E. Jephcott (Oxford, 1992)

Foucault, M., *The Order of Things: An Archaeology of the Human Sciences*, trans. A. Sheridan-Smith (1970; 2001)

Gregor, A. J., *A Survey of Marxism: Problems in Philosophy and the Theory of History* (New York, 1965)

Koselleck, R., *The Practice of Conceptual History: Timing History and Spacing Concepts*, trans. T. Presner (Cambridge, 2002)

Le Goff, J., *History and Memory*, trans. S. Rendall and E. Claman (New York, 1992)

Mali, J., *Mythistory: The Making of a Modern Historiography* (Chicago, IL, 2003)

Ricoeur, P., *Time and Narrative* (Paris, 1985), trans. K. Blarney and D. Pellauer (Chicago, 1988), 3 vols

Roberts, G. (ed.), *The History and Narrative Reader* (2001)

Snooks, G., *The Laws of History* (1998)

Stone, L., 'History and the Social Sciences in the Twentieth Century', in his *The Past and the Present Revisited* (Boston, MA, 1981), pp. 3–44

Comparative Time Cultures

Adam, B., *Timewatch: The Social Analysis of Time* (Cambridge, 1995)

Brody, H., *The Other Side of Eden: Hunter-Gatherers, Farmers and the Shaping of the World* (2001)

Fabian, J., *Time and the Other: How Anthropology Makes its Object* (New York, 1983)

Friedman, W., *About Time: Inventing the Fourth Dimension* (Cambridge, MA, 1990)

Gell, A., *The Anthropology of Time: Cultural Constructions of Temporal Maps and Images* (Oxford, 1992)

Lippincott, K. et al., *The Story of Time* (1999)

Nabokov, P., *A Forest of Time: American Indian Ways of History* (Cambridge, 2002)

Rosen, R. M. (ed.), *Time and Temporality in the Ancient World* (Philadelphia, PA, 2004)

Thapar, R., *Time as a Metaphor of History: Early India* (Delhi, 1996)

Thompson, E. P., 'Time, Work Discipline and Industrial Capitalism', in his *Customs in Common* (1991), pp. 352–403

Whitrow, G.J., *Time in History: Views of Time from Prehistory to the Present Day* (Oxford, 1989)
Zerubavel, E., *Time Maps: Collective Memory and the Social Shape of the Past* (Chicago, IL, 2003)

Measuring Time

Audoin, C. and Guinot, B., *The Measurement of Time: Time, Frequency and the Atomic Clock*, trans. S. Lyle (Cambridge, 2001)
Aveni, A.F., *Empires of Time: Calendars, Clocks, Cultures* (1990)
Bedini, S.A., *The Trail of Time: Time Measurement with Incense in South Asia/Shih-chien ti tsu-chi* (Cambridge, 1994)
Borst, A., *The Ordering of Time: From the Ancient Computus to the Modern Computer*, trans. A. Winnard (1993)
Galison, P., *Einstein's Clocks, Poincaré's Maps: Empires of Time* (2003)
Hannah, R., *Greek and Roman Calendars: Constructions of Time in the Classical World* (2005)
Holford-Strevens, L., *The History of Time: A Very Short Introduction* (Oxford, 2005)
Landes, D.S., *Revolution in Time: Clocks and the Making of the Modern World* (2000)
North, J., *God's Clockmaker: Richard of Wallingford and the Invention of Time* (2005)
Poole, R., *Time's Alteration: Calendar Reform in Early Modern England* (1998)
Richards, E.G., *Mapping Time: The Calendar and its History* (Oxford, 1998)
Waugh, A., *Time: From Micro-Seconds to Millennia – A Search for the Right Time* (1999)

Representing Time

Literary

Bal, M., *Narratology: Introduction to the Theory of Narrative*, trans. C. van Boheemen (Toronto, 1985)
Gibson, A., *Towards a Postmodern Theory of Narrative* (Edinburgh, 1996)
Kermode, F., *The Sense of an Ending: Studies in the Theory of Fiction* (New York, 1967; 2000)
ter Meulen, A.G.B., *Representing Time in Natural Language: The Dynamic Interpretation of Tense and Aspect* (Cambridge, MA, 1997)

Musical

Bohlman, P.V., *World Music: A Very Short Introduction* (Oxford, 2002)
McNeill, W.H., *Keeping Together in Time: Dance and Drill in Human History* (Cambridge, MA, 1995)
Griffiths, P., *Modern Music: A Concise History* (1994)
Wallin, N.L., Merker, B. and Brown, S. (eds), *The Origins of Music* (Cambridge, MA, 2000)

Visual

McQuire, S., *Visions of Modernity: Representation, Memory, Time and Space in the Age of the Camera* (1998)
Panofsky, E., 'Father Time', in his *Studies in Iconology: Humanistic Themes in the Art of the Renaissance* (Oxford, 1939), pp. 69–94

Rocker-Friedenthal, A., *The Enduring Instant: Time and the Spectator in the Visual Arts/Der bleibende Augenblick: Betrachterzeit in den Bildkünsten* (Berlin, 2003)
Sturgis, A., *Telling Time* (2000)

Future History

Buzan, B. and Segal, G., *Anticipating the Future* (1998)
Howe, L. and Wain, A. (eds), *Predicting the Future* (Cambridge, 1993)
Lewisohn, R., *Prophets and Prediction: The History of Prophesy from Babylon to Wall Street*, trans. A. J. Pomerans (1958)
Maddox, J., *What Remains to be Discovered: Mapping the Secrets of the Universe, the Origins of Life, and the Future of the Human Race* (1999)
Margolis, J., *A Brief History of Tomorrow: The Future, Past and Present* (2000)
Menzel, P. and D'Aluisio, F., *Robo Sapiens: Evolution of a New Species* (Cambridge, MA, 2000)
Morgan, C., *The Shape of Futures Past: The Story of Prediction* (Exeter, 1966)
Naughton, J., *A Brief History of the Future: The Origins of the Internet* (1999)
Pondisco, R., *The Future: An Owner's Manual: What the World Will Look Like in the Twenty-First Century and Beyond* (New York, 2000)
Rescher, N., *Predicting the Future: An Introduction to the Theory of Forecasting* (New York, 1998)
Toffler, A., *Future Shock* (1970)
Wagner, D. A. (ed.), *The Future of Literacy in a Changing World* (Cresskill, NJ, 1999)

Time Travel

Aldiss, B. and Wingrove, D., *Trillion Year Spree: The History of Science Fiction* (Thirsk, 1986; 2001)
Al-Khalili, J., *Black Holes, Wormholes and Time Machines* (Bristol, 1999)
Barksdale, E. C., *Enchanted Paths and Magic Words: The Quantum Mind and Time Travel in Science and in Literary Myth* (New York, 1998)
Davies, C., *How to Build a Time Machine* (2001)
Foote, B., *The Connecticut Yankee in the Twentieth Century: Travel to the Past in Science Fiction* (New York, 1991)
Gott, J. R., *Time Travel in Einstein's Universe: The Physical Possibilities of Travel through Time* (2001)
Kaku, M., *Parallel Worlds: A Journey through Creation, Higher Dimensions, and the Future of the Cosmos* (New York, 2005)
Parker, B., *Cosmic Time Travel: A Scientific Odyssey* (New York, 1991)
Pinsky, M., *Future Present: Ethics and/as Science Fiction* (Madison, NJ, 2003)
Roberts, A., *Science Fiction* (2000)
Telotte, J. P., *Science Fiction Film* (Cambridge, 2001)
Wolf, F. A., *Parallel Universes: The Search for Other Worlds* (1991)

Philosophy and Time

Cahn, S. M., *Fate, Logic and Time* (New Haven, CT, 1967)
Cleugh, M. E., *Time and its Importance in Modern Thought* (1937)
Cockburn, D., *Other Times: Philosophical Perspectives on Past, Present and Future* (Cambridge, 1997)

Craig, W. L., *The Tenseless Theory of Time: A Critical Examination* (Dordrecht, 2000)

Fraser, J. T. (ed.), *The Voices of Time: A Cooperative Survey of Man's Views of Time as Expressed by the Sciences and by the Humanities* (New York, 1966)

Jaques, E., *The Form of Time* (New York, 1982)

Le Poidevin, R., *Change, Cause and Contradiction: A Defence of the Tenseless Theory of Time* (Basingstoke, 1991)

Lewis, D., *On the Plurality of Worlds* (Oxford, 1986)

Loizou, A., *The Reality of Time* (Aldershot, 1986)

McLure, R., *The Philosophy of Time: Time before Times* (2005)

Raju, C. K., *The Eleven Pictures of Time: The Physics, Philosophy and Politics of Time* (New Delhi, 2003)

Wood, D., *The Deconstruction of Time* (Evanston, IL., 2001)

Time and the Cosmos

Albert, D. Z., *Time and Chance* (Cambridge, MA, 2000)

Baggott, J. E., *Beyond Measure: Modern Physics, Philosophy and the Meaning of Quantum Theory* (Oxford, 2004)

Barbour, J., *The End of Time: The Next Revolution in Our Understanding of the Universe* (1999)

de Grasse Tyson, N., Liu, C. and Irion, R., *One Universe: At Home in the Cosmos* (Washington DC, 2001)

Deutsch, D., *The Fabric of Reality* (1997)

Gribbin, J., *The Birth of Time: How We Measured the Age of the Universe* (1999)

Hawking, S. W., *A Brief History of Time: From the Big Bang to Black Holes* (1988)

Hoyle, F., Burbidge, G. and Narlikar, J. V., *A Different Approach to Cosmology: From a Static Universe through the Big Bang towards Reality* (Cambridge, 2000)

Lockwood, M., *The Labyrinth of Time: Introducing the Universe* (Oxford, 2005)

Prigogine, I. with Stengers, I., *The End of Certainty: Time, Chaos and the New Laws of Nature* (New York, 1997)

Siegfried, T., *Strange Matters: Undiscovered Ideas at the Frontiers of Space and Time* (Washington DC, 2002)

Silk, J., *On the Shores of the Unknown: A Short History of the Universe* (Cambridge, 2005)

Index

Page references in italics indicate illustrations.